REASON
AND
MORALITY

REASON
AND
MORALITY

Alan Gewirth

THE UNIVERSITY OF CHICAGO PRESS
Chicago and London

ALAN GEWIRTH is the Edward Carson Waller
Distinguished Service Professor of Philosophy at
the University of Chicago. He is a past president of
the American Philosophical Association, a fellow
of the American Academy of Arts and Sciences, and
the author of several books, including *Political
Philosophy* and *Marsilius of Padua and Medieval
Political Philosophy*.

The University of Chicago Press, Chicago 60637
The University of Chicago Press, Ltd., London

82 81 80 79 78   54321

Library of Congress Cataloging in Publication Data
Gewirth, Alan.
Reason and morality.
Includes bibliographical references and index.
1. Ethics.   I. Title.
BJ1012.G47   170   77-13911
ISBN 0-226-28875-7

FOR MARCELLA

CONTENTS

PREFACE

The most important and difficult problem of philosophical ethics is whether a substantial moral principle can be rationally justified. On the answer depends the possibility of construing the difference between moral right and wrong as objective and universal and hence as knowable by moral judgments on which all persons who use rational methods must agree. From Plato's Idea of the Good and Aristotle's rational mean to various doctrines of natural law, Kant's categorical imperative, and Mill's principle of utility, to mention only a few outstanding examples, moral philosophers have sought in diverse ways to provide affirmative answers to this problem. Other philosophers, in an equally long tradition from the ancient sophists and skeptics through Hume, Marx, and Nietzsche to contemporary emotivists and other noncognitivists, have given arguments of various sorts for a negative answer to the same problem. In a century when the evils that man can do to man have reached unparalleled extremes of barbarism and tragedy, the philosophic concern with rational justification in ethics is more than a quest for certainty. It is also an attempt to make coherent sense of persons' deepest convictions about the principles that should govern the ways they treat one another. For not only do the divergences among philosophers reflect different views about the logical difficulties of justification in ethics; the conflicting principles they uphold, whether presented as rationally grounded or not, have drastically different implications about the right modes of individual conduct and social institutions. The problem of whether any of these principles can be rationally justified is hence of first importance for the guidance of human life.

In addition to the participants in the perennial debate over justification, there have been many moral philosophers who have declined to concern themselves with the problem of rationally justifying a supreme moral principle. Intuitionists have held that moral principles are self-evident; others—traditionalists or conventionalists—have argued that it is sufficient to view certain principles as underlying the morality of their culture, tradition, social system, or historical epoch and to use the principles to systematize and elucidate that culture's more specific moral rules and judgments. This approach, however, incurs a severe difficulty. For so long as the rightness or correctness of the principle itself on which the whole system ultimately rests is not established, such a procedure still leaves the system without any warrant of its rightness or correctness. Partisans of opposed cultures, traditions, or social systems may each claim self-evidence for their own moral principles, and they hold that their respective rules and judgments are the morally right ones. Hence a moral principle's success in justifying or systematizing the subordinate rules or judgments of any one culture, ideology, or tradition does nothing, of itself, to prove their superiority over the moral rules or judgments of opposed cultures or traditions.

Recognition of this fact has supplied one of the strongest intellectual motivations for the various ancient and modern thinkers who have tried to provide a firm nonrelativist foundation for ethics. By giving a rational justification of one or another supreme moral principle, they have hoped to disprove or establish the wrongness of rival principles. No such attempt, however, has been judged generally successful by philosophers, for in each case its critics have been able to point out serious flaws.

In this book, while trying to profit from the work of my predecessors, I present a new version of a rational justification. The chief novelty is the logical derivation of a substantial normative moral principle from the nature of human action. Although the importance of action for morality has been recognized since the ancients, I undertake to show that the connection between them is much closer and more substantive than has hitherto been thought. My main thesis is that every agent, by the fact of engaging in action, is logically committed to the acceptance of certain evaluative and deontic judgments and ultimately of a supreme moral principle, the Principle of Generic Consistency, which requires that he respect his recipients' necessary conditions of action. To prove the thesis, I have argued that the very possibility of rational interpersonal action depends upon adherence to the morality that is grounded in this principle. Because every agent must accept the principle on pain of self-contradiction, it has a stringent rational justification that is at the same time practical because its required locus is the context of action. In addition to arguing for the principle from what I have called 'the normative structure of action,' I have also devoted two chapters to discussions of the principle's most salient applications for the distributive and substantive issues of both individual and social morality. The moral rules and judgments that constitute these applications share in one way or another the rational justifiability of the principle from which they are derived.

At various points I have indicated, with what I hope is due caution, how I have tried to avoid the familiar dangers confronting such a project, to which noncognitivists and other antirationalists have long called attention, including the pitfalls of logical gaps, circularity, lack of motivating force, excessive formalism or abstractness, vacuity, and so forth. Especially pertinent in this connection is my use of what I have called a "dialectically necessary method," as opposed to both dialectically contingent and assertoric methods.

Certain other features of the argument, though by no means novel, may be mentioned here both because of their central relevance for various additional hazards of this project and because they depart from some widespread tendencies in recent moral philosophy. I use 'reason' and 'morality' in senses that are morally neutral in that they do not incorporate any normative moral principle, including the one whose rational justification is at issue, while at the same time they do include chief components generally recognized in the meaning of each of these words. Thus I confine 'reason' to the canons of deductive and inductive logic, and in the definition of 'morality' I include both the 'formal' element of requirements for action that are categorically obligatory and the 'material' element of concern for other persons' interests. Since the extent of the 'other persons' and the nature of the 'interests' are explicitly left open, the definition fits the whole range of divergent moralities. And the inclusion of the formal element as a distinct part of the definition of 'morality' also leaves open, as a separate question, why a concern for the interests of other persons should be accepted as categorically obligatory by every agent. In addition to this neutrality-enforcing generality of the basic concepts, I have also refrained from claiming self-evidence for any substantial moral judgment or principle.

In an earlier version of this book, almost twice the present length, I examined in detail the concepts and problems of reason and of action, including such concepts related to action as voluntariness and forced choice. In reducing the book to its present size I have tried to eliminate all analyses not directly pertinent to the main argument. In a sequel, I intend to deal more fully with the sociopolitical issues discussed in the last chapter as indirect applications of the moral principle.

During my years of work on this book I have accumulated many

debts, which it is a pleasure to acknowledge. To the several generations of graduate students at the University of Chicago who have
given me written and oral critiques of the book's successive versions, I
must here content myself with a collective statement of thanks, for if I
were to try to single out a few of these students by name, I should
have to list over a hundred. Earlier versions of the main argument
were presented to my faculty colleagues at Chicago as well as at many
other universities, and also at a symposium session of the American
Philosophical Association, where the assigned commentators were
Jerome B. Schneewind and John R. Silber; in addition, during the past
decade I have published more than a dozen articles setting forth
various parts or versions of the main theses.[1] One of these papers was
my presidential address to the western division of the American
Philosophical Association, "The 'Is-Ought' Problem Resolved." From
all these presentations I have received many helpful criticisms, both
published[2] and unpublished. Among the unpublished communications
I wish especially to mention with thanks the critical comments by
Maurice Mandelbaum and Henry B. Veatch, each of whom gen-
erously wrote me several acute and instructive letters. I have also
received helpful written or oral communications from Bernard
Baumrin, Martin P. Golding, Kenneth E. Goodpaster, John Hooker,
Gerald L. MacCallum, Jr., Geoffrey R. Marnell, J. Roland Pennock,
Robert Simon, Marcus G. Singer, William David Solomon, Herbert
Spiegelberg, James P. Sterba, J. W. N. Watkins, and Carl Wellman. I
thank David Spitz for his kindness in arranging an informal faculty
seminar at the Graduate Center of the City University of New York
for the discussion of some of my views.

My initial thinking on the ideas from which this book developed
was facilitated by a fellowship from the Rockefeller Foundation, while
the culminating work during 1974–76 was immensely helped by
successive fellowships from the National Endowment for the Humanities and the John Simon Guggenheim Memorial Foundation. I
gratefully acknowledge the assistance of all these institutions, as well
as that of the University of Chicago for giving me, in addition to a
two-year leave of absence, a stimulating intellectual environment.

Besides incalculable encouragement and support, my wife Marcella
has given me the benefit of her biological and ecological expertise and
her general good judgment in connection with various of the problems
discussed here and in my other writings. I dedicate this book to her:
living proof of the unity of reason and love.

1

THE PROBLEM OF JUSTIFICATION

1.1. Persons guide their lives in many different ways. Among the various goals, rules, habits, ideals, and institutions that figure more or less explicitly in such guidance, morality has a unique status. For it purports to set, for everyone's conduct, requirements that take precedence over all other modes of guiding action, including even the self-interest of the persons to whom it is addressed. What, if any, is the warrant for such a claim of precedence? Does the claim have a rational basis, or is it simply a product of superstition or societal conditioning? And even if the authoritative precedence of morality can in some way be justified, does this help us to know which, if any, among the various competing moralities is itself right or justified?

As these questions suggest, from among the diverse meanings of 'morality' and 'moral' a certain core meaning may be elicited. According to this, a morality is a set of categorically obligatory requirements for action that are addressed at least in part to every actual or prospective agent, and that are concerned with furthering the interests, especially the most important interests, of persons or recipients other than or in addition to the agent or the speaker. The requirements are categorically obligatory in that compliance with them is mandatory for the conduct of every person to whom they are addressed regardless of whether he wants to accept them or their results, and regardless also of the requirements of any other institutions such as law or etiquette, whose obligatoriness may itself be doubtful or variable. Thus, although one moral requirement may be overridden by another, it may not be overridden by any nonmoral requirement, nor can its normative bindingness be escaped by shifting one's inclinations, opinions, or ideals.

It might be thought that this definition of morality makes it relatively easy to determine what is morally right, since one need only ascertain what is required for furthering the interests of one's recipients. But, on the contrary, determining the correct or justified criterion of moral rightness has been a perennial difficulty for moral philosophy. We may begin to see why this is so if we compare morality with other fields of practice. Even if moral requirements take precedence over all other practical precepts, in every field there are specific criteria of rightness that set requirements for correct or successful actions in that field and hence also for evaluating the actions as correct or successful. Now in various particular fields, such as chess, soccer, business, or medical practice, the specific requirements are derivable more or less directly from the commonly acknowledged ends or rules of the fields themselves, and the obligatoriness of the requirements for any person's conduct is contingent on his accepting these ends or rules.

In the field of morality, however, it is precisely the correctness of the ends or rules that is in question, while at the same time their obligatoriness is not thus contingent. Because of the overarching character of moral precepts as addressed at least in part to all agents and as concerned with the most important interests in a categorically obligatory way, there are deep conflicts about moral ends or rules: conflicts over which persons and which interests are to be favorably considered in action, and also conflicts between the interests of the agent and those of other persons. Consider, for example, the radically different moral criteria epitomized by such names as Nietzsche or Callicles, Kierkegaard or St. Augustine, Kant or Schweitzer, as well as the perhaps less radical but still marked divergences between Hegel, Marx, Spencer, and Mill. The disagreements between these thinkers do not represent merely different 'second-order' analyses of a commonly accepted body of 'first-order' moral judgments, in the way philosophers may differ about the analysis of knowledge while recognizing (except for some borderline cases) a commonly accepted body of knowledge. In contrast to these, the divergences among the above moral philosophers are disagreements of basic first-order moral principle about how persons ought to regard and act toward one another, about what interests of which persons are worth pursuing and supporting. And there is considerable evidence that many non-philosophers uphold, although less systematically, one or another of such divergent moral principles.

Because of these conflicts of principle, even if criteria of moral rightness are derivable from certain moral ends or rules about persons and their interests, there still remains the question of which among the competing ends or rules are themselves right or correct. And even if a certain set of ends or rules and hence a certain criterion of moral rightness could be shown to be somehow more correct or valid than its competitors, there still remains the further question of why this criterion's requirements should be accepted as categorically obligatory for each person addressed by them, especially when they are in conflict with what he considers to be his own personal interests or with the requirements set by particular groups to which he may belong.

In the light of these conflicts of criteria and interests, we may distinguish three central questions of moral philosophy. First, there is the authoritative question: Why should one be moral, in the sense of accepting as supremely authoritative or obligatory for one's actions the requirement of furthering or favorably considering the important interests of other persons, especially when these conflict with one's own interests? If this question is not to be circular, the criterion of its 'should' must be other than the criterion of moral rightness whose obligatoriness is in question. Second, there is the distributive question: Whose interests other than his own should the agent favorably consider in action? To which persons should the goods accruing from such consideration be distributed in actions and institutions? Third, there is the substantive question: Of which interests should favorable account be taken? Which interests are good ones or constitute the most important goods?

Just as the various answers to the distributive question have run a vast range of particularisms between the extremes of personal egoism and egalitarian universalism, so the answers to the substantive question have ranged from the extreme of nihilism, that no interests are of any value, to the extreme of complete inclusivism, that all interests are good simply by virtue of being interests. Since, however, interests may conflict, some ordering is necessary; hence the interests of which favorable account should be taken have been classified and upheld according to many different and intertwining poles: religious interests as against secular ones; pacific interests as against bellicose or militaristic ones; theoretical or intellectual interests as against activist or political ones, and both of these as against romantic or aesthetic interests; narrowly biological or economic interests as against more spiritual ones; pleasure or happiness as against duty or dignity or equality or collective control; freedom as against security or order; and so forth. The various answers to the distributive and substantive questions constitute conflicting criteria of moral rightness, while the authoritative question concerns the reasons for accepting one or another of these criteria as categorically mandatory for actions and institutions.

1.2. These questions are obviously of the first importance for human life and society, since their answers determine the most basic requirements of how persons ought to live in relation to one another. Now the fact that philosophers, theologians, statesmen, and many other persons have given and still give widely divergent answers does not itself prove that rationally justifiable answers are impossible or even especially difficult. It might, for example, be provable that many such persons have made mistakes of logic or empirical fact. The crucial difficulty, however, is that so far as has been shown up to the present, different persons may give conflicting answers to the authoritative question and uphold conflicting criteria of moral rightness, and thus conflicting moral judgments, even if they have made no logical or empirical errors.

In this respect, there is an important contrast between science and morality that poses a severe difficulty for the latter. Empirical fact can serve as a check or test of the correctness of the factual statements on which the natural sciences may be held to be ultimately based,[1] but it does not seem able to serve this function in the case of moral judgments. Compare, on the one hand, such statements as 'Mrs. Jones is having an abortion' or 'The Azande are going on a headhunt' with such other statements as 'Mrs. Jones ought to have an abortion' and 'The Azande ought to go on a headhunt.' Regardless of the precise role statements like the former pair play in scientific inquiry, we know, in a way that is not at all question-begging, both what it would mean for the statements to be true and, at least in principle, how to go about checking or confirming whether they are true. But in the latter pair of statements it is difficult to see even what it would mean for them to be true. To what facts does or could a statement like 'Mrs. Jones ought to have an abortion' correspond? If it is replied that the facts in question consist in our ordinary moral opinions or considered reflective beliefs, this would ignore that the opinions and beliefs in question disagree with one another, and that in any case the question is which among these opinions and beliefs are themselves correct or true. If it is replied further that the moral statement is true if it conforms to or is derivable from the 'moral point of view,' this has the difficulties that there may be quite opposed moral points of view and that the moral point of view in its favored egalitarian-universalist interpretation must itself receive adequate justification if it is to justify such judgments.

A further possible answer to the question of the correspondence-correlates of moral judgments might adduce a certain kind of naturalistic position. According to this, for moral judgments to be true would mean that the actions they endorse have certain positive consequences for human happiness. This, however, would beg the basic moral question of whether such consequentialism is the right meaning or criterion of the application of moral concepts like 'right' and 'ought.' Entirely apart from the issue of whether the concept of human happiness is a purely factual one, definable without considering different value criteria, it is surely not the case that any person who utters the 'ought'-judgments can mean by them nothing other than certain predictive facts about human happiness. What of persons who have quite different criteria for upholding such 'ought'-judgments, such as the will of God or the requirements of good breeding or the laws of the tribe? In addition, since one person's happiness may conflict with another's, there still remains the question of whose happiness should be given priority.

These differences are related to the diverse positions taken on the distributive and substantive questions about morality indicated above. A naturalistic position like the one just mentioned assumes a certain normative moral principle, such as that one ought to maximize human happiness. But this principle needs justificatory argument. Since persons may have different criteria as to the individuals or groups and the interests that should receive favorable consideration, what it would mean for such 'ought'-judgments to be true cannot, without further argument, be held to consist in some specified set of empirical data, as against what it means for a natural scientific or empirical statement to be true. Hence, moral judgments, unlike factual statements of the sorts on which the natural sciences ultimately rest, cannot be connected with empirical facts or observations in order to check their truth without begging basic moral questions—that is, questions of principle about the criteria of moral rightness and hence of the correctness of moral judgments. This issue, of what facts, objects, or relations may serve as the basis of the truth-value of moral judgments, I shall call the *problem of the correspondence-correlate* or, more generally, the *problem of the independent variable*, since the question primarily concerns whether there are any objective independent variables that serve to determine the correctness or rightness of moral judgments. This problem is obviously not resolved by invoking the semantic conception of truth according to which the sentence "Mrs. Jones ought to have an abortion" is true if and only if Mrs. Jones ought to have an abortion. For this tells us nothing about the status in fact or reality of what is referred to after the "if and only if," just as if one were to say that the sentence, "The Absolute Mind gyrates slowly on its axis" is true if and only if the Absolute Mind gyrates slowly on its axis.

5

It might be thought possible to evade the problem of the independent variable by opting for the 'performative' view of truth, according to which to call a moral judgment true is to endorse or affirm it. This would shift the emphasis from the content of the judgment to the speech-act of uttering it. Even with this shift, however, the view is mistaken: endorsement or affirmation is not present when one asks, 'Is it true that Mrs. Jones ought to have an abortion?' or when one hypothesizes, 'If it is true that Mrs. Jones ought to have an abortion, then there ought not to be laws prohibiting it.' In any case, the shift from content to speech-act does not answer the question of just how the contents of moral judgments may be true.

It may also be maintained, however, following a long tradition, that moral judgments have no correspondence-correlates or independent variables at all. Thus, in his classic attack on the thesis that moral distinctions are derived from reason, Hume declared that moral judgments, like the passions and actions they affect, are "original facts and realities, complete in themselves" and hence cannot represent or correspond to anything outside themselves, including empirical facts or logical relations. He also insisted, however, that for a judgment to be a moral one it must be made from a general, disinterested point of view stemming from a "sentiment common to all mankind."[2] Now it might be held that such a sentiment provides the independent variable for the rightness or correctness of all moral judgments. This position, however, would incur the serious difficulty that a consistent set of moral judgments is not provided in this way. Hume, of course, believed that moral sentiments qua moral are invariant and universal, in that the features of actions or qualities that give a spectator "the pleasing sentiment of approbation" are the same for all spectators, these features consisting in what is either useful or immediately agreeable either to the agent himself or to other persons. But even taking into account Hume's requirement that the point of view from which moral spectators judge is or must be general rather than self-interested, it is difficult not to see in his assertions about what universally and invariably pleases them the optimistic innocence of the Enlightenment. Hume himself had to admit that some moral judges or spectators approved of the "monkish virtues" that are quite different from the virtues he himself had denominated moral, and that many nations, in esteeming the martial virtues, have also departed from what gives his moral spectator a pleasing feeling of approval.[3] Hence, the deliverances of the 'moral sense' cannot supply a consistent independent variable for the rightness of moral judgments.

There are other ways of solving the problem of the independent variable, some of which will be considered below. If, however, it is held that there is no independent variable that determines the truth or at least the correctness of moral judgments, including not even one found within judgments themselves, then the entire normative quest to ascertain the criterion for distinguishing the morally right from the morally wrong, and hence for an answer to moral skepticism, is given up. This would mean that behind the claims to correctness found in differing moral judgments there are only insoluble conflicts, and that the only recourse is to a radical relativism in which the conflicting judgments made by different persons or groups are left at that: they are made by different persons or groups. In this view, the correctness of a morality is not a matter of knowledge or truth at all; rather, the moral judgments any person accepts as right or correct can ultimately reflect only his tastes, feelings, conditioning, conventions, decisions, or economic class, and it is only to such noncognitive bases that any moral evaluation can appeal. There is and can be no such thing as the objectively right or correct moral criterion or principle, and even if there were there would be no way of rationally knowing what it is, let alone of rationally convincing anyone else who has different moral criteria or principles or who has none at all because of his negative answer to the authoritative question.

In order to deal with this issue and with the authoritative, substantive, and distributive questions of morality, we must turn to the problem of whether some supreme moral principle can be rationally justified. For there are competing answers to each of these questions, answers that can be systematized so that they can be shown to rest on different underlying assumptions or supreme principles. But unless it can be shown which of these principles, if any, it is more rational to accept than its competitors, the multiplicity of answers will not advance us beyond the arbitrariness and skepticism just mentioned.

Is It Needless to Justify a Supreme Moral Principle?

1.3. There are familiar arguments against both the needfulness and the possibility of justifying a supreme moral principle. Such a principle serves to show or establish which particular moral judgments and general rules are right and which wrong, so that it also shows the rightness of acting in certain ways as against others. Since to justify something is to show or establish its rightness or correctness, the supreme moral principle provides the justification of all correct moral judgments and rules. But, it is held, one undertakes to establish the rightness of some X only when X's rightness has been called into

7

question. Now particular moral judgments and general moral rules are not such Xs, because they are in order just as they are. This is true not only in the general sense that making moral judgments is a recognized institution of our culture but also in the more specific sense that the particular moral judgments we make and the general moral rules we uphold are acknowledged to be right or correct.

This contention is closely related to intuitionism. Just as the older intuitionists held that one can see by direct intellectual inspection what ought to be done in each morally relevant situation, so some contemporary philosophers have held it to be self-evident that, for example, wantonly inflicting pain on another person is always at least prima facie morally wrong. Similar self-evidence has been held to attach to the obligations to keep one's promises and to tell the truth. Since we know such moral propositions, there is no need to justify them; hence too, a fortiori, there is no need to justify a supreme moral principle as the ground or justificans for justifying particular moral propositions or general rules.[4]

This position is sometimes buttressed by a comparison between ethics and empirical knowledge. In the latter we begin not with principles, let alone supreme ones, but with particular empirical perceptions. The truth of propositions describing these perceptions or their objects can be ascertained independent of recourse to general principles, while the latter are reached only by inference from the particulars. Hence, it is contended, in ethics too we should begin from the recognition that particular moral judgments are correct or justified independent of their relation to a supreme principle, and we should regard general principles only as inductive summations of such judgments.

The difficulty with this contention is similar to that we found above in connection with the suggestion that moral judgments are true by virtue of corresponding to empirical facts. How do we determine which particular moral judgments are correct in the first place? They all have competitors stemming from different moral principles, so that to uphold some as exclusively correct would, in the absence of further principled argument, reflect one's conditioning or prejudices rather than any independent correctness. Particular empirical propositions can be checked for their truth against empirical perceptions; but what similar independent variable or correspondence-correlate is there for moral judgments? The answer of the older intuitionists, that this independent variable consists in nonnatural facts ascertained by immediate intellectual inspection, raises more questions than it answers. The newer intuitionists are also faced with the difficulty that the alternatives to what is declared to be self-evident have been upheld by various philosophers and ordinary persons going back at least to Glaucon in the second book of Plato's *Republic*. These alternatives restrict in various ways both the persons whose interests are to be favorably considered and what those interests are. The classic conflicts of moral philosophy represented in these alternatives cannot be rationally resolved simply by refusing to contend with one of the competing positions. The accusation that upholders of such restrictive alternatives are 'blind' or 'mad' stops argument when argument on the distributive and substantive issues they raise is both needed and possible. The assertion of madness is also confronted by the fact that persons upholding and practicing the castigated alternatives emerge as quite 'normal' in the psychiatric sense.[5]

1.4. Closely related to the intuitionist position is a somewhat more linguistic or perhaps conceptual contention. The attempt to justify a supreme moral principle in order to determine which among various competing moral criteria is the right one, or which ways of life or kinds of society are morally right, is held to be needless because the answer can be read off from the very meaning of the word 'moral.' Two aspects of this meaning have been invoked by different philosophers; they bear, respectively, on the distributive and the substantive questions of morality. According to one aspect, morality is inherently egalitarian and universalist, so that it follows from the meaning of 'moral' that "moral rules must be for the good of everyone alike."[6] According to the other aspect, a moral consideration is one that, from the very concept of 'moral,' is concerned with the attainment of well-being and the avoidance of ill-being. This view is suggested by such a statement as the following: "A moral system seems necessarily to be one aimed at removing particular dangers and securing certain benefits, and it would follow that some things do and some do not count as objections to a line of conduct from a moral point of view."[7]

Two possibilities must be distinguished with regard to the meaning of 'moral' in such doctrines. 'Moral' may be used in an evaluative sense in which it means 'morally right' and is opposed to 'immoral,' or in a descriptive sense in which it is opposed to 'nonmoral.' Now if the above doctrines use 'moral' in its evaluative sense, they incur such difficulties as the following. How do they know which rules are morally right? Can considerations about the meanings of words alone settle substantive or distributive issues about the morally right way to act? The approach taken by these doctrines appears to try to answer by definition what has traditionally been recognized to need serious justificatory argument: the question of what is the morally right way to live. It is true that the views in question still provide room for argument; but not on the most basic normative issues. For the distributive doctrines exclude, by definition, moralities that are nonuniversalist or inegalitarian, and the substantive doctrines seem to overlook the fact that widely different ideals and conceptions of well-being and benefit have been upheld as morally relevant, right, or good by different persons or groups. It is indeed true and important to emphasize that the concept of morality, by definition, rules out from being 'moral' such pointless rules as those that would require, for example, that one wag one's little finger in a certain direction three times daily. But even here it is recognized that special 'backgrounds' must be excluded from the interpretation of such examples; for if there is a religious cult for which such finger-wagging is a significant form of worship, then the example no longer fulfills its purpose of being pointless or trivial.

What this indicates is that there is a mean between making the possible content of 'morality' so thoroughly a matter of personal decision that even completely trivial rules may be 'moral' ones, and restricting the content of 'morality' to such an extent that it excludes in advance many of the varying criteria that persons and groups have had of what interests are important as matters of well-being. Hence there still remains a need, which cannot be settled by a definition, to adjudicate rationally among different, competing moralities, for each of which supreme authoritativeness is claimed and each of which propounds different answers to the distributive and substantive questions about whose interests, and which interests, should be favorably considered in the various possible ways of life and society.

If, on the other hand, the above doctrines use 'moral' in its descriptive, morally neutral sense, then it must encompass or be compatible with all the different possible moral positions; it must include what they all have in common as against what is peculiar to one (presumably preferred) morality. Here the above doctrines incur the serious difficulty that the distributive and substantive contents they assign to 'moral' do not apply to all moralities; they take sides in support of one moral position as against other moral positions within the general sphere of possible moral rules and judgments.

A further difficulty of this approach is that it leaves unanswered the authoritative question of *why* one should be moral—that is, what justification there is for acting in accordance with the distributive or substantive contents they call 'moral.' If it is replied that 'moral' just means the way one categorically or overridingly ought to act, this incurs the problem of how this formal meaning is related to the meanings of 'moral' that incorporate certain contents. Such a formal definition still leaves unresolved the problem of the justification for answering the authoritative question on the same grounds as are used to answer the distributive and substantive questions. Even if 'moral' means acting in accord with the interests X of persons Y, what reason is there for any particular person or group to act in this way, let alone to regard such action as categorically obligatory? I conclude that the task of justifying a supreme moral principle is not made needless by definitions that attribute to 'moral' a certain favored distributive or substantive content.

This needlessness has also been upheld with regard to another function assigned to the supreme principle—that of resolving conflicts among particular moral judgments or rules. To the contention that this function requires that there be only one supreme principle, it has been objected that a plurality of principles, none of which is derivable from the others, can also serve to resolve conflicts. For if the principles are coherent with one another, they provide for a consistent set of moral judgments concerning actions or institutions. The actions required by one principle further the actions required by the others; or else they are substitutable for one another according to a regular pattern of choice. By virtue of such coherence, these multiple principles are themselves rationally justified without having to be shown to follow from some more general principle, and they give a rational justification of all the particular judgments that follow from them in these ways. They thereby show which among conflicting particular judgments are justified and which are not.[8]

There are at least two difficulties with this coherence view. First, it does not deal adequately with conflicts among the principles themselves. There are occasions when the requirements of one principle may clash with the requirements of another. To be sure, this clash sometimes arises because one of the principles has already been violated. But even in this case there is the problem of what to do about the violation, where this requires violating still another principle. For example, if someone's starving is the result of a morally wrong social system, this still leaves open the question of whether theft, physical assault, or some other morally wrong action is thereby justified. The coherence test provides no answer here. In addition, many conflicts among principles do not arise from prior violations; for example, the principle of avoiding needless suffering may clash with the principle of telling the truth when someone has incurred a fatal disease.

When it is said that the coherence view deals with conflicts by making actions or policies intersubstitutable according to a consistent pattern of choice, there still remains the question of what is to be done when one person's or group's choices conflict with another's. Since no overarching principle settles such conflicts, they are left unresolved.

Second, even if conflicts among duties or particular lines of action are resolved by such coherence, this still leaves open the question of rational justification. Actions or choices may be consistent and still be morally wrong: they may, for example, be those of a villain or a tyrant. Rational justification must hence be provided at a more fundamental level: the principle from which the various duties derive must itself be shown to be justified. Or, if there is more than one principle, then a basis for resolving potential conflicts between them must be indicated, and this basis must itself be justified. The basis in question would function as the supreme principle.

Is It Impossible to Justify a Supreme Moral Principle?

1.5. Whether or not the needfulness or desirability of rationally justifying one supreme moral principle is admitted, there remains the problem whether it can be done. A wide variety of arguments has been invoked for a negative answer. One argument is that morality lacks two conditions that must be fulfilled by anything that is to be justified. Since to justify something is to establish its rightness or correctness, the justificandum must be right or correct or at least be susceptible of rightness or correctness; also, it must be subject to human control. Both these conditions are to some extent denied to morality by Marx's doctrine that moral judgments and ideals reflect the underlying economic structure and power relations of a society in a given historical epoch. For this means that no morality is right or correct as having any independent validity, nor is a morality something that can be freely adopted in the light of personal reflection; rather, it is taken over from the general culture as part of the ideological superstructure necessarily erected on the economic base. A parallel position may be attributed to Freud, for whom moral ideals, though historically invariant, have no rightness or correctness, because they are the results of parental and societal conditioning aimed at repressing vital impulses. This idea is a partial echo of Nietzsche's denigration of 'slave' morality.

These negative views can be dealt with for the present by the familiar observation that they have positive accompaniments. Amid their common insistence, variously grounded, on the unjustifiability of traditional moralities, Marx, Nietzsche, and Freud upheld as correct their own moral ideals: nonexploitative and nonalienated relations among men; the glorification of the will to power; the ethics of self-knowledge and honesty. Since these thinkers regarded their respective ideals as right or correct and strove to have them accepted, each would have to admit that his moral principle fulfills both the above necessary conditions of being a justificandum.

The first condition of a justificandum is also denied to morality by extreme noncognitivists who assimilate moral judgments to ejaculations, commands, decisions, or expressions of emotion. Since considerations of right or wrong, correct or incorrect, do not apply to such things, moral judgments are not susceptible of any justification; hence their supreme principles cannot be justified.

Even if this extreme view about the nature of moral judgments were granted, it would not establish its negative conclusion. To justify something is to establish its rightness or correctness, and it may be right or wrong, correct or incorrect, to utter an ejaculation or command or to express an emotion in one sort of circumstance or another.

The negative conclusion is also untenable if applied to the contents rather than to the actual utterings of moral judgments interpreted in the above noncognitive ways. The one requirement is that these contents must be viewed as deriving not from involuntary reactions but from modes of thinking that are under the control of the persons who make the judgments. In the case of such nonpropositional utterances as commands, for example, their contents have some point or purpose, so that, by reference to this, arguments can be given for their justification or disjustification. Even in the case of such simple commands as the military 'Eyes right!' or 'Parade rest!' one can ask their point or purpose in the context of military training and operations: How do they contribute, for example, to the inculcation of discipline, obedience, or uniformity?

With respect both to speech-acts and to their contents, two sorts of relations of justifiability may be distinguished. One relation is external, where questions of their rightness or correctness are raised by persons other than the persons who utter the speech-acts. The other relation is internal, where questions of their rightness or correctness are raised, or claims as to their rightness or correctness are made, by the same persons who utter the speech-acts. Now both these relations pertain to moral judgments even when these are interpreted as nonpropositional. We have already seen how the external relation may pertain both to their uttering and to their contents. The internal relation, however, is essential to a judgment's being a moral one. A moral judgment is reflective: it does not consist merely in conforming to some accepted practice; it also carries with it an implicit claim, on the part of the person who sets forth the judgment, that he has made it after due consideration and that it is right or correct. The moral judgment made by A, that B ought to do X (where B may or may not be identical with A), is regarded by A as having a good reason in its support, even if this reason consists only in the value of adhering to custom. In view of this reflective claim, it is untenable to hold that questions of justification are irrelevant to moral judgments. For this would be to say that although claims of rightness are at least implicitly advanced by persons who make moral judgments, those claims are to be ignored in all considerations of the judgments.

1.6. A further argument for the impossibility of justifying a supreme moral principle attacks a basic assumption about the function of such a principle; namely, that it can resolve all moral conflicts and hence reconcile all justified or valid moral judgments or positions and systematize them under a single principle. The argument, which stems especially from intuitionists, contends that there are justified moral values or ideals that are or may be opposed to one another and none of which can be shown to be more justified than any of its alternatives. These ideals are defined by the priority they give to one or another substantive or distributive end or value. It is well known, for example, that liberty may conflict with equality and with order, justice with the general welfare and with mercy, and so forth. A principle that makes one of these values basic may hence conflict with a principle that upholds a different value. The attempt to find an ultimate moral principle by which such conflicts can be resolved consequently is doomed to failure: "since some values may conflict intrinsically, the very notion that a pattern must in principle be discoverable in which they are all rendered harmonious is founded on a false *a priori* view of what the world is like."[9]

In dealing with this difficulty, it is essential to consider certain alternatives about the relation of a supreme principle to moral ends or ideals. These ideals may be viewed in simple, unqualified terms, such as 'liberty,' 'equality,' and so forth; or they may be viewed in a more qualified way, such that they take account of at least some of the complexities of accommodating one ideal to another. In the former case, conflicts are probably unavoidable both conceptually and empirically, for the conceptual components of any one ideal as well as the consequences of its empirical implementation may be in opposition to the components and consequences of some other ideal. The case is different, however, if ideals are fitted into a more general framework wherein the claims of one are assessed by its relation to the claims of other ideals. Such mutual accommodation not only permits the resolution of conflicts between ideals but may even be held to be necessary for the genuine validity of each ideal. An obvious example is the need to restrain the freedom of an individual when he intends to use it to remove the life of another, innocent individual. Different modes of resolution are of course possible. But if a principle for one such resolution can itself be rationally justified, while the principles of other possible resolutions cannot be, then the former resolution is to this extent more correct than the latter. The inevitability of conflicts among ideals taken unqualifiedly is hence no bar to the possibility of a supreme principle that adjudicates conflicts among ideals suitably modified.

This adjudication, however, requires that there be some general criterion that can serve as a common denominator for weighing or assessing different values or ideals in relation to one another. Utilitarianism is a familiar example of an attempt to provide such a common denominator. But it has rivals, and there still remains the question whether any one general criterion or principle can be justified as against its rivals. The working out of an affirmative answer to this question is a main project of this book.

1.7. I turn now to some more formal arguments against the possibility of justifying a supreme moral principle. Since to justify something is to show or establish its rightness as satisfying some criterion, which is the justificans, this latter functions as the independent variable of the justification; as Wittgenstein said, "justification consists in appealing to something independent."[10] Now a supreme principle is what is logically first in some field, in that everything else in the field depends for its justification more or less directly on the principle, whereas the principle in turn is not dependent on or justified by anything else. But if the supreme principle is itself to be justified, then it becomes a justificandum, and as such it is logically posterior to and dependent on the justificans that justifies it. Consequently, the very idea of justifying a supreme principle seems contradictory, for it requires showing the dependence of what is independent, the logical posteriority of what is logically prior, giving the justification of that whose justification cannot be given.

The attempt to justify a supreme principle also appears to involve either an inevitable circularity or a certain superfluity. For the only things left to justify the supreme principle in any field are the very justificanda or consequents that it is the function of the principle itself to justify; hence, the justificanda can justify the principle only if it has already been assumed that the justificanda have themselves been justified by the principle. But if this assumption is made, then there is no need to justify the principle, for the latter could not have justified the justificanda unless it were already understood at that point to be itself in no need of justification. And if the principle is justified by the justificanda only because the latter have been justified by the principle, then the question of the principle's justification is obviously begged. Hence, the justification of the supreme principle is either circular or superfluous.

The above difficulties apply to the attempt to justify a supreme principle in any field, including logic and empirical science. It might be thought, however, that there can be cross-justification between fields, in that a supreme principle in one field can be justified through the principles of some other field. Whatever be the merits of this suggestion in general, its application to the supreme principle of morality seems very doubtful. For since, by definition, a supreme moral principle is an ultimate principle of practical justification, it cannot be justified by being derived from a superior practical principle, for there is none. Nor, it seems, can it be derived from some theoretical or factual principle, for since the latter of itself sets no practical requirements, it cannot justify a conclusion that sets such requirements.

This last point may be put somewhat more specifically as follows. The attempt to justify a supreme moral principle by deriving it from some superior principle or justificans incurs a dilemma. For the superior principle in question must itself be either moral or nonmoral. If it is moral, so that the justification given is also moral, then this obviously begs the question. For a moral justification of a supreme moral principle already assumes, in its criterion of justification, the very principle that is to be justified: the moral justificans is the same as the justificandum. If, on the other hand, the superior principle from which the supreme moral principle is derived is nonmoral, then it is doubtful on many grounds whether the moral principle can be justified at all. In particular, there is the logical question of how a moral principle containing an 'ought' can be derived from premises that do not themselves contain any 'oughts.' The familiar issues of naturalism and heteronomy arise here.

Can a Supreme Moral Principle Be Justified Inductively?

1.8. The above examination of the possibility of justifying a supreme moral principle has yielded negative results. It might be contended that this is because I have operated with an exclusively deductive conception of justification. Although some aspects of what may be considered an inductive justification have already been discussed above, I shall now consider more explicitly whether such a justification can be more successful. By an 'inductive' justification I shall mean a process of trying to establish the rightness or correctness of a moral principle where the process comprises any of the following: (a) the appeal to empirical facts either to refute or to confirm the empirical assumptions on which a moral principle rests; (b) generalizing from particular moral judgments to the general principle that systematizes them or that is implicit in them; (c) means-end calculation, including 'rational choice,' where a cause-effect relation is held to be established between action in accordance with a supreme moral principle and the attainment of desired ends; (d) arguing from the correctness or cogency of some specific choice-procedure to the correctness or cogency of the moral principle that would be chosen by the use of that procedure.

a. It has sometimes been held that all inegalitarian moral principles depend crucially on empirically false assumptions or correlations, such as that persons belonging to certain empirically discriminable groups—races, religions, nations, and so forth—have more of some desirable quality, such as intelligence or industriousness, than persons belonging to other such groups. Hence, all inegalitarian principles can be refuted by showing the falsity of the empirical correlations on which they depend, so that an egalitarian principle is left unchallenged and is hence justified, at least by default. Such justification is inductive in at least two respects: it examines the truth of empirical generalizations by considering particular cases, and this justification of the egalitarian principle can be at best only probable since it is impossible to examine all the empirical generalizations that might be asserted to uphold an inegalitarian principle.

This sort of argument would not work, however, against inegalitarian moral principles that do not rest on empirical correlations. Such principles directly assert that persons who have in superior degree certain unequally distributed desirable qualities, such as intelligence, industriousness, or political ability, should have superior rights. These assertions are justified by an appeal to elitist ideals about

17

maximal human development, with no attempt to correlate the persons who have these qualities with the members of other empirically discriminable groups. Aristotle and Nietzsche are at least partial examples of such an approach.

This consideration also shows the inadequacy of another sort of attempted empirical justification of an egalitarian-universalist moral principle. It is sometimes argued that because all persons equally have certain needs or desires, it follows that all persons ought equally to have the means of satisfying these needs or desires. Entirely apart from the gap here between 'is' and 'ought,' there is the further difficulty that the second type of elitist just mentioned can always deny, in the light of his inegalitarian ideal, that the needs or desires in question should all be given equal weight, because he denies that the persons in question are all of equal value, since they are unequal with respect to the quality that is crucially relevant for the allocation of rights.

b. Many moral philosophers have held that the only way any moral principle can be justified is by generalizing from persons' particular moral judgments to the general principle that is implied or presupposed by the judgments. The particular judgments are hence the justificantia, or independent variables, and the general principle is accepted as correct or valid insofar as it reflects in a general way what is judged to be right or wrong in those particular cases.

A more complex version of such an inductive justification has been upheld by Nelson Goodman in respect to the principles of deductive and inductive inference, and this in turn has been applied by John Rawls to the justification of a moral principle. The pattern of the justification is that general rules or principles of logical inference or of morality are justified by being shown to be in accordance with the particular logical inferences or moral judgments we actually make and accept, and the particular inferences or judgments are in turn justified by being shown to be in accordance with general rules or principles of inference or of morality. The circularity that is present here is held to be virtuous rather than vicious, because the justification of both the general principles and the particular inferences or judgments consists in their being brought into agreement or 'reflective equilibrium' with one another.[11]

Whatever the merits of such an inductive justification with regard to the principles of logical inference, it suffers from a serious difficulty when applied to morality—a difficulty already encountered above in my discussion of the possible self-evidence of a moral principle. The inductive justification assumes that we can differentiate the morally right from the morally wrong in persons' particular moral judgments and can hence infer what is the morally right general principle by generalizing from the morally right particular judgments. This would work well enough so long as there is no serious dispute over the particular judgments that are taken as the sources. But what if there is such dispute? What if the judgments are challenged by a Callicles, an Aristotle, or a Nietzsche? In this case, to appeal to the principles to settle the dispute would beg the question, since the principles rest exclusively on the particular judgments the opponents are disputing. A principle that shows that alternatives like those just mentioned are morally wrong must do so not simply because it is itself a generalization from the opposed alternatives—for this is question-begging—but because it has an independent rational justification of its own.

c. Some philosophers have tried to justify an egalitarian-universalist moral principle by an appeal to means-end calculation or 'rational choice' concerned with choosing the most efficient means to one's desired ends, where the chooser is an individual whose end is to maximize his own happiness or well-being. The main point, which goes back to Hobbes if not to Plato, is that the only way to be sure of attaining one's own happiness or of successfully pursuing one's interests is by giving equal consideration to the happiness or interests of all other persons who are affected by one's actions. On this view, prudence or self-interest and egalitarian morality coincide, at least so far as concerns the actions each of them requires, so that an egalitarian-universalist moral principle is justified by being shown to be in accord with rational self-interest.[12]

This argument is unsuccessful, however, in two respects. An individual whose sole concern is to pursue his own interests will at least sometimes, and perhaps often, be able to achieve his ends by violating either the legitimate interests of other persons or rules that aim impartially at the good of everyone. Moreover, practical acceptance of such impartial rules will at least sometimes, for some persons, result in the frustration rather than the realization of their self-interested desires. Hence, the causal relation the argument asserts to hold between acting in accordance with an egalitarian moral principle and furthering one's own interests breaks down in two ways.

An important attempt to avoid this result has been made by Rawls in his much more sophisticated and insightful version of the use of rational choice to justify an egalitarian moral principle. Rawls's salient addition consists in the double stipulation that persons who are choosing a basic moral principle for the constitution of their society are in an 'original position' of equality with respect to power and freedom, and that each is equally encumbered by a 'veil of ignorance' about his own particular qualities. Given these equalizing stipulations together with primarily self-centered motives, the persons in question will choose an egalitarian moral principle, which is therefore justified by rational choice.[13]

The argument to this egalitarian conclusion, however, is circular in important respects. For the veil of ignorance, in addition to its obvious nonrational (because noncognitive) features, is, like the assumption of original equality, a way of removing from the rational choosers' consideration certain factors, consisting in their actual empirical inequalities and dissimilarities, that together with their self-interest would strongly influence them to make inegalitarian choices. Neither of the stipulations by which Rawls avoids this inegalitarian result has any independent rational justification: persons are not in fact equal in power and ability, nor are they so lacking in empirical reason as to be ignorant of all their particular qualities. This latter stipulation, that of ignorance of particulars, goes far beyond the limited assumption of ignorance that actual rational persons make when they choose under conditions of uncertainty. Hence, Rawls's egalitarian conclusion is achieved only by putting into his justificans or premise an equality that cannot itself be justified either by empirical facts or by consideration of cognitive adequacy (as opposed to ignorance).

d. Some philosophers have tried to justify a moral principle by using what I shall call a *reflexive* method. By this method, one infers that a moral principle is correct or cogent from the fact that it would be chosen by a mental procedure that is itself correct or cogent, in that the procedure embodies such valuable mental characteristics as being fully informed, free, imaginative, sympathetic, calm, impartial, fair, willing to universalize, acting on principle, considering the good of everyone alike, and so forth. The most famous version of this reflexive method is the 'ideal observer' theory stemming from Adam Smith. Other versions of the method attempt to justify a moral principle or principles through a certain 'qualified attitude' or through the 'considered judgment of a competent person' or through a 'rational choice among ways of life' or through 'the moral point of view.'[14] Such methods may be classed as inductive in that the inference from the use of the mental procedures to the choice of certain moral principles is viewed either on a causal model or at least as establishing generalizations about principles from particular instances of use of the procedures.

These reflexive methods of justification all suffer, however, from a fatal dilemma similar to the one presented above in connection with a deductive justification of a supreme moral principle. The mental characteristics or procedures the methods regard as decisive in justifying one moral principle as against another are themselves either morally neutral or morally nonneutral—that is, normatively moral. If the characteristics are normatively moral, then the argument is obviously circular. For in this case a moral principle will have been justified by assumptions that are themselves normatively moral ones, about which mental characteristics or procedures are morally right as against morally wrong. But it is precisely these assumptions that had to be justified. Such characteristics as being fair, impartial, sympathetic, and considering everyone's good alike are among the obvious instances of this; for a person who is partial to himself (or to some favored group) in certain contingencies by making exceptions in his own favor, or who is lacking in sympathy for others who are suffering, is condemned on moral grounds. If, on the other hand, the mental characteristics or procedures in question are morally neutral, as is the case with being fully informed, imaginative, and calm, there is no guarantee that such nonmoral traits will lead to the selection of one moral principle as against another, or in particular to an egalitarian-universalist principle. A person may have such traits and still choose a moral principle that assigns superior rights in respect of well-being and freedom to persons of superior intelligence, political ability, and so forth.

I conclude that none of the varieties of inductive argument considered above is sufficient to justify a supreme moral principle.

Reason and the Generic Features of Action

1.9. A definitive justification of a supreme moral principle must provide, in a way that does not beg the question, determinate and conclusive answers to the three central questions of moral philosophy. The answers must be determinate in that the criteria of moral rightness they establish have certain definite contents such that the opposite contents cannot be derived from the principle that has been justified. The answers must also be conclusive in that they show that these criteria cannot rationally be challenged by any of their competitors and that it is categorically obligatory for all persons to act in accordance with them.

The thesis of this book is that such answers are to be obtained through an analysis of certain considerations about reason and action, as these considerations are reflected in their respective concepts. More specifically, the answers are provided by applying reason to the concept of action, where this concept represents the phenomena of human voluntary and purposive behavior. My thesis is a strong one in that I hold that the rational analysis of this concept is both the necessary and the sufficient condition of solving the central problems of moral philosophy. In the next two chapters I shall focus mainly on the arguments that show that the analysis is a sufficient condition of the solution, but I shall also indicate at several points how it is also a necessary condition. The establishment of these conclusions will require some detailed analyses of certain crucial aspects of human agency. The degree of detail to be presented in this and the following chapter is justified both because of its contribution to solving the central problems of moral philosophy and because the aspects I shall single out have not hitherto received the attention they require for this purpose. At the same time, I shall treat in much lesser detail other aspects of action that are of less direct importance for the problems of this book.

I use 'reason' in a strict sense as comprising only the canons of deductive and inductive logic, including among the latter its bases in particular sense perceptions. I also construe conceptual analysis on the model of deductive logic, in that when a complex concept A is analyzed as containing concepts B, C, and D, these concepts belong to A with logical necessity so that it is contradictory to hold that A applies while denying that B, C, or D applies. The concept of action, while representing actual phenomena of human conduct, will be obtained and used by such conceptual analysis. Although difficulties may be raised about the general justification of both deduction and induction, in the present context it must suffice to note that, because they respectively achieve logical necessity and reflect what is empirically ineluctable, deduction and induction are the only sure ways of avoiding arbitrariness and attaining objectivity and hence a correctness or truth that reflects not personal whims or prejudices but the requirements of the subject matter. Because of these powers of reason, reliance on it is not a mere optional or parochial 'commitment' parallel to the commitments some persons may make to religious faith, aesthetic rapture, animal instinct, personal authenticity, national glory or tradition, or other variable objects of human allegiance. An important point of contrast is that concerning each of these other objects one may ask for its reason in the sense of the justification for upholding it; and any attempt at such justification must make use of reason in the sense of deduction or induction or both. Even if it is held that one or more of these objects is an intrinsic good needing no external justification, the question may always be raised of how it bears on or is related to other goods; and to answer such questions reason must be used.

It is indeed the case that there have also been historical demands that reason itself in turn pass various justificatory tests set by religious faith, aesthetic rapture, and so forth. But the very scrutiny to determine whether these tests are passed must itself make use of reason. For example, salient powers of reason must be used in order to check whether the products of logical and empirical rationality are consistent with propositions upheld on the basis of faith, or whether the use of reason is compatible with the experiencing of aesthetic feelings, and the like. Thus any attack on reason or any claim to supersede it by some other human power or criterion must rely on reason to justify its claims. On the other hand, despite Hume's dictum that "reason is nothing but a wonderful and unintelligible instinct in our souls,"[15] the logical validity and necessity achieved by deduction and the empirical ineluctableness reflected in induction are directly constitutive of reason, and they give it a cogency and nonarbitrariness that provide a sufficient justification for relying on it.

How do the concepts of reason and action fulfill the justificatory task I have assigned to them in relation to the supreme principle of morality? Let us begin by recalling that the answer to the authoritative question of moral philosophy must indicate why action in accordance with a certain moral criterion is categorically obligatory in that its requiredness cannot rightly be evaded by any action or institution. Now such an answer is obtainable if a supreme moral principle can be shown to be logically necessary so that its denial is self-contradictory. For since the principle says that actions of a certain kind ought to be performed, the fact that the principle is necessarily true provides a conclusive justificatory reason for believing that the kinds of action the principle says ought to be performed ought indeed to be per- formed. But to have such a reason for believing this about certain actions is also to have a conclusive justificatory reason for doing the actions, so that the principle's normative necessity, whereby its require- ments for action cannot rightly be evaded, follows from its being logically necessary. For if one is conclusively justified in believing that one ought to do X, then, at least so far as concerns the ascertainable grounds for one's action, one is conclusively justified in doing X. And it is only by deductive rationality that such necessary truth can be established.

This brief answer incurs various difficulties about the relations between logical and moral necessity, and between reasons for believing and for doing. Waiving these for the present, I wish to emphasize a further gap whose bridging will show the central importance of the concept of action for the justificatory project. It is possible for a proposition or principle to be necessarily true only within the context of a system of arbitrary definitions and axioms from which it can be shown to follow by rigorous deductive reasoning, so that to affirm the premises and to deny the conclusion is to incur self-contradiction. But the premises need not themselves be necessarily true. Hence, the proposition would have only a kind of formal or relative necessity, as logically following from the system's premises; yet the system as a whole would be only contingent because it would have logically possible alternatives: its premises could be denied without self-contradiction. Indeed, the premises themselves may be false, and also the conclusions. If, then, the supreme principle of morality is to emerge as a necessarily true justificatum by a deductive argument, it seems that the formal necessity of its being entailed or deductively implied by various premises is not sufficient; there will also have to be a material necessity of the premises themselves. The content as well as the form of the justificatory argument will have to be necessary and not merely contingent, let alone arbitrary or false.

The need for such necessary content also follows from the concept of morality itself. As we have seen, judgments of moral obligation are categorical in that what persons morally ought to do sets requirements for them that they cannot rightly evade by consulting their own self-interested desires or variable opinions, ideals, or institutional practices. For moral judgments are critically evaluative of all of these. But such inescapable obligations cannot be derived from variable contents. Moreover, ultimate moral disagreements can be rationally resolved only if moral obligations are based on necessary contents. For if moral principles have contingent contents, so that their obligatoriness may vary with the variable desires or opinions of different protagonists, then no finality can be rationally imposed on their differing moral beliefs. To ascertain which among the various possible or actual moral principles are right or correct hence demands that one adopt a standpoint that is superior to these variable elements, so that it can be seen to impose rational requirements on them. Such a superior standpoint, to avoid the variability and relativism of the subject matter to which it is addressed, must have a rational necessity of content as well as of form. But how can such contentual necessity be established by reason?

To answer this question, the subject matter of morality must be considered; this consideration, being performed through conceptual analysis, is itself a product of reason in the sense of deductive rationality. If there is a subject matter with which all moralities and moral judgments must be concerned directly or indirectly, then this will provide a necessary content for all such judgments. If it can be further shown that this content has certain determinate logical consequences regarding the criteria of moral rightness, then the principle that upholds these criteria will emerge as materially or contentually as well as formally necessary. The subject matter of morality will thus be at least part of the justificans of the supreme moral principle; and since this justificans is contentually necessary, so too will be the moral principle that is its justificatum.

This necessary content of morality is to be found in action and its generic features. For all moral precepts, regardless of their further contents, deal directly or indirectly with how persons ought to act. The specific modes of action required by different moral precepts are, of course, highly variable. But amid these variations, the precepts require actions; and there are certain invariant features that pertain generically to all actions. I shall call these the *generic features* of action because they characterize the genus or category of action as a whole, as delimited by moral and other practical precepts. Thus, just as action provides the necessary content of all morality, so the generic features provide the necessary content of all action.

It will be of the first importance to trace how these features determine the necessities of moral rightness, so that from the 'is' of the generic features of action there is logically derivable the 'ought' of moral principles and rules. Insofar as these generic features of action constitute the justificans of the supreme principle of morality, the latter, as their justificatum, will also have a necessary content. These generic features, in turn, are ascertained by deductive rationality, so that the ultimate justificans of the supreme principle consists in reason.

Now just as the concept of reason, which I have confined to deduction and induction, is morally neutral and hence not question-begging, so too the concept of action that is to be used as the basis of the justificatory argument is morally neutral. For since this concept comprises the generic features of all action, it fits all moralities rather than reflecting or deriving from any one normative moral position as against any other. How, then, can it be shown that from such morally neutral premises there follow determinate, normatively moral conclusions about the necessary content of the supreme principle of morality? This question poses one of the major challenges the present work must meet. The answer consists in showing that, because of its generic features, action has what I shall call a 'normative structure,' in that evaluative and deontic judgments on the part of agents are logically implicit in all action; and when these judgments are subjected to certain rational requirements, a certain normative moral principle logically follows from them. To put it otherwise: Any agent, simply by virtue of being an agent, must admit, on pain of self-contradiction, that he ought to act in certain determinate ways.

The relation of action to morality bears importantly on the question raised earlier about the correspondence-correlates moral judgments must have if they are to be true by virtue of correspondence. Since action comprises the factual subject matter of moral and other practical precepts, it serves for moral philosophy a function analogous to that which empirical observational data may be held to serve for natural science: that of providing an objective basis or subject matter against which, respectively, moral judgments or rules and empirical statements or laws can be checked for their truth or correctness. It must be emphasized that this function is only analogous: a moral judgment does not become true simply by stating that some action or kind of action is actually performed. As we shall see, it is rather that action, through its generic features and normative structure, entails certain requirements on the part of agents, and moral judgments are true insofar as they correspond to these requirements and hence to the normative structure of action. But because action provides the necessary content of moral judgments, these are not left, so far as concerns truth, completely unsupported by relevant objective standards or data. Although the importance of action for moral philosophy has been recognized since the ancient Greeks, it has not hitherto been noted that the nature of action enters into the very content and justification of the supreme principle of morality.

1.10. Before tracing how determinate criteria of moral rightness are logically derived from the generic features of action, the content and context of these features must be further indicated. The word 'action' is used in many different senses, but the sense relevant here is that which is the common object of all moral precepts as well as of many other practical precepts that set requirements for action. Amid the immense variety of such precepts, they have in common that the intention of the persons who set them forth is to guide, advise, or urge the persons to whom they are directed so that these latter persons will more or less reflectively fashion their behavior along the lines indicated in the precepts. Hence it is assumed that the hearers can control their behavior through their unforced choice so as to try to achieve the prescribed ends or contents, although they may also intentionally refrain from complying with the precepts. From this it follows that action, in the strict sense that is relevant to moral and other practical precepts, has two interrelated generic features: voluntariness or freedom and purposiveness or intentionality. By an action's being voluntary or free I mean that its performance is under the agent's control in that he unforcedly chooses to act as he does, knowing the relevant proximate circumstances of his action. By an action's being purposive or intentional I mean that the agent acts for some end or purpose that constitutes his reason for acting; this purpose may consist in the action itself or in something to be achieved by the action. Voluntariness and purposiveness hence comprise what I referred to above as the generic features of action, since they are the most general features distinctively characteristic of the whole genus of action, where 'action' consists in all the possible objects of moral and other practical precepts in the respects just indicated. And it is these generic features that constitute the logical justificatory basis of the supreme principle of morality.

It may be objected that many and perhaps even all moral precepts address prospective agents not as unencumbered individuals who can make their own decisions de novo but rather as bearers of social roles defined by institutional rules. The primary morality, in this view, is that of 'my station and its duties' as derived from the requirements of groups, so that a person is an 'assemblage of roles': husband, father, voter, taxpayer, carpenter, union member, proletarian, buyer, bowling-team captain, or more generally a member of some national, religious, ethnic, or racial group or economic class, and so forth. What moral precepts assume or require about a person's conduct, then, is not that it is voluntary and purposive in that he initiates and controls his behavior in the light of his own aims, but rather that he conforms to the rules that define his various roles or status; and insofar as he conforms, it is these rules that control his conduct and set its purposes. Hence, voluntariness and purposiveness are not the generic features of all or even most actions in the sense in which 'action' has been defined.

This objection does not remove the point of the above delineation of action. As is indicated by such famous phrases as Marx's "Man makes his own history" and "Workers of the world, unite!" it is assumed even in 'social-role' moral precepts that, within limits, action is under the control of the persons or groups addressed by the precepts— that they can have knowledge of relevant circumstances and choose to act in one way rather than in another for purposes or reasons they accept. Even if moral precepts urge conformity to various social roles or institutions, and even if they assume that such conformity is already exhibited by the persons addressed, the point of setting forth the precepts is at least partly to reinforce an existing pattern of obedience and thereby to ward off potential disobedience. Thus the precepts assume that alternative behavior may be open to the persons addressed so that, to this extent, their behavior is under their control. This control may be dispositional rather than occurrent. In any case, even inaction, when it is intentionally engaged in by persons who dispositionally control their behavior, is a form of action. It is from the generic features of the actions that are the common objects of all such moral and other practical precepts that the supreme principle of morality is logically derived.

When it is said that action as envisaged by all moral (including social-role) precepts is voluntary and purposive, a distinction must be drawn between the general formal assumptions of all such precepts and their specific variable contents. These contents may not promote or provide for the further voluntariness or freedom and the various purposes of the agents to whom they are addressed. Indeed, they may be quite antithetical thereto, for in order to be moral they need take favorable account of the interests only of some person or persons other than or in addition to the agent or speaker. Nevertheless, insofar as they fulfill certain formal conditions, the precepts prospectively assume that the behaviors of the persons addressed will be voluntary and purposive. These conditions, which are found in all moral precepts, consist in certain minimal aspects of rationality and associated normativeness. The precepts must be presented not as mere incitements or goads to action, as threats or attempts at brainwashing, but rather as reasoned commands, as offering directives or guidance for action with the implicit assumption that these are the right ways to act because there are sound reasons for doing so (these need not be moral reasons). A related assumption is that these reasons can be reflectively understood by the persons to whom they are addressed. To the extent to which these conditions are fulfilled, the precepts, regardless of their further contents, are addressed to their hearers as persons who can control their behavior with a view to achieving the prescribed objectives. To say this is not, of course, to say that the hearers, who are prospective or actual agents, or all the other persons affected will necessarily agree with the reasons or the objectives, or that either the speakers or the hearers fulfill more than these minimal conditions of rationality.

To see more clearly how the generic features of action provide the necessary content of the supreme principle of morality, we must note that the features of the actions prescribed by moral principles and judgments are also found in the behaviors prescribed by technical, artistic, prudential, social, and other principles and judgments. Examples of these are situations where one person advises another on what to do in some technical context (such as how to give a karate chop or make a bomb) or where he decides what to do from a purely prudential or egoistic motive concerned only with his own purposes or well-being (such as how to swindle a rich widow), as well as in social contexts where some degree of reflective thought is assumed. Collectively these principles and precepts make up the field of what I shall call 'practice,' and the behaviors they prescribe are of the sort usually called 'intentional' actions. It is hence not open to an 'amoralist' or 'nihilist' to reject the ensuing argument from the generic features of action to the supreme principle of morality on the ground that, since he rejects all moralities, he rejects the present account of action that is derived from morality. My argument does not rest, in circular fashion, on any form of moral precept or judgment such as, 'One morally ought not to regard a behavior as an action unless it has features X and Y.' Nor does my argument assume that one already accepts any morality in general or in particular or that one upholds any norms other than those of deductive and inductive rationality. Rather, the present use of moral precepts is to provide clues to the relevant concept of action, that is, the concept from which the supreme principle of morality is logically derived. Since this concept also applies to practice and intentional actions, the nihilist or amoralist could reject this stage of the argument only by disavowing and refraining from all intentional action and from the whole sphere of practice.

In deriving the relevant features of action from the assumptions or envisagement of persons who set forth moral and other precepts about actions, I am not suggesting that the contents of these assumptions diverge from the realities of human conduct or behavior. The pattern of the argument is not: 'If action is to be as it is envisaged to be in moral and other precepts, then it must have features $F_1, F_2, \ldots, F_n$, although in reality $F_1, F_2, \ldots, F_n$ may or do not pertain to any human behavior.' The analysis of the concept of action is not to be regarded as yielding results that are merely 'conceptual' as opposed to 'real.' Rather, the concern is to differentiate, from the many and varied real features of human behaviors, those that constitute human action in the relevant sense. What the utterers of such precepts prospectively envisage about future actions falls within the real possibilities of human conduct.

A sign of the real status of actions as here characterized is that (waiving Cartesian doubts) they not only make up a large dimension of the human behavior encountered in ordinary experience but they also supply the data of empirical studies of human action. For example, action as treated here includes all four types of 'social action' distinguished by Weber, which are characterized, respectively, by means-end rationality, by dedication to an absolute value, by affectual behavior, and by conformity to tradition.[16] In this extensive way, the generic features of action pertain to historically diverse patterns of conduct, including not only moderns, ranging from capitalist entrepreneurs (or 'men of action') to unskilled laborers, but also medieval saints, warriors, and plebians, ancient sages, tyrants, and 'banausoi,' and exponents of many different ways of life in all eras in which persons control their behavior for ends they regard as worth pursuing. The unity and invariability of the concept of action as here analyzed do not debar the concept from being relevant to the diversities of problems, backgrounds, ideals, and modes of conduct that characterize morality and practice in their full historical complexity.

It must also be noted that the relevant concept of human action is not to be viewed as being exhaustively confined to behaviors that actually fall under past or present moral and other practical precepts, let alone to those that actually conform to such precepts. The precepts are divergent attempts to guide a vast mass of human behaviors. The features by virtue of which these behaviors can be thus guided may also belong to a host of other behaviors that are not and have not been the objects of such precepts. The generic features of the actions found in all these contexts provide the common basis from which the supreme principle of morality is logically derived.

The moral population addressed by moral precepts varies in part according to the substantive and especially the distributive criteria upheld in different moralities. The Machiavellian or Nietzschean elitist addresses at least some of his precepts to a much smaller group than does the Kantian or Millian universalist. In any case, it is this group of persons addressed by the precepts of each morality that comprises, from its standpoint, those who are moral agents as against being mere recipients of other persons' agency. But however much the persons addressed by various moral and other practical precepts may differ in other respects, it is true of all of them that they are assumed to be able to control their relevant behaviors by their unforced choice for reasons and purposes they can make their own. And as we shall see, by virtue of having these practical abilities, agents are logically committed to accept certain normative judgments, and ultimately a certain supreme moral principle.

1.11. The concepts of voluntariness and purposiveness, as well as of action itself, involve many controversial complexities that have generated a vast literature. Within the present limits of space I must confine myself to a few further considerations that are especially relevant to seeing how these features of action provide the justificatory basis of the supreme principle of morality.

First, then, voluntariness. For human behaviors or movements to be actions in the strict sense and hence voluntary or free, certain causal conditions must be fulfilled. Negatively, the behaviors must not occur from one or more of the following kinds of cause: (a) direct compulsion, physical or psychological, by someone or something external to the person; (b) causes internal to the person, such as reflexes, ignorance, or disease, that decisively contribute, in ways beyond his control, to the occurrence of the behavior; (c) indirect compulsion whereby the person's choice to emit the behavior is forced by someone else's coercion. Positively, the person must control his behavior by his own unforced and informed choice. This does not mean that whenever he chooses to do something he does it, for he may be unable to do it. It means rather that when his behavior is voluntary or free, his unforced and informed choice is the necessary and sufficient condition of the behavior. For all behaviors that are the objects of moral and other practical precepts, it is assumed that the persons addressed can control their behaviors in this way. When there is such control, the person chooses on the basis of informed reasons he has for acting as he does. Among other things, he knows what action he is performing, for what purpose, its proximate outcome, and his recipients. The self, person, or agent to whom the choices belong may be viewed as an organized system of dispositions in which such informed reasons are coherently interrelated with other desires and choices. Insofar as a person's behavior derives from this system, it is the person who controls his behavior by his unforced choice, so that it is voluntary. And because it is voluntary, it constitutes part of the justificatory basis of the supreme principle of morality.

In its most complete sense, 'choice' connotes antecedent, informed deliberation between alternatives and a reasoned decision based on that deliberation, with consideration being given to relevant aspects of the organized system of dispositions that constitutes the person and with knowledge of relevant circumstances. There are also less complete senses of 'choice,' where it still connotes a selection and decision from among available alternatives but with little or no antecedent deliberation. Within limits, choices may be foolish and uninformed; but when these limits are passed, the resulting behavior is no longer voluntary. The kleptomaniac's or berserk smasher's behavior is not controlled by his choice even in these less complete senses; he suffers severely diminished capacity to be aware of relevant circumstances, alternatives, and reasons and to select among them. We may, however, distinguish three different sorts of control and unforced choice on the part of a person that, when applied to his behavior, make it voluntary. (a) The control and choice may be occurrent, pertaining directly to the action as it occurs. (b) They may be dispositional, in that if the agent had chosen not to perform the action he would not have performed it. (c) They may be even more indirectly dispositional, in that although the action occurred despite the agent's choosing not to perform it, so that the action was not under his dispositional control of sort (b), still he could have controlled his getting into the situation where he could not thus dispositionally control his performing the action. In all three of these ways the agent's reasoned choice and control function as necessary and sufficient conditions of his action. Behavior is involuntary if it is not controlled by the agent in any of these three ways.

In all these kinds of choice, an important condition is that they must be unforced. For behaviors caused by forced choices are not fully voluntary, hence not actions in the strict sense, and hence not part of the normative structure from which the supreme principle of morality is logically derived. Paradigm cases of forced choice are found in slave and concentration camps and in most prisons, but a simpler example is provided by the gunman's saying to Smith, 'Your money or your life.' When Smith hands over his money, he controls his movement by his own choice. His choice, however, is forced because he is compelled to choose between two undesirable alternatives that someone else has set for him with the intention of causing him to choose one alternative by threatening that, in case of noncompliance, he will undergo the other, even worse alternative. Hence, although it is open to Smith to choose either alternative, both the constraining of the alternatives and the severe disadvantage of the threatened worse alternative serve in effect to force the choice of the other alternative. Forced choice thus has at least three interrelated aspects: compulsoriness, undesirableness, and threat. We may extend the concept of 'control' here: Smith is not in control of the situation whereby he must choose one of the two alternatives: if it were left to his own control, he would choose neither. When one's choice is unforced, on the other hand, one chooses on the basis of one's informed reasons that do not include these compulsory and other features.

Now insofar as actions comprise the possible objects of moral and other practical precepts in the ways indicated above, behaviors under forced choice may be actions. For an important kind of moral precept declares that some behaviors ought to be engaged in under the conditions of compulsoriness, undesirableness, and threat, and other behaviors ought not, that is, that among the alternative actions available to a person under forced choice where the well-being of other persons is involved, he morally ought to choose some alternatives rather than others. For example, if the gunman threatened to kill an innocent bystander if Smith did not surrender his money, then according to such a moral precept he ought to surrender it. What this shows is that while some aspects of the direct forced-choice situation are not under the person's control, other aspects are. This is why Aristotle called such behaviors 'mixed '[17]: they are 'voluntary' in that at the moment of his actual performance the person controls his behavior by his own choice, but they are 'involuntary' because they comprise the compulsory and other conditions noted above, so that the choice is forced. It remains, then, that behavior under forced choice has an irreducible involuntary or unfree component because of its combination of compulsoriness and threatened undesirableness. This component, as it confronts the prospective agent, is not subject to his control and hence is not itself an object of moral or other practical precepts. For this reason, voluntary or free action in the full or strict sense excludes forced choice, so that such choice is not included among the generic features of action that provide the justificatory basis of the supreme principle of morality.

It might be thought, however, that on the above account most and even all choices can be shown to be forced, so that no actions are fully voluntary. Consider such alternatives as: 'Take a pay cut or be fired,' 'Shave off your beard or I won't marry you,' 'Love your country or leave it.' According to a certain 'economic' view of choice and action, all choice is compulsory and between undesirable alternatives: "Everywhere we turn, if we choose one thing we must relinquish others which, in different circumstances, we would wish not to have relinquished. . . . Economics brings into full view that conflict of choice which is one of the permanent aspects of human existence. Your economist is a true tragedian."[18] In addition to the absence of threat, however, this extension of the concept of forced choice is to be rejected on at least one other ground. For according to the economic view everything short of the whole of all possible value would be 'undesirable,' since it regards as undesirable whatever contains less good than some other possibility one might want to have. This, however, assumes a fantastic exaggeration of human desire, on the model of Plato's insatiable tyrant or Freud's id.

Another possible reason for rejecting the above multiplication of forced choices is that the concept requires, besides the three features previously listed, a further condition: an intrusion into "the normal or natural or expected course of events" where this intrusion makes the alternatives "worse than they would have been in the normal or expected course of events."[19] This condition may serve at least in part to distinguish the gunman case from the other cases just mentioned. There still remains, however, the question of how choice is to be construed where in "the normal or natural or expected course of events" the alternatives for one's choice are already very undesirable, threatening, and externally induced. Surely the forcedness of choice is not removed when these features are a regular part of someone's life or of the institutional structure of a society. To take a less extreme example from the large-scale development of modern technological systems, when industrial workers function as cogs in a vast machine and as dominated by huge impersonal corporations, their choices to work under such conditions might be held to be forced by the threat of unemployment and the unavailability of alternative conditions. Even if the threatened undesirableness and compulsion do not occurrently stem from an individual agent like the gunman, concepts like powerlessness, alienation, and meaninglessness may be used to characterize the workers' situation.

To deal with this issue in the light of the various examples given above, it must be recognized that forced choices may vary in degree. Three bases of this variation may be distinguished, reflecting the criteria of forced choice previously indicated: first, how bad, in the eyes of the chooser, is the worse of the two alternatives between which a choice must be made (undesirableness); second, whether any further alternatives may be opened up (compulsoriness); third, and especially important, to what extent rational procedures are made available to the coerced person or group (threat). Consider, for example, the differences between the gunman and the pay-cut cases. In the gunman case, one of only two alternatives set by someone else must be chosen at once, one of the alternatives is death, no appeal or argument is permitted. But in the pay-cut case, the choice between pay cut and loss of livelihood may not have to be made at once; there may still remain such alternatives as organizing on the part of the workers, collective bargaining, and setting up rules that provide for all concerned protections from a jungle situation. The opening up of such alternatives may tend toward a greater equalization of power among the persons concerned as against a monopoly of threats on one side; but also, as against a bare forced-choice situation, it provides opportunities for giving and weighing reasons for one course as against another. This aspect serves to remove, in important degree, the threats, undesirableness, and compulsoriness noted above. But although the forcedness of choice may vary in these ways, this does not entail that voluntariness and hence action are subject to similar variations. Although they may vary in other ways, these do not include compulsoriness and threatened undesirableness. In the strict sense action involves unforced choice based on one's informed reasons, so that the conjoint conditions indicated above are absent. And it is from action in this strict sense that the supreme principle of morality is logically derived.

In addition to problems raised by forced choice, my thesis that the generic features of action include voluntariness or freedom may also be criticized on the ground that legal precepts providing for strict liability or collective responsibility have as their objects behaviors that are not subject to the individual's control and knowledge. Since legal precepts are practical and are akin to moral precepts in certain respects, it may be contended that these provisions of the law disprove my thesis that the objects of all such precepts are voluntary actions. It may also be argued that my exclusion of such behaviors from the sphere of 'action' reflects an individualist, normatively moral out-look,[20] so that my starting point is not morally neutral after all. It must be noted, however, that the relevant concept of action concerns behaviors as prospectively envisaged by those who give moral and other practical precepts rather than as involved in the manifold operational problems of the actual execution of the precepts. The question is: When actions are morally or practically advised, urged, or prescribed, what features must the speakers assume that the actions will have in relation to their hearers on whom these actions are urged? As I have previously indicated, an assumption of moral and much other practical discourse is that the hearers can understand and reflect on the reasons for performing the actions and can then proceed to perform them. The behaviors dealt with in provisions for strict liability and collective responsibility are actions in the relevant sense only insofar as the persons addressed can at least prospectively control their behavior so as to conform to these provisions. Where this ability to control is absent, the idea of reason-giving that is essential to moral and many other practical precepts is also absent, unless the control in question is exercisable by the persons addressed at some stage prior to the behavior in question. That there is such prior ability to control one's behavior is, indeed, an assumption of these legal precepts.

According to the thesis of hard determinism, all events, including even the agent's own choices, are caused by forces beyond his control. If this thesis is true, then there are no unforced choices based on one's own informed consideration of reasons for action, so that no human behaviors are voluntary or free in the sense discussed above; instead, all occur ultimately from what I have called 'direct compulsion.' From this it would follow that there are no actions in the strict sense having a normative structure from which the supreme principle of morality can be derived. I shall briefly indicate four reasons why this thesis of determinism should not be viewed as invalidating the above account of voluntary action. First, the thesis itself is far from being proved as an explanation either of all events in general or of human actions in particular. Second, regardless of the logical or metaphysical status of the thesis, it must still leave room for the distinctions indicated above. No thesis can be regarded as plausible that denies the differences among the following kinds of behaviors: those involving forced choices of the gunman type; those where one makes no choices, whether in direct compulsion (such as when one is struck by lightning or is physically pushed around by someone else) or in internally caused nightmares; and those where, after prolonged deliberation on relevant reasons culminating in a carefully considered choice, one embarks upon some planned, more or less extensive activity.

Third, the determinist thesis is unable to account for itself, and indeed it is at odds with itself. If the thesis is true, then the intellectual or cognitive operations of its upholders, including their choice or decision to maintain the thesis, far from proceeding in terms of independent careful consideration of reasons or arguments, are themselves only the effects of inexorable forces beyond the upholders' control. But if this is so, why should the thesis that results from these operations be accepted as valid or true? If, on the other hand, the thesis does indeed rest on the intellectual examination of reasons or arguments and a considered choice based thereon, then the thesis is false as a universal account of human behaviors. Fourth, the determinist thesis is unable to account for the difference between the relation of physical or psychological cause and effect and the relation of logical or evidential ground and consequent. According to the thesis, all relations involving human behaviors are of the former kind; but for the thesis to be tenable as an explanatory doctrine, some relations (those entering into the thesis itself, including the formation, understanding, and choice of it) must be of the latter kind. To be sure, computing machines can be constructed that embody logical relations in physical cause-effect operations. But the constructors themselves, at an earlier or a later remove, must proceed by their own independent, intellectual understanding of logical relations as distinct from physical ones. Choices may indeed be extensively affected by previous psychological conditioning. But such conditioning may take a variety of forms. Even when strong emotional factors are invoked, these and other conditioning influences need not be exhaustive determinants of a person's choices; he may still reflectively consider various reasons for alternative actions and choose among them on the basis of such consideration. It is when a person controls his behavior by such unforced choices based on his own informed reasons that his action is fully voluntary, and it is such voluntariness that provides part of the normative structure from which the supreme principle of morality is logically derived.

1.12. I shall now briefly consider certain aspects of purposiveness as a generic feature of action. As in the case of voluntariness, I shall confine myself to aspects that enter into the rational justification of the supreme principle of morality. When moral and other practical precepts enjoin certain behaviors on persons, the speaker assumes not only that his hearers can control their behavior through their unforced choice, so that they act voluntarily, but also that they will do so with a view to attaining ends or goals that constitute their reasons for acting. This point holds as much for deontological as for teleological moral precepts; in the case of the former it is conformity to certain moral rules that directly constitutes the purpose or intention of the actions urged on persons. In urging or advising that such actions be performed, the deontologist assumes that the persons he addresses are in any case acting with a view to certain purposes or objectives, and he tries to show what they ought to aim at when moral issues are at stake, even if, in a narrower sense of 'purpose,' he denies that moral actions have any purpose.

The behaviors that are the possible objects of these and other moral precepts are hence not aimless but rather goal-directed, at least in the sense that they envisage more or less clearly a certain content to be effected or achieved, even if at one level this content consists only in a certain mode of acting or in observance of certain rules or formal requirements. The persons who engage in this behavior are regarded not merely as loci of movements but as controlling their movements for reasons they can make their own, because they want to engage in that behavior either for its own sake or for some result to be achieved thereby. These reasons or wants are the purposes of their actions, and the purposes may violate as well as conform to moral precepts; they may also be indifferent to the precepts. But in any case the agents are assumed to be capable of reflecting on the purposes for which they act, even if they do not always do so. The purposive feature of action thus extends from the direct content of the action as intended by the agent to whatever more distant end he may aim at according to his motives for acting. In this whole range, the agent's aims or intentions are wants or desires, so that in every action an agent acts more or less reflectively in accordance with his wants. These wants, however, need not be hedonic or inclinational; they may consist simply in the intentions with which actions are performed.

Such purposiveness is as necessarily connected with action in the strict sense as is the feature of voluntariness or freedom. In choosing to perform some definite action, the agent must more or less clearly envisage that action: he must know what action it is that he is choosing to perform; that is, he must intend that action in the sense of having it more or less in view and wanting to perform it. He must intend it, moreover, either for its own sake or for the sake of some consequence he wants to achieve by the action, or both. Thus intention or purpose, in the sense of the desired content of an action, is the other side of the control and choice that constitute voluntariness or freedom and that are concerned with bringing about that desired content.

Just as control and choice may be dispositional as well as occurrent, so it is with purposiveness. Agents may not always have purposes clearly in view; in particular, 'purposive' must not be identified with 'purposeful,' where the latter connotes a deliberate, resolute design and its determined pursuit. The purposes for which persons act may be habitual, results of long-standing goal-directed behavior where the goals have ceased to occupy the center of attention. Such habits, however, do not indicate the complete absence of purposiveness, but only that the purposes can be achieved without being explicitly considered or aimed at. That they are still latently present, however, would be shown if attempts were made to interfere with the agent's attaining them. A person may eat, for example, out of habit and while thinking of many other things; but if his food is taken away when he is only half-finished, or if food entirely different from his usual preferences is substituted, his purposes in eating would return to the forefront of attention.

Purposiveness has a procedural as well as a substantive aspect. Just as 'intention' may refer both to intending and to what is intended, so 'purpose' may refer both to 'purposing' and to the object or end aimed at. Purposing is conative and dynamic; it consists in trying to achieve some end. The purpose in the sense of having achieved the end aimed at, on the other hand, is consummatory. Now in its conative aspect purposiveness, like voluntariness, is procedural and instrumental, since trying to achieve consists in events or operations engaged in with a view to achieving. Nevertheless, these two features of action can still be distinguished in that conative purposiveness consists in the agent's aiming at an end or goal, whereas voluntariness consists in the agent's controlling his behavior. Thus purposiveness as conative and instrumental, unlike voluntariness, involves intrinsic reference to the end or goal the agent envisages for his action. Because of this, purposiveness makes a distinct contribution to the normative structure of action from which the supreme principle of morality is logically derived.

To this account of the necessary connection of purposiveness and action, two interrelated objections may be made. One, which especially reflects a deontological position, is that in obeying moral precepts persons may act simply from a sense of duty or in accordance with moral rules and not for the fulfillment of any end or purpose. This objection is based on two assumptions: that to act for a purpose is to act to fulfill some want or desire, and that wants or desires are always hedonic or inclinational. The deontologist, following Kant, holds that moral duties are meant to curb person's inclinations, so that action in accordance with moral precepts cannot consist in acting according to one's wants.[21] A second objection accepts the second of the two deontological assumptions but rejects the first. This objection, while agreeing with my account that all action is purposive, holds that purposive action requires only that the agent have certain endeavors or intentions, but not necessarily any wants or desires. The basis of the objection is that persons may engage in purposive action without having any positive liking for or hedonic inclination toward that which it is their purpose to do or to bring about, even as a means to something else that is desired.[22]

These objections do not, however, show that agents, including moral agents, do not act for purposes or that they do not in any sense want or desire to do what it is their purpose to do. It is important to remember that 'wanting' has not only an inclinational or hedonic sense, but also an intentional sense.[23] In the inclinational sense, to want to do X is to take pleasure in doing X or to like doing X; but in the intentional sense, to want to do X is simply to intend to do X, to regard one's doing X as having some point or purpose even if one doesn't like doing it. In this intentional sense, a person may want or desire to do something because he regards it as his duty or role or as a means toward avoiding a worse alternative or for some other reason, even though he takes no pleasure in doing it, has no feeling of inclination toward doing it, and indeed does it very reluctantly. As we shall see, it is because of this general connection of purposiveness with wanting that every agent implicitly makes certain value judgments from which, through several further steps, the supreme principle of morality is logically derived. It will hence be helpful to consider further how wanting enters into purposive action.

What is common to all cases of wanting to do something is that the agent has some sort of pro-attitude toward the purpose of his action. This pro-attitude comprises at least three main features. First, there is selective attention: in acting for some purpose E, the agent turns his attention to E as against other possible objects of his attention. This attending need not be completely exclusive in its objects, nor need it be very intense in its quality; but still, in a relative sense, it involves focusing on E sufficiently to constitute an awareness of E in contradistinction to other objects. Second, having this pro-attitude toward E is directive or vectorial: other things being equal, the agent tends to move himself toward the attainment of E rather than other possible objects. Although not all pro-attitudes may involve such a tendency, it is present when there are no opposed attitudes or when these do not outweigh it. Third, this tendency is accompanied by some sort of favorable interest in or mind-set toward attaining E, as against being indifferent or hostile toward it. This favoring need not be vehement, nor need it be hedonic or inclinational. But it comprises a positive intending to have E, such that interference with its attainment would cause at least momentary annoyance or dissatisfaction. It follows from this that there are no indifferent actions, 'indifferent' meaning that the agent does not care at all whether he performs the action or not. For even if he regards his action as morally indifferent or as not making any difference on some other specific criterion, by the very fact that he aims to do the action he has a pro-attitude toward doing it and hence a positive or favorable interest in doing it. At least in this relative sense, the agent in acting for some end or purpose E wants to have or attain E as the chosen or intended object of his endeavor. And since purpose or intention, like wanting, need not be hedonic, it can be a feature even of such moral action as is performed from a sense of duty.

It is this more general sense of 'wanting,' as against the more narrowly hedonic one, that removes the otherwise paradoxical import of the position that every agent does what he wants to do. The narrower sense often figures alone in psychological descriptions, as in the two following characterizations, the first of psychopathic personalities, the second of masochists: "They merely wish to do what they want to do when they want to do it; they are grown-up children of the Pleasure Principle, often with normal egos, but without fear of intrapsychic punishment because of defective super-ego functions." "They tend not to assert themselves, not to do what they want, but to submit to the factual or alleged orders of these outside forces."[24] Neither of these characterizations removes the generalization I have presented here, that all agents, not only psychopaths and not excluding masochists, perform their actions because they want to do so, for the sake of some purpose whose attainment they desire. But the more general meaning of 'want' must here be kept in view. And of course there still remains the separate question whether psychopaths and masochists act voluntarily.

It is important to have seen the connection presented above between purposiveness and wants or desires. For from this connection stems the fact that the agent necessarily regards his purposes as good and hence makes an implicit value judgment about them; and from this, in turn, there necessarily follow other judgments, both evaluative and deontic, that finally entail the supreme principle of morality as a principle that every agent is logically committed to accept.

In the broad senses in which each of them has been explicated here, voluntariness and purposiveness exhaust the generic features of action. This can be seen by noting some of the ways in which they have been or may be distinguished, despite their close interrelation as concerned with reasons for acting. Voluntariness involves a procedural aspect of actions in that it concerns the way actions are controlled as ongoing events. Purposiveness, on the other hand, in addition to having the distinct procedural aspect mentioned above, also involves the substantive aspect of actions, the specific contents of these events. Voluntariness refers to the means, purposiveness to the end; voluntariness comprises the agent's causation of his action, whereas purposiveness comprises the object or goal of the action in the sense of the good he wants to achieve or have through this causation. Thus voluntariness is a matter of initiation or control while purposiveness is at least in part a matter of consummation. Other candidates for generic features of action, such as adherence to rules or principles, deliberation or calculation of consequences, and so forth, either do not characterize all actions or else are derivative from and subsumable under one or the other of the two features discussed above.

Before undertaking to show how action, with its generic features of voluntariness and purposiveness, logically commits all agents to acceptance of a certain determinate moral principle, I must discuss certain aspects of method, bearing on the way judgments in general are connected with action. The point of this discussion is that certain judgments, in a certain sequence of argument, are necessarily attributable to every rational agent. What I shall call the dialectically necessary method explains the basis of this attribution. The method shows how the argument from the generic features of action to the supreme principle of morality is not only one that is presented here for the reader's consideration, but also that every agent logically must give his assent to the argument insofar as he is rational.

The Dialectically Necessary Method

1.13. As so far analyzed, action has been seen to comprise, in addition to bodily movements, such mental factors as choosing and intending. These, in their broadest aspects, are modes of thinking, at least of practical thinking; they consist not merely or even primarily in incipient behaviors, but also in such occurrent or dispositional mental states or events as wanting, envisaging, reflecting, heeding, deliberating, attending, deciding, valuing, caring, and so forth, all of which may enter into the proximate causal background of actions. Now it has long been recognized that language is connected with thought, as expressing and communicating it. This is as true of practical as of theoretical thinking. Hence, to the extent to which such practical thinking is attributable, and to some extent necessarily attributable, to the agent who performs actions as analyzed above, to the same extent linguistic expressions or judgments are also attributable to him. This does not mean that he necessarily speaks aloud or mutters to himself vocally, but rather that in acting and thinking as he does the agent uses or makes judgments that can be expressed in words. To say that they are so expressible is not, of course, to say that they are actually expressed.

These linguistic expressions or equivalents of the agent's practical thinking can correctly be attributed to him in either direct or indirect discourse. Thus, if Jones chooses to do X for purpose E, he can be depicted as saying, 'I choose to do X for purpose E.' The psychological verb may also figure only implicitly in the judgment, taking such forms as, 'I will do X for purpose E' or 'X is to be done by me for purpose E.' Although the difference between these modes of expression may be important for some contexts, they may be treated as practical equivalents in others. Also, in addition to performative, prescriptive, and other nondescriptive judgments, the agent's action can be expressed by him simply as, 'I do X for purpose E.' This form of statement is not 'ascriptive' but straightforwardly descriptive, as indicating what the agent does and is aware of doing. In making such a statement the agent may not be performing the very action mentioned in the statement (as in 'I hereby marry you'), nor need he be accepting responsibility for the action. Instead, he may simply be reporting what he does or has done. Diary entries and other narrations are familiar examples of such descriptive reports of one's own actions.

When the mental events that enter into practical thinking are given such linguistic renditions, it may be objected that they construe the agent as performing at least two 'acts,' a mental one and a linguistic one, where he has performed only the mental one. It may also be objected that he is here credited with an unrealistic degree of self-consciousness: persons who act and make choices do not always or even usually have a distinguishable explicit awareness of doing so, let alone an awareness that they express in words. These objections, however, misconstrue the linguistic expressions as separate occurrences of speech, instead of as being the verbal counterparts of the actions with their included mental events. Just as choosing and intending are often not occurrences separate from the actions that manifest them, so the linguistic expressions are dispositional rather than occurrent; they represent the main content of what the agent would veridically say if he were asked to describe what he has done. Or, to put the point in a related way, the agent in acting from this choice 'says in his heart' that this action from this choice was performed or was to be performed by him.[25]

It will be convenient at some points to render the agent's practical thinking in its equivalent linguistic expressions. To proceed in this way will be to use what I shall call a 'dialectical' method. Among the wide variety of meanings attached to the word 'dialectical' in philosophy, one of the most central and traditional (going back to the Socratic dialogues and to Aristotle) refers to a method of argument that begins from assumptions, opinions, statements, or claims made by protagonists or interlocutors and then proceeds to examine what these logically imply. It will be in this sense that my method is dialectical. Two kinds of beginning points and hence two kinds of dialectical methods may be distinguished. The dialectically contingent method begins from singular or general statements or judgments that reflect the variable beliefs, interests, or ideals of some person or group. The dialectically necessary method begins from statements or judgments that are necessarily attributable to every agent because they derive from the generic features that constitute the necessary structure of action. The method I shall use here will be a dialectically necessary one, since this reflects the objectivity and universality reason achieves through the conceptual analysis of action. I shall, then, view the agent as a person who is rational in that he is aware of and can give expression to the generic features that conceptual analysis shows to pertain necessarily to his actions, including the logical implications of these features. It is important to note, however, that it is not the dialectically necessary method that determines the generic features of action and hence the general standpoint of agency itself, since the contents of these features are independent of what any agent may think they are. But once these features have been ascertained, as indicated above, the method operates to trace what judgments and claims every agent logically must make from within this standpoint.

A certain complexity of the dialectically necessary method should be noted. As dialectical, the method proceeds from within the standpoint of the agent, since it begins from statements or assumptions he makes. The dialectical method must thus be distinguished from an assertoric method that is not limited to such a purview. For example, it is one thing to say assertorically that X is good; it is another thing to say dialectically that X is good from the standpoint of some person, or that some person thinks or says 'X is good.' Where the assertoric statement is about X, the dialectical statement is about some person's judgment or statement about X. But whereas the dialectical method is relative to persons in this way, the dialectically necessary method propounds the contents of this relativity as necessary ones, since the statements it presents reflect judgments all agents necessarily make on the basis of what is necessarily involved in their actions. For example, the method does not proceed by saying merely that some person happens to say or think that X is good; rather, the method proceeds by saying that every agent necessarily says or thinks that X is good. The basis of this necessity is found in one or another aspect of the generic features of action and hence in the rational analysis of the concept of action. Thus, although the dialectically necessary method proceeds from within the standpoint of the agent, it also undertakes to ascertain what is necessarily involved in this standpoint. The statements the method attributes to the agent are set forth as necessary ones in that they reflect what is conceptually necessary to being an agent who voluntarily or freely acts for purposes he wants to attain.

The dialectically necessary method thus combines aspects of what Aristotle distinguished as 'demonstrative' (or apodictic) and 'dialectical' reasoning.[26] For its necessity reflects the 'essential nature' of action. It might be held that action did not, for Aristotle, have an essential nature because he thought that such a nature can be attributed only to entities or kinds that are not dependent on human action for their inherent characteristics. On the other hand, the generic features of action are not themselves controllable or changeable by human action as are the things that depend on human actions for their existence or characteristics. In any case, it is important to distinguish the Aristotelian essentialism and its consequent necessity from that of Leibniz. There is no commitment in Aristotle, or in the present account, to the idea that necessary propositions are true 'in all possible words,' in the sense in which the 'possible' reflects the infinity of logical possibilities. The dialectical necessities that derive from what every agent must say or think because of the nature of action reflect the necessities of this existing world, including the limits set by its own structure and potentialities.

If the dialectically necessary method reflects such essential necessities, why should my argument be based on agents' statements or judgments at all? Why can't I dispense with the dialectical element and confine myself simply to the necessities of action? This question will be answered in some detail below (3.10). Here it must suffice to point out that, by remaining within the standpoint of the agent and the judgments he necessarily makes or accepts, the dialectically necessary method is able to avoid certain difficulties that confront naturalistic approaches to ethics, including relativism and the justification of value judgments on the basis of empirical facts. And although the method's analysis of the agent's judgments that are logically involved in purposive action may not correspond to the explicit awarenesses of some particular agent, there are also phenomenological correlates of the results of such logical analysis.

1.14. An important use of the dialectically necessary method consists in the tracing of certain entailments. The purposiveness that is a generic feature of all action will be seen to reflect certain evaluations on the part of the agent; these, expressed as value judgments, will be found to entail further judgments because of their background in the generic features of action and in related conceptual considerations. Now a certain caution must be noted here about entailment-transfers. If one proposition p entails another proposition q, this does not entail that someone's believing or judging that p entails his believing or judging that q. Logical relations which hold between propositions or statements do not necessarily also hold between beliefs or assertions of the respective propositions or statements. On the other hand, where the entailments are simple and direct, there is no fallacy in making such entailment-transfers by attributing to the agent belief in or acceptance of certain propositions on the basis of their being entailed by other propositions he accepts. The justification for such attribution is that since the entailments are readily ascertainable, awareness of them can safely be attributed to any person who is able to control his behavior by his unforced choice with a view to achieving his purposes. I shall henceforth refer to the agent who grasps or accepts such entailments as a *rational agent*. It is to be noted that the criterion of 'rational' here is a minimal deductive one, involving consistency or the avoidance of self-contradiction in ascertaining or accepting what is logically involved in one's acting for purposes and in the associated concepts.

In addition to such deductive rationality, a certain minimal inductive rationality may also be attributed to the rational agent. The caution I have just indicated about entailment-transfers applies also to calculation-transfers and value-transfers. If X is a necessary condition of Y or a means to Y, that some person is aware of Y and wants to have Y does not entail that he is aware of X either in itself or as a means to Y. And if he values or wants to have Y, this does not entail that he values or wants to have X. One aspect of this latter entailment is sometimes put as, 'He who wills the end wills the means.' The possible falsity of this dictum stems not only from the possible failure of calculation-transfer but also from the fact that one may not will the means because one puts superior value on certain counterconsiderations. For example, if Smith and Jones are competing for some highly valued job and Smith is aware that the only way to beat out Jones is to tell a certain lie about him, it does not follow that Smith wants to tell the lie. Here, although Smith wills the end in that he wants to get the job and thus beat out Jones, he does not will the means. The dictum can be saved only if the means—telling the lie about Jones—is made part of the full description of the end. The inductive rationality I shall attribute to the rational agent will have to take account of these difficulties of calculation-transfer and value-transfer. As with the entailment-transfers of the agent's deductive rationality, however, the other transfers will be so minimal that they can be safely attributed to the rational agent.

The use of the dialectically necessary method requires a certain sequence of argument. In this sequence, only those propositions are accepted, either as definitively justified or as warranting favorable consideration, that emerge successively from the conceptual analysis of action and of the agent's necessary beliefs. Thus the whole structure of argument leading to the rational justification of the supreme principle of morality will consist only in such rationally necessary propositions. If, at any stage of this sequence, some particular agents or groups of agents have contingent beliefs or principles that are opposed to such propositions, this opposition will carry no justificatory weight. For a main point of confining the argument to rational necessities is to attain an objective standpoint from which such beliefs or principles can be critically evaluated. The dialectically necessary method attains such a standpoint by restricting the propositions it admits as justified to those that follow from the concept of action, including the beliefs or judgments every agent is necessarily warranted in having on the basis of his acting for purposes he wants to achieve.

It will be by the application of this nonarbitrary, rationally grounded method to the generic features of action that we shall see that every agent, on pain of self-contradiction, must accept a certain supreme principle of morality. In virtue of this, the principle will emerge as categorically obligatory and as having a strictly rational justification.

2

THE NORMATIVE STRUCTURE OF ACTION

The main thesis of this book is that every agent, by the fact of engaging in action, is logically committed to accept a supreme moral principle having a certain determinate normative content. Because any agent who denies or violates this principle contradicts himself, the principle stands unchallenged as the criterion of moral rightness, and conformity with its requirements is categorically obligatory.

The basis of this thesis is found in the doctrine that action has what I have called a normative structure. In this chapter I undertake to prove this doctrine in three main steps. First, every agent implicitly makes evaluative judgments about the goodness of his purposes and hence about the necessary goodness of the freedom and well-being that are necessary conditions of his acting to achieve his purposes. Second, because of this necessary goodness, every agent implicitly makes a deontic judgment in which he claims that he has rights to freedom and well-being. Third, every agent must claim these rights for the sufficient reason that he is a prospective agent who has purposes he wants to fulfill, so that he logically must accept the generalization that all prospective purposive agents have rights to freedom and well-being.

I shall now present detailed arguments in support of each of these steps. The arguments will proceed by the use of the dialectically necessary method, and their general aim will be to show that action as the voluntary pursuit of purposes commits the agent to accept certain normative judgments on pain of self-contradiction. This means that the very possibility of purposive action is dependent on its having a certain normative structure. And it is from the judgments that are necessarily constitutive of this structure that the supreme principle of morality is logically derived.

Purposiveness and Goods

2.1. It was noted above (1.12) that purposive action is conative and dynamic in that the agent tries by his action to bring about certain results or consummations that he wants at least intentionally, even if not inclinationally, to attain. From this conativeness it follows that the purposes for which he acts seem to him to be good. Hence, he implicitly makes a value judgment about this goodness. Suppose the fact of the agent's performing a purposive action is expressed by him in such a descriptive statement as 'I do X for purpose E.' Because of the presence of purposiveness in action, from the standpoint of the agent this statement entails 'E is good.'

The doctrine that every agent acts for ends or purposes that seem to him to be good has behind it a long tradition in philosophical psychology. In some parts of the tradition 'good' is distinguished from 'best,' so that the problem of 'weakness of will' or 'incontinence' is not directly raised; for the thesis that the purposes for which one acts seem to the agent to be *good* is not refuted by the phenomenon of weakness of will whereby the agent acts against his judgment of what is the *best* course of action open to him. In any case, there is an opposed doctrine that, while admitting the relevance of purpose in characterizing action, holds that there is no need that the agent's purposes seem good to him. If he is asked why he wants to get or do something, he may answer that he simply wants to, that he has no reason for it, and hence a fortiori that he does not want it for any good reason or for any good that may be produced by his action.

In the present context, however, this position presents no important obstacle to my inference from something's being the agent's purpose to his regarding it as good, if some appropriate distinctions are recognized, especially the distinctions between nonreflective valuing and reflective appraising, between moral and nonmoral goods, and between wanting something for its own sake and wanting it as a means to something else. In acting, the agent envisages more or less clearly some preferred outcome, some objective or goal he wants to achieve, where such wanting may be either intentional or inclinational. He regards this goal as worth aiming at or pursuing; for if he did not so regard it he would not unforcedly choose to move from quiescence or nonaction to action with a view to achieving the goal. This conception of worth constitutes a valuing on the part of the agent; he regards the object of his action as having at least sufficient value to merit his acting to attain it, according to whatever criteria are involved in his action. These criteria of value need not be moral or even hedonic; they run the full range of the purposes for which the agent acts, from the momentarily gratifying and the narrowly prudential to more extensive and long-range social goals. Now 'value' in this broad sense is synonymous with 'good' in a similarly broad sense encompassing a wide range of nonmoral as well as moral criteria. Hence, since the agent values, at least instrumentally, the purposes or objects for which he acts, it can also be said that he regards these objects as at least instrumentally good according to whatever criteria lead him to try to achieve his purpose.

The agent may or may not reflectively appraise or evaluate his purpose on various criteria before, after, or perhaps even during the time he acts to attain it; and the result of the appraisal or evaluation may conflict with the valuing in which directly consists his wanting to do what he does. Such reflection on one's purposes is, indeed, a central aspect of agency viewed not merely as a sequence of particular occurrences but in its broader scope as comprising longer-range plans and goals. But it is an excessively intellectualistic restriction of judgments of good to hold that because in some particular case an agent may not reflectively appraise or evaluate his action in the light of further criteria, it follows that his direct wanting to perform the action involves no judgment of at least immediate good on his part. On the contrary, the primary, although by no means the only, basis of judging something to be good is precisely its connection with one's pro-attitude or positive interest or desire whereby one regards the object as worthy of pursuit. And since it is admittedly some desire, at least in the intentional sense of wanting, that provides one's purpose in acting, it follows that an agent acts for a purpose that constitutes his reason for acting and that seems to him to be good on some criterion he implicitly accepts insofar as he has that purpose.

This purpose need not consist in some further end to which the action is regarded as a means; the agent may want and hence value the action for itself. He may also value the action only as having been arbitrarily chosen by him from among various alternatives, where he had to make some choice but was indifferent as to the alternatives. In addition, the agent may act for a purpose that seems to him to be bad on various criteria. He may regard it as morally bad in that he thinks it wrongly frustrates the interests of other persons; and he may also regard it as bad on legal and even prudential grounds, as when he believes that the purpose for which he performs his action, although it conforms to his immediate or short-range desire, goes counter to his long-range interests, or when the range of alternatives open to him is so small that he regards his action as having little value for him. Psychological literature is full of cases where persons renounce the ends they had previously considered good: "They realize that they do not value such purposes or goals even though they may have lived by them all their lives up to this point."[1] Nevertheless, whatever be the relation of the agent's past or future purposes or criteria to his present ones, in all such cases he still controls or directs his present, ongoing actions for the sake of something he wants. Even in the case of arbitrarily chosen actions he at least wants to perform some action rather than none. So long as this wanting is not a case of forced choice in the sense discussed above, it constitutes a valuing on the part of the agent so that, to this extent, he regards the purpose or object of his action as good, whatever his further beliefs about the conformity of his action to moral, legal, or even prudential criteria. In such cases, the agent's judgment of the goodness of his immediate purpose may be accompanied or followed by further judgments of the badness of his action on some other criterion. But this is no more anomalous than the fact that he may want to do something in the intentional sense of 'wanting' although he may not want to do it in the inclinational sense.

It is important to keep in mind that the position upheld here bears on the relation between purpose, valuing or wanting, and *seeming* good to the agent, not *being* good. This difference stems from the use of a dialectical rather than an assertoric method. The position is hence not subject to attack from the usual version of the 'open question' test: even if E is someone's purpose, something he wants or values, it still makes sense to ask whether E is good. For the test to apply here, it would have to make sense to ask whether E *seems* good to the person whose purpose it is. Apart from various other difficulties with the 'open question' test, this amended version of the question in terms of 'seeming good' is to be dealt with by means of the distinctions indicated above.

To say that the agent regards his purposes as good, or that he implicitly says of his purpose E, 'E is good,' is not to run afoul of the distinction between attributive and predicative uses of 'good.'[2] When the agent says that E is good, he need not be construed as thinking that 'good' is independently adjectival, like 'red,' as against its presupposing some substantive to which 'good' is attributed, as when one asks, 'a good what?' It was noted above that the agent regards his purposes as good according to whatever criteria are involved in his action. The purposes for which he acts may encompass a wide range of reasons, but in any case they provide the substantives to which 'good' is at least implicitly attached when the agent says or thinks of them that they are good. Amid these different substantives and criteria, however, 'good' has the common illocutionary force of expressing a favorable, positive evaluation of the objects or purposes to which it is attributed. To hold that these objects are good is to value or prize them, and to say that they are good is to give expression to these attitudes. Thus far, then, we have seen that every agent makes an implicit judgment that the purposes for which he acts are good.

2.2. The agent's positive evaluation extends not only to his particular purpose but also a fortiori to the generic features that characterize all his actions. These features hence constitute, in his view, what I shall call *generic goods*. Since his action is a means of attaining something he regards as good, even if this is only the performance of the action itself, he regards as a necessary good the voluntariness or freedom that is an essential feature of his action, for without this he would not be able to act for any purpose or good at all. The freedom thus valued consists both in his controlling each of his particular behaviors by his unforced choice and in his longer-range ability to exercise such control. It hence includes both occurrent and dispositional noninterference with his actions by other persons or things, except insofar as such interference may help to assure either his freedom in respects he values more or his attainment of other valued purposes. In one respect there are degrees of necessity here. The loss of dispositional or long-range freedom, such as by imprisonment or enslavement, makes all or most purposive action impossible, while to lose some occurrent or particular freedom debars one from some particular action but not from all actions. Nevertheless, the loss of freedom in a particular case deprives one of the possibility of action in that case.

Although voluntariness or freedom, unlike purposiveness, is not conceptually tied to ends or purposes, the agent's control of his own behavior serves, and is at least sometimes perceived by him as serving, as a means to attaining his ends. He not only controls his behavior, but he wants to control it with a view to such attainment, so that any threat to this control is perceived as a threat to his getting what he regards as good. In addition to this instrumental value, the agent also regards his freedom as intrinsically good, simply because it is an essential component of purposive action and indeed of the very possibility of action. This is shown by the fact that when he is subjected to violence, coercion, or physical constraint, he may react negatively, with dislike, annoyance, dissatisfaction, anger, hostility, outrage, or similar negative emotions, even when he has no further specific end in view. Although, as we have seen, a certain degree of voluntariness or freedom is exhibited even in forced choice (1.11), what the agent regards as a necessary good is that control of his behavior that is not inextricably linked, as in forced choice, with an involuntary or unfree component consisting in threatened undesirable alternatives imposed on him by other persons. For it is the uncoerced or unforced aspect of his action that enables him to pursue what he regards as good.

The thesis that agents regard their freedom as good and indeed as a necessary good is not contradicted by such phenomena as the 'escape from freedom' where persons try to reject the ability and need for making choices by putting their destinies into the hands of dictators or total institutions. Such persons are agents so long as they control their conduct by their own unforced occurrent or dispositional choices; and they regard this control as good at least in its bearing on their attainment of their ends, whatever they may be. The persons are still agents at the point where they intentionally give up such control; and they are at least prospective agents so long as it remains under their dispositional control whether they will resume occurrent control of their behavior. But if their surrender of control is permanent in that they no longer have even dispositional control of significant phases of their behavior, then they cease to be agents with respect to these phases and the considerations advanced above no longer apply to them in these respects. Such cases, however, may correctly be regarded as pathological, because, so far as the historical record indicates, they mainly occur when basic well-being—persons' ability to obtain the minimal necessities required for agency—is so severely threatened that only surrender of their freedom seems to offer any relief. Such threat may arise either from adverse social conditions or from individual life histories marked by insecurity and dependency.[3] Thus it still remains true that agents value their freedom or voluntariness as a necessary good so long as the possibility remains of successful purposive action—that is, of action that is able to fulfill and maintain at least those purposes required for the continuation of agency. This valuation is expressible in a corresponding judgment.

2.3. In addition to the voluntariness or freedom of his actions, the agent also values their generic purposiveness as a necessary good. Since he regards each of the particular purposes for which he acts as good, he regards as good in each case an increase in his level of purpose-fulfillment whereby he achieves the goal for which he acts. But viewed more extensively over the whole range of his actions, their generic purposiveness may be seen from the standpoint of the rational agent to encompass three kinds of goods. First, he regards as good those basic aspects of his well-being that are the proximate necessary preconditions of his performance of any and all of his actions. Second, he regards it as good that his level of purpose-fulfillment not be lowered by his losing something that seems to him to be good. Third, he regards it as good that his level of purpose-fulfillment be raised by his gaining something that seems to him to be good, namely, the goal or objective for which he acts. I shall refer to these three kinds of goods as *basic goods, nonsubtractive goods*, and *additive goods*. Each of these is necessarily involved in all purposive action as viewed by the rational agent, the first kind as its preconditions, the other two kinds as constitutive of his purposes. Each of the three kinds of good is hence also involved in the value-judgments that express his view of the goodness of the purposes for which he acts. I shall subsequently show that, in relation to the agent's conception of his well-being, the three kinds of goods must be given a generic-dispositional interpretation.

The basic goods, which are the general necessary preconditions of action, comprise certain physical and psychological dispositions ranging from life and physical integrity (including such of their means as food, clothing, and shelter) to mental equilibrium and a feeling of confidence as to the general possibility of attaining one's goals. At several points above it has been noted that among different persons and groups there is a large variety of criteria of human goods or well-being (1.1,4). Such variation does not, however, affect the present position about the contents of basic goods. For the assertion that agents necessarily regard these contents as good is made within the context of purposive action; it indicates the preconditions necessary to the existence of any agent's purposive actions viewed generically and collectively. Hence, since the agent regards his purposes as good, he must, insofar as he is rational, regard these conditions as at least instrumentally good, whatever his particular contingent and variable purposes and evaluations. At the extreme he may, of course, have it as his purpose to put an end to all his purposive actions; but at this point, when he ceases to be an agent, the argument no longer applies to him.

The argument from the agent's evaluation of his purposes and purposive actions as good to his similarly valuing their necessary preconditions is an inference drawn according to the dialectially necessary method in the way indicated above. Since the argument proceeds from within the standpoint of the agent, it is not affected by evaluations made from other standpoints. Since, however, agency is the necessary and universal context of the whole sphere of practice, the standpoint of the agent occupies a superior position in relation to these other standpoints.

Besides basic goods, the agent also necessarily values what I have called nonsubtractive goods. These goods consist in his retaining and not losing whatever he already has that he regards as good. Hence, to lose a nonsubtractive good is to suffer a diminution of the goods one already has; it is to have one's level of purpose-fulfillment lowered. Now every agent, so far as he can, brings it about that his level of purpose-fulfillment is not decreased or lowered by his action, in that he does not lose something that seems to him to be good. The goods in question include the basic well-being of the first dimension of purposiveness, so that there is in this respect a continuum between basic and nonsubstractive goods. But nonsubtractive goods also include, more specifically, whatever else, before his acting, the agent has and regards as good.

The words 'nonsubtractive' and 'additive' as applied to the goods possessed by some persons are second-order, relational, aggregative expressions. They refer to goods in a certain quantitative relation to other goods, the relation obtained by comparing different states or stages of someone's possession of goods. If at time t some person A had X units of goods, and at time t_1 he also has the same X units of goods, then he has not lost any units. The relation between these two states is nonsubtractive. But since not to lose units of good is better than to lose some units, A thereby has a nonsubtractive good. 'Nonsubtractive' here refers both to the relation between the two states and to the X units of good A still has in the latter state. If, on the other hand, at time t_1 A has X + 1 units of good, then A has gained a unit, and the relation between the two states is additive. Hence, A has an additive good, where 'additive' refers both to the relation between the two states and to the added unit of good.

As is shown by the history of utilitarianism and similar atomistic approaches to action and value in psychological and economic theories, to talk about 'units' of good is quite artificial. I have done so, however, in order to bring out somewhat more graphically what is meant by 'levels of purpose-fulfillment' and by the raising or lowering of these levels. Since every agent acts for purposes that seem to him to be good, to achieve his purpose is to raise his level of purpose-fulfillment by comparison with his state before achieving his purpose. This raising is good from the agent's standpoint precisely because he regards his purposes as good. To be sure, there may be costs in respect of the effort expended and other factors the agent may view as subtracting from his total good. It seems clear, however, that he regards the achievement of his purpose as more than compensating for these losses; otherwise he would not act toward this achievement.

The particular contents of nonsubtractive and additive goods are relative both to each person's status quo regarding his possession of goods and to what he views as goods. A bottle of wine may be an additive good for the poor man but not for the rich man with a well-stocked wine cellar, for whom the various bottles he keeps are nonsubtractive goods. For the nondrinker, on the other hand, none of these are goods. The pauper who sees and picks up a dollar bill acquires a much greater additive good than does the affluent person who picks one up. Despite this familiar relativity, we shall see that it is possible to indicate the general contents of certain standard kinds of nonsubtractive goods, and hence implicitly also of additive goods. The basis of these contents is in the conditions of successful purposive action; such goods are hence part of the generic features of action since they are included within the generic purposiveness of action. These conditions build on, but are not identical with, the basic goods that are the necessary preconditions of action.

The third kind of good involved in the generic purposiveness of action is that which I have called 'additive.' In acting for a purpose, the agent intends to achieve the purpose for which he acts and hence to gain something that seems to him to be good. Such gain is an increase in his level of purpose-fulfillment, and he necessarily regards it as good, since it directly reflects the conative nature of his action, that for the sake of which he puts forth whatever effort enters into his action.

Two different meanings of 'additive good' should be distinguished. In one meaning, an additive good is any positive object of any purpose, whatever any agent aims to attain through action. In another meaning, an additive good is only such a positive object of a purpose as is not comprised within basic and nonsubtractive goods. Thus, on the first, inclusive meaning, if someone is acting to save his life or to ward off a physical attack, these purposes constitute additive goods for him, since they are the direct objects of his purposive action. On the second, exclusive meaning, however, these purposes would constitute only basic or nonsubtractive goods but not additive ones, since they are concerned with maintaining a necessary precondition of all his action or with retaining some good he already has. The exclusive meaning is comparative and substantive, since it refers to certain contents of purposes as against others; it compares these contents with those that are more directly tied to the conditions of purposive action. The inclusive meaning, by the same token, is more general and noncomparative. To avoid confusion, I shall use 'additive goods' in the exclusive sense, so that additive goods are not basic or nonsubtractive.

In discussing nonsubtractive and additive goods I have referred to considerations of 'loss' and 'gain.' These considerations are entirely general, in two respects. First, the agent regards fulfillment of his purposes as good regardless of their specific contents. His criteria for this goodness may be of different sorts at different times: sensory, economic, technical, aesthetic, legal, moral, and so forth. At some points, he may evaluate his purpose by several different criteria that may yield conflicting evaluations. But in all cases his direct purpose is to gain something he values, and this may either include or presuppose his not losing something he values or his avoiding something he disvalues, where he would regard failure in such avoidance as itself a loss.

Second, and more important, the considerations of 'loss' and 'gain' are general with respect to the varying criteria of different agents; they are by no means confined to balance-sheet egoists. The considerations apply just as much to an altruist (for whom his fulfillment of other persons' interests constitutes his gain), to an ascetic (each of whose failures to maintain a completely nonhedonic mode of life is a loss), to a voluptuary (whose gains and losses are assayed by narrowly sensory hedonic criteria), and to a masochist (for whom pains and suffering are gains). In some pathological cases the masochist's behavior may be more involuntary than voluntary, so that he is not fully a purposive agent in the strict sense understood here. For example, his choices may derive from unconscious internal compulsions; while ignorant of the sources of these compulsions he may at the same time eagerly seek out their objects.[4] The masochist, then, would be included among agents only so long as his conduct does not stem from such compulsions; but in any case he too is concerned with nonsubtractive and additive goods, losses and gains.

What I have tried to show, then, is that all purposive action is valuational, and that agents regard as good not only their particular purposes but also the voluntariness or freedom and purposiveness that generically characterize all their actions. Their valuation of this generic purposiveness, in turn, extends to the basic, nonsubtractive, and additive goods. The presence of choice and purpose in action hence gives it a structure such that, from the standpoint of the agent, 'I do X for purpose E' entails not only 'E is good,' but also, 'My freedom and my purposiveness with its three dimensions are necessary goods.' Thus from the standpoint of the agent the 'fact-value' gap, even if not the 'is-ought' gap, is already bridged in action. On the basis of his engaging in purposive action every agent is logically committed to accept this value judgment about necessary goods, and we shall see how this in turn requires him to accept certain judgments about rights. But first we must note how the basic, nonsubtractive, and additive goods considered so far are tied still more directly to the general conditions of agency.

2.4. With regard to all three kinds of goods, we must distinguish between *conative* and *achievemental* modes of purposive action. In every case the agent tries to bring it about that he achieves his purpose, that he gains something that seems to him to be good or at least does not lose something that seems to him to be good. But he does not always succeed in achieving his purpose. In one respect, then, it is the conative rather than the achievemental mode that necessarily characterizes all purposive action and constitutes purposiveness as a generic feature of action. On the other hand, the conative mode is a means to the achievemental mode of purposive action and is so regarded by the agent. The point of trying is to succeed, so that the concept of action takes on a further normative connotation, that of successful action. In this respect it is the achievemental mode that for the agent necessarily constitutes purposiveness as a generic feature of action.

There is, however, an intermediate position on this question of purposiveness as a generic feature of action, a position that also pertains, mutatis mutandis, to voluntariness or freedom. To see this, we must recognize another distinction that so far has been only briefly noted. All three of the kinds of goods previously discussed may be viewed either particularly-occurrently or generically-dispositionally. Viewed in the former way, they consist in the particular purposes any person may actually try to fulfill by his actions, including maintaining particular basic goods, retaining the particular goods he already has, and obtaining further particular goods. Viewed in the latter way, the three kinds of goods consist in the general conditions and abilities required for fulfilling any such particular purposes. In this generic-dispositional view, the emphasis falls not on particular goods for which the agent occurrently acts, but rather on the general necessary conditions that enable him to act for any purposes he might have and that he would hence regard as generically good. To refer to these abilities as 'dispositional' is not to deny that they must be exercised if they are to function as goods for the agent. Thus, just as the basic goods consist in the necessary preconditions of action, so the nonsubtractive goods viewed generically-dispositionally consist in the abilities and conditions required for maintaining one's level of goods and for retaining undiminished one's capabilities of action, and the additive goods consist in the abilities and conditions required for improving one's level of goods and for increasing one's capabilities of action. Since these conditions and abilities are concerned with action, I shall also refer to them, respectively, as basic, nonsubtractive, and additive capabilities of action.

Goods as viewed generically-dispositionally are at a high level of generality, for they are second-order goods. The basic, nonsubtractive, and additive capabilities of action are general goods for retaining and obtaining more specific and particular goods. They are also second-order abilities or powers, for they are abilities to retain and expand one's capacities for particular actions.

Because of this generality, the generic-dispositional view of goods has an invariability that is lacking at the level of particulars. Where the particular purposes for which different persons act may vary widely, the capabilities of action required for fulfilling their purposes and for maintaining and increasing their abilities are the same for all persons. Consider, for example, some of the standard extreme cases of divergent purposes, such as those of the religionist who wants to dedicate himself to God even if this means losing his earthly life, or of the intellectual who welcomes blindness because it enables him to concentrate on his philosophical inquiry. It may be thought that the capabilities of action required for fulfilling such purposes have little or nothing in common with those required for fulfilling the purposes of the person dedicated to this-worldly success or to militaristic prowess. Nevertheless, so long as the religionist and the intellectual are agents, acting for purposes they want to achieve, they must satisfy the necessary general conditions of agency. They must control their behaviors by their unforced choices, they must be able to make certain minimal plans for what they will do in order to achieve what they want, and they must have or maintain the general abilities and conditions required for exerting such control and making such plans. The need for and positive evaluation of these capabilities are hence common to all such agents amid their diversities of particular purposes and values. This point was already noted above when I indicated how the concepts of 'loss' and 'gain' apply to the purposive actions of all agents, including ascetics as well as voluptuaries and altruists as well as egoists. To this extent, the relativity objection fails: goods viewed generically-dispositionally as the general capabilities of action are necessarily and objectively goods for all purposive agents. Recognition of this is an important step toward seeing how the generic features of action provide the rational justification of the supreme principle of morality.

2.5. Every agent must regard these capabilities of action not only as goods but also, because they are required for all purposive action, as necessary goods. His positive evaluation of these capabilities is itself a central part of the generic features of action. This evaluation is primarily dispositional rather than occurrent. The agent may not, and usually does not, make an explicit, positive evaluation of the purpose-facilitating abilities and conditions, but that he would do so if his possession of these capabilities were threatened would be shown at least by his self-protective actions. For him not to evince such an evaluation in these circumstances would be for him not to value his generic ability for purpose-fulfillment at all, and hence to cease being even a prospective rational agent.

The generic-dispositional goods have a further important role in the agent's values. For he regards his capabilities of action as constituting his own well-being as an agent. For him to function as an agent is to have and exercise these capabilities, including the second-order abilities to retain and expand his first-order abilities to act to fulfill his purposes. It would be contradictory for an agent to hold that certain general abilities and conditions are required for his purpose-fulfilling activity in the generic sense just indicated and also to hold that these are no part of his well-being. For this would be to hold that what enables him to be an agent and a successful agent is at the same time no part of what enables him to function well as a person and an agent. Such a position would begin to make sense only if a person were somehow to distinguish what he is as an agent from what he is in some other capacity. Now it is indeed true that persons are not only or always agents; they may also be recipients of other persons' agency, and when they are asleep they may not be involved in actions or transactions at all. Nevertheless, insofar as practical 'oughts' apply to them and they are concerned with their fulfillment of their purposes, they are at least prospective agents, and in this crucial role their well-being is centrally constituted by what enables them to act with some hope of fulfilling in general the purposes of their action.

Although agents often identify their well-being with their possessing certain particular goods, in such cases the well-being characterizes them not simply as agents but in some more restricted capacity. It is also true that in some respects no sharp line can be drawn between the general capabilities and the particular goods because the former are exercised for the sake of the latter; and an agent who seldom or never achieved his particular purposes would also probably not have the general capabilities for achieving them. Well-being in the inclusive sense is hence to be understood as a continuum that comprises having the general capabilities and successfully exercising them. Since, however, agency is the condition of pursuing particular goods, the agent's well-being is to be identified primarily even if not exclusively with the general abilities and conditions required for attaining any of his purposes. It is these abilities that are necessary goods for the agent, and they are states or dispositions of the agent himself as they impinge on his purposive pursuits. Although the conditions of these pursuits may include circumstances that are distinct from the agent, such circumstances are for his well-being and hence are a part of his well-being.

The distinction between the particular-occurrent and the generic-dispositional views of purposes and goods also obviates the objection that the agent's well-being is not to be identified with the capabilities of action required for the fulfillment of any of his purposes because he may act for many purposes that are opposed to his well-being. He may smoke cigarettes, thereby subjecting himself to the danger of lung cancer and heart disease; he may vehemently cling to certain childish practices, thereby stunting his psychological growth and condemning himself to immaturity. Although such actions and purposes may evince his preferences, they are not thereby good for him; although they are what he is interested in, they are not therefore in his interest or part of his well-being. Since, however, the capabilities of action with which the agent's well-being is primarily equated are generic and dispositional, they may be turned in different directions, so that the agent can learn from experience to avoid their harmful applications. In any case it is not the particular purposes and outcomes but rather the generic abilities and conditions that for the agent primarily constitute his well-being, since they are the necessary conditions of all his pursuits of his purposes. It must also be kept in mind that the main point I am here upholding is the dialectically necessary one that any rational agent must regard these abilities and conditions as constituting his well-being because of their strategic relation to all his purposive actions irrespective of the more particular contents he may assign to various of his purposes. Thus, just as we saw earlier that, from the standpoint of the agent, his statement 'I do X for purpose E' entails 'E is good,' which in turn entails 'My freedom and my purposiveness with its three dimensions are necessary goods,' so we have now seen that this last statement is equivalent to 'My freedom and well-being are necessary goods.'

2.6. It may be helpful at this point to summarize the relation of well-being and purposiveness both to one another and to the generic features of action. As those features that are found in every action, whether or not it achieves its purpose, the generic features comprise occurrent voluntariness or freedom and purposiveness in the conative mode, whereby the agent tries to attain something he regards as good; and since such purposive attempts require certain minimal abilities and conditions, the generic features include well-being in that component of it that consists in having the basic goods, the necessary preconditions of all actions. But the generic features of action taken in this all-inclusive way do not include purposiveness in the achievemental mode, or well-being insofar as it comprises having the abilities and conditions for retaining the goods one already has and for obtaining further goods. For sometimes an agent may lack these abilities and hence fail to retain or obtain the respective goods. Similarly, purposiveness as a generic feature of action does not include all the components of well-being but includes only its component of basic goods. On the other hand, the generic features of action do include the agent's positive evaluation of the whole of his freedom and well-being in the generic-dispositional sense just considered; this positive evaluation does not, however, extend to the elements of involuntariness found in forced choice. Moreover, the generic features of successful action also comprise purposiveness in the achievemental mode and well-being in all three of its dimensions; and here purposiveness and well-being are identical. For in successful actions the agent achieves his purposes, so that he has not only the minimal abilities required for any purposive pursuits but also the further abilities and conditions needed for avoiding losses and making gains.

An agent may perform some successful actions without having well-being in all three of its dimensions; and he may have such well-being and yet not succeed in some particular action. Nevertheless, well-being in its three dimensions is a generic feature of successful action when such action is regularly and predictably accomplished. The rational agent's purview is not only occurrent but also dispositional; he considers himself not only as a present agent but also as a prospective one who has desires and purposes even when he is not currently acting. Thus "the object of man's desire is not to enjoy once only, and for one instant of time, but to assure forever the way of his future desire." Well-being requires that actions be successful "in a complete life. For one swallow does not make a summer, nor does one day; and so too one day, or a short time, does not make a man blessed and happy."[5]

Although every agent regards his whole well-being as a necessary good because of its relation to his purpose-fulfillments, its components fall into a hierarchy determined by the degree of their indispensability for purposive action. The basic capabilities of action, whereby the agent has basic goods, are the most necessary of all, since without these he would be able to act either not at all or only in certain very restricted ways. Among these basic goods there is also a hierarchy, headed by life and then including various other physical and mental goods, some more indispensable than others for action and purpose-fulfillment. Of the other two kinds of capabilities, the nonsubtractive rank higher than the additive because to be able to retain the goods one has is usually a necessary condition of being able to increase one's stock of goods. Thus the hierarchy of well-being corresponds somewhat to the 'hierarchy of needs' developed in psychological theories.[6] In what follows, it will be important at some points to emphasize these degrees of necessity, but at many others it will be sufficient to refer without differentiation to freedom and well-being as necessary goods. For, viewed generically-dispositionally, freedom and well-being are collectively the most general and proximate necessary conditions of all the agent's various purpose-fulfilling actions. Similarly, the distinctions between conative and achievemental purposiveness, and between action and successful action, can be elided in some contexts below so long as the several ways in which the generic features are necessary for action are kept in view.

We have now seen that every agent must hold or accept that his freedom and well-being are necessary goods. We have thereby taken a major step toward seeing how every agent is logically committed to accepting a certain supreme principle of morality, and hence how such a principle is rationally justified on the basis of the generic features of action.

Generic Rights and Right-Claims

2.7. Since the agent regards as necessary goods the freedom and well-being that constitute the generic features of his successful action, he logically must also hold that he has rights to these generic features, and he implicitly makes a corresponding right-claim.

In view of the crucial importance of this thesis for my overall argument, I shall begin by asking two broad complementary questions. (a) If a rational agent is to claim any rights at all, could anything be a more urgent object of his claim than the necessary conditions of his engaging both in action in general and in successful action? (b) If he regards these conditions as indeed necessary for the very possibility of his agency and for his chances of succeeding in his actions, then must he not hold that all other persons ought at least to refrain from interfering with the conditions? Since this 'ought' entails correlative rights insofar as it signifies what the agent regards as his due, the latter question may also be put in the following equivalent form: Must not the agent hold that he has rights to these necessary conditions of his agency?

Although each of these questions involves various complexities about the nature and justification of rights and right-claims, it is at least initially plausible that each question is to be answered in the affirmative, because of the conceptual connection between rights and necessary goods. I shall now try to reinforce this initial plausibility by presenting some detailed analyses of the questions, as well as detailed arguments for an affirmative answer especially to the second question.

This second affirmative answer—that every agent must hold that he has rights to the necessary conditions of agency, freedom and well-being—entails that action has a deontic as well as an evaluative structure. Through its deontic structure, action encompasses not only the agent's evaluative judgments about the necessary goodness of his having freedom and well-being but also deontic judgments he makes or accepts that he has rights to these generic features of action. I shall hence call them *generic rights*. They are generic in that they are rights to have the generic features of successful action characterize one's behavior: the right to freedom, consisting in noncoercion or noninterference by other persons, so that one's behavior is controlled by one's own unforced choice; and the right to well-being, consisting in the three kinds of good viewed generically-dispositionally, so that one has the general abilities and conditions required for maintaining and obtaining what one regards as good. These rights are also generic in one or another of two further senses: either they subsume other rights in that the others are specifications of the rights to freedom and well-being, or they take precedence over other rights in that the latter, if they are to be valid, must not violate the rights to freedom and well-being. In these respects, they may be called 'fundamental rights.' They are also constitutive rights in that their objects are the proximate necessary conditions of all agency. And they are 'human rights' in that they are rights that all humans have as human agents (and all humans are actual, prospective, or potential agents: see 2.22; 3.4). It is these rights that directly enter into the supreme principle of morality. And it is because every agent is logically committed to holding or at least accepting that he has these rights that he is also committed, on pain of self-contradiction, to accepting the principle.

Before considering how the agent's statement, 'My freedom and well-being are necessary goods,' entails his further statement, 'I have rights to freedom and well-being,' let us examine what the latter statement adds to the former. A complete rights-statement has the following structure: 'A has a right to X against B by virtue of Y.' There are five variables here: first, the subject of the right, that is, the person who is said to have the right (A); second, the nature of the right that is had, including its modality or stringency and the meaning of the statement that someone has the right; third, the object of the right, what it is a right to (X); fourth, the respondent of the right, the person or persons against whom the subject has the right (B); fifth, the justifying reason or ground of the right, that by virtue of which the right is had (Y).[7] The logical or conceptual relation that freedom and well-being as necessary goods bear to their being the objects of rights derives most directly from the last variable, the justifying reason or ground of the rights. But the other variables are also important for ascertaining what the rights-statement adds to the statement about necessary goods.

In the agent's statement, 'I have rights to freedom and well-being,' the subject of the rights is the agent himself, the same person for whom freedom and well-being are necessary goods. The object of the rights is these same necessary goods. Now in rights-judgments, the subject who is said to have rights is not always the same as the person who makes a claim or a rights-judgment attributing the rights to the subject. Moreover, a rights-judgment need not be set forth independently; it may, instead, figure as a subordinate clause wherein the attribution of rights to the subject is only conditional. In all cases, however, there is assumed some reason or ground that is held, at least tentatively, to justify that attribution. This reason may, but need not, be some moral or legal code. In the present case, where what is at issue is the justification of a moral principle, such a principle cannot, of course, be adduced as constituting the justifying ground for the attribution of the generic rights to the agent. Rather, in his statement making this attribution, the justifying reason of the generic rights as viewed by the agent is the fact that freedom and well-being are the most general and proximate necessary conditions of all his purpose-fulfilling actions, so that without his having these conditions his engaging in purposive action would be futile or impossible. Because of this necessity, the agent who is the subject of the generic rights is assumed to set forth or uphold the rights-judgment himself, as knowing what conditions must be fulfilled if he is to be a purposive agent; and he upholds the judgment not merely conditionally or tentatively but in an unqualified way.

Between the agent's statement that his freedom and well-being are necessary goods and his further statement or claim that he has rights to these goods, there are the important differences that in the latter statement the goods are set forth not merely as valuable or desirable but as objects to which the agent is entitled or which he ought to have as his due, and the agent is in the position not only of valuer or evaluator but also of claimant. The claim-making may be only implicit or dispositional, a matter of attitude, of how the agent regards himself in relation to other persons; but in any case he here lays claim to freedom and well-being as goods to which he is entitled—which are due him. It is this entitlement that directly constitutes the nature of the rights he claims for himself. His right-claim hence has a certain illocutionary force; it is prescriptive, for in setting it forth he advocates or endorses that he have freedom and well-being. This advocacy is stronger than that involved in judgments the agent might make that it is right or permitted or not wrong that he have freedom and well-being. The difference consists both in a further aspect of the nature of the right-claim and in the fact that the right has a respondent. For the right-claim is an explicit or implicit demand made on all other persons that they at least refrain from interfering with the agent's having freedom and well-being. This demand is regarded as having a certain ground consisting in the fact that freedom and well-being are necessary goods to the agent.

Because of this groundedness, which constitutes the justifying reason for the demand, the right-claim takes the correlative form of an 'ought'-judgment addressed to all other persons, that they ought at least to refrain from interfering with the agent's having freedom and well-being. This correlativity amounts to logical equivalence so that there is a mutual entailment between the agent's right-claim and this 'ought'-judgment. Although not all 'ought'-judgments entail or are correlative with rights-judgments, the entailment holds when the person making the 'ought'-judgment regards it as setting for other persons duties that they owe to him. For when duties are owed to him, he has a right to their performance or to compliance with them. Now the agent regards in this way the 'ought'-judgment that other persons ought at least to refrain from interfering with his having freedom and well-being. For he does not view the judgment as stating merely an obligation that has some general ground not primarily related to himself; rather, he regards it as stating that something is due or owed to him, to which he is entitled by virtue of its being required for all his purposive actions. The agent holds that other persons owe him at least noninterference with his freedom and well-being, not because of any specific transaction or agreement they have made with him, but on the basis of his own prudential criteria, because such noninterference is necessary to his being a purposive agent.

With regard to the right to freedom, no anomaly arises from the facts that freedom consists, in part, in noninterference with one's action by other persons, and that the 'ought'-judgment that is correlative with the generic right-claim holds that all other persons ought at least to refrain from interfering with the agent's freedom. For what the agent here demands is that noninterference with his actions is not to be interfered with; that is, that the state or condition of himself whereby he is not interfered with in initiating or controlling his actions is to be maintained or continued without interference from other persons. In addition, just as freedom also has a positive component consisting in the effective ability to act, so the agent's right-claim also entails, in a secondary way, that under certain conditions other persons ought to assist him to have freedom and well-being. These conditions occur when failure to give such assistance would result in his failing to have these necessary goods (see 4.7 ff.).

The 'oughts' or obligations of other persons that are here correlative with the agent's generic rights are quite strict. The actions and, more usually, the omissions of which they are predicated are regarded by the agent not merely as preferable or fitting, as generous, supererogatory, or matters of grace, but rather as required or mandatory, so that he holds that he is entitled to redress and his respondents are subject to severe censure and other appropriate countermeasures, at least by himself, if the required conduct is not forthcoming. This mandatoriness is a logical consequence of the fact that the objects of the generic rights are necessary goods and are so regarded and claimed by the agent. I shall here use 'obligation' and 'duty' interchangeably with these strict 'oughts,' although the former terms are sometimes used in more restricted and specific senses to signify the requirements that stem, respectively, from prior agreements and from one's job, office, or station. One basis for the present less-specialized use is that, so far as my argument has gone, no justification has yet been given for deriving specific requirements from agreements and offices. We are still at a primary stage where the ground of moral and legal duties and obligations is being laid, so that moral and legal rules cannot yet be appealed to for the justification of such requirements.

It has been pointed out that some rights—the so-called liberties— entail no obligations, positive or negative, on the part of other persons.[8] If Jones has a right to win his race with Smith in the sense that he has no duty to refrain from winning it or that it is all right for him to win, this does not entail that Smith ought to refrain from interfering with Jones's winning, let alone that he ought to assist Jones's winning, since Smith too has such a right to win the race. This qualification does not, however, have any important bearing on the agent's claim to have the generic rights. For this claim is stronger than the assertion that his having freedom and well-being is merely permissible or all right. Since his claim is concerned with his having the generic abilities and conditions required for achieving any of his purposes, what he claims are the rights not merely to try to have freedom and well-being but actually to have them, so that the rights entail the strict obligation of other persons at least not to interfere with the right-holder's having them. This obligation, in turn, affects the rights of these other persons, a result that will be examined at a later stage.

Against the thesis that every agent necessarily holds that he has the generic rights, it may be objected that such a judgment on the part of the agent must be pointless. For one cannot rationally hold that one has a right to do or have what one cannot help doing or having; in this respect the concept of having a right, like the concept of 'ought,' implies both 'can' and 'may not.' But since the agent cannot avoid that the generic features of action characterize his actions and hence himself qua performing actions, it is not the case that he may not have these generic features. Hence it is pointless for him to hold that he has a right to them.

There are two replies to this objection. First, although, as we have seen, regularly successful action is characterized by voluntariness or freedom and well-being in all three of its dimensions, not all actions are successful. Some actions do not manage to attain nonsubtractive and additive goods, and their agents may lack the abilities and conditions required for such attainment. Since well-being in its full scope consists in having these nonsubtractive and additive capabilities as well as the basic ones, the agent in claiming a right to well-being does not claim a right to what he necessarily has already. Second, the objection fails even with regard to freedom and basic well-being. Although these necessarily pertain to every agent, a person is not always an agent. He claims the right to freedom and well-being not only as a present agent but also as a prospective agent; and in the latter capacity he does not necessarily have freedom and well-being. There is always the possibility of interference with his agency and hence of his losing the freedom and well-being that agency requires. It is within this broader, prospective context that he, even as an agent, claims the right to have freedom and well-being.

2.8. It might be contended that in attributing right-claims and 'ought'-judgments to the agent I am already equipping him with moral concepts, so that moral rules or criteria are at least implicitly invoked here. This would incur the problem of how moral concepts can be derived from the considerations so far adduced, since the agent's purposes and the goodness he attributes to them are not, as such, moral ones. The concepts of 'rights' and 'ought' as here invoked by the agent are not, however, moral. As they are used in different contexts, these concepts may be of various normative kinds other than moral, such as prudential, aesthetic, logical, or legal, depending on the criteria on which the right-claims and 'ought'-judgments are grounded. Now the criteria or grounds to which the agent appeals to justify his having the generic rights are, so far, not moral ones: they do not refer to the most important interests of at least some persons other than the agent (see 1.1).

It is worth noting more explicitly that attributions of rights do not operate only in moral or legal contexts. Although these are indeed their main fields of application, the concept of having a right is used in connection with many kinds of justificatory criteria other than moral and legal ones, for the concept is a general normative one. Consider the following statements where the criterion of having a right is intellectual or logical: (a) "We hope ultimately to show the logical right to the use of such [teleological] concepts by deducing them as secondary principles from more elementary objective primary principles." (b) "I conclude then that the necessary and sufficient conditions for knowing that something is the case are first that what one is said to know be true, secondly that one be sure of it, and thirdly that one should have the right to be sure. This right may be earned in various ways...." (c) "I am not in any sense claiming that the customary vocabulary of introspection is 'illegitimate.' Rather, I am merely claiming the same legitimacy for the neurological vocabulary—where 'legitimacy' means the right to be considered a report of experience." (d) "We award ourselves the right to believe a great variety of things whose truth is in no way a matter of our experience: we believe things about other people's minds, or about the meaning of their words, or about the existence of physical objects independent of ourselves...." (e) "The sceptic may still insist that we have no right to make the assumption that other things are known, and if he likes he may therefore declare all epistemic statements unfounded." (f) "I don't think that the non-cognitivists realize that they make this assumption, but without it, they have no right to draw the conclusions they do." (g) "He certainly can go beyond Peano arithmetic, and he is perfectly justified in claiming the right to do so." (h) "The right to have one's conjectures taken seriously must be earned by prolonged immersion in the historical sources." (*i*) "So if we carefully ponder Leibniz's Law and the alleged objections, if we consider its connections with other propositions we accept or reject and still find it compelling, we are within our rights in accepting it." (*j*) "One kind of negative change in strength has some historical right to the term inhibition." (*k*) "Or again there is a parallel between inferring and arguing soundly or validly and stating truly. It is not just a question of whether he did argue or infer but also of whether he had a right to, and did he succeed."[9]

There is no oddity about the above statements. Oddities arise only if the rights to which they refer are assumed to be moral (or legal) ones. For it can then be pointed out that the operations or attitudes to which persons are here said to have rights may not meet moral criteria, and that moral criteria may indeed justify the opposed operations or attitudes.[10] Now the objects of the rights which the above statements claim, deny, or otherwise refer to are intellectual operations: they are rights to assert, believe, assume, consider, infer, or perform other intellectual operations or adopt other intellectual attitudes. And the grounds on which they base these assertions or denials of rights do not stem from any legal or moral rules; they consist rather in intellectual criteria having to do with empirical evidence, logical validity, inductive probability, systemic fruitfulness or parsimony, or similar intellectual considerations. The applications of these criteria, however, to which rights are here claimed, presuppose the generic right to freedom in the specific form of intellectual freedom; for there would be no point in holding that persons have or do not have these intellectual rights unless they were free to consider the relevant intellectual criteria and to make up their own minds accordingly. In saying that persons have a right to X, where X is such an intellectual operation or attitude, the writers are saying that the persons are entitled to X and may claim X as their due on the basis of intellectual or logical justificatory criteria. The writers are also implying that other persons ought, on the basis of these same criteria, to refrain from intellectually interfering (by way of denial or contradiction) with the performance of the intellectual operations in question, and that intellectual censure may be warranted for noncompliance.

To hold that the above references to intellectual rights are merely metaphorical, that they all derive ultimately from moral or legal attributions of rights, would be to ignore the autonomy both of the operations and of the criteria that are held to ground the rights in question. These intellectual or logical criteria are indeed normative ones, but not all norms are moral or legal; hence, too, while all attributions of rights are normative, they are not all moral. This point is closely connected with one about justification: the rightness or correctness a justification establishes need not be moral, and justification has no necessary connection with justice.

Let us return to the right-claims and 'ought'-judgments I have said every agent must make on the basis of his regarding freedom and well-being as necessary goods. The criteria on which he grounds these 'rights' and 'oughts' are not moral but rather prudential: they refer to the agent's own freedom and well-being as required for his pursuits of his own purposes, whatever they may be. 'Prudential' is here not identical with 'egoistic,' for the purposes the agent pursues, and for whose achievement he requires freedom and well-being, need not be exclusively self-interested ones. He might even be an altruist who wants mainly or solely to advance the interests of other persons. But for his actions to succeed even in such purposes he still needs freedom and well-being. In any case, it is directly because freedom and well-being are necessary goods for his own purposive actions that the agent holds that he has rights to them, regardless of what may be the specific contents of his purposes and actions. In holding that all other persons ought at least to refrain from interfering with his having freedom and well-being, the agent likewise appeals not to moral criteria but to prudential ones. This 'ought'-judgment is made from within the agent's own standpoint in purposive action: what grounds his judgment is his own agency-needs, not those of the persons about whom he makes the judgment. On this ground he sets forth a requirement for the conduct of other persons, that they at least not interfere with his having freedom and well-being. He thus claims freedom and well-being as his prudential due, in that, from within his own prudential standpoint as a prospective purposive agent, other persons owe him at least noninterference with his having the necessary goods of action. It is on his own necessary prudential needs of agency that he bases his claim, directed though it is to other persons.

Because of this prudential basis, it may be objected that even if the agent regards his freedom and well-being as necessary goods and hence demands that they not be interfered with, it does not logically follow that he must claim rights to them. Such demands, after all, may be made by gangsters and many other persons who do not invoke rights; the demands may be more equivalent to snarls or threats than to right-claims: 'Don't interfere with me—or else!' In addition to being a demand, then, the objection continues, a right-claim or rights-talk in general must have four further interrelated characteristics, none of which necessarily pertains to the demand every agent makes that his freedom and well-being not be interfered with. First, in order to be a right-claim the demand must purport to be valid, justified, or legitimate; this is why it asserts that something is due the demander, that he is entitled to it, and not merely that he wants, values, or insists on having it. Second, this entitlement must be based on rules or other reasons; it is these that confer or bestow the right by providing its justification, and the speaker who claims or upholds the right is committed to accepting these rules or other reasons. Third, rights-talk and rights-claims presuppose the existence of a community to which the talk or claims are addressed and which understands and recognizes such talk and the common rules that provide the justification or legitimacy of the rights. Thus, for the agent's demands to be a right-claim, the persons he addresses would have to care about his freedom and well-being and agree that the requirements of his acting entitle him to have these goods. But since his ground is prudential, not moral, why should these other persons accept or credit his demands? Fourth, the community addressed by right-claims must be a legal and political one. For when rights are claimed to objects as general and central as freedom and well-being, the claimants advocate that they be incorporated in a legal system so that they can be sufficiently protected. Hence, the objection concludes, political and legal rights and duties must take precedence over the generic rights of action. Unless the agent recognized the existence and legitimacy of some government to whom to address his right-claims, he would not make any such claims.

This objection with its various components is only partly correct. There is indeed a difference between mere demands and right-claims because the latter purport to be based on justifying reasons. As was shown above, however, these reasons need not be moral ones. The agent's demand is based on the most fundamental of all specifically practical justifying reasons. For what greater justification could any person have for claiming any rights relevant to action than that their objects are necessary for his engaging in any purposive actions at all or for his succeeding in any such actions? Such a claim goes beyond the demands of gangsters or any other particular persons concerned with particular actions for particular purposes, since its object is the necessary condition of all agency. Thus although the agent's right-claim is prudential, it is far from being arbitrary. He claims as his prudential due certain general goods that every other prospective agent can likewise recognize as necessary for his respective agency. This prudential due constitutes, from within the agent's standpoint of purposive agency, an entitlement to have other persons at least refrain from interfering with his freedom and well-being. As we have seen, the generic rights are constitutive of the whole context of agency. Each agent, at the present stage of the argument, proceeds from within his own standpoint in this context. Since this standpoint is decisive for him as an agent, he regards as his entitlement or due whatever is required for his being an agent. Thus he holds that he is entitled to freedom and well-being because of the genuine necessity, generality, and fundamental character of the justifying reasons on which his claim is based.

As was noted above, the concept of a right involves the concept of something due to the subject or right-holder, something to which he is entitled. Only when the concept of 'ought' includes this concept of an entitlement or something due is it logically correlative with the concept of a right. Just as we have seen that rights and right-claims are found in many normative contexts in addition to moral and legal ones, so too with entitlements and 'dues,' despite their legalistic tenor. Artists, athletes, scientists, workers, businessmen, wives, husbands, and many other persons are variously entitled to honor, money, support, and many other emoluments—they can claim these as their due—on the basis of a large variety of criteria. These criteria or 'titles' need not include or rest on prior agreements or transactions with other persons, or even their more general approval. Insofar as the claims are addressed to other persons these must indeed have some understanding of the criteria, as well as of the possible reasonableness of the claims; but their actual assent to the claims or criteria is not required.

Now all the varying criteria of entitlements are practical ones, since they are tied to various kinds of activity. But the generic features of action are the most general context of any and all activities. Hence, when the agent claims rights to the necessary conditions of action, he holds that he has an entitlement that is logically prior to all others, because the criterion on which it is based consists in the very possibility of engaging in any actions at all and of general success in such actions. Every agent must hold, from within his own prudential standpoint in purposive action, that he is entitled at least to noninterference with his freedom and well-being, not only because these are the bases of all other entitlements but also because they are constitutive of the very standpoint from which he proceeds as an agent. Since he here proceeds solely from within this standpoint, its necessary conditions provide the basis for his addressing to other persons the requirement that they at least not interfere with his having these conditions. This requirement, then, embodies the agent's claim of an entitlement, so that he here claims rights to freedom and well-being.

Although the agent's right-claim is in this way based on a justifying reason, he need not yet conceive the reason as a general rule. It will indeed be shown that the agent is logically committed to accepting a certain generalization on the basis of his particular right-claim; but in the first instance, at the present stage of the argument, his claim is a particular one concerned only with the justification that his own agency-needs provide for his having the rights of freedom and well-being. So far as the agent's claim has gone, these rights are generic in that their objects are the most general features of his own purpose-achieving actions, but not yet in that they also pertain to all other prospective agents.

The above objection's reference to a community is correct in one sense, but not in the extensive way in which it is presented. Since the agent's claim to have the generic rights entails that all other persons ought at least to refrain from interfering with his freedom and well-being, he implicitly addresses his reason-based demand to all other persons. In this way he assumes that these other persons understand and can comply with the demand. But it is not the case that they must constitute a community that accepts or 'recognizes' rules on which the right-claim is based. Such a view is unduly conservative; it ignores that the persons addressed may not yet accept certain right-claims or the rules underlying them. The claims of the abolitionists and of the opponents of apartheid are familiar examples.

The persons addressed may, indeed, be a community in some broader sense as accepting more general moral or other rules; in this way even the references to the logical or intellectual rights mentioned above assume a community of persons who recognize and accept the relevant logical or intellectual criteria. At the present stage of the argument, however, where other persons have been introduced only as addressees of the agent's right-claim, they are a community only in the sense of accepting deductive and inductive criteria of reasoning and, as prospective agents, of having the same general conative motivations as characterize all agents. But the argument has shown that these criteria lead to the recognition that the agent's reason for his own right-claim reflects the conceptual and causal relations that freedom and well-being bear to action. In any more extensive sense of 'community,' the generic rights as claimed by the agent are logically prior to a community, in that they derive their validity not from the community but rather from his own needs with regard to action. A community, indeed, will be legitimate, so far as the agent is concerned, only if it respects his generic rights. He is aware, however, that his addressees, being themselves actual or prospective agents, are at least capable of such respect. It will be shown below, moreover, that to avoid contradicting himself the agent must admit that other persons have the same rights to freedom and well-being against himself as he here claims against them. In this way the initial prudential ground of his right-claim will logically lead him to recognize a moral ground for the rights of all other prospective purposive agents (3.5).

Although the most basic rights of freedom and well-being must be incorporated in a legal system, this does not hold for all rights, such as one's right that promises made by another person to oneself be kept or the right to be told the truth. In their primary use, moreover, rights are claimed not against governments but against other persons.[11] The main justification of government is, indeed, to protect the most basic of these rights; but this shows that the normative existence and implicit claiming of the rights are logically prior to the government that is appealed to for their protection, and the primary respondents of the rights are other persons; government's function is to help assure that these persons fulfill their correlative duties. The agent, then, need not directly invoke or recognize a government or a legal system in claiming the generic rights; for making these claims, it is sufficient in the first instance that he urge the requirement that all other persons respect the necessary conditions of his engaging in purposive action.

2.9. As we have seen, the necessary goodness of the agent's having freedom and well-being is the initial ground of his claim that he has the generic rights. But it is important to be especially cautious here. For there is no direct entailment from 'X is good for A' to 'A has a right to X,' or from 'A regards X as good' to 'A claims a right to X.' Indeed, a certain deontological doctrine holds that rights are so completely unique among normative concepts that they cannot be explicated by or be grounded on any considerations of good and bad, benefit or harm. This doctrine appeals to such arguments as that persons who stand to benefit from certain treatment do not therefore have a right to it, even when there is a duty to provide the treatment. In addition to the debatable cases of animals and babies, this argument is illustrated by the case where the ground of the duty is a promise by one person A to another person B that A will provide certain beneficial treatment to a third person C. Here it is B who has the right that A provide the treatment, but it is C who will benefit from the treatment. From this it is concluded that benefiting or deriving good from something X cannot be the ground of any right to X or of any claim to have this right.[12]

In opposition to this deontological view, I hold that in the case of every right and right-claim, its object is something that is held to be good. More specifically, a necessary condition of any person's claiming a right to anything X is that X seems to him to be good. He need not think that it is morally good, or good in terms of his own self-interest, but he must think that it is directly or indirectly good according to whatever criteria he accepts in the given situation. By 'indirectly good' I refer mainly to two kinds of cases. One is where the claimant does not regard as good the specific object of his right-claim but holds that this object, insofar as he claims a right to it, is a specification of some more general good. For example, he may claim for himself or for others the right to ingest heroin or to perform some other action that is harmful to the agent, not because he regards the action itself as good but because he holds it to be an exercise of individual freedom, which he regards as good. A second kind of indirect good is found where a person has and claims a certain right by virtue of certain rules he upholds and regards as good, even though he may not regard as good every application of the rules. For example, he may have, by virtue of some political office he occupies, the right to pardon convicts. He may not welcome his having this right, so that he does not regard it as directly good; but he regards it as good insofar as it derives from the rules that determine the power of his office, his having of which, or the rules of which, he considers good. If he did not at all consider the rules to be good, or consider it to be good that he has the office, then he would not claim to have the rights that derive from the rules determining the powers of the office. Either he would not consider these powers to be his rights at all or he would at least not lay claim to these powers.

To lay claim to something X as one's right is contrasted with the situation where one makes no claim to have it as one's right. Such claiming or laying claim, when done explicitly, is a purposive action. Now we saw above that in the case of all his actions the agent regards their purposes as good. Hence, unless the claimant regarded his claiming a right to X as having a purpose he considers good, he would not explicitly make the claim. To be sure, it might still be argued that this good purpose may consist in the claiming itself or in some goal beyond the X that is the direct object of the right-claim. But it is difficult to see how, in either of these cases, the purpose in question could be considered good without X itself being regarded as at least instrumentally good. This connection between rights and good also obtains when the person in question does not explicitly lay claim to X as his right but merely thinks he has a right to it. There would be no point in his thinking this unless he regarded X as directly or indirectly good.

This position holds even in such anomalous cases, which figure in some idealist theories, as where a convicted criminal claims punishment as his right. For the basis of this claim is the right to be treated as a mature person who is responsible for his actions; and such treatment is regarded as a good by the person who makes the claim. A parallel consideration applies to the argument outlined above, where the person to whom certain beneficial treatment is owed is not the same as the person who has a right, by virtue of a promise made to him, that the treatment be provided. The latter person would not claim it as a right that the promise be kept unless he thought it good that the treatment be provided, even if the good of the treatment that is the content of the promise is not provided directly to him or for his own self-interest.

But even if it is a necessary condition of someone's claiming a right to X that X seem to him to be good, it is hardly a sufficient condition. There would be a tremendous proliferation of right-claims if each person were to claim a right to all the myriad objects he considered good, or even to all those that constituted purposes of his particular actions. There are cases, moreover, where an agent performs actions he admits he has no right to perform. The purpose of his action seems to him to be good on one criterion, such as a prudential one, but he does not think that this goodness gives him a right to perform the action because he acknowledges that its criterion is outweighed in importance by other, opposed criteria. For example, he may rob a poor widow in order to buy himself a transistor radio. In such cases the agent may admit that, in final analysis, he has no right to perform the action according to the criterion he regards as having superior authority.

The final ground for maintaining that the agent must hold that he has rights to the generic goods of freedom and well-being is that, unlike the particular goods or purposes for which he may act, the generic goods are the necessary conditions not merely of one particular action as against another but of all successful action in general. Right-claims are thus essentially linked to action because, just as actions themselves are conative and evaluative, so right-claims are demands on the part of agents that the essential prerequisites of their actions at least not be interfered with. It was very likely for this reason that Jefferson included life, liberty, and the pursuit of happiness among the inalienable rights of man. If 'happiness' is understood as well-being, these rights are inalienable because, being necessary to all action, no agent could waive them or be deprived of them and still remain an agent.

It is also primarily for this reason that the agent's necessary right-claim is directly limited to his having freedom and well-being. Particular agents may, of course, claim all sorts of objects as their rights. But since these objects are not necessarily connected with their claimants' being agents, they may have a kind of arbitrariness, as opposed to the rational necessity to which the argument must be confined if its content is itself to be rational. This point is closely related to my previous distinction between necessary and contingent contents (1.9). Contingent contents may vary with the arbitrary whims of the protagonists, whereas necessary contents are those to which any agent must be committed on pain of ceasing to be an agent, along the several degrees of necessity distinguished above. Adherence to these contents is rational because, like the natural scientist's ultimate adherence to empirical facts, the necessary contents provide a subject-matter that is a genuinely independent variable for the agent's, and eventually the moralist's, judgments, as opposed to the contents that are dependent on those judgments for their being asserted or upheld.

2.10. I come now to my own more direct argument for the thesis that every agent must hold or accept, at least implicitly, that he has rights to freedom and well-being. The argument depends on the point made above, that such a right-claim is correlative with and logically equivalent to a strict 'ought'-judgment that other persons ought at least to refrain from interfering with the agent's freedom and well-being. If these were not logically equivalent or at least correlative, the right-claim would lose its distinctive point; it could no longer be construed as a demand addressed to other persons based on a reason consisting in the necessity or requiredness of freedom and well-being for the agent's action. For the agent to hold that he has rights to freedom and well-being but that nonetheless it is permissible for other persons to interfere with these would be to remove or at least strongly to dilute his conviction that they are necessary goods for him. For in regarding them as necessary for his agency he holds that they must be kept inviolate, so that interference with them is impermissible. Conversely, since the agent regards the 'ought'-judgments as imposing restrictions that he is entitled to have other persons respect in their conduct toward him, the judgments entail that he has rights to the objects of these restrictions.

The argument may now be put as follows. Since the agent holds that freedom and well-being are necessary goods for all his actions, he also holds that it is necessary that he at least not be interfered with by other persons in having freedom and well-being. For if he were thus interfered with, he could not have what is required for him to act. Now these ascriptions of necessity, about necessary goods and the necessity of noninterference, are not mere means-end statements of a purely 'factual' sort. On the contrary, because of the agent's practical conative attachment to the generic features of his successful action, the ascriptions carry his practical advocacy or endorsement. In saying that freedom and well-being are necessary goods for him, the agent is not merely saying that if he is to act, he must have freedom and well-being; in addition, because of the goodness he attaches to all his purposive actions, he is opposed to whatever interferes with his having freedom and well-being and he advocates his having these features, so that his statement is prescriptive and not only descriptive. Similarly, in saying that because freedom and well-being are necessary goods for him it is necessary that other persons at least not interfere with his having these goods, he is not merely stating a 'factual' connection between his having X and other persons' not interfering with his having X, or between its being necessary that he have X and its being necessary that other persons not interfere with his having X. In addition, he is setting forth a practical requirement he endorses, that other persons not interfere with his having freedom and well-being.

This requirement constitutes a strict practical 'ought' in the view of the agent. The necessary and sufficient conditions of some person's addressing such an 'ought' to other persons are four: first, he sets forth a practical requirement for their conduct that he endorses; second, he has a reason on which he grounds this requirement; third, he holds that this requirement and reason justify in some way preventing or dissuading the persons addressed from violating the requirement; fourth, he holds that fulfillment of the requirement is due to himself or to the persons in whose behalf he sets it forth. The reasons and justifications here referred to need not be moral ones, just as strict practical 'oughts' are not only moral ones; their criteria may be prudential (as in the present case) or legal as well as of other sorts. It must also be kept in mind that an 'ought'-judgment that one person A addresses to another person B may be prudential because it is intended to serve not B's purposes but rather A's. Now, as we have seen, the agent's reason for his requirement that other persons not interfere with his freedom and well-being is that these are necessary for all his pursuits of his purposes, and this too is what justifies for him preventing any violations of the requirement. Hence, the agent is saying that because freedom and well-being are necessary goods for him, other persons strictly ought at least to refrain from interfering with his having them. And this is equivalent to saying that he has a right to them, because the agent holds that other persons owe him this strict duty of at least noninterference. It must be kept in mind that the agent here proceeds from within his own standpoint of purposive agency, including the entitlements called for by that standpoint.

Another way of presenting this argument shows more explicitly that if any agent denies that he has the generic rights, then he is caught in a contradiction. Suppose some agent were to deny or refuse to accept the judgment (1) 'I have rights to freedom and well-being.' Because of the equivalence between the generic rights and strict 'oughts,' this denial of (1) would entail the agent's denial of (2) 'All other persons ought at least to refrain from interfering with my freedom and well-being.' By denying (2), the agent would have to accept (3) 'It is not the case that all other persons ought at least to refrain from interfering with my freedom and well-being.' But how can any agent accept (3) and also accept (4) 'My freedom and well-being are necessary goods'? That he must accept (4) we saw above; for by virtue of regarding his purposes as good the agent must also a fortiori value his freedom and well-being as required for achieving any of his purposes. Hence, insofar as he is a purposive agent, that is, an agent who wants to achieve the purposes for which he acts, he must want his freedom and well-being to be kept inviolate, so that they are not interfered with by other persons. He must want this, moreover, not as a mere favor from other persons but as setting a requirement for their noninterference that they are obligated to obey, such that from his own standpoint as a purposive agent, severe censure and even coercion are warranted if they violate the requirement. Hence, the agent must accept (2). Consequently, since (2) is logically equivalent to (1), the agent contradicts himself if he denies (1). He must therefore accept, on pain of contradiction, that he has the generic rights.

Still another way to put this point is as follows. As we have seen, for the agent to regard his freedom and well-being as necessary goods is for him to hold that they should be kept inviolate. But if he accepts (3), which is entailed by his denial of (1), then he accepts that it is permissible that other persons interfere with or remove his freedom and well-being. He hence shows that he regards his freedom and well-being with indifference or at least as dispensable, so that he accepts (5) 'It is not the case that my freedom and well-being are necessary goods,' where 'necessary' has, as before, a prescriptive force and not only a means-end sense. Therefore, if the agent were to deny that he has rights to freedom and well-being, he would again be caught in a contradiction: he would be in the position of both affirming and denying that his freedom and well-being are necessary goods, that is, goods that he values as the necessary conditions of all his actions and that must hence not be interfered with or removed from him by other persons.

This contradiction may be brought out still more explicitly by using the practical-prescriptive 'must' to render both 'necessary' and 'ought.' Thus (4) 'My freedom and well-being are necessary goods' may be rendered as (4_a) 'I must have freedom and well-being,' for this expresses the agent's resolve to have what he recognizes to be indispensable for his engaging in purposive action. Similarly, (2) 'All other persons ought at least to refrain from interfering with my freedom and well-being' may be rendered as (2_a) 'All other persons must at least refrain from interfering with my freedom and well-being,' for this 'must' also expresses the agent's resolve that the necessary conditions of his engaging in purposive action not be obstructed. Now (4_a) entails (2_a). For if the agent must have freedom and well-being, then, from the standpoint of his own purposive action, whatever interferes with his having these must be rejected or removed, including interference by other persons. (I shall discuss the question of conflicts below.) It would be contradictory for him to accept both that he must have freedom and well-being and that other persons may interfere with his having these, *where the criteria of the 'must' and the 'may' are the same, consisting in the agent's own requirements for agency.* Hence, from the agent's standpoint, the necessity of his having freedom and well-being entails the necessity of other persons' at least refraining from interference with his having them. This latter necessity is equivalent to a strict practical 'ought' that he implicitly addresses to all other persons, and hence is also equivalent to a claim that he has a right to the necessary goods of freedom and well-being.

It is to be noted that the agent is caught in the above contradiction only so long as the goods in question are necessary ones. He would not contradict himself if he were to deny or refuse to accept that he has rights to goods other than necessary ones. For it is only to necessary goods that the 'must' indicated above applies, and with it the requirement that they be kept inviolate. Other goods, by definition, are dispensable, so that, from the agent's standpoint, it is not the case, at this stage of the argument, that interference with them is impermissible so that other persons strictly ought to refrain from interfering with them. In contrast, the necessary goods of freedom and well-being are the general, truly grounded requirements of his own conditions of purposive action. The generality of these requirements explains further why the agent does not rationally claim for himself more particular rights on the same basis as he claims the generic rights. For example, he does not move from (4_b) 'I must have a motorcycle' to (2_b) 'All other persons must at least refrain from interfering with my having a motorcycle.' Since his having freedom and well-being is tied to the general condition of his agency, it has an ineluctableness within the context of action that is not had by the objects of his particular, dispensable desires. Thus, the objects to which the agent necessarily claims rights are only those goods that are truly necessary for his action or his successful action in general.

2.11. It may be objected that the above inference from (3) to (5), and hence from (4_a) to (2_a), is not valid, for an ethical egoist of the universalist sort might consistently accept (3) while rejecting (5). He would accept (3)—'It is not the case that all other persons ought at least to refrain from interfering with my freedom and well-being'— because, holding that each person ought to act only for his own respective self-interest, the universal ethical egoist would deny that any person A ought to refrain from interfering with the freedom and well-being of any other person B, including the egoist, when such interference is in A's self-interest. At the same time the universal ethical egoist would reject (5)—'It is not the case that my freedom and well-being are necessary goods'—since he would hold that his own freedom and well-being are necessary goods because they either constitute or are means to his self-interest.

It is worth dealing with this objection and its related ramifications in some detail because of the superficial resemblance of the position defended here, about the agent's claiming the generic rights for himself, to certain egoistic positions. To begin with, we must note that the universal ethical egoist as just depicted does not proceed from within the standpoint of his being an individual agent who has purposes he want to fulfill. Rather, his standpoint is that of the upholder of a universal principle that prescribes how all agents ought to act. Hence, there still remain the questions of what is the justification of this principle and why the individual agent should accept it, as universal, in preference to his own conative concerns as an agent. It might be thought that universal ethical egoism is consistent with those concerns or even that it supports them. As we shall see, however, this view is mistaken. In any case, since the agent's concern is necessarily with his own having the necessary goods of freedom and well-being (regardless of the various specific purposes for which he may use them), he will not accept a principle that permits or requires other persons to interfere with his having these necessary goods. In addition to these considerations, acceptance of the egoist's universal principle at this stage would violate the sequence required by the dialectically necessary method, wherein only those propositions are to be accepted that logically emerge successively from the conceptual analysis of action and of the agent's necessary beliefs (1.14).

It must also be noted that the universal ethical egoist's acceptance of (3) gives it a different meaning from that in which (3) was rejected above by the agent. For when the agent says that all other persons ought at least to refrain from interfering with his freedom and well-being, the criterion of this 'ought' is his own general agency-needs or prudential purposes. But when the universal egoist denies that all other persons ought at least to refrain from such interference, the criterion of his 'ought' is rather the purposes or self-interest of all the persons who are the subjects of the 'ought'-judgment. It is, however, the former criterion, not the latter, that the agent must uphold from within his own standpoint in purposive action. Hence, the justification for his accepting the universal egoist's criterion becomes even more problematic.

The contention of the universal ethical egoist as given above incurs a familiar but severe difficulty even if we reinterpret (3) in accordance with his own intention so that the criterion of its 'ought' is the respective self-interest of each and all of the persons who are the subjects of the judgment. For in rejecting (5)—or, what is the same thing, in accepting (4) 'My freedom and well-being are necessary goods'—the ethical egoist holds that his freedom and well-being should be protected and not interfered with. But if at the same time he accepts (3) as reinterpreted, so that he accepts that other persons may or ought to interfere with his freedom and well-being when this is conducive to their own self-interest, then he drops his opposition to this interference. He would hence be in the position of both upholding and not upholding or even rejecting the conditions that enable him to be a purposive agent: the position of believing that these conditions both should not be interfered with and may be (and even should be) interfered with.

It might be contended that the universal ethical egoist can still accept (3) without incurring any practical inconsistency. For although his position requires that, in final outcome, of any two persons A and B, A ought to kill B when this is to A's self-interest and B ought to kill A when this is to B's self-interest, there is no inconsistency here, for in each case A or B ought to perform these killings only if he can; that is, each of them should *try* to perform these actions.[13] The same difficulty, however, would still arise. How can any agent B accept that other persons are permitted or ought to try to interfere with his freedom and well-being (including that they kill him) when he also holds that his freedom and well-being are necessary goods? There is, indeed, a possible answer to this question (see 2.13), but it does not fall within egoism. Universal ethical egoism requires that the egoist take impartially the position of each person acting for his own respective self-interest and that he have the criterion of his 'oughts' reflect their respective self-interests, even when this is opposed to his own self-interest as an agent, with its freedom and well-being. But as an agent, he must also regard his freedom and well-being as necessary goods, and hence he cannot impartially accept as criterion of his 'oughts' the self-interest of other persons when this conflicts with his freedom and well-being. Thus, a person cannot consistently be both an agent and a universal ethical egoist. Since, qua engaging in purposive action, he must be an agent, he cannot consistently be a universal ethical egoist. Hence, the agent logically must reject the criterion of ethical egoism with its acceptance of (3) while rejecting (5).

Attempted answers to this argument may proceed in several interrelated ways.[14] It may be said that although the universal ethical egoist must indeed believe that other persons ought to interfere with his freedom and well-being when this is for their self-interest, it does not follow that he must *want* them to do this. Since, out of his concern for his own self-interest, he doesn't want them to interfere with his necessary goods, while he does want to maintain these goods, he is not committed to wanting incompatible goals. And his practical decisions about his own actions, being in accord with his wants, will similarly not conflict with one another. This reply is buttressed by the egoist's conception of human life as an arena of competition and conflict. In a competitive game one believes that one's opponent ought (in the light of the game's objectives and rules) to make a certain move, while at the same time one believes that one ought, if possible, to prevent him from making that move. These two 'ought'-beliefs do not involve a practical inconsistency, for one's desires and resulting actions will follow the second, self-interested 'ought,' not the first, impartial one. Hence, the universal ethical egoist, even while holding that he ought to pursue only his own self-interest, can be quite consistent in holding that each person ought to act only for his own respective self-interest even if this harms the interests of other persons, including himself. For in his life his wants and his resulting actions will likewise follow only the 'oughts' that prescribe that he act for his own self-interest but not also the 'oughts' that say other persons ought to act for their respective self-interests.

These replies incur serious difficulties that may be summed up in a pair of dilemmas. The first dilemma arises from the contention that the universal ethical egoist may believe that all other persons ought to act only for their respective self-interests while at the same time he does not want them to act in this way. In order for his position to be one of universal ethical egoism, it must not only hold that each person ought to act exclusively for his own self-interest but it must use 'ought' in the same sense. The position would not be one of *universal* egoism, and it would involve an equivocation at least of illocutionary force, if its 'oughts' did not apply to other persons' actions in the same sense or with the same force of 'ought' as that with which they apply to the egoist's own actions.

But this nonuniversality and equivocation are in fact incurred by the egoist's position. For his 'ought' as he applies it to his own actions is unqualifiedly prescriptive; it sets a conclusive requirement for his actions. The egoist definitively endorses his own acting for his self-interest, even if this endorsement involves not necessarily any public promulgation but rather his sincere belief and private advocacy: this is what his 'ought' signifies. On the other hand, when he differentiates his 'ought'-beliefs about how other persons ought to act from his wants or desires as their actions, he shows that his 'ought' as he applies it to other persons' actions is not unqualifiedly prescriptive but is at most hypothetical and prima facie. His endorsement of their acting for their own self-interests is not at all definitive or a matter of even private advocacy; it is rather of the form: If they are to play the game of life according to the rules of egoism, then they ought to act for their self-interest. But since he doesn't want them to play according to these rules (for their doing so would attack his own self-interest), the 'ought' he uses or upholds for other persons' actions is at most tentatively prescriptive, not definitive. Thus the purportedly universal ethical egoist's position is in fact not universal, for it does not apply to all other agents in the same way as it applies to the egoist himself; and it is at least illocutionarily equivocal, for the 'ought' it uses for the actions of all other persons does not have the same intentional sense or prescriptive force as the 'ought' it uses for the egoist's own actions.

If, on the other hand, the ethical egoist does indeed maintain universality and avoid equivocation, so that he upholds for all other persons as well as for himself (even if only in his private beliefs) unqualified, definitive 'oughts' that conclusively endorse their acting for their respective self-interests, then he incurs the previous problem of incompatible, self-defeating directives. He would then believe that other persons definitively ought to violate his own self-interest while also believing that he definitively ought to violate theirs. This, then, is the universal ethical egoist's first dilemma. If he is to avoid upholding incompatible and self-defeating directives, he must at least incur equivocation, and his egoism cannot be universal. But if he avoids equivocation and maintains universality, he must uphold incompatible and self-defeating directives.

It might be contended that this dilemma does not affect the universal egoist's position because the specific illocutionary force of his 'ought' as applied to other persons' actions is irrelevant to its general action-guiding quality. He might say, 'I still believe that other persons ought to act for their own self-interests; this "ought" is sufficiently action-guiding, it says or indicates what other persons are to do, regardless of the specific strength of my endorsement of their doing it.' If, however, his position is to be an action-guide at all, even if only in his private thinking, then it still incurs to this extent the problem of incompatible, self-defeating goals. The universal egoist cannot consistently have it both ways: he cannot hold that his differentiation of his wanting from his mere 'ought'-beliefs extricates him from the difficulty of having incompatible goals while at the same time he holds that his universal egoistic 'ought'-beliefs indicate the goals for which all persons are to act. If he maintains the latter at all, then at whatever level he maintains it he is caught in a practical inconsistency.

To understand the second dilemma that confronts the universal ethical egoist, we must consider his analogy of human life to a competitive game. The equivocation about 'ought' just noted is not or is at least not necessarily incurred in the context of competitive games. For when competitor A thinks, 'My opponent ought to do X and I ought to prevent him from doing X,' these 'oughts' occur in the context of his overall, definitive commitment to the rules of the game. Thus, both the above 'oughts' are qualified or hypothetical ones; they logically occur as consequents whose antecedent is: 'The game ought to be played according to its rules and related objectives.' It is this latter 'ought' that carries A's unqualified or conclusive endorsement. For games are structured by rules that set requirements or 'oughts' that must be accepted by the competitors regardless of their other, particular self-interested wants, so long as they play the game. This is why A believes both the conflicting 'oughts' given above, and why these two 'oughts' are not equivocal in force since they both carry the same qualified endorsement. They amount in effect to believing that each competitor should try to do his best (within the rules of the game) to defeat the other in accordance with the game's objectives.

Now suppose we try to rescue the universal ethical egoist from his first dilemma by applying this competitive-games model. In this case he would avoid the above equivocation about his 'oughts' by maintaining that his overall or unqualified commitment is to the 'Formal' Basic Rule of the Universal Egoistic Life-Game: each and every person ought to act only for his own respective self-interest. It would be to the competition and conflict of his universal egoistic life-game that he would give his primary allegiance, and it would be its 'ought' that would have his unqualified endorsement.

Such an endorsement, however, would commit the universal ethical egoist to the self-subverting 'oughts' indicated above, and hence to endorsing the violation of his own egoistic aims. Thus the egoist incurs a second dilemma. If he maintains his universal egoism with its primary, definitive commitment to the Formal Rules of the Universal Egoistic Life-Game, then he is not really an egoist in the sense of a person whose primary, definitive commitment is to the pursuit and maximization of his own self-interest, for he would endorse directives that violate his self-interest. If, on the other hand, he maintains this latter, egoistic commitment as his primary and definitive one, then he cannot maintain his *universal* egoism with its primary, definitive commitment to the universal life of struggle and conflict.

The competitive-game model is a dangerous one for the egoist. Although a famous football coach is alleged to have said, "Winning is not the most important thing; it is the only thing," the rules of games prohibit certain ways of 'winning' and indeed prescribe that under certain conditions some competitors must lose. The egoist, on the other hand, is committed to winning, that is, advancing his self-interest, in whatever ways he can. This commitment is indeed in conformity with part of the rules of universal ethical egoism. But by the same token it stands in opposition not only to the limiting rules and commitments of competitive games but also to the other part of the rules of universal ethical egoism which prescribe that other persons ought to frustrate his self-interest whenever it is in their self-interest to do so.

In view of these dilemmas, including the possibly disastrous implications of the universal ethical egoist's theory for his own self-interest, the agent who recognizes that his freedom and well-being are necessary goods for him qua agent will refuse to accept this theory. It must also be noted that freedom and well-being are required for participation in competitive games and in the conflict situations that characterize the egoist's view of life. This holds even if the 'games' are such potentially lethal ones as Russian roulette or dueling. So long as one continues to be an agent, then, one must implicitly claim rights to freedom and well-being and must hence hold correlatively that other persons ought at least to refrain from interfering with one's having these necessary goods.

The above dilemmas also enable us to see, at the current stage of the argument, two of the crucial differences between universal ethical egoism and the present thesis that every agent necessarily claims for himself the rights to freedom and well-being. The rational agent whose beliefs and claims are here analyzed confines himself to what he is logically justified in claiming from within his own context of purposive action; hence he limits his claims to the necessary goods or conditions of agency. The ethical egoist, on the other hand, directs his claims or 'oughts' to his whole self-interest taken globally or without any limits. Such an unlimited claim, however, does not have the same rational justification as the above limited one, where 'rational' is taken in the strict sense of what cannot be denied within the context of action without self-contradiction. One can be an agent without having many components of what one might take to be one's overall self-interest (including Cadillacs and extensive political power; or alternatively all the books or paintings one might desire; or alternatively . . .). On the other hand, one cannot be an agent without having freedom and well-being. Thus the present argument abstracts from the divergent and possibly idiosyncratic desires or self-interests that may characterize different agents. The argument for every agent's having to make an implicit right-claim holds only insofar as the object of the right-claim is the necessary goods of action. As we have seen, if he were to deny that he has rights to these goods, he would contradict himself. But he would not contradict himself if he were to deny that he has rights to other goods.

Second, the rational agent recognizes that in order to have freedom and well-being he must uphold certain limits or requirements on the part of all other persons: that they ought at least to refrain from interfering with his freedom and well-being, and that in certain circumstances where he cannot have these by his own efforts they ought to assist him to have these. (For several reasons he will not claim the right to such assistance regardless of his own efforts or abilities; for one thing, as we shall see below, he is aware, as rational, that he would logically be subject to such claims from other prospective agents and would hence be burdened with an unfulfillable profusion of claims to assistance.) These limits or requirements that the rational agent upholds with regard to the actions of all other persons constitute his claim that he has the generic rights. The

88

universal ethical egoist, on the other hand, just as he upholds no limits with regard to the components of his own self-interest or his self-seeking actions, also upholds no limits with regard to the self-seeking actions of other persons. Thereby he is inevitably caught in the dilemmas and incompatible directives indicated above.

2.12. Let us now consider another kind of objection against my above argument that every agent must accept or hold on pain of self-contradiction that he has the generic rights. This objection is that the agent need make no right-claim or 'ought'-judgment at all, either positive or negative. He need not accept either statement (2) given above or its negation (3), for he might be an amoralist who disavows for himself all uses of moral or deontic concepts. Thus, in refusing to accept such a judgment as (1) 'I have rights to freedom and well-being' and hence also (2) 'All other persons ought at least to refrain from interfering with my freedom and well-being,' the amoralist agent would not therefore have to accept (3) 'It is not the case that all other persons ought at least to refrain from interfering with my freedom and well-being.' He would indeed accept (4) 'My freedom and well-being are necessary goods,' in that these are required for his pursuit of all his purposes. But on the basis of this evaluative premise he would not make or accept any right-claims or 'ought'-judgments, either positive or negative, so that he would not be in the position even of denying that persons ought to do or refrain from doing certain things, such as interfering with his freedom and well-being. For, as an amoralist, he would deny that concepts like 'ought' and 'right' have any valid application, at least in his own case. Instead, he would commit himself only to such a resolutive statement as (6) 'I'll do what I can to get what I want.' He might, for example, be the kind of person who holds, like Callicles, Thrasymachus, or Nietzsche, that power is the only thing that counts, so that normative claims about rights and justifications are useless and unnecessary. Such a statement of his as (6) would not involve him in the contradictions elicited above, for these all depended on the agent's having to accept the negative 'ought'-judgment (3).[15]

In dealing with this objection, it must be recalled that although (1), (2), and (3) are normative and deontic judgments, they are not moral but rather prudential (2.8). The question raised by the amoralist's objection, then, is whether he can disavow all use of even prudential deontic judgments. That the answer is negative can be seen once it is assumed that the amoralist is a rational and conatively normal person (and if this assumption is not made, then there is no point in arguing with him). By 'rational' I mean that he accepts the reasons of deductive and inductive logic, including the evidence of empirical facts. By 'conatively normal' I mean that he has the self-interested motivations common to most persons and is willing to expend the effort needed to fulfill them; in other words, he is at least a prospective agent. Now such a rational and conatively normal person must make or accept for himself at least instrumental prudential 'ought'-judgments. For suppose something Z threatens his basic goods and hence his basic well-being, and he believes that the necessary and sufficient condition of his avoiding Z is his doing X. Then, given certain minimal qualifications, he must make or accept for himself such a prudential and prescriptive 'ought'-judgment as (7) 'I ought to do X.' The qualifications in question are that he believes doing X is in his power and that he does not believe there is any superior counter-consideration to his doing X. The latter qualification is here a minimal one, in that the superior counterconsideration in question would have to be one that overrides the amoralist's basic well-being. Since the amoralist, by definition, has no moral convictions, these could not figure for him as superior counterconsiderations.

Now (7) is a deontic judgment in the sense indicated above: it sets forth a prescriptive requirement for action, grounded on a justifying reason consisting in a certain end: the preservation of his basic well-being. That the requirement it sets forth is prescriptive is shown by the fact that the presumed amoralist, being conatively normal, actively wants the end in question and is prepared to do what he believes is necessary to secure it. The 'ought'-judgment (7) is hence not a mere theoretical means-end statement indicating a cause-effect relation to which the amoralist has no practical or prescriptive attachment. On the contrary, (7) signifies both the amoralist's awareness of what he must do to get something he wants and his resolve to act in the required way. He could fail to accept (7) only at the price of not being rational or not being conatively normal, or both.

Even an amoralist, then, so long as he is rational and conatively normal in the senses indicated above, must use the practical concept of 'ought.' Apart from being addressed to the agent himself rather than to other persons, it is the same concept as figured in (2) and (3) above. A person who did not use this concept would not be aware that any requirements or constraints were ever set for his conduct for any reason whatever, including his own self-interested desires. Even if the latter were his only desires, he would not be able to distinguish what he ought and ought not to do with a view to satisfying them. So soon as any person begins to deliberate between alternative courses of action to achieve any purpose of his, and thereby rules out some alternatives and accepts others, he necessarily uses the concept of 'ought.'

There still remains the question of how such a prudential 'ought'-judgment as (7), when made by an amoralist, is related to the more complex 'ought'-judgments (2) and (3) above that were in various ways correlative with right-claims. Although the criterion of each of these 'oughts' is the same, consisting in the agent's purposes or self-interest, (2) and (3) are more complex than (7) because (7) is self-directed, laying a practical requirement only on the agent or the person whose well-being is directly at stake, whereas (2) and (3) are other-directed, laying practical requirements on other persons at least to refrain from interfering with the agent's well-being. The agent's right-claim (1) is correlative only with the more complex, other-directed 'ought'-judgments, so that the proof that he must use such a self-directed 'ought'-judgment as (7) is not yet a proof that he must make or accept a right-claim like (1). The question, then, is whether and how the agent must move from a self-directed 'ought'-judgment like (7) to an other-directed 'ought'-judgment like (2): 'All other persons ought at least to refrain from interfering with my freedom and well-being.'

The answer to this question can be seen from the consideration that the agent's self-directed requirement entails correlative requirements on other persons. If a person accepts that he ought to do X, on some criterion of 'ought,' then he must also accept that he ought, according to that same criterion, to be free to do X in that his doing X ought not to be prevented or interfered with by other persons. To put it somewhat more formally, (7) 'I ought to do X' entails (8) 'I ought to be free to do X,' where to be free means at least not to be prevented or interfered with by other persons, and where the criterion of 'ought' is held constant. For insofar as such nonprevention or noninterference is a necessary condition of one's doing X, one's acceptance for oneself of the requirement that one do X entails at least an implicit acceptance of the requirement that there be no interference with one's doing X. To reject the latter requirement, so far as one is aware of it, would be to reject also the former requirement, for one cannot rationally both accept that something ought to be done and reject a necessary condition of its being done. This connection must, indeed, take account of what was said above about the difficulties of calculation-transfer and value-transfer (1.14). But the inference from doing X to being free to do X is quite direct. And if one believes that the necessary condition of one's performing some action is repugnant or otherwise unacceptable, then, where it is indeed necessary to the performance of that action, one will not accept the requirement that the action itself be performed.

One objection to my position that (7) entails (8) is that this does not hold for competitive situations, including situations where interference with one's doing something is expected or accepted. Consider the following assertions: 'I ought to rob this bank'; 'I ought to win this tennis match'; 'I ought to win this contract.' Assume that in each case the 'ought' is not merely predictive but rather sets forth what each speaker accepts as a prescriptive requirement for his action grounded in what he takes to be a justifying reason; and assume also that the 'winning' mentioned in the last two assertions signifies either a culminating action or a sequence of actions. Each speaker, however, recognizes that opposition to and interference with his respective projects is or may be forthcoming: from the police, from his tennis competitor, from his business rival, each of whom has his own justifying reason for interfering. In view of this recognition, how can the speakers hold that they ought to be free to perform their respective actions? For this would mean that the police, the tennis competitor, the business rival ought not to interfere with the actions; but this would go counter to the speakers' recognition that in each case there are justifying reasons for such interference, so that the respective opponents ought to interfere. Hence it is false, at least for such competitive situations, that (7) 'I ought to do X' entails (8) 'I ought to be free to do X.'

The answer to this objection is that it does not take account of the proviso that there must be the same criterion of 'ought' if (7) is to entail (8). The would-be thief's statement 'I ought to rob this bank' has as its criterion, presumably, his own self-interest as reflected in his need or desire for money; legal criteria as accepted by the police are irrelevant to him. Hence, on his criterion his statement does entail 'I ought to be free to rob this bank' and hence that other persons, including the police, ought to refrain from interference with his robbery. On the other hand, the tennis player's statement 'I ought to win this match' has as its criterion not only his self-interest but also the rules of tennis, including the requirements of good sportsmanship. Because of his acceptance of this multiple criterion, his statement does not entail that his opponent ought not to interfere with his winning the match (for according to the rules the opponent ought to do his best to win), but only that his opponent ought not to interfere with his trying to win the match according to the rules. Thus the tennis player's statement means, 'I ought to try to win this match,' and this entails, 'I ought to be free to try to win this match.' As for the businessman's statement 'I ought to win this contract,' it is to be construed on the same model as that of the tennis player, except that the criterion of its 'ought' comprises rather the legal rules of business competition and the economic rules of entrepreneurship. On the other hand, the business-man may use threats or terrorism to get rid of his rival bidders for the contract; in this case his statement is to be assimilated to that of the bank robber. Thus, so long as the same criteria are maintained, (7) entails (8).

A related objection to this position would invoke the same egoistic doctrine considered earlier. A universal ethical egoist, while accepting (7), would reject (8) because he would hold that other persons ought to interfere with any action of his whenever they believe that it threatens their own self-interest or that their interfering with it would advance their own self-interest. Thus, for the universal egoist, (7) does not entail (8). Here, however, the same criticisms apply against universal ethical egoism as were presented above. It must also be noted that although the same criterion of universal egoism grounds the 'oughts' of both (7) and (8), the criterion is specifically different. For when the egoist says, 'I ought to do X,' his criterion is that of his own self-interest; but when he goes on to say that other persons ought to prevent him from doing X if they can, the criterion of this 'ought' is these other persons' self-interest. To maintain that the same general criterion of the principle of universal egoism grounds both statements would be true; but it would overlook the way in which, in keeping with the principle, the general criterion becomes particularized in dealing with different persons. Thus, if the same criterion of the egoist's own self-interest is maintained for each use of 'ought,' then his statement (7) 'I ought to do X' does entail (8) 'I ought to be free to do X.'

This point can be extended to deal with other objections against the entailment of (8) by (7) based on giving different qualifications to the 'ought' and the 'do' in (7) and in (8). For example, 'I (prima facie) ought to do X' does not entail 'I (conclusively) ought to be free to do X,' nor does 'I (legally) ought to do X' entail 'I (morally) ought to be free to do X.' Again, 'I ought to (attempt to) do X' does not entail 'I ought to be free to (succeed to) do X.' Such objections can be met by avoiding these diversities of qualification. In the present context, the criterion of the 'oughts' in (7) and (8) is directly neither moral nor legal but rather prudential. And each of them, like their respective uses of 'do,' refers to a conclusive requirement for achieving the doing of X, not merely for attempting that doing. For it will be recalled that the agent regards the doing of X as necessary for preserving his basic well-being.

93

Other objections against the position that (7) entails (8) can be answered in a parallel way by noting other relevant qualifications. Thus it may be objected that (8) goes beyond what is asserted by (7) because 'free to do' is a dispositional concept and hence refers to a greater time slice than simply 'do.' This objection may be answered in either of two ways. Most directly, (8), like (7), may be interpreted as episodic. 'I ought to be free to do X' would then mean that on certain datable occasions there ought to be no impediments to one's doing X, namely, on those occasions when one ought to do X. Thus, (8) would not go beyond (7). Less directly, both (7) and (8) might be interpreted as dispositional, so that (7) would say that one ought to do X on whatever occasions one chooses to do so, and (8) would then mean that on any such occasions one ought to be free to do X.

Still another objection to the entailment from (7) to (8) is that it is impossible to satisfy the condition that the same criterion must ground the respective 'oughts.' Since (7) 'I ought to do X' is a prudential judgment, it may also be rendered, at least in part, as (7_a) 'It would be prudent for me to do X.' But (8) 'I ought to be free to do X' cannot be similarly rendered, even in part, as (8_a) 'It would be prudent for me to be free to do X.' For since one's being free to do X involves noninterference by other persons with one's doing X, (8_a) would mean (8_b) 'It would be prudent for other persons not to interfere with my doing X.' Here, however, the prudential consideration in question consists in the self-interest or purposes of these 'other persons,' whereas in (7_a) it consists rather in the agent's own self-interest or purposes. Hence the same criterion does not ground the respective 'oughts' in (7) and (8).

In reply, it must be kept in mind that the entire sequence of statements is made by the agent from within his own standpoint in purposive action. Hence the correct way to state the point misleadingly expressed in (8_b) is as follows (8_c): 'It would be conducive to my prudential purposes that other persons not interfere with my doing X.' In (8_b) this is misleadingly expressed, among other reasons, because the 'for' in 'prudent for other persons not to interfere' suggests the meaning 'for the sake of (or for the prudential purposes of) those other persons,' whereas the required meaning is rather that other persons' not interfering would serve the purposes of the person who makes the statement. To preserve the meaning of (8), any proposed rendition of it must maintain the central idea that the judgment is presented from within the purposive standpoint of the person who makes the judgment. Thus in making such an 'ought'-judgment as (8) 'I ought to be free to do X', the agent is propounding, for the sake of his own prudential purposes, requirements or restrictions as to the conduct of other persons, so that the same prudential criterion grounds the 'oughts' in (7) and (8).

The entailment from (7) to (8) answers the question raised earlier of whether and how any agent must move from a self-directed 'ought'-judgment like (7) ('I ought to do X') to an other-directed 'ought'-judgment like (2) ('All other persons ought at least to refrain from interfering with my freedom and well-being'). For (8) uses the concept of 'free,' which is other-directed in that it has at least the negative meaning of one's not being interfered with by other persons. Thus (8) 'I ought to be free to do X' entails (9) 'All other persons ought at least to refrain from interfering with my doing X,' where the criterion of both 'oughts' is the same. Now, since the sole reason for the agent's accepting the requirement that he do X, according to the example given before, is that he regards his doing X as a necessary and sufficient condition of preserving his basic well-being, (9) entails (10) 'All other persons ought at least to refrain from interfering with my basic well-being.' Here, as before, the 'ought'-judgments (9) and (10) are prudential ones in the sense that they are concerned to further the interests or purposes not of the subjects of the judgments but rather of the agent who addresses the judgments to those subjects. He here holds that noninterference with his basic well-being is a requirement whose fulfillment is owed to him by all other persons because of the necessity of such noninterference for his continuing to be at least a prospective agent capable of achieving his purposes. Thus, by virtue of the correlativity of right-claims and strict 'ought'-judgments, (10) entails (11) 'I have a right to basic well-being.' This is, of course, an essential part of (1) 'I have rights to freedom and well-being.' That the amoralist logically must accept the remainder of (1) can be shown by the same arguments that led to his having to accept (11). Thus even an amoralist must accept and hence claim at least implicitly that he has prudential rights to freedom and well-being.

This restriction to the prudential does not depart from the standard concept of rights. It has long been recognized that assertions of rights are often linked to high valuations of individual liberty; indeed, Marx went so far as to say that rights-talk, including the French Declaration of the Rights of Man, is essentially egoistic.[16] In any case, when an individual agent claims for himself the generic rights to freedom and well-being, the fact that in the first instance he grounds this claim on his own needs as an agent does not preclude it from having the normative and prescriptive force traditionally associated with invocations of rights.

2.13. In addition to the egoist and the amoralist, the 'fanatic' may also be invoked against the thesis that every agent must hold that he has the generic rights. A fanatic is a person who agrees to the overriding of his own self-interest when this conflicts with some ideal he sincerely upholds.[17] At the extreme, there is the fanatical racist who sincerely believes that all persons of black ancestry should be enslaved or even killed, and who, on learning that he himself has black ancestry, offers himself to be slaughtered. A fanatic of this latter kind is in the position of saying, 'If I were of black ancestry, I would not have any rights to freedom and well-being.' But this contradicts my thesis that every agent must hold that he has rights to freedom and well-being.

It might seem that the simplest way of dealing with the fanatic is to assert that he is too irrational or conatively abnormal to be taken seriously. This, however, would overlook some important similarities to persons who are taken quite seriously. Other words for the fanatic as here defined are 'idealist' and 'person of principle'; for if anyone accepts a general principle requiring some counterinclinational treatment, such as legal punishment, for certain kinds of action such as wanton killing or cheating on one's income taxes, then if he is a person of principle he accepts that he ought himself to undergo such punishment if he were to perform such actions. In one familiar use of the word there is nothing unduly 'fanatical' about accepting this, even though to be deprived of liberty or property runs counter to one's usual inclinations.

The most direct answer to the question of how the existence of such 'fanatical' agents is compatible with my thesis is that the thesis deals with what is generically involved in agency: the generic rights are justified and upheld as being the proximate necessary conditions of action as such. So long as the racist or any other fanatic is prepared to act in support of his ideal, he has purposes he wants to fulfill. Hence, he must, if he is rational, hold that he has the generic rights required for his purpose-fulfilling actions, even if the purposes in question are ultimately designed to prevent his continuing to be an agent.

It must also be noted that the racist, like other fanatics, already has a specific principle on which he is prepared to act. In holding that if he had certain qualities he would no longer have rights to freedom and well-being, the fanatic is giving priority to a specific normative criterion for having such rights. This principle, however, is on a different level from the beliefs every agent must have about his own generic rights insofar as he confines himself to what pertains to himself as an agent, as against being a person who has a specific normative principle. Since persons may act on many other principles, there arises the question of the rational justification of the fanatic's principle as against these others. But, so far as the present stage of the rational argument has gone, none of these specific principles is logically necessary: all of them can be denied or rejected by any agent without self-contradiction, since they have not yet been shown to follow from the concept of action. Now it will be recalled that the use of the dialectically necessary method requires that the whole sequence of argument leading to the supreme principle of morality must respect the restriction that only those propositions are to be accepted as warranted that necessarily follow from the concept of action. Contingent beliefs or principles about the criteria for having rights, as upheld by some agents as against others, cannot be accepted into the sequence of argument, since an important goal of the argument is to attain a rationally necessary vantage point from which such beliefs can be critically evaluated (1.14). Whatever the specific contents of these beliefs or principles, they must, if they are to be justified, satisfy the normative rational requirements based on the conditions of action as such. Hence, the racist fanatic is premature in appealing to a specific normative principle whereby he would reject the generic rights in his own case or in that of any other person. His principle or ideal does not yet carry any justificatory weight with regard to ascertaining what is generically involved in action, so that it is not yet to be credited as a possible basis for coercing or harming anyone, including the fanatic himself, or for opposing the thesis that every agent must hold that he has the generic rights (see also 2.19, 22, 23).

2.14. Still another objection to this thesis might come from a radical social critic who contends that every action in his era reflects an evil social order. Actions do not occur in isolation; they require a social matrix that, at a minimum, provides conditions of stability and predictability without which the dynamic purposiveness of action, with its aims and plans, is futile. But if this matrix is unjust or even murderous, then the actions it supports will in turn support it unless they are dedicated to changing it; hence the actions take on the moral viciousness of the society. Persons who have this view of their society and of its vitiating influence on their actions would deny that they have any right to the generic features of action or, indeed, that their freedom and well-being are necessary goods.[18] A similar conclusion might be reached on the basis of the view that human nature is radically evil. An agent who has this view would not regard his purposes as good, nor would he think that he has rights to the freedom and well-being that are the necessary conditions of his actions.

Although such extreme positions raise important problems, they do not remove the facts that action is voluntary and purposive and that its purposiveness involves, on the part of the agent, a judgment of at least relative good. No matter how much he may deny his agency by proclaiming himself a passive victim of uncontrollable psychological or social forces, he is still in at least proximate control of his conduct, and he regards what he does as at least relatively worth doing, since otherwise he would not act at all. Moreover, even if he disapproves of his particular actions because of what he takes to be their vicious causal or environmental background, he will still maintain that he has a right at least to generic freedom and well-being. For these are the conditions of his very assertion of the wrongness of his society or his psyche, and they are also the conditions of whatever action he may take to overcome or lessen this wrongness.

2.15. The thesis that every agent must implicitly hold that he has rights to freedom and well-being also incurs the historical objection that although actions and agency are presumably coeval with most of the existence of the human race, the concept of a right is of much more recent origin. For rights are goods to which individuals are entitled as their due, and which they may rightly claim from other persons or from society. Hence, it is sometimes contended that rights are conceived and invoked only where the freedom and well-being of individual persons are viewed as having supreme importance. In premodern Western societies and in non-Western ones, however, superior value is attributed to the group, clan, or tribe or to a social or divine order in which the individual as such has a subordinate role. Hence there is no place in such societies for the concept of a right. This negative conclusion applies even to Roman law. Thus the objection is that it is anachronistic to attribute to premodern agents claims or judgments that they have rights to freedom and well-being.[19]

In dealing with this objection, it is important to note certain distinctions bearing on the five variables differentiated above in the concept of a right (2.7). It is one thing to say that there is no concept of a right at all in premodern societies or legal systems, and it is a quite different thing to say that this concept is not tied, for its justifying ground, to a certain exalted view of human individuals as contrasted with the social, natural, or divine order. The idea of entitlements or of rightful claims or powers had by individuals as subjects of rights might be maintained even if these entitlements are not derived from the nature of man but rather are subordinated to or derived from various social requirements.

It is also important to distinguish between having or using a concept and the clear or explicit recognition and elucidation of it. Not all concepts that are had or used are clearly analyzed, just as not all users of a language are theorists or analysts of it. Thus persons might have and use the concept of a right without explicitly having a single word for it; a more complex phrase might signify or imply the concept, such as that some persons have strict duties toward other persons, with sanctions for nonfulfillment, or that persons ought or ought not to be allowed to have or do certain things.[20]

The various justifying grounds of rights must also be further distinguished: a right might be upheld on moral criteria although it has no legal recognition; and if it is legally recognized, this might be with varying degrees of stringency or priority so far as concerns its protection or enforcement. Among legal as well as moral rights there are also distinctions as to their objects: these might be specific and relatively narrow, as in rights based on contracts or other phases of private law, or they might be general and broad, as in the constitutional and other rights invoked in public law. The respondents of the rights may correlatively vary from particular individuals to all mankind. Finally, the subjects of the rights may vary according to all the dimensions indicated earlier in the distributive problem of morality, from particular individuals or groups demarcated in various ways to all humans equally (cf. 1.1). Thus rights might be invoked and used without being 'human' or 'natural'; they may be restricted to certain individuals or groups while still being rights.

When such distinctions are recognized, it becomes less easy to credit the assertion that the concept of a right is peculiarly modern. For this would mean that premodern societies had no idea of entitlements due to individuals, not only with regard to property and contracts but also in connection with abstention from and punishment for crimes. The lack of this idea would entail that in such societies it was not held that at least some persons had rights to be free from physical assault or from other sorts of harms, or to own property and to make and collect on binding agreements or to engage in other sorts of transactions, or to have certain kinds of political authority. 'Some,' of course, does not mean 'all' or even 'most'; thus the historical universality of the concept of rights is compatible with the historical existence of markedly inegalitarian societies and drastic restrictions on the distribution of rights. In addition, the fact that in many or most societies only some agents have effectively had rights to freedom and well-being does not contradict the thesis that all agents implicitly hold that they ought to have these rights. The concept of 'having' a right is ambiguous as between the effective and the normative, between that which is socially recognized or legally enforced and that which ought to be recognized or enforced. The thesis upheld here has the latter, normative content, although, as we have seen, its criterion for having rights is at this stage prudential rather than moral.

A brief survey indicates that the negative view that restricts the concept of rights to the modern era is mistaken as a historical thesis. To begin with, it is significant that among the historians who deny that the concept of a right is found in Roman law, one writer nevertheless affirms that the Romans 'approached' this concept, although it was 'vague' and 'undifferentiated,' and another explicitly makes copious and repeated use of the concept of a right in expounding various provisions of Roman law.[21] Such use might be interpreted as meaning not that the concept of a right is found in the Roman legal texts but only that recourse to the concept is helpful in expounding texts in which no such concept occurs. But it is difficult to see how the exposition could escape the charge of distortion unless the texts expounded contained at least implicitly the concept used in the exposition. The more likely explanation involves one of the distinctions mentioned above: that the Romans had and used the concept of a right but did not invoke or analyze it as fully and explicitly as is done in modern legal texts. But from this it follows that the concept of a right, so far as concerns its justifying ground, is not restricted to a peculiarly modern doctrine of the equal worth of all individuals.

A similar point may be made in connection with feudalism. The panoply of agreements between lords and vassals was conceived to generate rights as well as duties on both sides. As McIlwain has put it: "The feudal relation is created by a solemn reciprocal engagement confirmed by an oath on one side and considered equally binding on both—it is contractual; but the rights so created on both sides are legal rights, they can be judicially interpreted only by the whole body of the peers of the fief, not by the lord. Theoretically, there never was a period when rights were more insisted upon."[22]

It is true that in the organic, inegalitarian social philosophies of Plato and Aristotle, assertions of rights as pertaining to all persons can hardly be found. But, as we have seen, rights-judgments need not be restricted to egalitarian-universalist positions. Plato's and Aristotle's doctrines in support of hierarchic political orders are readily interpreted as resting on the natural right of the wiser to rule those who are less wise; and rights are also implicit in their discussions of property and in Aristotle's analyses of the divergent grounds on which different groups in the state lay disputatious claim (*amphisbētousi, diamphisbētousi*), even justly (*dikaiōs*), to political authority. Moreover, echoes or anticipations of egalitarian rights can be found in these philosophers' descriptions of the claims of the democrats that every man should have the authority (*exousia*) to do as he likes.[23] Still more directly, the Greek concept of *isonomia*—meaning literally 'equality of law'—has been interpreted as involving "an equal right in the law-making, law-administering, law-enforcing power of the state."[24] Closely related to this is such a passage as that wherein Euripides writes that "when the laws are written down the weak and the wealthy have equal rights (*dikēn isēn*)."[25]

The concept of rights is also found in primitive societies. The recognition that such societies have legal systems has led to detailed descriptions of the structuring of their social relations by a network of rights and obligations. As Malinowski wrote of the Melanesians, "There is a strict distinction and definition in the rights of every one and this makes ownership anything but communistic."[26] These rights entail correlative obligations, with elaborate provisions for sanctions in case of nonperformance by the members of each community: "If at any time previously these have been guilty of neglect, however, they know that they will be in one way or another severely penalized. Each community has, therefore, a weapon for the enforcement of its rights: reciprocity." The rights in question extend beyond property to a variety of other relations, including marriage, maternity, economic exchange, protection against physical assault; and these relations are regulated by legal rules. But the rules, in turn, are both known to and internalized by the individual members of the community, who obey and also sometimes break the rules. This is to say that the individuals know their rights and duties: what entitlements they as well as others have. "Far also from being exclusively a group affair, his rights and his duties are in the main the concern of the individual, who knows perfectly well how to look after his interests and realizes that he has to redeem his obligations."

The concept of a right is not, then, restricted to modern Western societies. Hence, it is not anachronistic to attribute to every agent the implicit judgment that he has rights to freedom and well-being. While the objects of these rights are, as we have seen, very general, they do not depart in principle from the contents that have been upheld for rights in many other times and places. The agent's judgment about his rights, resting as it does on the prudential grounds of what is proximately required for agency and for successful action, reflects practical necessities that transcend the historical peculiarities of different social orders.

2.16. The upshot of this section is that the concept of a right is essentially connected with action. From the standpoint of the agent, his statement, 'I do X for purpose E' entails not only 'E is good' and 'My freedom and well-being are necessary goods,' but also 'I have rights to freedom and well-being.' Thus the analysis of action shows how, beginning from a descriptive concept and a factual statement, evaluative and deontic judgments can be logically derived therefrom. To be sure, the derivation is only within the standpoint of the agent, as the use of the dialectically necessary method requires; the judgments are not yet presented as independently assertoric or apodictic. Nevertheless, it is important to have seen in this way that deontic judgments necessarily follow from the concept of action. An important consequence of these considerations is that in the logical structure of action both the gap between fact and value and the gap between 'is' and 'ought' are bridged. To bridge the latter gap it is not necessary to appeal to institutional rules that govern practices like promising; claims of rights and correlative 'oughts' are logically involved in all purposive action.

Another consequence of the above considerations bears on the necessary content of moral argument. Many philosophers have held that all moral argument is ad hominem,[27] in that the only way for anyone to seek to resolve moral disagreements is by dealing with the implications of statements made by his interlocutor as to what is morally right or wrong. Such philosophers have therefore also held that an insuperable obstacle is posed if one's interlocutor refuses to use moral language in the first place and therefore will not enter the arena of moral debate. The above argument, however, has shown that no agent can rationally support such a refusal to use moral language, since right-claims are logically implied in all purposive action. To be sure, not all right-claims are moral ones; further devices are required in order to move from normative prudential discourse to moral discourse. But to have shown that normative rights-language is inescapable for any agent is at least an essential preliminary to these further devices; once this step has been taken, it can also be shown that the reason for which an agent claims his rights to freedom and well-being must be generalized to apply to other persons as well.

I also suggest that it is the valuational and justification-claiming features of action stressed in the above argument that provide the elemental basis of human rights. Philosophers have often asked about the logical and ontological grounds of such rights: where they come from, what is the status of right-claims, and so forth. Persons are not born having human rights in the sense in which they are born having legs; and while rights may be bestowed by positive laws, it is correctly felt that this basis is too contingent and conventional to ground human rights. The doctrine that rights are grounded in human worth or dignity is more promising; but often this is just another way of saying that human persons are right-bearing entities. To say that rights are demands or claims set forth by persons still leaves unsettled the question of what warrant there is for these demands. Although Hart has tried to derive the 'natural' right to be free from the assumptions of specific transactions like promising,[28] this incurs the difficulty that promising already presupposes a rule (or institution) to the effect that saying 'I promise' in certain contexts generates rights and obligations.

Such presupposition holds for specific rights where these are not viewed as parts of the generic rights. The latter rights, however, do not similarly presuppose some rule, for since their objects are the necessary conditions of all action, the generic rights supply the basis of all practical justificatory rules and hence are not themselves based on such rules. In the case of the rights attached to promising and similar specific institutions, on the other hand, there still remains the problem of how the rules on which they are based are themselves justified; until such justification is provided, the derivation of rights from them is left inconclusive. I shall indicate below that the rights and obligations of promising are derived from the rights of freedom and well-being, rather than the reverse (4.14 ff.).

The argument in this section supports the view that rights are necessarily rather than contingently connected with being human, for I have held that the basis of rights must be sought in the conviction necessarily held by every human agent that he has rights to the necessary conditions of action by virtue of his having purposes and pursuing goods. There is, of course, an important difference between believing that one has inherent rights and genuinely having them. But if argument is to establish the truth of the latter, it must begin from the beliefs each human agent necessarily has about his own rights of action. Once these beliefs are given, it can be shown by a further dialectically necessary argument that the agent must admit that such rights equally belong to all other prospective human agents. By admitting this, he is logically committed to accept the supreme principle of morality. But before this can be shown, we must carefully examine the basis for such an extension of the agent's rights-judgment.

The Criterion of Relevant Similarities

2.17. Every right-claim or attribution of a right is made on behalf of some person or group under a certain description or for a certain reason that is held to justify the claim. This reason need not be set forth explicitly, but the person who upholds the right must at least have it implicitly in view as the justifying ground of his claim. Without such a reason, he would be making not a right-claim but only a peremptory demand akin to that voiced by a gunman. The reason given for the right-claim must ultimately be advanced as a sufficient reason, one that provides a sufficient justifying condition for the person's having the right. Just as, in general, 'X is a sufficient condition of Y' means that if X occurs then Y must also occur, so 'X is a sufficient justifying condition of Y' means that if X occurs then Y must be justified or established as correct. To take a tentative example, if 'X' is that A has promised B to lend him ten dollars and if, given this promise, it must be justified or established as correct that B has a right to receive ten dollars from A, then A's promise is a sufficient justifying condition of B's having this right.

If the reason given for a right-claim is advanced not as a sufficient justifying condition but only as a necessary condition, or as neither necessary nor sufficient, then it can always be challenged with regard to whether it suffices to justify the right-claim. It is a question of understanding the justifying grounds for the right-claim by developing them to the point where they are held, by the person who adduces them, to succeed in the justificatory task he assigns them. If they are to be regarded as being thus successful, they must constitute sufficient reasons or grounds for the right-claim. For, by definition, anything short of a sufficient condition is such that, even if it obtains or is valid, the question still remains open whether the right-claim is justified.

A justificatory reason for a right-claim may or may not explicitly adduce, as the ground of the right, some description or descriptive characteristic of the person for whom the right is claimed. In either case, however, the reason implicitly refers to such a descriptive characteristic, and it can be reformulated, with no change of meaning, as giving such a description. Thus, in my example of the right derived from a promise, the justificatory reason does not explicitly adduce a description of B, the person who has the right; but implicitly it says that B has this right by virtue of having the description or descriptive characteristic that he is the person to whom A has made the promise.

Now whatever the description under which or the sufficient reason for which it is claimed that a person has some right, the claimant must admit, on pain of contradiction, that this right also belongs to any other person to whom that description or sufficient reason applies. This necessity is an exemplification of the formal principle of universalizability in its moral application, which says that whatever is right for one person must be right for any similar person in similar circumstances. But this formal moral principle, in turn, derives from a more general logical principle of universalizability: if some predicate P belongs to some subject S because S has the property Q (where the 'because' is that of sufficient reason or condition), then P must also belong to all other subjects $S_1, S_2, \ldots, S_n$ that have Q. If one denies this implication in the case of some subject, such as S_1, that has Q, then one contradicts oneself. For in saying that P belongs to S because S has Q, one is saying that having Q is a sufficient condition of having P; but in denying this in the case of S_1, one is saying that having Q is not a sufficient condition of having P. The principle of universalizability even in its moral application is not itself a substantial normative moral principle, not only because, depending on the criterion it uses for relevant similarities or for the property Q, it gives results that are morally quite diverse and even opposed to one another, but also because it simply explicates what is involved in the concept of 'because' as signifying a sufficient reason. Hence, in using the principle of universalizability to establish the supreme principle of morality I shall not be using a substantial moral principle.

Apparent exceptions to the logical principle of universalizability arise when the reason given is not in fact taken to be sufficient. When it is said that S has P because S has Q, what may be meant is that S has certain other characteristics R that, when combined with Q, are sufficient for its being the case that S has P. On this interpretation of the 'because,' it would not logically follow that other subjects that have Q have P, because these other subjects may not have R, and Q is a sufficient condition for P only when combined with R. I shall refer to such cases as that of R as 'additional conditions.' For example, if it is said that a car skidded because it was traveling sixty miles per hour on an icy road, this would not justify the generalization that all cars that travel sixty miles per hour on an icy road will skid, if what was implicitly understood in the initial statement was that the car's skidding in the situation described had as contributing factors that the car was of light construction, had worn tires, and was being driven with no regard for circumstances of weather. Such complexity of additional conditions is a standard feature of causal explanations that adduce sufficient conditions.[29]

Additional conditions differ, however, with regard to their degree of generality. One kind is illustrated in my example, where the skidding was held to have as its sufficient condition a quite specific set of characteristics of the car, the driver, and the road. At the other extreme are additional conditions that are maximally general, as when it is understood that certain universal physical laws obtain. For without these laws the conditions described would not be sufficient to generate the skidding. Since, however, the laws obtain in all cases, they are implicitly assumed and require no separate explicit statement.

The logical principle of universalizability is given a deontic or moral application by interpreting the predicate P in the above pattern as a deontic or moral predicate. It may then be formulated, among other ways, as follows: if one person S has a certain right because he has quality Q (where the 'because,' as before, is that of sufficient condition, now understood as justificatory), then all persons who have Q must have such a right. Other familiar deontic or moral formulations of the principle are that what is right in one case must be right in all similar cases and that whatever rule one applies in one's own case one ought to apply in all similar cases. Such formulations are sometimes said to be principles of 'formal justice.'[30] In each of these the criterion of relevant similarities, which gives content to formal justice, is the same as the sufficient reason for which, or the description under which, a person is held to have a certain right. Hence, for other persons to fulfill this sufficient reason is for them to be similar to the first person in respect of having the descriptive characteristics that were held to justify his having the right.

The apparently egalitarian import of the moral principle of universalizability is severely restricted by the fact that the principle allows complete variability with respect to content. One kind of contentual variability is that the actions it is right to perform, according to the principle, may vary indiscriminately in accordance with the variable inclinations or ideals of agents; this violates the requirement of categoricalness for a supreme moral principle. Another kind of contentual variability is especially pertinent in the present context. For the universalizability principle sets no limits on the criteria of relevant similarity or the sufficient reasons for having the right to perform various actions, so that agents or other protagonists can tailor these criteria or reasons to suit their own variable desires or prejudices. Thus, so far as the principle is concerned, some person may without inconsistency claim the right to inflict various harms on other persons on the ground that he possesses qualities that are had only by himself or by some group he favors; or, alternatively, on the ground that his recipient possesses qualities quite different from his own. He may claim that he has the rights in question because, for example, he is white or male or American or highly intelligent or a laborer or a capitalist, or for that matter because he is named Wordsworth Donisthorpe or because he was born on such and such a date at such and such a place, and so forth. And, depending on the property he adduces as a sufficient reason for his right-claim, he will be logically required to grant only that these maleficent rights belong to all other persons who have this property, including, at the extreme, the class consisting only of one member, himself. Even if it is insisted that the agent, in order to apply the principle, must imagine himself as being in the position of the recipient, this still leaves it open that fanatical agents may be willing to be recipients of such harmful actions. Such variability as to the criteria of relevant similarities serves to remove the contentual egalitarianism that might otherwise be thought to characterize the principle of universalizability.

2.18. Some philosophers have held that such variability as to the criterion of relevant similarities is inevitable. Since all persons are similar in some respects and dissimilar in others, and since persons can hence be classified in many different ways, what anyone takes to be relevant qualities or similarities must be entirely relative to his own particular purposes or moral principles. An extreme version of this general position declares that since moral principles are not susceptible of proof or justification, the relativity of criteria of relevant similarities to moral principles entails that the criteria themselves are ultimately arbitrary.[31] A less extreme version of this position is found among some expositors of utilitarianism, who suggest that from a utilitarian standpoint qualities of persons or acts are relevant to justice insofar as they causally affect the production of good or bad consequences. Entirely apart from the well-known difficulties that beset all utilitarian attempts to provide grounds for justice, it is clear that this general position, if sound, would make impossible the project of the present work. For the purpose of all the steps of my argument, including the current one aiming at the rational justification of a criterion of relevant similarities, is to set forth a rational justification of a supreme moral principle. Hence I cannot, without self-contradiction, accept the view that all criteria of relevant similarities are arbitrary because moral principles are not susceptible of justification. Nor can I, without vicious circularity, appeal to my own moral principle in order to justify the criterion of relevant similarities.

Other philosophers have tried to establish criteria of relevant similarity that avoid the arbitrariness and relativity of the above general position. It has been suggested, for example, that which qualities of persons or acts are relevant to justice or to moral rightness is to be determined by the specific purposes of the positions, rules, or institutions for which the qualities are to be selected.[32] The trouble with this suggestion is that the purposes in question may themselves be unjust or otherwise immoral, so that to distinguish between qualities of persons or acts on the basis of these purposes would promote injustice rather than justice. Another suggestion has been that which qualities are relevant to justice or to moral rightness is to be determined by means of reciprocal acceptability—that is, by considering whether differentiations of treatment in terms of those qualities are acceptable to persons regardless of whether they themselves have the qualities and hence regardless of whether they are on the active or on the passive side of transactions according to rules that determine treatment of persons by possession of those qualities.[33] This criterion, however, unless specified in further ways, would prohibit acts and rules that are ordinarily regarded as just or otherwise morally right, such as punishment and differential academic grading. And it would permit acts and rules that are ordinarily regarded as unjust or otherwise morally wrong, for a 'fanatic' may uphold various discriminatory ideals regardless of their harmful impact on his own interests if he were to have the qualities in question.

Some of these difficulties are avoided by John Rawls's acute stipulation that persons must commit themselves in advance as to the contents of rules and hence as to the criteria of relevant similarities, from an 'original position' wherein they are completely ignorant of all their particular personal qualities, including their relative power or ability. Such a stipulation does indeed serve to remove the self-partiality of some criteria. If one deprives persons of all knowledge of their own specific characteristics, then it is plausible to assume that they will choose egalitarian principles of justice.[34] But how cogent is this as an argument for the validity or rationality of egalitarian principles that are to operate in the actual world of persons who are in fact unequal in power and ability and who know their specific characteristics (see 1.8)? Since the assumption of persons' total ignorance of their particular qualities, being factually false, is hardly rational, how can it be rationally justifiable to rational persons in the real world to which Rawls intends that his principles of justice be applied? There is an important difference in this respect between Rawls's argument and at least some examples of the abstract simplified models to which it might otherwise be assimilated. For the writers who develop these models acknowledge that in taking as their units individuals whose choices or preferences are given equal weight in the ensuing 'social choice' or 'constitution' or 'economic welfare function,' they are making ethical value assumptions.[35] One might try to assimilate Rawls's double assumption of rationality and ignorance to the game theorists' and economists' models of risk-taking under conditions of uncertainty. But those models do not extend the uncertainty factor so drastically as is done in his assumption of persons' total ignorance of their specific characteristics.

2.19. The difficulties of all these views on criteria of relevant similarity may be summed up by noting that they either admit of some sort of substantive or moral variability or are based on dubious or untenable assumptions. In order to follow my own resolution of these difficulties, it must be recalled that in the present context I am concerned with the claim that, as we have seen, is implicitly made by every agent that he has rights to freedom and well-being. We have also seen that the agent's justifying reason for claiming these rights is that freedom and well-being are the proximate necessary conditions of all his purposive actions (2.7 ff.). But their being such conditions serves, for the agent, to justify his having them as rights only because he is an actual or prospective agent who has purposes he wants to fulfill. If he were not such a purposive agent, having no concern for fulfilling his purposes, then he would not regard his freedom and well-being either as necessary goods or as rights. On the other hand, so long as the agent fulfills the description of being a prospective agent who has purposes he wants to fulfill, he must hold that he has rights to freedom and well-being. It is hence this description of the agent that constitutes, from his own standpoint, the sufficient justifying condition for his right-claim, and that constitutes also the criterion of relevant similarity when it is said, in accordance with the principle of universalizability, that the rights the agent claims for himself he logically must admit belong also to all other persons who are relevantly similar to himself. The agent is rationally entitled to adduce only this description as his sufficient reason, so that his criterion of relevant similarity is exempt from substantive and moral variability.

The agent's description of himself as a prospective purposive agent is both a necessary and a sufficient condition of the justifying reason he must adduce for his claim to have the generic rights. That it is a necessary condition can be seen from the fact that every agent performs his actions by virtue of having purposes whose fulfillment he regards as good. And it is because freedom and well-being are required for such purposive actions that every agent claims the rights to these generic features of action. If agents had no purposes, they would not claim any rights to act or to have freedom and well-being. The justifying reason for every agent's claim to generic rights must hence refer to a description of him involving the purposes for which he acts: that he is a prospective agent who has purposes he wants to fulfill.

This description of the agent is also a sufficient condition of the justifying reason he must adduce for his having the generic rights. If the agent were to maintain that his reason must add some qualifying restriction to this description, and must hence be less general than his simply being a prospective purposive agent, then he could be shown to contradict himself. Let us designate by the letter D such a more restrictive description. Examples of D would include, 'My name is Wordsworth Donisthorpe,' 'I am highly intelligent (or benevolent),' and other descriptions like those mentioned earlier. Now let us ask the agent whether, while being an agent, he would still hold that he has the rights of freedom and well-being even if he were not D. If he answers yes, then he contradicts his assertion that he has these rights only insofar as he is D. He would hence have to admit that he is mistaken in restricting his justificatory description to D. But if he answers no, that is, if he says that while being an agent he would not hold that he has these rights if he were not D, then he can be shown to contradict himself with regard to the generic features of action. For, as we have seen, it is necessarily true of every agent both that he requires freedom and well-being in order to act and that he hence implicitly claims the right to have freedom and well-being. For an agent not to claim these rights, at least implicitly, would mean that he does not act for purposes he regards as good at all and that he does not regard the necessary conditions of his actions as necessary goods. But this in turn would mean that he is not an agent, which contradicts the initial assumption. Thus, to avoid contradicting himself, the agent must admit that he would hold that he has the rights of freedom and well-being even if he were not D, and hence that the description or sufficient reason for which he claims these rights is not anything less general or more restrictive than that he is a prospective agent who has purposes he wants to fulfill.

I shall call this the Argument from the Sufficiency of Agency (ASA), since it says that the fact of being a prospective agent who has purposes he wants to fulfill provides for any agent a sufficient (as well as necessary) justificatory reason for his implicit claim to have the generic rights. It is important to keep in mind that the ASA does not of itself deal with the justification of claims to more specific rights. These will require further considerations, which I shall discuss subsequently. But since freedom and well-being are proximately required for all agency, as the common denominators that must be had by every purposive agent regardless of the different specific purposes for which different agents may act, the agent's claim to have these as rights is based simply on the general consideration of his having purposes as a prospective agent. The generic scope of the rights claimed must be matched by a corresponding generality of the qualities adduced by any agent to justify having the rights. For if the justifying qualities were more restrictive, they would not justify the full range of the rights each agent must claim for himself to the proximate necessary conditions of his engaging in action.

This point can be further connected with the requirements of rational justification whereby the rational excludes what is arbitrary. For any agent's procedure in trying to justify his claim to the generic rights is arbitrary so long as he is permitted to pick and choose according to his own predilections from among the varying descriptions, contents, or criteria of relevant similarities that may enter into his right-claim. The only way to halt this arbitrariness, and hence to establish his claim on a rationally justified basis, is to restrict its justification to what is necessarily and universally connected with its subject matter, as against what is optional or left to the agent's discretion. Now no matter in how many ways the agent in making his right-claim might choose to describe himself or to give sufficient reasons for his action, the description and sufficient reason he cannot reject is that he is a prospective agent who has purposes he wants to fulfill. For it is this description that is necessarily and universally, hence invariably, connected with the generic features of action, which supply the contents to which every agent claims the rights. Hence, insofar as the agent's necessary right-claim is restricted to what he is rationally justified in claiming, his claim that he has rights to freedom and well-being must refer to himself qua prospective agent who has purposes he wants to fulfill. Thus, once again, the generality of the objects of the rights requires a corresponding generality of their subject.

It is also this generality that explains why, in the necessary description or sufficient reason of his having these rights, I have referred to a *prospective* agent who has purposes he wants to fulfill.' For the agent claims these rights not only in his present action with its particular purpose but in all his actions. To restrict to his present purpose his reason for claiming the rights of freedom and well-being would be to overlook the fact that he regards these as goods in respect

111

of all his actions and purposes, not only his present one. To be a prospective agent, then, is not necessarily to be an actual agent; it is rather to have desires or goals one wants or would want to fulfill through action. A prospective agent is so called not only from his prospects, which at some points may be meager, but also from his prospecting—his occurrently or dispositionally looking ahead in some way to acting for purposes he regards as good.

Since, then, to avoid contradicting himself the agent must claim he has the rights of freedom and well-being for the sufficient reason that he is a prospective agent who has purposes he wants to fulfill, he logically must accept the generalization that all prospective agents who have purposes they want to fulfill have the rights of freedom and well-being. This generalization is a direct application of the principle of universalizability; and if the agent denies the generalization, then, as we have seen, he·contradicts himself. For on the one hand in holding, as he logically must, that he has the rights of freedom and well-being because he is a prospective purposive agent, he accepts that being a prospective purposive agent is a sufficient condition of having these rights; but if he denies the generalization, then he holds that being a prospective purposive agent is not a sufficient condition of having these rights.

2.20. Let us now consider the ways an agent may try to evade such generalization of his right-claim to all other prospective purposive agents. First, he may give no justificatory reason at all for his right-claim; hence, a fortiori, he does not supply a justificatory reason that can be generalized to other persons. This, however, has already been considered and rejected at the beginning of the present section. If the agent does not even implicitly have and give a justificatory reason, then he makes not a right-claim but a peremptory demand. But, as we saw in the preceding section, the agent must make the right-claim I have attributed to him. Hence, he must implicitly have and give a justificatory reason for it.

It must be kept in mind that what is primarily involved here is not merely giving reasons to others in the sense of overt communication with them, but also having reasons for one's own right-claim. The issue is not only or mainly the rhetorical one of what to say to other persons, but rather the logical one of the agent's own rationale for his conviction that he has rights to freedom and well-being. Since he intends to act for purposes that seem to him to be good, and since he requires freedom and well-being for such action, this requirement constitutes a reason no agent can evade as the basis of his claim that he has the corresponding rights.

A second way an agent may try to evade generalizing his right-claim beyond his particular case is by not having or giving sufficient reasons for his right-claim. He may insist that his justificatory reasons constitute at most necessary conditions, so that in claiming that he has rights to freedom and well-being he has omitted other reasons that are required for the full justification of his right-claim. Thus he may declare, for example, that his being a prospective purposive agent is only a necessary condition of his having these rights; further necessary conditions are that he is highly intelligent and benevolent; but even these are not yet sufficient justifying conditions. Hence, while he would indeed be logically committed to holding that all persons who have rights to freedom and well-being are prospective purposive agents who are highly intelligent and benevolent, he would not be logically committed to hold the converse generalization. And this process may continue with the agent maintaining at each point that he has not yet arrived at sufficient justifying conditions for having the generic rights.

There are at least three considerations that may seem to support this failure to give sufficient justifying conditions. One bears on the parallel case of trying to explain historical events. It is usually quite difficult to ascertain the sufficient conditions for the occurrence of a historical event because of the complexity of the causal background; hence, historians usually confine themselves to setting forth necessary conditions.[36] Insofar as the explanation of a historical event is similar to the justification of a right-claim, in that in each case one or a group of propositions or judgments is set forth as providing a reason or rationale for what is signified by another proposition or judgment, the difficulties of giving sufficient conditions in the historical case might seem to support a similar restrictiveness in the case of rights. A second consideration bears on the justification of specific rights. To recur to my earlier example of the right derived from a promise, it is notorious that such a right may be overridden by more pressing requirements of well-being. Thus B's right to be lent ten dollars, as promised him by A, would be removed at least temporarily if A needed the money to buy medicine for his wife. Consequently, A's promise to B is not a sufficient justifying condition of B's having the right, at least as a conclusive or actual right; and such lack of sufficiency also characterizes the reasons or conditions that might be adduced to justify other specific rights. In the parallel case of legal rights, it has been argued that all of them are 'defeasible' in that they can be terminated in a number of different ways, so that sufficient conditions for their being valid cannot be given.[37] It may be argued, third, that no general sufficient condition can be given by the agent for his having the rights of freedom and well-being because the particular situations in which he would use or exercise these rights may differ in various and unpredictable ways, and a concomitant variety and unpredictability must attend his justifications of these uses.

Although these considerations are indeed suggestive, they do not carry over to the present context. For I am here concerned not with specific rights but with generic ones, and with the general conditions of their being possessed and claimed by agents. It must also be kept in mind that, in accordance with my dialectically necessary method, I am here concerned with the sufficient conditions of the justification of the generic rights from within the standpoint of the agent himself and not as determined by legal or other criteria that may be external to that standpoint, and whose own justificatory status has not yet been established. From the agent's standpoint, his having the generic rights to freedom and well-being is sufficiently justified by his being a prospective agent who has purposes he wants to fulfill. For these rights are the proximate prerequisites of all his purposive actions and hence of all the goods he may seek to attain by action. This sufficiency of justification from within the standpoint of the agent is hence not affected by the complexities either of normative criteria external to that standpoint or of the variety of causal and other background circumstances.

It is important to note the precise limits of this dialectical justification of the generic rights from within the standpoint of the agent. I have argued that from the standpoint of the agent himself, being a prospective purposive agent is a sufficient justifying condition for having the generic rights. This does not entail, however, that I am committed to holding that the exercise of these rights may never be rightly overridden. Such overriding might be justified on the basis of two kinds of criteria, which must be carefully distinguished. One kind would be introduced as completely independent of the agent's own standpoint, with no attempt to indicate any positive relation between them. This approach would hence leave unelucidated, at least to the agent, the warrant of such a criterion, including the question of why any agent should accept it as normatively binding for him. The other kind of criterion would be positively related to the agent's own standpoint, in that it would have been shown that he must be committed, on rational grounds, to subsuming his individual standpoint under that criterion. I shall deal with these grounds in chapters 4 and 5. From this it will follow that the justifying condition that was sufficient, from the agent's individual standpoint, to justify his having the generic rights is no longer sufficient to justify his exercising these rights in certain sorts of circumstances. It is obviously of first importance to deal with these points sequentially. I am here concerned with what is justified from within the agent's own standpoint in purposive action; the introduction of further criteria, which the agent himself must rationally accept, will be dealt with later.

2.21. I shall now consider somewhat more extensively a third way an agent may try to evade the generalization to all other prospective purposive agents of his right-claim to freedom and well-being. This way would be for him to maintain that although he supplies sufficient conditions for justifying his having the generic rights, the conditions must include additional characteristics besides simply being a prospective agent who has purposes he wants to fulfill. This addition, as made by the agent, would preclude that all prospective purposive agents have the characteristics that enter into his own sufficient justifying reason. The addition also entails that this sufficient reason is not, and logically need not be, the same as the reason given by other agents for their respective claims to have the generic rights.

The additional characteristics adduced by the agent for this restrictive purpose may be of two kinds. One kind is purely individual, in that the characteristics pertain to only one person, usually the agent himself. The other kind is particular, in that the characteristics pertain to more than one person, to some special or partial group of persons short of all prospective purposive agents. Hence there occur two kinds of objections to my above universalization of the agent's right-claim: an individualizability objection and a particularizability objection. Although I think both kinds of objections can be satisfactorily answered by the Argument from the Sufficiency of Agency (*ASA*) presented above, it may be helpful to deal with each of them in somewhat fuller detail.

The individualizability objection holds that when the agent gives a sufficient justificatory reason for his having the generic rights, this reason may be so individualized that it pertains only to the agent himself. The point is that since the agent claims the generic rights for himself, his reason for this claim must consist in his own having of his own purposes that he wants to fulfill for himself. Hence, as formulated by the agent, his reason for his right-claim must include 'egocentric particulars'—expressions whose denotation is relative to the speaker himself, such as 'I' and 'my.' The agent would be in the position of saying, 'I have the generic rights because *I* want to fulfill *my own* purposes.' Since other persons may not have or want to fulfill the agent's purposes, the agent's reason for his right-claim comprises characteristics of himself that are not had by other persons, and his reason is not the same as the reasons other persons give for their right-claims. Thus the universalization of the agent's right-claim would be not, 'All prospective agents who have purposes they want to fulfill have the generic rights,' but rather, 'All prospective agents who have *my* purposes that *I* want to fulfill have the generic rights.'

To make this individualizing restriction even more explicit, the agent (whom I shall call 'X') may insist that other indexical expressions referring uniquely to himself, such as his own proper name, must be included in the sufficient justifying reason he gives for his right-claim: 'I have the generic rights because I am a prospective agent named X who wants to fulfill X's purposes.' The universalization would now be: 'All prospective agents named "X" who want to fulfill X's purposes have the generic rights.' Thus in each case the universalization of the agent's right-claim would be logically restricted so as to entail only that the agent himself has the generic rights, not that all prospective agents have them.

The intuitive reaction to this latter way of individualizing the agent's right-claim is that the properties it adduces, such as his proper name, are irrelevant to his or anyone else's reason for claiming or having the generic rights. Thus the *ASA* is applicable here; one would ask the agent, 'Wouldn't you claim the rights to freedom and well-being even if your name weren't "X"?' If he replies, 'No; only one's having the noble name "X" justifies one's having these rights,' then he can be refuted by the consideration, which has been elaborated above, that the rights to freedom and well-being must be claimed, at least implicitly, by every agent who acts for purposes he regards as good. Hence, X would claim to have these rights for a justificatory reason even if his name were not 'X.' It follows that being named 'X' is not any necessary part or condition of his justificatory reason for claiming to have the generic rights; or, to put it otherwise, his justificatory reason can be sufficient without including or having in the background his being named 'X.'

What, however, of the version of the individualizability objection that uses speaker-relative expressions like 'I' and 'my'? It might seem that this cannot be dealt with as was the version that used such indexical expressions as 'X.' Suppose one were to ask the agent, 'Wouldn't you claim for yourself the rights to freedom and well-being even if you didn't have your own purposes you wanted to fulfill?' The answer would have to be that in this case he would not claim these rights for himself, where such a right-claim has as its reason his own having purposes and wanting to fulfill them by action.

It still remains, however, that the agent has the same sufficient reason for claiming the generic rights as have all other agents. For the reason he gives, 'I want to fulfill my own purposes,' is also the reason had or given by all other agents, since each wants to fulfill his own respective purposes. Consequently, the universalization of the agent's right-claim must extend to all other prospective agents. It may be objected, however, that the first agent's reason for his right-claim is not the same as other agents' reasons, because the words 'my' and 'his' are referentially ambiguous when they are used to refer to the respective persons' purposes. To stop this ambiguity, we must give the first agent's reason not as wanting to fulfill 'his' purposes but as wanting to fulfill the purposes of X or of someone named 'X'; and this is not the reason for other persons' claiming the generic rights for themselves. Here the argument returns in part to the proper-name version of the individualizability objection, which I have already answered through the *ASA*. The argument may also be interpreted, however, as turning not on X's name but on his being the unique person he is. For X would not claim the generic rights for himself if he did not want to fulfill the purposes of the unique person X, and this is not the same reason as that for which other persons claim the generic rights for themselves.

To deal with this argument, it is important to be clear as to what is meant by 'the same reason' when it is affirmed or denied that X has the same reason for claiming the generic rights as have other prospective agents. The concept of 'the same reason' can be atomized in several ways. It may be declared that no one person ever does something twice for the same reason, even where that something is, for example, brushing his teeth on two successive evenings, because the state of intention or desire that constitutes his reason for acting on the first occasion is numerically different from that which constitutes his reason for acting on the later occasion. Even if we dismiss this psychologistic-occurrent interpretation of a 'reason' for an interpretation that focuses on the contents of the reason, it may still be declared that no two persons ever do anything for the same reason even when they are cooperating toward a common objective, such as oarsmen on a crew trying to win a race. For oarsman X is trying to fulfill the purposes of the unique person X, while oarsman W is trying to fulfill the purposes of the unique person W.

Such atomizations, however, erroneously assume that if the concept of sameness is to be correctly applied to a reason, the reason must have the numerical identity that pertains to a single individual who has the reason, even if not to a single state or pulsation of his consciousness. If this assumption were correct, then no sense could be made of enduring character traits either of a single individual who performs many numerically diverse actions for the same reason, or of many individuals who have similar enduring character traits so that the actions of all of them are performed for the same reason. Nor could sense be made of the ways in which different individuals may cooperate in order to achieve a common objective, so that they perform their diverse actions for the same reason. In all such cases, the concept of 'the same reason' involves not a uniqueness that is restricted to a single individual or a single state of intention, but rather a generality or similarity of purposes or motivations that may be common both to one individual agent at different times and to many individual agents.

This generality or similarity also pertains to cases of competition. When X and W are having a race, X's reason for running is to have X win the race and W's reason is to have W win the race. Nevertheless, they are running for a generically same or similar reason: to succeed in winning the race (S). Thus, if X expresses his reason or purpose as 'I want that I have S,' this statement is a token of a type that can be truly uttered by W and by any other competitors in the race as well. While each of these tokens has a different reference so far as concerns the 'I,' they all have a common meaning in that they express the qualitatively same desiderative attitude toward the (numerically or generically) same object. Hence, those other persons' reasons for performing their actions are the same as X's reason.

To consider somewhat further this qualitative sameness of the reasons for which different persons may act, let us assume that X and W are personal egoists, so that the following statements are respectively true of them: 'X wants to benefit X,' 'W wants to benefit W.' What makes the X-statement a statement of X's reason for acting is that it expresses a prorelation between his desiderative attitude or striving on the one hand and his being benefited on the other. The relation itself is a general one—it does not itself mention X. And this same relation also obtains in the case of the W-statement as a statement of W's reason for acting. In each case, the reason may be analyzed into two proper-name relata and the relation between them. The reasons differ in their respective relata (X and W), but they are the same not only in the relation of 'wanting to benefit' but also in the reflexivity of each relation. For each reason expresses the qualitatively same desiderative attitude toward benefiting the person who has the attitude. Now suppose X were to insist that the reflexive relation provides no reason for acting at all unless it relates the specific relata X and X—that is, 'X wants to benefit X.' Even so, he could not deny that the same reflexive relation is an essential component of, and makes a crucial contribution to, W's reason as well as to X's, so that the reasons are to that extent the same. The fact that the respective relata or referents are different means not that the reasons are not the same at all (since the relations themselves are the same) but only that X has the same relation toward, and hence the same reason for, claiming the generic rights for himself (namely, that he wants to benefit himself) as W has for claiming the generic rights for himself. Thus, even on the assumptions of personal egoism and the uniqueness of individual agents, their reasons for acting and for claiming the generic rights for themselves may be the same. It follows that the individualizability objection is mistaken when it appeals either to proper names or to other unique properties as grounds for holding that the sufficient justificatory reason some agent gives for his having the generic rights may be so individualized that it pertains only to that agent himself.

2.22. Let us turn to the particularizability objection. According to this, an agent may contend that he has the generic rights not simply qua prospective purposive agent but only because and insofar as he has certain more specific characteristics that pertain only to some partial group short of all prospective purposive agents. The favored characteristics may be those of belonging to some particular race, religion, nation, or economic class, or they may be such characteristics as a certain high level of intelligence or benevolence or having a certain kind of knowledge or purpose. Hence, the agent would be logically committed through the principle of universalizability to holding only that the members of this particular group have the generic rights.

To this contention the *ASA* furnishes an adequate reply. Even if the agent were to lack these favored characteristics, he would still hold that he has the generic rights, since it is necessarily true of every agent that he implicitly claims the generic rights for himself on the ground of their necessity for his purposive pursuits. Hence, the sufficient reason for which he claims the rights must adduce simply the characteristic of being a prospective purposive agent, so that he must admit that all other prospective purposive agents also have these rights.

Before accepting this egalitarian universalist conclusion, let us see how it can cope with objections drawn from the concept of agency, since it is from an implication of this concept that the conclusion is held to follow. If agency itself were to involve various inegalitarian differentiations, this would create problems for the egalitarianism inferred from it. To begin with, it must be noted that not all entities that pursue or seem to pursue purposes are agents in the sense used here. Animals other than humans lack for the most part the ability to control their behavior by their unforced choice, to have knowledge of relevant circumstances beyond what is present to immediate awareness, and especially to reflect rationally on their purposes. These abilities are also lacked to some extent by children and by the insane and other such mentally deficient persons. Hence, these groups are in varying degrees and on different grounds excluded from the class of prospective agents. Children are potentially such agents, while mentally deficient persons can attain the requisite abilities only in part.

If, however, there are these degrees of approach to full-fledged agency, then are there not also degrees of agency itself, so that 'normal' adult human agents are unequal to one another as agents? Most obviously, some persons are superior to others in practical intelligence; hence they are superior agents, since they can act more effectively to achieve their purposes and can also achieve a wider range of purposes. This superiority bears at least in part on the same characteristics—ability for self-control, knowledge of relevant circumstances, reasoned reflection on purposes—whose lack was held to exclude animals from the class of agents, actual or prospective.

Two inferences might be drawn from such unequalizing differentiations among human agents. One is that the description or sufficient condition that justifies having the generic rights is not simply the nonrestrictive characteristic of being a prospective purposive agent, which pertains to all normal adults; it is rather the restrictive characteristic of having the capacity for agency in superior degree. It was on such an exclusivist criterion—the ability to exercise rationality, especially in deliberating and foreseeing consequences—that Aristotle based his attribution of freedom and of fullness of well-being to a restricted group of humans, while calling those who lacked this deliberative ability natural slaves.[38] Thus only the superior agents would have the generic rights. The other inference that might be drawn is that although all human agents have the generic rights, these rights belong in greater degree to superior agents. For since the qualities that justify having the rights are unequally distributed, the rights too should be unequally distributed. Hence, superior agents should have greater rights to freedom and well-being: more power to choose and control their own and other persons' participation in transactions and more means of fulfilling their purposes.

Because of the general importance of the premise on which the latter inference is based, I shall state it more formally and explicitly as follows. When some quality Q justifies having certain rights R, and the possession of Q varies in degree in the respect that is relevant to Q's justifying the having of R, the degree to which R is had is proportional to or varies with the degree to which Q is had. I shall call this the *Principle of Proportionality* (*PP*). Thus, if x units of Q justify that one have x units of R, then y units of Q justify that one have y units of R. Such proportionality is a pervasive feature of traditional doctrines of distributive justice.[39]

Now the *PP* is true, but only if it is interpreted correctly; and it is easily misinterpreted. The main misinterpretation bears on the justifying quality Q, including the respects in which it does or does not vary in degree. For example, in the United States a citizen's legal right to vote is largely determined by his age, which may hence be viewed as at least part of the quality Q that legally justifies his having this right. But although citizens vary with respect to age, it does not follow that older citizens have more legal right to vote, or a legal right to more votes, than do younger citizens. This example shows that for the *PP* to be interpreted correctly, the justifying quality Q must be precisely stated. It is the quality or property of being at least eighteen years old that legally justifies or determines that a citizen has the right to vote; and the possession of this quality is absolute, not varying in degree, because that one is at least eighteen years old is not affected by how much older than eighteen one may be. Hence, the *PP* is not pertinent in this situation, or rather it is pertinent only as a limiting case: since the Q does not vary in degree, neither does the R.

Let us now apply this consideration to the generic rights. As we have seen, what justifies for every agent his having these rights is that he is a prospective agent who has purposes he wants to fulfill; I shall call this quality 'P.' Does P vary in degree? To answer this question properly, we must note that it has two distinct meanings: (*a*) Are there degrees of approach to being P? (*b*) Are there degrees of actually being P? The answer to (*a*) does not determine the answer to (*b*), nor conversely. In fact, the answer to (*a*) is yes; the answer to (*b*), no.

To understand this, let us recur to the example of having the legal right to vote, restricting ourselves again to the legally justifying quality or property of being at least eighteen years old. Since children who are sixteen years old are closer to being eighteen than children who are ten years old, it follows that (*a'*) there are degrees of approach to being at least eighteen years old and hence, according to the *PP*, there are corresponding degrees to which citizens approach having the right to vote. These degrees of approach might bear, for example, on being eligible for voter education classes, for serving on youth advisory boards, and so forth. On the other hand, as we have seen, once one is eighteen years old one absolutely possesses the quality of being at least eighteen years old, so that (b') there are no degrees of actually being at least eighteen years old and hence of actually having the right to vote. By way of contrast, in some cases there may be variations in the degree both of approaching the having of some quality and of actually having that quality. For example, (a'') there are degrees of approach to being a tall human being, and (b'') there are also degrees of actually being a tall human being.

In a way that is similar to the voting example, there are degrees of approach to being prospective purposive agents (P), but there are not degrees of actually being such agents, at least in the respect in which this quality is relevant to the justification of having the generic rights. That there are degrees of approach to being P can be seen by returning to my previous considerations about children, mentally deficient persons, and lower animals. To be P, that is, a prospective purposive agent, requires having the practical abilities of the generic features of action: the abilities to control one's behavior by one's unforced choice, to have knowledge of relevant circumstances, and to reflect on one's purposes. These abilities are gradually developed in children, who will eventually have them in full; the abilities are had in varying impaired ways by mentally deficient persons; and they are largely lacking among animals, although some animals may have some of them in rudimentary forms. Since the quality that determines whether one has the generic rights is that of being P, it follows from these variations in degree, according to the Principle of Proportionality, that although children, mentally deficient persons, and animals do not have the generic rights in the full-fledged way normal human adults have them, members of these groups approach having the generic rights in varying degrees, depending on the degree to which they have the requisite abilities. The reason for this proportionality is found in the relation between the generic abilities of action and the having of purposes one wants to fulfill. For the lesser the abilities, the less one is able to fulfill one's purposes without endangering oneself and other persons.

There are not, however, degrees of actually being prospective purposive agents, at least in the respect that is relevant to the justification of having the generic rights. Even if one concedes, with Aristotle and others, that some agents are superior to others in the abilities listed above, it is not simply the having of these abilities that is the relevant quality determining for each agent his claim to have the generic rights. For if a person of superior practical intelligence had no purposes, he would make no claim to have any right to act and hence to have freedom and well-being. On the other hand, as we have seen, he would claim these rights even if he lacked superior intelligence or other superior practical abilities so long as he was a prospective purposive agent. It is hence by virtue of being a prospective agent who wants to fulfill his purposes that the person of superior intelligence makes this right-claim. To this extent, however, such a person is in no different position from that of other prospective agents, and he can claim no rational justification, simply as a person of superior intelligence, for any rights of action. For in relation to the claim to have the generic rights, actually being a prospective agent who has purposes he wants to fulfill is an absolute quality, not varying in degree. The purposiveness in question does not itself vary in degree; it is not affected, for example, by whether one has more or fewer purposes in view, by whether one has them more or less intensely, by whether or not one organizes them under a few leading purposes, and so forth.

In this connection it is important to distinguish two questions: (c) What characteristics or abilities must one have in order to be an agent? (d) What aspect of being an agent is the justifying ground for claiming to have the generic rights? The version of the particularizability objection we have been considering assumes that the answer to the first question, with its possible variations in degree of practical effectiveness, also constitutes the answer to the second question. But this, as we have seen, is not the case. The criterion for answering (c) refers to the generic abilities of action, whereas the criterion for answering (d) refers to the desire to fulfill one's purposes among persons who have these abilities. Thus it is not the case that two completely different criteria are used to answer (c) and (d). Rather, the answer to (d) takes as decisive one component or aspect of the answer to (c). What justifies this specification of criteria is that the determination of the characteristics required for being an agent is not itself subject to the views, claims, or desires of agents, as is the determination of what aspect of agency serves to justify for each agent his claim to have the generic rights (1.13). Thus the answer to (c) falls outside the dialectically necessary method, unlike the answer to (d). Once it is determined what constitutes being an agent, the dialectically necessary method takes over, with its focus on what must be claimed or upheld by every agent from within his own standpoint in purposive agency. It is from within this standpoint that every agent implicitly claims to have the generic rights, and the criteria or qualities on which this claim is based, taken as a whole, also justify the varying exclusions of children and others indicated above.

We have seen, then, that although there are degrees of approach to being a prospective purposive agent, there are not degrees of actually being such an agent in the respect that is relevant to the justification of having the generic rights. It is not the generic features or abilities of action as a whole that directly lead an agent to hold that he has rights to freedom and well-being; it is rather that aspect of the features or abilities whereby he pursues purposes he regards as good. The necessity of freedom and well-being for acting to attain anything he considers worth striving for is the consideration that moves the agent to regard these as necessary goods and to hold that he has rights to them. In relation to the justification for having the generic rights, then, being an agent is an absolute or noncomparative condition. Wherever there is an agent—a person who controls or can control his behavior by his unforced choice with knowledge of relevant circumstances in pursuit of purposes he regards as good—there is an implicit claim to have the generic rights. This claim on the part of the agent is not affected by degrees of practical ability or agency. Hence, the Principle of Proportionality does not apply to this claim, and the *ASA* still provides the basis for dealing with the sufficient justifying condition for claims to have the generic rights.

In the light of this conclusion, let us return to the version of the particularizability objection which asserts that the person of superior practical intelligence should have superior or exclusive generic rights. I shall here deal only with the claim to superior rights, since if this is refuted, then so too is the latter, exclusivist claim. The basic argument is that if an agent has rights to freedom and well-being, then a superior agent (which, ex hypothesi, the person of superior intelligence is) has superior rights to freedom and well-being. Now this argument commits a non sequitur. The antecedent of the argument, properly expanded, says that the reason why a person has rights to freedom and well-being is that he is a prospective agent who wants to fulfill his own purposes. The consequent says that if one prospective agent X has greater ability to achieve X's purposes than another prospective agent Y has to achieve Y's purposes, then X has superior rights to freedom and well-being. This consequent does not, however, follow from the antecedent, since the reason the consequent gives for having superior generic rights is quite distinct from the reason the antecedent gives for having the generic rights. Wanting to fulfill one's own purposes through action is not the same as having the ability to fulfill one's own purposes through action. While it is true that to act requires certain abilities, what is crucial in any agent's reason for acting is not his abilities but his purposes.

To justify the claim of superior rights, the argument from superior intelligence would have to include one or both of two further assertions: (a) that those who have superior intelligence will necessarily use it to fulfill not only their own purposes but also the purposes of all or many other prospective agents; (b) that those who have superior intelligence also have more valuable purposes. Neither of these assertions, however, is plausible. Assertion (a), moreover, would involve an implicit admission that the action-rights of the more intelligent agents, so far as they claim to fulfill the purposes of persons of inferior intelligence, must be evaluated by reference to those purposes. But since without some sorts of basic controls on the part of the inferior agents it is quite unlikely that their purposes would be sufficiently provided for by the superior agents, the claims of the latter to superior rights are further weakened.

2.23. Let us now consider a different version of the particularizability objection. Some agent, while granting that he would claim the generic rights even if he were to lack certain more restrictive characteristics D, might hold that he would not then be justified in making such a claim. He might contend that knowing as he does the difference between having and lacking D, he is convinced that D is a necessary justifying condition of having the generic rights, so that merely being a prospective purposive agent is not sufficient. D might consist, for example, in a certain minimum of education or benevolence or in a true as opposed to a false consciousness of the forces at work in one's society or in some other moral or intellectual characteristic, or in some combination of these. The agent in question would distinguish between two different standpoints: that of an (actual or prospective) agent, who necessarily holds that he has the generic rights regardless of whether or not he has D, and that of a hypothetical beholder of himself or others who has the superior vantage point provided by an awareness of D and of its necessary relation to having the generic rights. From this superior vantage point, the agent would put a hypothetical distance between himself qua agent (who necessarily claims the generic rights) and himself qua contemplating himself or someone else as lacking D. In the latter situation he would be able to deny that as an agent he would have the generic rights, since in lacking D he lacks a necessary condition of having rights to freedom and well-being. Hence, the fact that every agent necessarily holds that he has the generic rights does not prevent some agent from hypothetically conceding that, lacking D, he should not have these rights.

This objection rests on a basis similar to that of the 'fanatic' considered above (2.13) and is to be answered in a similar way. The objector adopts a standpoint other than or additional to that of agency, and he holds that this additional standpoint, epitomized in his upholding of D, is superior to that which rests on the criteria of agency itself. Even if such specifications of D as superior knowledge or benevolence build on the requirements of agency rather than being antithetical to them, there still remains the question of why any actual or prospective agent should accept these added requirements as necessary criteria of his having the generic rights. For the criteria are not necessarily connected, as are freedom and well-being, with being an agent. A rational justification must still be provided for holding that D is a necessary condition of having the generic rights, and this the objector is not yet in a position to give.

The objection's differentiation of the standpoint of the agent from that of a hypothetical beholder might be defended on the ground that it yields a broader perspective than is afforded by the context of agency. On the other hand, there are compelling reasons for not preferring the hypothetical contemplative standpoint to that of the agent himself. Since the generic rights are rights to the proximate necessary conditions of action, the standpoint directly relevant to them is that which is set by the requirements of action, and hence of the agent who is actually or prospectively involved in action. The relevance of the more restrictive characteristics D to the justification of having the generic rights, on the other hand, remains to be established. If a person who had D had no purposes, he would make no claim to have the generic rights. On the other hand, once he has purposes as a prospective agent, he necessarily claims to have these rights, since otherwise his having purposes would be futile. He would be in the impossible position of both wanting to achieve some goal and being indifferent to the necessary conditions of his achieving the goal. It is hence by virtue of being a prospective agent who wants to fulfull his purposes, and not by virtue of having D, that the person who has D claims the generic rights for himself. This sufficient condition justifying the right-claim, since it derives from within the context of agency that is directly relevant to the generic rights, takes precedence over rival conceptions of the sufficient justificatory condition.

Similar considerations apply to such a contention as that although every agent may claim he has the generic rights, only those agents who have earned these rights through their own efforts are justified in making this claim. This contention may be explicated as follows. Since the generic rights entail correlative duties on the part of all other

3

THE PRINCIPLE OF GENERIC CONSISTENCY

The Derivation of the Principle

3.1. In the last chapter I was concerned primarily with the individual agent and the generic features of his action. Other persons figured in the analysis insofar as these features include the agent's implicit claim that he has rights to freedom and well-being, because this right-claim entails a correlative judgment that other persons ought at least to refrain from interfering with the agent's having freedom and well-being. But apart from this negative relation, the actions in question might be purely personal or individual, affecting no other persons except as possible interferers with the action. Morality, however, is primarily concerned with interpersonal actions, that is, with actions that affect persons other than their agents (1.1). I shall refer to such actions as *transactions*, and to the persons affected by them as *recipients*. I shall also say that both the agent and his recipients *participate* in transactions, although the former does so actively and the latter passively, by undergoing or being affected by the agent's action toward him. At some points when a person performs an action that does not affect other persons, I shall refer to him as an *actor* rather than as an *agent* in order to confine the latter term to the transactional relation where he has a recipient.

There are many kinds and degrees of one person's 'affecting' another, ranging from the most casual encounters to the most intimate and enduring forms of contact. But even if there is a continuum rather than a sharp differentiation here, it is possible to specify, in the various modes of affecting, certain aspects that especially make them morally relevant. These aspects are found where what is affected is the recipient's freedom and well-being, and hence his capacity for action. It is especially when one person's action toward another has such an impact that his action on that other is a transaction. In contrast to actions that impinge on other persons only by way of example or beliefs, in a transaction one person affects or tends to affect the proximate capacity of some other person or persons to behave freely and to maintain and acquire the other conditions necessary for action. Such modes of affecting in transactions can be most readily recognized in their negative forms: when one person coerces another, hence preventing him from participating freely or voluntarily in the trans-action, or when one person harms another, hence preventing him from participating purposively or with well-being in the transaction. Each of these modes of affecting will be analyzed further in the next chapter.

This characterization of transactions also helps to clarify the distinction between agents and recipients. As so far presented, this is the distinction between persons who act and other persons who are affected by their actions; and, to connect this with the point just made about transactions, the other persons are affected in ways that bear on their proximate capacity for action. This distinction is not removed by the consideration that societies consist of interdependent persons, each of whom is affected by the actions or nonactions of other persons, so that all persons are in some sense mutually agents and recipients to one another. On this view, *interaction* rather than *transaction* is the correct term for all human interpersonal relations. From some global perspective this organicist contention may have a point. There still remain, however, more or less stable interrelations where one or more persons is agent and another person or group is recipient. In one standard kind of transaction, two persons, X and Y, participate in an interrelation with one another that fulfills the following conditions: (*a*) X initiates and controls his participation in the interrelation with a view to furthering some purpose of his own and hence of attaining some additive good. His well-being, defined as the abilities and conditions required for his having basic, nonsubtrac-tive, and additive goods, is at least maintained in the course of his participation in the interrelation, and so too is his freedom. (*b*) The character of Y's participation—whether Y also controls his partici-pation in the interrelation while at least maintaining his well-being—depends on X, in that X may or may not coerce Y and may or may not harm him. (*c*) During or immediately before the period of his interrelation with X (as described in *a* and *b*), Y does not stand toward X or toward any third person Z in the relation in which X stands to Y.

As examples of such interrelations, consider the cases where, on the one hand, X, after careful planning, hits Y over the head with a club in order to rob Y of his money, and where, on the other hand, X asks Y to lend him some money, and Y then decides either to lend or not to lend it. In both these cases, X participates voluntarily and purposively in his interrelation with Y. But in the first case Y's participation is involuntary and contrapurposive, not according with his inclinational or intentional wants, whereas in the second case it is voluntary and purposive. These contrary features of Y's participation, moreover, depend on X, for since X is in each case performing a voluntary action, how he will undertake to deal with Y is under X's control. But since, on the other hand, Y does not initiate or determine these respective interrelations with X, the character of Y's participation therein does not similarly depend on himself. It is open to X to try either to coerce Y or to win Y's unforced consent. It is also open to X to try either to lower or to raise (or at least leave unchanged) Y's well-being. Which of these generic modes—voluntary or involuntary, purposive or contra-purposive—will characterize Y's participation in his interrelation with X therefore comes to depend on X. In such interrelations there are genuine transactions wherein X is the agent and Y the recipient. Since X is the agent, it is necessarily true of him that he participates voluntarily and purposively in his transaction with Y. With respect to Y's participation, however, the most that can be said is that it is necessarily true of him that he will participate either voluntarily or involuntarily and either purposively or contrapurposively. Which of these modes of participation will be true of Y depends upon X. These distinctions are not altered by the fact that both voluntariness and purposiveness may vary in degree.

In the above account of transactions, two aspects of the agent's relation to his recipient were intermingled: that the agent initiates the transaction and that he controls or determines both his own partici- pation therein and the generic character of the recipient's participa- tion. These two aspects may, however, be found separately. In particular, the person who initiates the transaction may not be the same as the person who controls or determines whether the other person will have or maintain well-being. To take an extreme example, suppose A is drowning and calls out for help to B, who can easily rescue A by throwing him a rope; but B instead lets A drown. It might be held that there are really two transactions here: one where A calls out to B, the other where B refuses to help A. From the standpoint of the conditions of agency at stake in this situation, however, it would be quite artificial to split up the event in this way. Even if the separation is made, so that A is the agent in the first transaction and B in the second, it could not correctly be said that B 'initiates' the second transaction, since his refusal to help A is itself a reaction to A's appeal for help. In any case, while transactions may be individuated in different ways, what is decisive so far as concerns morality is their impact on freedom and well-being, and more generally on the conditions of agency. In this respect, there is a single transaction in the above example, in that the whole sequence of events from A's call for help to B's refusal to help bears drastically on A's well-being, since A drowns. A's call to B for help, however, taken as a distinct transaction, has no particular impact on B's freedom or well-being; moreover, B would continue to be free and to have well-being even if he threw the rope to A. In the single whole transaction, then, A is the initiator, while B controls or determines both the character of his own participation in the transaction and the crucial impact on A's well-being. Because of this control, it is B rather than A who is the agent in the transaction, and A is the recipient.

That agents and recipients can be distinguished in this way does not preclude, of course, that a person who is an agent in one transaction may become a recipient in another. Human interrelations may be analyzed into a series of transactions, and there is a frequent interchange of roles. In what follows I shall usually refer to 'the agent' and 'the recipient,' but the fixity assigned to these concepts will be one not of persons but rather of roles or functions within the transactional relations that are of primary concern to morality.

Although I have thus far discussed the distinction between agent and recipient in relatively simple bilateral situations, the distinction is also found in more complex human interrelations, including those structured by various institutional rules. It was noted earlier that for an action to be voluntary the agent must know its relevant circumstances, including its recipients and its outcome (1.11). Such knowledge is much more difficult to achieve when transactions affect persons far beyond the agent's immediate ken; thus the worldwide repercussions of contemporary transnational corporate entrepreneurs, with their effects on the ecological environment of future generations, are vast both in space and in time. The scope of such effects makes the question 'Who is my recipient?' even more poignant and difficult than the biblical 'Who is my neighbor?' Nevertheless, the great expansion of human communication facilities is a part of the very technological growth that drastically multiplies the recipients whose freedom and well-being are affected by transnational agents. Thus it becomes possible to know how agricultural and commercial policies in the United States affect the lives of Chilean copper miners and South African villagers. The vast increase in the scope and intricacy of human transactions does not, then, remove the distinction between agents and recipients, between those who have the power to make decisions and policies carrying even a global impact and those who may bear the results of this impact in a greatly reduced ability to control aspects of their lives that bear significantly on their own capabilities of agency.

3.2. Let us now relate these considerations to the conclusion reached at the end of chapter 2. We saw there that every agent must claim, at least implicitly, that he has rights to freedom and well-being for the sufficient reason that he is a prospective purposive agent. From the content of this claim it follows, by the principle of universalizability, that all prospective purposive agents have rights to freedom and well-being. If the agent denies this generalization, he contradicts himself. For he would then be in the position of both affirming and denying that being a prospective purposive agent is a sufficient condition of having rights to freedom and well-being.

As we also saw in the preceding chapter, the statement that some person or group of persons has a certain right entails a correlative 'ought'-judgment that all other persons ought at least to refrain from interfering with that to which the first person or group has the right. Since, then, the agent must accept the generalized rights-statement, 'All prospective purposive agents have rights to freedom and well-being,' he must, on pain of contradiction, also accept the judgment, 'I ought at least to refrain from interfering with the freedom and well-being of any prospective purposive agent.' The transition here from 'all' to 'any' is warranted by the fact that the 'all' in the generalization is distributive, not collective: it refers to each and hence to any prospective purposive agent.

Now the recipients of the agent's action are prospective purposive agents insofar as they can operate voluntarily and purposively, controlling their behavior by their unforced choice with a view to fulfillment of their purposes and having knowledge of relevant circumstances. When it is said that the recipients can operate in these ways, this 'can' is a dispositional one, referring to the long-range abilities (whatever their hereditary and environmental sources) that enter into such modes of operation. It would hence be irrelevant for an agent to argue that because he has previously assaulted someone or otherwise made him unable to operate freely and with basic well-being, his victim is not a prospective purposive agent and does not have the rights referred to in the above generalization. The 'ought'-judgment entailed by the generalization logically must be accepted by the agent as binding on all his conduct toward other prospective agents, so that in coercing or harming any of them he violates a requirement he is rationally obliged to accept.

When some person is a recipient in a transaction, he does not actually choose or initiate and control his conduct with a view to fulfilling some purpose of his. Nevertheless, he is still a prospective agent who has purposes he wants to fulfill, at least in the dispositional sense that he has wants or interests that are of concern to him. It would be incorrect to think that purposive participation is not attributable to the recipient because only agents have purposes. For someone to have a purpose it is not necessary that he actually try to achieve it; he may, like the recipient, be passive and quiescent. His purpose will correspondingly vary from the remotely dispositional and diffuse to the proximately occurrent and specific. In each of these kinds of situation, the recipient regards his purposes and objects as good. This goodness extends through the same range of basic, nonsubtractive, and additive goods as do the purposes of the agents: the recipient, too, regards as good and has as his at least dispositional purposes that he maintain the necessary preconditions of actions, that he not lose in transactions something that seems to him to be good, and that he gain in transactions something that seems to him to be good. For the recipient, too, his well-being consists especially in his having the general conditions and abilities required for his fulfilling such purposes.

3.3. Since the recipients of the agent's action are prospective agents who have purposes they want to fulfill, the agent must acknowledge that the generalization to which we saw that he is logically committed applies to his recipients: they too have rights to freedom and well-being. Their right to freedom means that just as the agent holds that he has a right to control whether or not he will participate in transactions, so his recipients have the right to control whether or not they will participate. Hence, the agent ought to refrain from inter-fering with their freedom by coercing them: their participation in transactions must be subject to their own consent, to their own unforced choice. The recipients' right to well-being means that just as the agent holds that he has a right to maintain the conditions and abilities required for purposive action, so his recipients also have the right to maintain these. Hence, the agent ought at least to refrain from harming his recipients by interfering with their basic, nonsubtractive, and additive goods, especially when these are viewed generically-dispositionally. In certain circumstances, moreover, when his reci-pients' well-being cannot otherwise be maintained through their own efforts, their right to well-being entails that the agent ought to act positively to assist them to have these conditions or abilities.

It follows from these considerations that every agent logically must acknowledge certain generic obligations. Negatively, he ought to refrain from coercing and from harming his recipients; positively, he ought to assist them to have freedom and well-being whenever they cannot otherwise have these necessary goods and he can help them at no comparable cost to himself. The general principle of these obligations and rights may be expressed as the following precept addressed to every agent: *Act in accord with the generic rights of your recipients as well as of yourself.* I shall call this the *Principle of Generic Consistency* (*PGC*), since it combines the formal consideration of consistency with the material consideration of rights to the generic features or goods of action. The two components of the *PGC*, requiring action in accord with the recipients' generic rights of freedom and of well-being, I shall call the *generic rules.*

The *PGC* is a necessary principle in two ways. It is formally or logically necessary in that for any agent to deny or violate it is to contradict himself, since he would then be in the position of holding that rights he claims for himself by virtue of having certain qualities are not possessed by other persons who have those qualities. The principle is also materially necessary, or categorical, in that, unlike other principles, the obligations of the *PGC* cannot be escaped by any agent by shifting his inclinations, interests, or ideals, or by appealing to institutional rules whose contents are determined by convention. Since the generic features of action are involved in the necessary structure of agency, and since the agent must hold that he has rights to these features simply insofar as he is a prospective purposive agent, he rationally must accept that his recipients also have these rights insofar as they too are prospective purposive agents. In this regard, the *PGC* is unlike those moral principles whose contents are contingent and normatively escapable in that they reflect the variable desires or opinions of agents.

I shall now try to explicate the *PGC's* direct content somewhat more fully. To act in accord with someone's rights is to see to it, so far as one can, that one fulfills the correlative obligations. Since the rights have certain objects—they are rights to have or do something X—the content of the obligations, what the respondent B ought to do, is determined by what is required if the subject or the right-holder A is to have or do X. Sometimes, as in the case of the right to freedom of speech or movement, all that is required for B to act in accord with A's right is for B to refrain from interfering with A's speaking or moving. Here, then, the correlative obligation is only negative. At other times, however, the obligation is positive, as in the case of the right to have food where A is starving from lack of food and cannot obtain food by his own efforts. In such a case, for B to act in accord with A's right to food requires that B give food to A if he can. Positive obligations, requiring positive actions, clearly make more demands on the respondents than do negative obligations, so that the conditions of their fulfillment raise many more questions about comparative abilities, costs, causes, and other variables. The relevant assistance or positive action often requires a context of institutional arrangements, as against the negative obligations that may be independently fulfilled by respondents. I shall discuss these qualifications below.

What, then, does it mean for an agent to act in accord with his own generic rights? In such a case the agent is the subject or holder of the rights, but he is not necessarily also the respondent of the rights. Rather, in acting he sees to it that he at least occurrently maintains his own freedom and well-being so that these are not interfered with by other persons without his consent. Just as we have noted that the agent necessarily manifests or embodies the generic features of action in his conduct and necessarily claims at least implicitly to have freedom and well-being as his rights, so in his particular actions he necessarily acts in accord with his own generic rights. This is to say that at least on the particular occasions of his acting he maintains the essential conditions of his agency against any attempts by other persons to violate these conditions without his consent. Such violation may indeed occur, but then he is no longer an agent or acting in that situation.

That the agent acts in accord with his right to well-being does not mean that he is infallible in ascertaining what is required to fulfill his purposes and that he invariably acts conformably to this ascertainment. It means, rather, that he tries to fulfill his purposes and to see to it that without his consent other persons do not interfere with his maintaining the conditions that, so far as he is aware, are required for such purpose-fulfillment. Undoubtedly this process is marked by varying degrees of knowledge, rationality, and resoluteness among different agents. But this variation does not remove the generalization that, whatever their different purposes and abilities, agents act in accord with their own rights to freedom and well-being as required for their actions in pursuit of their purposes. Nor is this generalization removed by the fact that in some contexts persons may operate under conditions of compulsoriness and external threat; for in such cases there is forced choice rather than action in the strict sense. The generalization is not affected even by such an extreme case as that of suicide. For insofar as the would-be suicide maintains the conditions of action in the strict sense, including the absence of internal causes that remove his own control over his behavior (1.11), he still sees to it that other persons do not interfere with his freedom and well-being without his consent. It is also true, however, that in such a limiting case, where he intends to cease being an agent, he maintains these necessary goods only in the strictly temporary frame required for his final action aimed at losing them. This extreme, untypical case of agency does not, however, affect what holds true in the standard conditions and generic features of action.

From the preceding account of what it is to act in accord with someone's rights, it should also be clear what it is for the agent to act in accord with the generic rights of his recipients. In so acting, he refrains from interfering with their freedom and well-being without their consent, and he assists them to have these conditions where they would otherwise lack them and cannot maintain them by their own efforts. In contexts where this inability is widespread, the assistance in question should take the form of agents' supporting and contributing to institutions or social arrangements that more directly provide such assistance. It is necessarily true of the agent that he participates voluntarily and purposively in the transactions he initiates or controls with regard to his recipients, and that he claims for himself the rights to freedom and well-being in all such transactions. If the agent acts in accord with his recipients' generic rights, then, at least so far as his action is concerned, his recipients also participate voluntarily and purposively in their transactions with him so that their own freedom and well-being are also protected. Whether the recipient's participation in the transaction is voluntary or involuntary depends upon the agent, in that the latter can refrain from acting on his recipient until and unless the recipient has freely consented to participate. It also depends upon the agent whether the recipient's participation is purposive or contrapurposive, in that so far as concerns his action's intended and foreseeable effect on the recipient, the agent can see to it that he at least refrains from bringing about or contributing to a diminution of his recipient's well-being or capacity for purpose-fulfillment, and, in certain circumstances, he assists him to maintain well-being.

The obligations set by the *PGC* consist primarily in the modes of action just described, but they also involve correlated modes of respect. Every agent ought to respect his recipients' freedom and well-being as well as his own. Such respect includes not only action but also certain related dispositions: a recognition of the rights of others, a positive concern for their having the objects of these rights, and a positive regard for them as persons who have rights or entitlements equal to his own as well as the rational capacity to reflect on their purposes and to control their behavior in the light of such reflection.

Fulfillment of these obligations is also necessary for the agent's strict rational autonomy. Viewed etymologically, 'autonomy' means being a law (*nomos*) unto oneself (*auto*), or setting one's law for oneself. Now there may be many different kinds of law set by many different kinds of self. All cases of autonomy, nonetheless, are in a broad sense rational; but it is important to distinguish this broad sense from the strict sense. In the broad sense every person who sets laws for himself, or decides on his own principles of conduct, is rationally autonomous in that the law or principle he decides on is a general reason or criterion, and he subsumes particular cases under it. This criterion or principle, however, need not itself be rational, for it may be based on a faulty use of reason, including false but corrigible beliefs or invalid inferences. Thus a person who is rationally autonomous in the broad sense may use general criteria that reflect personal prejudices or benighted customs; he may be a racist, a perfervid nationalist, or otherwise wedded to irrational principles opposed to the *PGC*. Nevertheless, he will have chosen these reasons or principles for himself and may try to fashion a coherent plan of life on their basis.

If, on the other hand, one is rationally autonomous in the strict sense, then the general principle one chooses for oneself will have been arrived at by a correct use of reason, including true beliefs and valid inferences. In the strictest sense, these beliefs will reflect necessary features of the subject matter. This is the case with the agent who understands and accepts the *PGC* and with it the duty of respecting both the principle itself, as based on reason, and his recipients as having rights he rationally must respect. All normal human beings have the capacity to be rational in this strict sense, in that they have, at least in an elementary way, the empirical and logical abilities in question. Hence, they are all capable of being rationally autonomous in the strict sense, and it is to all of them that the *PGC* is addressed.

The agent's freedom or voluntariness of action is thus not violated when he is subjected to the duties or requirements imposed by the *PGC*. He is still left in control of his behavior by his unforced choice. The *PGC*'s directives addressed to him, moreover, are based on rational grounds whose rightness he is proximately capable of understanding. The *PGC* hence indicates to him that, as rational, he must choose to act in accordance with its requirements rather than in the other ways left open to him. Such choice is not forced because it is based on rational criteria he accepts, and indeed accepts as categorically obligatory for his actions. In choosing to comply with the PGC the agent is rationally autonomous in the strict sense.

The PGC's precept, "Act in accord with the generic rights of your recipients as well as of yourself," does not mean that the agent violates the precept whenever he ceases to act; it does not prescribe continuous or unremitting action. As the reference to 'recipients' indicates, the precept means that *when* the agent engages in transactions by acting toward other persons, he should respect their generic rights as well as his own. But the other duties of respect, as dispositional, are more generally incumbent on him. As we shall also see, there are certain sorts of circumstances when inaction on the part of some person is itself a kind of action that violates the precept, in that it is in disaccord with the generic rights of his recipients.

It is important to note here a certain connection between action and judgment. When an agent violates the PGC by intentionally infringing a generic right of his recipients, he in effect denies that they have this right and he thereby ceases so far forth to be rational. By 'in effect denies' I mean that even if the agent does not say anything, he shows by his action that he thinks or judges that his recipients do not have this right. This point is an application of the dialectically necessary method. Since the agent is in control of his conduct and knows what he is doing, his action is reflected in his at least implicit judgments. This relation was found beginning with the earliest stages of the argument leading to the PGC; for example, the agent's action in pursuit of his purpose E which he regards as worth pursuing was depicted as his saying or thinking, 'E is good' (2.1). At the present stage, the agent has arrived at the PGC as the logical consequence of previous judgments that, as rational, he must accept. He is hence aware of the requirement the principle sets for all his actions. To say that he is aware of the requirement is not, of course, to say that he explicitly thinks of it or that he always complies with it in all his actions toward other persons. When he does comply with it, he accepts it practically—that is, in his actions—and is thus rational as an agent. This practical acceptance is reflected in his implicit affirmation or judgment whose content is the PGC, or at least in his implicit judgment that the persons toward whom he acts in that action have the relevant generic right. When, on the other hand, the agent violates the PGC in some particular case by intentionally infringing a generic right of his recipients, he practically rejects the principle in that particular action. This rejection is reflected in his implicit judgment that his recipients do not have that right; hence, he in effect denies that they have the right, and to this extent he ceases to be rational. It should be added, however, that the agent's recognition that, like all humans, he may violate rational criteria in his actions is itself an indispensable part of his empirical rationality. The rational agent will therefore make or at least accept provision for rules that take care of such possible weaknesses of will and lapses from rationality on the part of some agents (see 5.7 ff.).

3.4. The *PGC* is an egalitarian universalist moral principle since it requires an equal distribution of the most general rights of action. It says to every agent that just as, in acting, he necessarily manifests or embodies the generic features of action—voluntariness and purposiveness—and necessarily claims the generic goods as his rights, so he ought to accept that his recipients, too, should manifest or embody these same generic features and have these same generic goods as their rights. The agent must hence be impartial as between himself and other persons when the latter's freedom and well-being are at stake, so that he ought to respect their freedom and well-being as well as his own. He should therefore treat other persons as well as himself as persons and not as things or objects whose only relation to himself in transactions is that of facilitating his own purpose-fulfillment. To violate the *PGC* is to establish an inequality or disparity between oneself and one's recipients with regard to the generic features and rights of action and hence with regard to whatever purposes or goods are attainable by action. The equality required by the *PGC* runs in both directions. It does not require that an agent surrender his own freedom or well-being for the sake of his recipients. They have a right to a parity of generic goods with him but not to a disparity in their favor any more than in his own.

The moral population or community to which the *PGC* applies comprises all prospective purposive agents. It was noted earlier that children, mentally deficient persons, and animals are in varying degrees and on different grounds excluded from the class of prospective purposive agents, but that these grounds for exclusion do not justify any more restrictive criteria for the distribution of the generic rights (2.22). To have the generic rights one must be a prospective purposive agent, which requires certain practical abilities; but given these, the generic rights must be granted regardless of varying degrees in which different prospective agents have the abilities. For the ground on which agents claim to have the rights consists not in the abilities themselves but in the purposes whose attainment through these abilities the agents regard as good.

Two interconnected questions arise here: about the relation of excluded groups to the rights upheld by the *PGC*, and about the extension of the class of prospective purposive agents. The first question is to be answered through the Principle of Proportionality (2.22). The degree to which different groups approach having the generic features and abilities of action determines the degree to which they have or approach having the generic rights. It must be emphasized that the acceptance of such proportionality is not antithetical to my previous insistence that in respect of having the generic rights, agency is an absolute or noncomparative condition. The point is that once a person is an actual or prospective agent, he has the generic rights in full; but if he does not fully attain to the generic features and abilities of action, then he has the generic rights in proportion to his degree of attainment of agency. As we saw earlier, the reason for this proportionality is found in the relation between the generic abilities of action and the having of purposes one wants to fulfill. The less the abilities, the less one is able to fulfill one's purposes without endangering both one's own and others' purpose-fulfillment.

Children are potential agents in that, with normal maturation, they will attain the characteristics of control, choice, knowledge, and reflective intention that enter into the generic features of action. A potential agent is not the same as a prospective agent, for the latter already has the proximate abilities of the generic features of action even if he is not occurrently acting. Insofar as children are not such prospective agents, they are not among the recipients whose right to freedom the *PGC* requires agents to respect fully. But insofar as children are potential agents, they have rights that are preparatory for their taking on the generic rights pertaining to full-fledged agency. In keeping with these preparatory rights, the *PGC* requires that children be given a kind of upbringing that will enable them to become both agents who can make their behavior conform to the *PGC* and prospective agents whose generic rights must be respected by agents. The preparatory rights include as much respect for freedom and well-being as is consistent with this goal of agency. Hence, children must increasingly participate actively in decisions affecting themselves as they increase in maturity. Rules providing for education, parental guidance, and other policies and institutions affecting children are justified and indeed required because of their contribution to such fostering of children's fully having the generic abilities and rights of action.

Insofar as mentally deficient persons are not able, even as physical adults, to exercise the kind of control over their behavior that normal prospective agents do, they do not have to the same degree the right to freedom. Since for any prospective agent the point of having and respecting the generic rights derives from their necessary contribution to action in pursuit of purpose-fulfillment, persons who are not capable of such action have the right to freedom only to the extent to which their free conduct would not directly interfere with the conditions of their own freedom and well-being or with the generic rights of other persons. But to the extent to which mentally deficient persons have human potentialities, the *PGC* requires both that these be protected and that efforts be made to effect whatever improvements may be possible in the direction of normal agency.

In the case of children and mentally deficient persons, the Principle of Proportionality requires only so much diminution of the generic rights, especially freedom, as is needed for the protection of their own well-being and their maturation into full-fledged agency. The lesser practical abilities of such persons justify their having lesser rights only because of the bearing of the abilities on their own fulfillment of their purposes. In the case of the human fetus, on the other hand, the crucial issue is the justification of abortion, which involves its death and hence the complete loss of the generic rights. If there were no conflict between the rights of the fetus and the rights of the mother, the Principle of Proportionality together with the *PGC* would require simply that the fetus, while of course having no right to freedom, have such right to well-being as is required for developing its potentialities for growth toward purpose-fulfillment.[1]

When there is such conflict, however, the mother's generic rights should take priority. The Principle of Proportionality together with the *PGC* makes clear why this is so. The justifying criterion for having the generic rights is that one is a prospective agent who has purposes he wants to fulfill. When someone is less than a full-fledged prospective agent, his generic rights are proportional to the degree to which he approaches having the generic abilities constitutive of such agency, and the reason for this proportionality is found in the relation between having the rights and having the generic abilities required for acting with a view to purpose-fulfillment. The fetus, of course, lacks the abilities, except in a remotely potential form. In addition, it also lacks any purposes of even the most rudimentary sort, because of its lack of any physically separate existence and of even an initial acquisition of memories. Hence its generic rights, by comparison with the rights of its mother, are minimal.

These lacks on the part of the fetus do not characterize even newborn infants. They are physically separate from their mothers and they at once display, although in very rudimentary form, distinct purposes or desires. They soon develop memory patterns and experiences that bear on their seeking to fulfill their desires and on having further purposes and values. In addition, the considerations that may justify abortion do not even begin to support infanticide because there is no comparable conflict between the rights of infants and of their mothers.

It must also be recognized, in accordance with the Principle of Proportionality, that the justification of abortion and hence of abrogating the fetus's generic rights may vary in degree. To begin with, as was noted above, the fetus approaches having the generic rights to the extent to which it approaches having the generic practical abilities and the corresponding purposes or desires. Hence, a six-month fetus has the right to well-being to a greater degree than does a three-month fetus, and the latter more than a four-week fetus, and so forth, so that there is correspondingly less justification for abortion the greater the approach to maturation. In addition, much depends on the nature of the conflict between the fetus's rights and those of the mother. The conflict involves that the mother's generic rights to the use of the abilities required for purpose-fulfillment are threatened by the fetus's being carried to full term. With regard to well-being, the threat may be the mother's death, or severe diminution of physical or mental health, or lesser but still sizable losses. With regard to freedom, the threat may be a continuation of the kind of severe violence or coercion that occurs when impregnation is due to rape or seduction or other causes beyond the mother's ability to control. In all such cases, abortion is justified regardless of the fetus's stage of development. For the mother, as a purposive agent, already has the generic practical abilities and the purposes to which these are directed, and their being lost, endangered, or attacked for the sake of the fetus would involve that the generic rights of someone who has them in full would be drastically subordinated to a minimal possessor of these rights. Here again the case of infants is different, for there is no comparable threat to the mother's generic rights, and the infant already has its own desires and purposes stemming from its separate physical existence.

In cases where the threat to the mother's rights is less severe, the justification of abortion is correspondingly less, and the fetus's stage of development becomes a more relevant consideration. Here, however, it is also important to consider the relation between the mother's generic rights and the prospects for the fetus's development of the generic abilities required for purpose-fulfillment. As we have seen, if there is no conflict of rights, then the fetus, because of its human potentialities, has such right to well-being as is required for developing its potentialities for growth toward purpose-fulfillment. But the prospects for fulfilling this right are often meager when the mother's physical, psychological, or social circumstances render her unable or unwilling to give her baby the nurturing care it needs. In such cases the mother's rights to freedom and well-being are threatened and with them also the aforementioned right of the fetus. It is vitally important that concern for the fetus's right to life be matched by concern for its right to adequate nutrition and other components of basic well-being. Too often the advocates of the former right show marked indifference to the latter. Where the prospects of fulfilling the latter right are poor, this fact, together with the fetus's lack of practical abilities and purposes, may also justify abortion. Such facts and policies are tragic at best, and it is a matter of the greatest moral urgency that the circumstances and behaviors that generate them be avoided to the fullest possible extent.

Let us now consider the relation of animals other than humans to the moral population to which the *PGC* applies. Since they lack the potentialities for agency, animals are not included among the recipients whose generic rights must be fully protected even in a preparatory way. But they have feelings parallel to those that enter into the generic features and abilities of action. Every rational agent, being also an animal, has various feelings, and these affect his pursuits of his purposes and the physical background that makes those pursuits possible. The suffering of pain is a debilitating experience, and the *PGC* prohibits its wanton infliction on others as violating the rights both of freedom and of well-being. Since all animals that have pain-receptors are similar in respect of such debilitation, the *PGC*'s prohibition applies to all of them. In Bentham's famous statement, "the question is not, Can they *reason*? nor, Can they *talk*? but, Can they *suffer*?"[2] This point is an application of the Principle of Proportionality in its limiting case: to the extent to which animals have in a similar way the quality or property of being debilitated by pain, they have in a similar way the right justified by this quality, the right to immunity from wanton infliction of pain.

When, however, the freedom and well-being of animals conflicts with those of humans, the generic rights of the latter take priority, for the reasons indicated by the Principle of Proportionality. Where allowing animals whatever degree of freedom they are capable of, without control by humans, would be dangerous to the latter as well as to the animals themselves, the freedom of animals must be subordinated to that of humans. And to the extent to which the eating of animal flesh is needed for the physical well-being of humans, the killing of animals is also justified on this ground.

Since the condition of being a prospective agent who has purposes he wants to fulfill is an absolute quality with regard to humans' having the generic rights, it is not affected by the variable circumstances of old age or physical handicaps that may characterize different human beings. This absoluteness in having the generic rights applies even to a certain degree of human brain damage, so long as there remains the possibility of recovery and hence of resuming the general practical abilities indicated above. Thus, with the exceptions noted in the quite different cases of children, mentally deficient persons, and fetuses, the moral community that has the generic rights extends to all human beings. In the case of criminals, who have voluntarily removed themselves from this community by violating the *PGC* in its most important requirements, the principled infliction of punishment serves not to continue their exclusion from the community but rather, through the *PGC*, to restore their membership in it (5.8).

3.5. The *PGC* is the supreme principle of morality, taking precedence over all other moral or practical principles of interpersonal conduct. For since its content is the generic features that necessarily enter into all action, the *PGC* bears on all actions or pursuits of purposes and hence of goods. Any other moral principles either are inconsistent with the *PGC*, in which case they involve contradictions and are morally wrong, or else are specifications of the *PGC*, dealing only with certain kinds of actions or purposive pursuits, so that its moral provisions are more extensive than theirs. Since their contents are related to the contents of the *PGC* as species to genus, the other principles must conform to the *PGC* if they are to be morally right. This relation will be analyzed more fully in the next two chapters.

A question may be raised about the correctness of calling the *PGC* a moral principle. For the *PGC* is logically derived from the agent's claiming the generic rights for himself. The criterion of this right-claim, however, is prudential, not moral, since the agent claims these rights for his pursuits of his own purposes. How, then, can the *PGC* as a moral principle be derived from claims or judgments that are themselves not moral?

To answer this question it must be kept in mind that the meaning of 'moral' here, as applied to a principle or a judgment, is that it, or the person making or upholding it, takes favorable account of the interests or well-being of at least some persons or recipients other than the agent or speaker (1.1). The *PGC* reflects such a social concern despite its derivation from a prudential antecedent. The derivation accomplishes the transition from the prudential to the moral at the point where, through the principle of universalizability, the agent logically must acknowledge that the generic rights he claims for himself are also had by all prospective purposive agents. For at that point he admits that the sufficient reason he must adduce as justifying his own having the generic rights also justifies that these rights are had by all other persons who fulfill that sufficient reason. It is also in this way that the generic rights themselves become moral rights. They are moral rights in that, by the very fact of the agent's attribution of them to his recipients, he is required to take favorable account of the freedom and well-being of his recipients. His attribution of these rights to himself could be considered moral only if he was prepared to admit that other persons also have such rights.

The transition from the prudential to the moral and social is thus, in the first instance, not motivational but logical. The reason why the agent must endorse the generic rights of his recipients is not the Hobbesian prudential or contingent one that if he violates or fails to endorse these rights for others he may probably expect them to violate his own rights, but rather the logically necessary one that if there is a sufficient condition that justifies the agent's having the generic rights, then it must justify that these rights are had by all other persons who satisfy that sufficient condition. As we shall see, the prudential reason is of considerable importance where the agent's motivation for accepting the *PGC* is in question (3.26). But if the basis of the *PGC* as a moral principle were only prudential, its validity or requiredness would be contingent on the degree to which an agent could not in fact pursue his purposes without endorsing other persons' having the generic rights. Hence, there would be many kinds of circumstances in which the agent would have no moral obligations to respect his recipients' generic rights. Since, however, the basis of these obligations is logical, their validity is necessary independent of such considerations.

Let us look somewhat more closely at this transition from the prudential to the moral. As we have seen, the agent's rights-judgment (1) 'I have rights to freedom and well-being' entails his holding (2) 'All other persons ought to respect my freedom and well-being.' In (2) the criterion of the 'ought' is the same as the criterion of 'have rights' in (1), namely, the agent's own prudential pursuit of his purposes. As we have seen, (2) as said by the agent is not a moral judgment despite the fact that it requires the other agents addressed ('all other persons') to consider favorably the interests of someone other than themselves, because the speaker, the original agent, addresses the requirement to them for the sake of his, not their, interests. Hence, as used by him, (2) is a prudential 'ought-judgment, even though the persons addressed might themselves regard it as a moral judgment.

We have also seen that through the principle of universalizability and the rationally justified criterion of relevant similarity, (1) entails (3) 'All prospective purposive agents have rights to freedom and well-being.' Just as in (1) the criterion of its 'have rights' is the prudential purposes of the subject of the judgment, so too in (3) the criterion of 'have rights' is the prudential purposes of the 'all prospective purposive agents' who are the subjects of the judgment. Nevertheless, (3) as said by the original agent is a moral judgment precisely because its criterion is not his own interests or prudential purposes but rather the interests or prudential purposes of persons other than himself the speaker. He thus has to accept a judgment that he must favorably consider the prudential purposes or interests of persons other than himself. The agent is logically compelled to make this transition from a prudential to a moral judgment, because if he did not he would be in the position of denying what he had previously had to affirm, namely, that being a prospective purposive agent is a sufficient justifying condition for having rights to freedom and well-being. So too when (3) entails (4) 'I ought to respect the freedom and well-being of any (and every) prospective purposive agent', the criterion of this 'ought' is the interests or prudential purposes of the subjects or right-holders in (3), namely, any and every prospective purposive agent. For this reason (4) too, as said by the original agent, is a moral judgment because it requires him to consider favorably the interests of persons other than himself. Thus the entailment from (1) and (2) to (3) and (4), proceeding throughout from within the standpoint of the individual agent, logically requires him to move from prudential judgments to moral ones. On pain of self-contradiction, the agent must move from right-claims and 'ought'-judgments concerned with upholding his own prudential purposes to right-claims and 'ought'-judgments concerned with upholding the prudential purposes of all other prospective purposive agents.

The arguments in this section have presented the concluding steps of the rational justification of the supreme principle of morality. A distinction must, of course, be drawn between the intricacies of philosophical analysis I have used in developing the whole justification and the thought-processes normally followed by rational moral agents. But although agents are not usually philosophers, the central sequence in the above analysis has not departed from the structures of thought and action available to agents. Thus I have used a dialectically necessary method that, beginning from statements or judgments necessarily attributable to every agent, has proceeded to trace by conceptual analysis what these logically imply (1.13, 14). The main point may be put succinctly as follows. What for any agent are the necessary goods of action, namely, freedom and well-being, are equally necessary goods to his recipients, and he logically must admit that they have as much right to these goods as he does, since the ground or reason for which he rationally claims them for himself also pertains to his recipients. The many complexities of the applications of this doctrine, including the various ways the principle is able to account for justified departures from equality of rights, will be explored in the next two chapters.

My justification of the *PGC* has been rational in that it has argued from what is necessarily involved in the concepts of action and reason. The argument, then, has been primarily deductive, including the use of the principle of universalizability to bring out the inconsistency that results from denying a certain entailment based on the idea of a sufficient reason as applied in justification of a right-claim.

How does my justificatory argument cope with the formal difficulties I set forth in the first chapter, including the logical impossibility of deriving a supreme principle from some superior source and of deriving the moral from the nonmoral, and the accompanying dangers of circularity (1.7)? My answer comprises three main points. The first is that my justificatory argument has appealed to general principles of reason, including especially the requirement of logical consistency. Second, my argument has proceeded by an analysis of the concepts of action and reason. Since action is the primary genus of morality, in that moral rules are precepts as to how persons should act, the first two points amount to saying that a moral principle is deduced from rational considerations about the features that necessarily pertain to all action. Since these considerations are logically prior to specifically moral considerations, because the moral is subsumed under the rational and the practical, there is no circularity in the argument and the difficulties of deriving a moral principle from some superior principle are to this extent resolved. A moral principle is indeed logically first in the field of morality, but this field belongs to the wider fields of rationality and action, and a moral principle can be noncircularly deduced from principles of these wider fields without losing its logical primacy within the field of morality itself. At the same time, the *PGC* is also the supreme principle of the whole field of action because of its derivation from the generic features and normative structure of action.

Third, this deduction also resolves the problem of how a moral principle with its 'ought' can be derived from a superior principle that does not contain any 'ought.' I have not directly defined 'ought' in terms of 'is'; rather, I have held that the application of 'ought' is entailed by the correlative concept of having a right. The agent's application of this concept, in turn, has been derived from the concept of goods that are the necessary conditions of all his actions, since he necessarily claims that he has rights to these goods. And the agent's application of the concept of good, finally, has been derived from his acting for purposes. Since the agent's assertion that he acts for purposes is an empirical, descriptive statement, I have in this indirect way derived 'ought' from 'is.' Thus I have argued that right-claims with their correlative obligations or 'oughts' are logically involved in all purposive action. Hence, the sequence from action to morality is from an 'is' to an 'ought'; but the 'is,' action with its generic features, has been seen to be a context that implicitly contains an 'ought,' and the argument has shown how this 'ought' is made explicit. This 'ought,' moreover, is a moral one not only because, pertaining to all action, it is normatively inescapable in the practical order, but also because it involves requirements as to how agents are to take favorable account of their recipients' interests where their freedom and well-being are mutually involved.

These considerations also bear on the ways in which my use of the principle of universalizability surmounts the difficulties characteristic of most moral applications of it. These difficulties, to which I called attention above, arise from the variabilities in content that the principle admits: variabilities in the actions it is right to perform and in the criteria of relevant similarities (2.17, 18). My argument avoids these difficulties because it substitutes rational necessities for these contingent contents.

First, as to the actions it is right to perform, whereas the usual applications of the principle allow agents to choose and describe these actions according to their own inclinations or ideals, regardless of how their recipients might react to them, my application of the principle restricts the agent's action-descriptions to necessary contents, that is, to the generic features of action—voluntariness and purposiveness—and to the necessary goods of freedom and well-being. The agent must act in accord with his recipients' rights to these goods. Unlike the actions permitted by the usual applications of universalizability, these features and goods are necessarily acceptable to the recipients because they embody the necessary conditions of freely acting for one's purposes.

Second, as to the criteria of relevant similarities, whereas the usual applications of universalizability allow agents to choose and describe these according to their own desires, my application restricts these criteria to descriptions that are necessarily and universally connected with action, namely, the description of being a prospective agent who wants to fulfill his purposes. Because this description pertains equally to all agents and recipients, my application of universalizability necessarily entails an egalitarian-universalist moral principle, as against the inegalitarian and particularist moralities permitted by the usual applications of universalizability. Both these shifts in respect to content, from variable to necessary features of action and criteria of relevance, result from applications of reason in that basic respect in which it requires avoidance of contradiction and is opposed to what is arbitrary. In this respect, reason requires that the features of action and criteria of relevance that give content to the logical form of universalizability not be permitted to vary according to the agent's contingent predilections, but that they reflect necessary and universal aspects of their subject matter.

As so far presented, then, the *PGC* presents rationally grounded answers to each of the three central questions of moral philosophy (1.1, 2). It answers the distributive question—which persons' interests ought to be favorably considered in action—by providing that each agent must respect the generic rights of all his recipients: all prospective purposive agents equally have these rights. It answers the substantive question—which interests ought to be favorably considered—by holding that freedom and well-being, because of their necessity for action, should be the primary goods, although further discriminations are possible within these. The authoritative question—why anyone should be moral in the sense of taking favorable account of the interests of other persons—is answered by noting that this is required by reason in its most rigorous interpretation of avoiding self-contradiction, so that no person's action can be rationally justified if it violates the *PGC*. This consideration also epitomizes the rational justification of the *PGC* itself as the supreme principle of morality. By virtue of these answers and their supporting arguments, the *PGC* fulfills the requirement that the supreme principle of morality must be supremely criteriological in that it sets forth the basic substantive and distributive criteria of moral relevance for actions and institutions.

The Formal Necessity of the Principle

3.6. The *PGC* is formally or logically necessary in that any agent who denies or refuses to accept it contradicts himself. Let us now look more closely at this necessity. The *PGC* was presented as an imperative. Although imperatives may be denied and may figure in such logical relations as contradiction, it will be convenient to restate the *PGC* as a grammatical indicative, in such a propositional form as: 'Every agent ought to act in accord with the generic rights of his recipients as well as of himself.' This restatement in terms of 'ought' simply returns the *PGC* to the considerations about rights and 'oughts' that were discussed in chapter 2. It also has the advantage that by being stated in propositional form, the *PGC* is at least open to being considered as true or false. I shall discuss below how the truth of the *PGC* can be construed in terms of correspondence.

Since every agent must accept the *PGC* on pain of contradiction, the *PGC* has been shown to be a necessarily true principle. A main element in this necessary truth is formal, in that the *PGC* follows from antecedent propositions through the principle of universalizability and hence through a formal consideration of logical consistency. It is important, however, to examine further how this formal consideration bears on the *PGC*'s necessity. So far as my present argument has gone, the *PGC* has been shown to be necessarily true not directly or in itself, but only at two removes. If we take as the criterion of a statement's being necessarily true that its denial is self-contradictory, then a statement is necessarily true directly or in itself if its denial can be shown to be self-contradictory through a consideration only of the definitions or meanings of its directly constituent terms together with the logical principle of identity. Thus, to take a hoary example, 'All bachelors are unmarried' is necessarily true directly on this criterion because (assuming existential import) its denial, 'Some bachelors are not unmarried,' can be shown to be self-contradictory through the definition of 'bachelors' as 'unmarried males.' For, by substituting 'unmarried males' for 'bachelors' in the denial, it then says, 'Some unmarried males are not unmarried.' But this violates the logical principle of identity, which says, 'All A is A,' so that it cannot be the case that some A is not A.

Now it might be thought that the *PGC* is in this way necessarily true directly. For when the *PGC* tells the agent that he ought to act in accord with his recipients' rights, it tells him nothing he didn't already know simply from the meaning of 'rights.' For the term 'rights' means, at least in part, that in accord with which one ought to act, or that with which one ought to refrain from interfering. Hence, since generic rights are rights to generic goods, the *PGC* may be reformulated as follows: 'Every agent ought to refrain from interfering with those generic goods of his recipients and of himself with which he ought to refrain from interfering.' The denial of this statement can, of course, be shown to be self-contradictory through a consideration of the meanings of its directly constituent terms.

This argument does not, however, show that the *PGC* is necessarily true directly. For the *PGC* says not only that one ought at least not to interfere with that to which one's recipients have rights; it also says that both the agent and his recipients have the generic rights, and it goes on to make explicit what is the agent's duty in light of this fact. Thus the *PGC*, unlike purely formal principles of justice, provides a substantial criterion for distinguishing morally right from morally wrong actions. That the agent and his recipients have the generic rights is a substantial proposition whose denial cannot be shown to be self-contradictory simply by a consideration of the meanings of its directly constituent terms together with the principle of identity. Rather, the *PGC* is in this respect more like a theorem than an axiom. Its necessary truth follows from antecedent propositions, including those about the agent's necessary goods, such that, if one accepts these propositions, then one cannot consistently deny the *PGC*, including its claim that agents and their recipients have the generic rights. This, then, is the first remove at which the *PGC* is necessarily true: to show that its denial is self-contradictory requires also a consideration of these antecedent propositions from which it is logically derived.

There is a second remove. The *PGC* has thus far been shown to be necessarily true only as a theorem that is upheld *by the (any) agent.* We may distinguish between assertoric and dialectical statements of the principle, or indeed of any proposition. An assertoric statement is of the form '*p*'; a dialectical statement is of the form 'S thinks (or says, or accepts) that '*p*'; a dialectically necessary statement is of the form 'S logically must (on pain of contradiction) think (or say, or accept) that *p*.' Similarly, with regard to the *PGC* we must distinguish between its assertoric form: 'Every agent ought to act in accord with the generic rights of his recipients as well as of himself,' and its dialectically necessary form: 'Every agent logically must accept that he ought to act in accord with the generic rights of his recipients as well as of himself.' Now strictly speaking it is the latter, dialectically necessary statement that I have thus far shown to be necessarily true, since it logically follows from other necessarily true statements about what every agent logically must accept. This is part of the dialectically necessary method to which I have previously referred.

3.7. As so far presented, then, the *PGC* is necessarily true neither directly in itself nor simply as a derived assertoric theorem, but rather as part of a complex dialectically necessary proposition that says the agent must accept the *PGC* on pain of contradicting other statements he logically must accept. But this now raises the following question. If what is necessarily true is not the *PGC* stated assertorically but rather the dialectically necessary statement, then what is the logical status of the *PGC* when taken by itself? When it is stated assertorically or independently— (1) 'I ought to act in accord with the generic rights of my recipients as well as of myself'—the *PGC* is necessarily true only when and as it is said by the agent. When it is stated dialectically, as part of a compound proposition that states what every agent must say or accept—(2) 'Every agent logically must accept that he ought to act in accord with the generic rights of his recipients as well as of himself'—the whole compound proposition is necessarily true.

Thus far, then, the *PGC*'s necessary truth has been shown to depend directly or indirectly on its dialectical linkage to the agent's statements or beliefs. I now want to examine some arguments for the view that the *PGC* is also necessarily true when it is stated assertorically and independent of this linkage : (3) 'Every agent ought to act in accord with the generic rights of his recipients as well as of himself.' If (3) is juxtaposed with the dialectically necessary statement of the *PGC* (2) given just above, it can be seen that the logical transition from (2) to (3) is obvious, given the premise that agents ought to do what they logically must accept that they ought to do. This premise is also obvious; for what stronger ground can be given for someone's having a duty than that he logically must accept that he has the duty? For since he logically must accept that he has the duty, he contradicts himself if he denies that he has the duty. And from this it follows that he necessarily has the duty, so that the following assertoric statement is necessarily true and must be accepted for himself by every agent: 'I ought to act in accord with the generic rights of my recipients as well as of myself.'

This conclusion may also be upheld by recalling that the agents to whom the *PGC* and moral judgments generally are addressed are assumed to be rational, in the sense of being agents who are capable of attending to and being influenced by rational considerations (although, of course, this capacity may often not be exercised, or may be exercised incorrectly, in relevant circumstances). These rational considerations, as previously indicated, are those required by the canons of deductive and inductive logic. Now what a rational agent ought to do, at least so far as he is able to ascertain, is what he is rationally justified in thinking he ought to do. But what he is rationally justified in thinking he ought to do is what he logically must accept that he ought to do. For what he logically must accept is such that he contradicts himself if he fails to accept it; and by contradicting himself he loses a necessary condition of rational justification. We have already seen in some detail, however, that what any agent logically must accept that he ought to do is to act conformably to the *PGC*—that is, to act in accord with the generic rights of his recipients as well as of himself. Consequently, what a rational agent ought to do is to act in accord with the generic rights of his recipients as well as of himself. Thus again the *PGC* has been shown to be necessarily true when stated assertorically. Both of the above arguments began from the dialectically necessary statement of the *PGC*: 'Every agent *logically must accept that he* ought to act in accord with the generic rights of his recipients as well as of himself'; but each argument then showed that the emphasized words can be elided, as a consequence of the logical import of what is meant by 'logically must accept.'

3.8. These arguments for the assertoric detachability of the *PGC* incur difficulties, which I shall now examine by noting some parallels to the *PGC* in its dialectical and assertoric forms. Compare the following two statements: first, the dialectically necessary statement: 'Every rational advertiser must claim that the products he advertises are good'; second, the assertoric statement: 'The products he advertises are good.' The former, dialectical statement may be admitted to be true, since it would be quite irrational, at least in the sense of counterproductive and self-defeating, for an advertiser not to claim that his products are good—that is, that they are worthwhile, valuable, pleasing, helpful, or have some other relevant sort of goodness. We might put it even more strongly: to be an advertiser is to aim to sell or to advance the selling of some product or object; but to deny that this product is good or to withhold all claims about its being good in relevant respects would be to go counter to this aim and hence would constitute not being an advertiser. It would be self-contradictory, therefore, to deny the dialectical statement, 'Every rational advertiser must claim that the products he advertises are good,' so that this statement is a necessary truth. From this, however, it by no means follows that the detached assertoric statement, 'The products he advertises are good,' is itself necessarily true, or indeed true at all. On the contrary, it may be and often is quite false. Thus the necessary truth of a compound, dialectical statement does not entail the necessary truth of its constituent assertoric statement. From this it seems to follow that the necessary truth of the dialectical statement 'Every agent logically must accept the *PGC*' does not entail that the *PGC* itself, in its assertoric form, is necessarily true or even plausible.

The analogy and argument can be pushed further. It might be thought that the *PGC*'s undeniability by any agent can be used to establish the moral rightness of acting according to the *PGC* only if there is implicitly assumed some such premise as (4) 'What logically must be accepted by every agent is right,' or (5) 'Every agent ought to act according to what follows from the concept of being an agent.' For my argument has indeed proceeded from the dialectical necessities of what the agent logically must accept as following from the concept of being an agent. But if (4) or (5) must be assumed, then the whole argument for the *PGC* will rest not on factual and logical antecedents alone but on a normative or evaluative premise; moreover, the question will then arise of the truth or warrant of this premise. In addition, the question will arise of why being an agent must be given such pride of place. For just as it may be said of the *PGC*'s premise, 'What logically must be accepted by every agent is right,' that it obtains or is true within the context of action or from the standpoint of the agent, so it may be said of the analogous premise that grounds the advertiser's statement—'What logically must be accepted by every advertiser is right'—that it obtains or is true within the context of advertising or from the standpoint of the advertiser. In each case, both the premise and its derivative statement or theorem would have not an absolute truth but a truth relative to a given context or from a given standpoint—that of action and the agent in the one case, that of advertising and the advertiser in the other. The truth of the *PGC*, then, as resting on its premise, would not be any greater or more assured when it is stated assertorically than the truth of the assertoric statement 'The products I advertise are good' as resting on *its* premise. But this is a reductio ad absurdum, for the advertiser's statement may often be false.

A similar difficulty arises if the argument is held to depend on such a premise as (5) 'Every agent ought to act according to what follows from the concept of being an agent.' For then the question will arise of why the same contention should not be made about other concepts. Consider, for example, such parallels as these: 'Every tyrant ought to act according to what follows from the concept of being a tyrant,' or 'Every sadist ought to act according to what follows from the concept of being a sadist.' These would indeed be cases of doing one's own thing, with a vengeance. And if, to rule out such parallels, one insists that only what follows from the concept of being an agent is good or right, then the question again arises of how this exclusive proposition is to be proved.

An obvious and important difference between the case of agency and the *PGC*, on the one hand, and the cases of the advertiser, the tyrant, and the sadist, on the other, is that a greater necessity and universality attach to the former: being an agent is much more inevitable and pervasive than being one of these other things. But it is very important to be cautious in interpreting this difference, since otherwise it is difficult to see how such a criterion can serve to exclude other more doubtful principles or statements that also rest on considerations of necessity and universality. Suppose we hold, following Freud, that there is some neurosis to which all humans are inevitably subject, so that they are all necessitated to accept some such statement as, 'I ought to kill my father (or mother).' Or suppose we hold, following Marx, that there is some ideological belief of 'false consciousness' to which all the persons of a given epoch must subscribe, such as 'All persons ought to obey their lords.' Surely the necessity and universality of such beliefs would be no guarantee of their truth or correctness.

3.9. I now want to resolve these difficulties, starting with the one just presented. The difference between the *PGC* on the one hand and the 'Freudian' and 'Marxist' precepts on the other is not only that the latter are explicitly set forth as pathological, but also that, as a consequence, they are regarded by their respective authors as having genuine alternatives within the respective contexts of their application. Having an Oedipus complex or being a victim of 'false consciousness' is a condition that must be worked through and superseded, for such conditions are products of compulsion and ignorance; once they are understood by the persons subject to them, their obligatoriness is disavowed. The *PGC*, on the other hand, derives from the generic features that are essential to all agency and hence to all pursuits of any goods. The *PGC* is a product not of ignorance but rather of rational awareness of what logically follows from being an agent, so that its obligatoriness is not overcome but rather is established and reinforced by rational understanding of its basis. Thus there are no rationally tenable normative alternatives to the *PGC* in the context of action. The generic features of action and the conclusions that follow from them can be known by every rational person; as such, they are matters of self-knowledge for agents, in contrast to the Freudian and Marxist parallels.

My argument, then, does not rest on the premise, 'What logically must be accepted by every agent is right,' unless the criterion of 'right' is taken to be rational or logical in the way just indicated. But so interpreted the 'premise' is not a normative moral one but is rather the premise assumed by all uses of reasoning.

There are also important differences between the cases of agency and of advertising that refute the conclusions drawn from the analogies presented above. Agency and its logical consequences, including the *PGC*, have a rational necessity and universality that do not pertain to advertisers or to any other specific kinds of agents as such. One may be a rational agent without being an advertiser; and indeed a concern for rationality in the sense of empirical truthfulness may lead to one's ceasing to be an advertiser in certain circumstances. Thus the connection between being an advertiser or even a rational advertiser and saying or thinking 'My products are good' is by no means necessary. An advertiser may feel compelled to proclaim in public his statement about the goodness of his product, but he may disavow it *in foro conscientiae*, and he may stop advertising some particular product that he finds to be not good. In addition, being an advertiser is not necessarily relevant to being subject to practical precepts in general, for one may be subject to such precepts even if one is not an advertiser. On the other hand, one cannot, while being an agent, cease to regard one's freedom and well-being as goods that are necessary for all one's actions; hence, an agent cannot rationally hold that he does not have rights to freedom and well-being, and so too with the other logical consequences of his agency, including the *PGC*. He may, indeed, refrain from some particular action, but this does not affect his logical commitment to the generic features of his agency. He cannot stop being an agent except at a prohibitive price; and, even so, the steps he intentionally takes to this end would themselves be actions and exhibit the generic features of agency. Being an agent is necessarily and universally relevant to being subject to practical precepts, since it is to agents that all practical precepts are addressed. The *PGC*, as the logical consequence of these features, has a necessity and universality that go beyond the normative statements made by advertisers or any other restricted class of agents. Since no agent can deny the *PGC*, on pain of contradiction, the *PGC* is necessarily true within the whole sphere of practice.

These considerations also apply to the case of the tyrant presented above. A connected point is that what follows from the concept of being an agent must take precedence over what follows from the concept of being a tyrant because agency, being universal and necessary relative to tyranny, sets the general requirements within which options like that of tyranny must operate. Insofar as the tyrant engages in actions, he has a choice whether to act tyrannicallly or not, and hence whether to be a tyrant or not. But he has no choice whether to be an agent or not, except at the prohibitive price indicated above. Hence, since being an agent has normative implications, these are normatively inescapable for the tyrant: they set obligations for him that are binding for him antecedent to any more specific obligations or rights he may claim.

3.10. The above arguments have not proved that the *PGC* can be completely severed from its dialectical linkage to what agents must say or accept. The arguments have indicated how necessary and universal is the *PGC*'s connection with being an agent and with the normative judgments that necessarily accompany agency. This connection shows that the *PGC* has a certain relative status: its truth or correctness cannot be completely separated from what agents must accept. But this relativism is not in any important way a limitation on the status of the *PGC* as a moral principle. Since the *PGC* logically must be admitted by every agent, it is necessary and universal in the context of action, and it is this context that is relevant to morality. Thus the *PGC* has as much necessity and universality as can be attained by any substantial normative moral or practical principle.

This point also bears on the question whether the derivation of the *PGC* from 'is'-statements about action and purposes satisfies the condition of providing a moral 'ought'-judgment that is categorical. It may be contended that the answer is negative, on the ground that there is a conflict between the categorical and the dialectical. Since my argument has been dialectical in that it proceeds from within the standpoint of the agent, including the evaluations and right-claims he makes, the *PGC* and the ensuing 'ought'-judgments I have derived are valid, so holds the objection, only relative to the agent's standpoint, but not absolutely. Even if the agent is logically compelled to uphold certain 'ought'-judgments, given his initial statement that he performs actions for purposes, this does not establish that those judgments are really correct or binding. Hence, their 'oughts' are not categorical.

My reply to this objection is that the dialectically *necessary* aspect of my method gives the *PGC*'s 'ought' a more than contingent or hypothetical status. Since moral 'oughts' apply only or primarily to the context of action and hence to agents, to have shown that certain 'ought'-judgments logically must be granted by all agents, on pain of contradiction, is to give the judgments an absolute status, since their validity is logically ineluctable within the whole context of their possible application. It will be recalled that in my original specification I said that for 'ought'-judgments to be categorical the practical requirements they set forth cannot rightly be evaded by any action or institution, so that their bindingness is not contingent on the agent's variable self-interested desires or on social institutions that may themselves be lacking in moral justification (1.1). This condition of categoricalness is fulfilled by the *PGC*'s 'ought.'

In my subsequent discussions I shall usually state and refer to the *PGC* in its independent assertoric statement. This will involve no distortion or fallacy; for since the whole of moral discussion is assumed to be addressed to actual or prospective rational agents, it will not be necessary at each point to reiterate that the moral principle in question is such that it logically must be admitted by every agent.

If, however, the specific formulations of the dialectically necessary method may be dispensed with from this point on, then why did this method have to be used in the first place? Why could not the whole sequence of the argument for the *PGC* have been stated assertorically and hence more simply, without the complicating apparatus of what the agent logically must say or admit at each step beginning from his statements of the goodness of his purposes (2.1)?

To answer these questions, we must recall that many naturalistic moral philosophers have accepted the doctrines that all human actions aim at purposes their agents regard as good and that, more generally, value concepts logically arise from the natural facts of persons' desires, interests, or strivings. But there is a crucial difference in the way these doctrines are interpreted. The naturalists directly equate or identify good with such objects of striving or desire. We find this all the way from Aristotle's dictum that the good is that at which all things aim, to R. B. Perry's definition of value as any object of any interest.[3] This naturalistic equation, however, incurs several serious difficulties. One is that of justifying the use of value concepts and moral concepts on the basis of a nonvaluational starting point. How does the fact that something is desired establish that it is good? And what is the warrant for holding that persons have rights to something because they necessarily want it, or that certain 'oughts' are normatively binding on all persons because their objects are desired by the agent? From the difficulty of answering such questions arises the charge that naturalists present illicit inferences. To be sure, 'good' could be defined at least in part as 'object of a purposive action,' and 'having a right to X' could be defined in part as 'X is necessary for action.' But in addition to questions about the plausibility and scope of these definitions (How are they related to other uses of 'good' and 'rights'?), this approach would omit the conativeness that characterizes the agent's own attitude toward his purposes and that serves to ground his attributions of good and rights.

A closely related difficulty is that of relativism. Since different agents have different and even conflicting purposes, not all their objects can be good, and such naturalistic definitions provide no way of deciding among them. Some naturalists have tried to resolve this difficulty by holding that there are certain objects for which all humans strive and which therefore are universally good. In addition to such very general objects as pleasure or happiness, the most obvious candidates are such biological conditions as life, health, and physical integrity. But, as we have seen, it has been pointed out that religionists, romantics, intellectuals, and others may choose physical suffering, blindness, and even a martyr's death in preference to the biological conditions upheld by the naturalists (1.1,4; 2.4). And as for pleasure and happiness, either they are so general that they have no determinate contents or, if they are given certain determinate contents, then the thesis that all humans desire them turns out to be false. Hence, the naturalists are unsuccessful in trying to move logically from certain objects purportedly desired by all persons to what is good.

The use of the dialectically necessary method has enabled my above argument to avoid these difficulties. Where the naturalists simply equated good with the objects of persons' purposive strivings, the dialectical method has operated within the conative standpoint of the agent and has described and analyzed what he rationally thinks, says, or claims from within his own standpoint. The naturalistic method is external and theoretical: it purports to describe action and its objects from the standpoint of an external observer. The dialectical method, on the other hand, is internal, conative, and practical, for it portrays action and its objects as these are viewed by the purposive agent himself from within his own conative standpoint. And the method is dialectically necessary insofar as this portrayal is restricted to what every purposive agent is logically or rationally justified in claiming from within this standpoint. Thus, there is a difference between arguing, as the naturalists do, 'A does X for purpose E; therefore, E is good,' and arguing, as above, 'A does X for purpose E; therefore, A thinks (or holds) that E is good.' The latter statement is not, like the former, open to the charge that it goes beyond the evidence by illicitly moving to a value conclusion from a limited factual premise. To put it in somewhat different terms, from an agent's purposive action something can safely be inferred from within his own standpoint about his values, about what he regards as good; but an inference cannot be drawn with equal directness or security, externally to his own standpoint, about the value or the genuine goodness of what he values. The latter, external inference goes beyond the evidence; the former, internal inference does not. Similarly, from 'A needs freedom and well-being in order to act' (or 'Freedom and well-being are necessary conditions of A's acting'), it does not follow that 'A has rights to freedom and well-being.' A person who accepts the former statement may without contradicting himself reject the latter. On the other hand, from 'A regards his freedom and well-being as necessary goods,' or 'A implicitly says, "My freedom and well-being are necessary goods,"' it does follow that 'A rationally holds that he has rights to freedom and well-being,' or that 'A rationally says, "I have rights to freedom and well-being."' As we have seen, A contradicts himself if he accepts the former enclosed statement and rejects the latter. In this inference, too, the dialectically necessary internal element is indispensable for avoiding an illicit evaluative extension beyond what is warranted by the factual antecedent.

Although my argument has been dialectical in this way, proceeding from within the conative standpoint of the agent, it overcomes the difficulty of relativism. More generally, the argument is able to move from the internal standpoint of the agent to the external rational justification of the *PGC* as categorical and objectively valid. Since my method is dialectically necessary, the value-judgments and right-claims it elicits from within the standpoint of the agent are presented as having to be made or accepted by every agent on pain of irrationality. This is different from the purportedly apodictic or assertorically necessary method of the naturalists. They tried to argue that certain states or dispositions must be desired *tout court* by all persons—a proposition we saw to be false; but the above dialectically necessary argument has been rather that certain states or dispositions must be desired or valued by all persons insofar as they are rational agents.

It is from the requirements imposed by agency and recognized by rational agents, rather than from objects purportedly desired by all persons, that the dialectically necessary argument has proceeded. Since, however, agency is the context of morality and of practice in general, restricting the argument to what must be accepted by rational agents does not prevent the argument from applying to all morality and practice. In this way the dialectically necessary method is indispensable for avoiding both relativism and illicit inference from facts to values. In addition, as will be shown below, the method, by involving the rational agent in its successive steps, provides for his rational consent to its various requirements, including those of the criminal law (5.10,11).

THE MATERIAL NECESSITY OF THE PRINCIPLE

3.11. The logical structure of the *PGC* is similar to that of traditional principles of formal justice, with their requirements of impartiality, mutuality, and reciprocity. The main logical feature of all such principles is interpersonal consistency as comprised in universalizability: what is right for one person must be right for any relevantly similar person. The principles require that one act toward others according to the same rules as one upholds for oneself. Violations of each principle incur self-contradiction because they entail holding that a mode of action or treatment that is right in one case, as determined by a rule one accepts, is not right in a relevantly similar case, where this relevant similarity is also determined by the rule.

Like other consistency principles, the *PGC* applies universalizability by setting up a symmetrical relation between the agent and his recipients. In the case of the *PGC*, this is the relation of having generic rights with regard to someone else: If the agent has generic rights with regard to his recipient, then the latter must have generic rights with regard to the agent. For A to have generic rights with regard to B means that B ought to respect or not interfere with A's freedom and well-being. Thus the *PGC* says that the agent ought to respect the generic rights of his recipients (they have generic rights with regard to him), just as he necessarily holds that his recipients ought to respect his own generic rights (he has generic rights with regard to them).

Now it is clear that the relation of having generic rights with regard to someone else is not definitionally symmetrical; it is not, in this respect, like the relations of being a sibling or being equal. For the interpersonal generic rights relation to be symmetrical, several substantive conditions must be fulfilled, the most obvious being that the two relata—agent and recipient—must be relevantly similar to one another. The *PGC* and the steps leading to it establish that these relata necessarily fulfill this and other conditions. It is for this reason that the symmetricalness that the *PGC* upholds is more invariant than that found in other principles of consistency or formal justice. To see this, we must pursue some further comparisons.

In addition to the *PGC*, two chief versions of consistency principles may be distinguished. One version is that of simple consistency. It says that one should apply the same rule in similar cases, or, more copiously, that if one holds that a rule is right or ought to be observed, then it ought to be applied impartially to all cases that fall under it. A second version is that of appetitive-reciprocal consistency, or the Golden Rule. This says that one should act toward other persons according to the same rules one would want them to apply to oneself. There is an obvious parallelism between such principles and the *PGC*'s requirement that an agent should act in accord with his recipients' generic rights as well as his own. Put in terms of rules, the *PGC* says that one should act toward other persons according to the same rules upholding generic rights as one applies in relation to oneself. In each case there is the idea that one must impartially apply to other persons the same general rules one applies to oneself insofar as the other persons are relevantly similar to oneself. Inconsistency is incurred if one accepts for oneself a rule of action one rejects for other persons, or conversely.

It must be noted that this consistency requirement pertains only to transactions. If there is no action of one person on another, then one may, without inconsistency, apply to oneself a rule of action that one does not apply to others. Consider, for example, a punctilious person's rule, 'Chew each mouthful thirty times.' Since in chewing he does not act on other persons, no question of interpersonal consistency arises as to any relation between rules he applies to himself and to other persons, for he applies no rule to the others.

Violation of each of the consistency principles incurs self-contradiction once it is assumed in each case that the agents and recipients to whom the principles refer are relevantly similar to one another. For since each principle requires the application of the same rule to relevantly similar cases, violation of the principles would involve that one both accepts and rejects a general rule requiring certain treatment for all persons who are similar to one another in fulfilling a certain relevant description as indicated in the rule. The violator would be in the position of upholding both members of an inconsistent pair of judgments: (1) 'All Q ought to receive treatment P' and (2) 'It is not the case that this Q ought to receive treatment P.' In the simple consistency principles, (1) represents the content of any general rule accepted by the agent, and his violation of the principle commits him to saying that this rule that ought to be applied to all the cases that fall under it need not be applied in some case that falls under under it. In the appetitive-reciprocal principle, (1) represents a general rule embodying the kind of treatment that the agent desires for himself and that he is logically committed to apply to other persons insofar as he holds that he ought to have this treatment because he has some generalizable quality Q. The denial of the principle involves the agent in holding that some person who has this quality Q need not be treated in that way. In the *PGC*, (1) represents the rules defined by the generic rights that the agent necessarily upholds for himself as a prospective purposive agent and that he is logically committed to granting to his recipients: 'All my recipients ought to have their freedom and well-being respected by me.' The agent violates the *PGC* in a particular case when he holds that the freedom or well-being of some recipient of his need not be respected by him.

3.12. Despite these similarities between the *PGC* and the other principles, there are also some crucial differences, which stem from the fact that the *PGC* has a necessary content as well as a necessary form. There are three interrelated aspects of this necessary content. The first bears on the rules of action or treatment required by each principle. The simple consistency version leaves the contents of these rules completely indeterminate: it provides no substantive criterion of when a rule is right. Hence, this version is at most a principle of judicial impartiality, and it involves complete substantive and moral variability: any possible rule, no matter what its content, is compatible with the principle. The appetitive-reciprocal version provides for a kind of legislative as well as judicial impartiality, since it requires not only that one judge and act according to general rules but also that the rules have a certain impartial content in that they must be acceptable to the agents who make and act according to them not merely qua agents but also qua recipients. But this version still leaves too large a residue of substantive and moral variability. For a rule that is acceptable to the agent qua recipient may be quite unacceptable to other recipients. In extreme cases, agents may be 'fanatics,' willing to uphold certain 'ideals' even if their consequences run counter to their self-interested inclinations. Hence the test of the agent's wishes for himself qua recipient could justify rules that impose on their recipients such hardships as racial discrimination and even genocide, and they could disjustify social rules other persons may regard as highly desirable.

Unlike the other two principles, the *PGC* provides for moral rules determinate contents that do not admit of such variability. For its requirement that the agent act in accord with the generic rights of his recipients is not contingent on whatever he may happen to accept or on his variable self-interested desires or ideals; hence the rules of action the *PGC* requires are similarly noncontingent. Since the generic rights of recipients, like those of the agent himself, have determinate contents consisting in the necessary conditions of action from which the *PGC* itself is derived, the rules that follow from the *PGC* are similarly determinate in content. They set forth specific ways in which such respect is to be fostered, and these ways cannot be tailored by the agent to fit his own variable predilections. Also, unlike the rules stemming from the other consistency principles, the requirement that the agent act in accord with his recipients' generic rights is necessarily acceptable to the recipients, because the objects of these rights are necessary goods: they embody the freedom and well-being that are directly involved in acting for one's purposes. At the same time, the PGC's requirement is also acceptable to the agent in that he is to act in accord with his own generic rights as well as those of his recipients. In the next two chapters I shall discuss the PGC's provisions for resolving further conflicts between agents and recipients.

3.13. A second difference between the PGC and the other consistency principles with regard to content concerns the criterion of relevant similarities. All three principles hold that what is right in one case must be right in any relevantly similar case. The simple consistency principle, however, determines the criterion of this relevant similarity only by some general rule whose contents are left completely indeterminate; hence, a like indeterminacy characterizes what is taken to be a relevant similarity. The appetitive-reciprocal principle determines the criterion by means of reciprocal acceptability, by considering whether differentiations of treatment in terms of the qualities taken to be relevant are acceptable to the agent not only qua agent but also qua recipient. This criterion, however, has the same difficulties as we saw in connection with the rules themselves: it allows the agent to tailor the criterion according to his own variable desires regardless of their impact on his recipients.

The PGC does not have this substantive and moral variability because, as we saw above, it determines the criterion of relevant similarity by qualities whose possession by the agent is necessary to his being an agent (2.19). This necessity is such that the agent contradicts himself if he adduces any less-general qualities as the sufficient justifying reason for his having the generic rights. And where the variable criteria allowed by the other principles may serve to ground rules that are seriously inegalitarian in that they differentially affect the freedom and well-being of persons according to the self-interested desires of agents, such a basis for inegalitarianism is not permitted by the PGC. The qualities determined to be relevant to the similarities provided for by the PGC are had equally by agents and recipients. On the other hand, some of the specific rules justified by the PGC provide for a differential status among agents and recipients, as in the differences between judges and defendants, umpires and players, teachers and students. Here again, however, the criteria of relevant similarities and differences are determinate, since, as we shall see, the criteria must conform to rules that must themselves be justified by the *PGC*.

3.14. A third, and most important, aspect of the *PGC*'s necessary content in contrast to the other consistency principles bears on the precise respect in which the principles are necessary by virtue of their denials involving self-contradiction. All consistency principles have applications that combine singular reasoned moral judgments with their corresponding universalizations. Their form is: 'I ought to do (or have) X (or I have a right to do (or have) X) because I am Q; therefore, all Q ought to do (or have) X (or, all Q have a right to do (or have) X).' Now, with the consistency principles other than the *PGC*, necessity pertains only to the combination of the singular and its corresponding universalization; the combination cannot be denied without self-contradiction because each member of the combination entails the other. But neither member is logically necessary of itself. Thus, the singular antecedent judgment is contingent; one can fill in whatever one likes for 'do (or have) X' in the antecedent, but given this antecedent one must accept the universal consequent on pain of contradiction.

The *PGC* and its applications, on the other hand, have a necessary antecedent; necessity pertains to the antecedent by itself, not merely to the combination of the antecedent singular and its corresponding universalization. For by virtue of the generic features and normative structure of action, every agent must accept for himself, 'I have rights to freedom and well-being because I am a prospective purposive agent.' Since this right-claim and its accompanying reason are the antecedent of the *PGC* and its applications, the agent must accept the consequent, which is the *PGC* and its applications, on two grounds: not merely because he *has* affirmed the antecedent, but because as an agent he *must* affirm the antecedent. Thus the *PGC* is materially as well as formally necessary.

This point may be presented more fully as follows. Violations of each of the three kinds of consistency principle incur self-contradiction in that the violators are in the position of accepting both some general rule: (1) 'All Q ought to receive treatment P,' and a particular judgment that is inconsistent with it: (2) 'It is not the case that this Q ought to receive treatment P.' So far as concerns what is common to all three consistency principles, however, the general rule (1) is not by itself necessarily true so that its denial is necessarily false; rather, what is necessarily true is the joint assertion of (1) and denial of (2), and what is necessarily false is the joint assertion of both (1) and (2). Now if two judgments are inconsistent with one another, it is indeed logically impossible to act according to both of them simultaneously. But this still leaves open the question of which member of the inconsistent pair is to be accepted and which rejected. For inconsistency can be avoided, and consistency maintained or restored, by rejecting either of the two mutually inconsistent judgments.

In the cases of the simple and appetitive-reciprocal consistency principles, it is left both logically and factually possible to avoid inconsistency by accepting either member of an inconsistent pair and rejecting the other. For example, if some person holds both (3) 'All persons of black ancestry ought to be enslaved' and (4) 'I, if I should turn out to have black ancestry, ought not to be enslaved,' then to avoid inconsistency he must reject one or the other member of this contrary pair. But if he is a 'fanatic,' he may accept (3) and reject (4), so that he accepts that if he should turn out to have black ancestry, he too ought to be enslaved. Although such a view would go counter to persons' usual inclinations, there is nothing impossible about it either logically or factually (see also above, 2.13,23).

From this possibility of accepting either member of an inconsistent pair of judgments, it follows that there is a severe limitation on the justificatory power of the simple and appetitive-reciprocal consistency principles. For such principles are unable to prove the moral wrongness of any action, judgment, or rule where the agent or judge is willing to undergo the same kind of action or judgment he applies or wants to apply to others, no matter how severe the hardship this inflicts on the others or how unwilling they themselves may be to undergo it. Thus these principles cannot show the moral wrongness of such rule as that persons of black ancestry ought to be enslaved, in any case where a person is willing to accept such a rule for himself.

In contrast to the patterns of moral argument provided by the other consistency principles, the *PGC* does not leave it open to an agent or judge to reject either member of an inconsistent pair. For, as we have seen, the *PGC* has a necessary content deriving from the necessary connection between being an agent, holding that one has the generic rights, and being logically committed to acknowledging that all one's recipients also have these rights. Since in any proposed moral rule it is not open to the agent who upholds the rule to deny that he has the generic rights or to reject them for himself, it is also not open to him to evade the rightness of the consequent this antecedent entails, that his recipients also have the generic rights. Because of this necessity, the rules deriving from the *PGC* cannot be rejected without self-contradiction: their necessary truth, unlike that of rules which fall under the other consistency principles, pertains to the rules themselves as derived theorems and not merely to the combination of a rule with the denial of a singular judgment which is inconsistent with the rule. The agent must accept (5) 'All prospective purposive agents have the generic rights,' and hence also (6) 'I ought to act in accord with the generic rights of my recipients'; nor can he reject any specific rule of such action. But if an agent A coerces or harms some recipient B, or holds that he is justified in coercing or harming B in some way not itself justified by the *PGC*, then A also accepts (7) 'B, a prospective purposive agent, does not have the generic rights,' and also (8) 'It is not the case that I ought to act in accord with B's generic rights.' Now (5) and (7) are mutually inconsistent, and so too are (6) and (8). But A cannot, without contradiction, reject (5) and (6) since these logically derive from the necessary structure of action. Consequently, A must reject (7) and (8) and with them the legitimacy or rightness of coercing or harming B. Thus the *PGC*, unlike the other consistency principles, provides for the categorical rejection of immoral actions and rules whereby the agent acts in accord with his own generic rights but not in accord with those of his recipients.

It follows that such a rule as (3) 'All persons of black ancestry ought to be enslaved' is directly refutable through the *PGC*. A person who accepts such a rule necessarily contradicts himself. This self-contradiction is not contingent on his also accepting such a judgment as (4) 'I, if I should turn out to have black ancestry, ought not to be enslaved.' Rather, acceptance of (3) by any agent necessarily condemns him to self-contradiction because (3) is inconsistent with (5) 'All prospective purposive agents have the generic rights'; and every agent logically must accept (5).

This necessity of the *PGC* can also be brought out by noting its contrast with such a superficially similar principle as 'Act in accord with the legal rights of your recipients as well as of yourself,' which I shall call the 'principle of legal consistency.' The substitution of 'legal' for 'generic' removes from this principle the material necessity that pertains to the *PGC*. A person cannot remain an agent if he rejects the *PGC*, because if he rejects it then he logically must reject the antecedent statement, 'I have the generic rights.' Since the generic rights are rights to the necessary conditions of action, to reject these rights is to incapacitate oneself for action and hence to cease being an agent. On the other hand, a person can be an agent while rejecting at least some and perhaps most of his legal rights. These rights might include, for example, the ownership of slaves, the *jus primae noctis*, and other emoluments whereby some persons victimize others. Because of the possibility of this rejection, the statement 'I have legal rights' does not provide for the principle of legal consistency the same necessary antecedent as 'I have the generic rights' provides for the *PGC*. Hence, any agent can reject the principle of legal consistency without self-contradiction.

3.15. It will be helpful to pursue further the relation between the *PGC* and the Golden Rule, which I have also called the principle of appetitive-reciprocal consistency. As we have seen, an important similarity is that each principle requires that an agent treat his recipients according to the same rules the agent wants for his own treatment. Thus the *PGC* provides that just as the agent necessarily values the generic rights for himself and wants other persons to act on him in accord with his generic rights, so he ought to act on other persons in accord with their generic rights. As we have already noted, an important difference from the Golden Rule is that whereas the *PGC* focuses on what the agent necessarily values or wants with regard to how he is to be treated, namely, that he be acted on in accord with his generic rights, the Golden Rule leaves completely open and indeterminate the content of the agent's wants for himself. But this contrast has a further aspect, bearing on the level at which the actions required by each principle are described. The Golden Rule leaves it open to the agent to describe his actions at differing levels of generality. He would want other persons to ply him with gin, hence he ought to ply others with gin; he would want other persons to give him a certain drink, or certain refreshments, or certain delectables . . . or certain treatment, hence he ought to give them the same. But which level of generality is the right one? Different answers may yield extremely unpalatable results, as where a sadomasochist holds that he ought to inflict pain and suffering on other persons because he would want them to inflict pain and suffering on him.

The *PGC* deals with this issue by confining itself to the maximally general, or generic level, at which actions can be described, namely, their voluntariness or freedom and purposiveness or well-being, and to the corresponding rights. This level does not have the variability or the multidescribability of the actions referred to in the Golden Rule. Since these generic features and rights are necessarily acceptable to all agents and recipients, they do not have the potential for evil and suffering that more specific levels of action-description provide.

The *PGC*'s restriction to the generic level of act-descriptions also has a rational justification that the Golden Rule's variability lacks. For when it is left open to the agent at which level he will describe his actions, even if he always describes them truly, this means that he can consult his own predilections and even arbitrary whims as to how he wants to be treated by others. But the *PGC* removes such potential arbitrariness; it describes actions only at a level that imposes itself on the agent and is not subject to his arbitrary choices or preferences. No matter in how many ways he might describe his action, he cannot evade the description of it as voluntary and purposive. And since these generic features are necessary to all action, they must take priority for the agent over the particular purposes for which he may contingently act. For the necessary features of action set the limits for all particular kinds of action. More specific descriptions of actions are permitted, but only in the context of rules that are themselves justified by the *PGC*.

Applications of the *PGC*, unlike those of other principles appealing to consistency or universalizability, cannot be immoral because they cannot be tailored, in their antecedents, to the agent's varying inclinations or ideals without regard to the generic rights of their recipients. The *PGC* hence provides in its applications an indefeasible guarantee of reciprocal fairness both to agents and to recipients. The *PGC* is a principle not only of judicial or legislative impartiality but also of constitutional impartiality. Unlike the principles of simple and of appetitive-reciprocal consistency, the *PGC* does not provide merely for impartiality in the application of specific rules regardless of their contents, and not merely for impartiality in the contents of such rules insofar as they must be acceptable to the agent qua recipient; it provides also for impartiality in the more complete and substantive sense that the contents of the rules must be in accord with the generic rights of all their recipients. The full scope of the derivation of specific rules from the *PGC* involves various complexities that will be explored in the next two chapters. But the general conception of individuals and of society that emerges from the *PGC* is that of an association of persons who mutually respect one another's freedom and well-being. With the *PGC*, unlike the other forms of consistency principle considered above, it is impossible to justify, and it is indeed mandatory to disjustify, any forms of racism or tyranny that involve the unqualified infliction of coercion and harm on innocent persons— that is, of coercion and harm that take no positive account of the generic rights of the persons affected. The *PGC* puts a premium on freedom and on mutual accommodation of well-being; these have an obvious application in the sociopolitical sphere as the principles of equal freedom and common good. Any moral principle that, unlike the *PGC*, fails to make these norms of central importance is to that extent suspect.

ANALYTIC TRUTH AND MORALITY

3.16. The *PGC*'s necessity as discussed above involves the following points: (*a*) The predicate of the *PGC* logically follows, although through several intermediate steps, from the concept of being a rational agent, where 'rational' means adhering to the criteria of deductive and inductive logic. This logical following holds for both the dialectical and the assertoric statements of the principle. To put it otherwise, the meaning of the *PGC*'s predicate term is entirely included, although implicitly, in the meaning of its subject term. By way of brief summary: an agent is a person who initiates or controls his behavior through his unforced, informed choice with a view to achieving various purposes; since he wants to fulfill his purposes he regards his freedom and well-being, the necessary conditions of his successful pursuit of purposes, as necessary goods; hence he holds that he has rights to freedom and well-being; to avoid self-contradiction he must hold that he has these generic rights insofar as he is a prospective purposive agent; hence he must admit that all prospective purposive agents have the generic rights; hence he must acknowledge that he ought at least to refrain from interfering with his recipients' freedom and well-being, so that he ought to act in accord with their generic rights as well as his own.

(*b*) The term 'agent' as I have used it here is to some extent a technical term or a term of art; it is not as current in ordinary language as is, for example, 'bachelor.' The term is defined through consideration of the characteristics understood to pertain to the possible addresses of practical precepts that are held to be based on reason. (*c*) The term 'agent,' or the concept of an agent, has objective reference, not only in the sense that it refers to all the persons who have the characteristics by which the term was defined but also in the sense that most adult human persons have or can have these characteristics. In addition, they can have the characteristics signified by 'rational.' (*d*) Hence, the *PGC*'s predicate also refers to most adult human persons. To put it otherwise, most adult human persons, all of whom are agents in the sense defined, do in fact have the obligations stated in the *PGC*'s predicate. It is indeed possible to be an agent and to violate or fail to fulfill these obligations; but it is not possible to be an agent and fail to have these obligations, or to be a rational agent and fail to accept them as justified.

These points raise many difficulties, both separately and in combination. To waive the problems of such words as 'meaning' and 'concept,' the first point has as consequence that the *PGC* is analytically true, true by virtue of the meanings of its terms. There are familiar difficulties with the notion that any moral judgment is analytic; more generally still, objections have been brought against the very idea of a proposition's being analytic as contrasted with synthetic,[4] and also against construing the results of philosophical analysis as analytic propositions or as finding 'conceptual connections' rather than ordinary Humean regularities or empirical correlations.[5] As we saw earlier, the *PGC* is analytic not directly but rather derivatively, because its predicate follows from the meaning of its subject only through several intermediate steps. But each of these steps follows successively from the meaning of 'agent.' It is for this reason that denying the *PGC* involves one in self-contradiction and hence debars one from being a rational agent.

This derivativeness, combined with the second point about the partially technical meaning of the term 'agent,' sharply differentiates the *PGC*'s analyticity from such a paradigm of analytic truth as 'All bachelors are unmarried.' The meanings by virtue of which the latter is analytic are conventional definitions of terms as used in ordinary language; but the meanings by virtue of which the *PGC* is analytic are more like theoretical concepts that have been elaborated on the basis, in part, of systematic empirical considerations. The concepts of 'action' and 'agent' from which my argument began were defined by examining the characteristics human behavior must have insofar as it is to be a possible object of practical, and especially moral, precepts. This examination was in part empirical and inductive in that it consisted in looking both at the kinds of precepts that have been set forth in the contexts of practice and morality and at the generic features of the kinds of behaviors with which these precepts have been concerned. But the examination was also conceptual in that it dealt with the concepts of 'moral precepts' and of 'action' as circumscribed by such precepts. These concepts are not entirely different from the meanings these words have in ordinary language. On the other hand, unlike 'bachelor' and 'unmarried,' the words 'moral precepts' and 'action' as I have used them reflect a systematizing of ordinary usage in the context of an overall theory whose basis is ultimately empirical, and they involve a much greater conceptual complexity than does 'bachelor.'

These considerations, which develop the third and fourth points listed above, bring the difficulties to a head. How can the *PGC* be both analytic and empirically based, both true by virtue of meanings and objectively referential? A traditional definition of analytical propositions is that they are true by virtue of meanings and independent of matters of fact; yet I seem to want to have it both ways. If the *PGC* is true by virtue of meanings, then it is indeed necessarily true; but this necessity is obtained precisely because the proposition is not dependent (or contingent) for its truth on facts about the world, but only on meanings of words or concepts that are as they are entirely by one's own decisions or by conventional usage. If, on the other hand, the *PGC* is true of facts or objects in the world, then, since these can be ascertained only through experience that is limited in its reach, the *PGC* would be inductively derived and hence would be only probable or contingent, not necessary.

3.17. To begin to deal with these familiar arguments, it must be noted that if all analytic truths must be of the direct, conventional sort typified by 'All bachelors are unmarried,' then it indeed follows that the *PGC* is not analytic, but it also follows that there can be statements that are neither analytic nor synthetic.[6] The *PGC* can be considered analytic, however, if the meanings or concepts by virtue of which an analytic statement is true may include those that have been defined by a series of systematic theoretical considerations resting in part on empirical inquiry and in part on logical criteria of consistency. It is the empirical inquiry that gives the concepts their objective reference. But the resulting definitions and propositions culminating in the *PGC* do not have the tentativeness characteristic of empirical knowledge, for at least two reasons. First, their empirical base is a comparatively limited one, consisting in actions, the kinds of behaviors that are the objects of moral and other practical precepts. The argument leading to the *PGC* begins from definitions of such behaviors, and it is a matter of experience that there are such precepts and that the behaviors they undertake to guide have, as such, certain features. In this respect the definitions differ, for example, from the equations erected for such terms of physical science as 'momentum' and 'kinetic energy,' with their dependence on complex findings that are both experimental and systematically theoretical. Although the practical precepts and behaviors from which my inquiry began also involve many complexities, the resulting concept of action or agency can be given a definition that is kept fixed within the context of the ensuing argument while reflecting the empirical realities on which it is based. For the kinds of phenomena in question are held to be sufficiently understood for the purposes of the inquiry, although if the inquiry were of a different sort (such as metaphysical or psychological), its conclusions would be severely limited in modality by the large penumbra of insufficiently understood features of human action. This limitation to the purposes of the inquiry does not, however, remove the objective reference of the definitions and conclusions, because these are concerned with actions and agents as empirically delimited by the requirements and assumptions of practical precepts.

The legitimacy of such fixity, as opposed to tentativeness, is also supported by a second consideration. The meanings or concepts from which the analytic truth of the *PGC* follows have a normative component. It is more directly from the concept of a rational agent, an agent who can adhere in his judgments to the criteria of deductive and inductive logic, that the various statements are derived that culminate in the *PGC*. Although the criteria of rationality also involve many complexities, these can be restricted for the purposes of the present inquiry, since they largely rest on the basic consideration of consistency in the sense of avoiding self-contradiction. This elemental component, which is logically (although not of course directly morally) normative, gives the ensuing definitions and propositions an invariability that is not affected by the possibility of diverse empirical findings. At the same time the requirement of the capacity for rationality does not exclude any normal human agent, actual or prospective.

The *PGC* is similar to many other analytic statements in having its necessary truth derive not merely from idiosyncratic or even conventional meanings but rather from concepts that signify objective properties. For example, it is an analytic truth that if X is longer than Y and Y is longer than Z, then X is longer than Z; but the transitive meaning of 'longer' on which this truth is based derives not merely from linguistic usage but rather from factual characteristics of this relational property itself. It is because the relation of one thing's being longer than another is transitive and because persons are aware of this transitivity that in their linguistic usage 'longer than' signifies a transitive relation. Similarly, even if my statements are analytic that all behaviors delimited by moral and other practical rules are voluntary and purposive, that agents make implicit claims that they have rights to freedom and well-being, and so forth, this analyticity depends not on my idiosyncratic decisions or even on conventional linguistic usage alone, but rather on the properties of the relevant actions and agents, as signified by the respective concepts. Some analytic truths arise because persons can conceptually understand extralinguistic properties and make linguistic classifications based on that understanding. More generally, to characterize some statement as analytic is by no means necessarily to hold that it is 'purely linguistic' or that there are not good extralinguistic reasons for the classifications of the meanings of the terms comprising the statements.[7]

With other analytic statements, as with the *PGC*, the derivation of their concepts from extralinguistic experience need not entail contingency. The existence of different colors and of comparative lengths is known only through experience; but this still permits such necessary truths as: 'Nothing can be red and green all over,' 'Everything red is extended,' and 'If X is longer than Y and Y is longer than Z, then X is longer than Z.' Such truths are not synthetic, since their being true follows from the meanings of their constituent terms, and these meanings have been fixed by the mind as concepts that signify the relevant empirical properties and relations. Now the experience from which the *PGC* derives, of what practical and moral precepts there are and what their correlative behaviors are like, is obviously more complex and theory-laden than the experience of colors and lengths; and this leads to a much greater possibility of variety and of concomitant need to revise the resultant generalizations. Nevertheless, the classifications of these precepts and behaviors are also affected by conceptual considerations about what can count as relevant precepts and behaviors. These considerations are not arbitrary or 'linguistic.' They lead to assigning certain meanings to 'action,' 'agent,' and so forth; but the considerations are fixed by the complex requirements that enter into being the sorts of practical precepts from which the whole inquiry begins and by the additional requirement of rationality.

3.18. Thus far, I have held that the *PGC* and its entailed moral judgments are analytically true in that their predicates logically follow from the concept of being a rational agent. According to this account, moral judgments are primarily concerned to attribute duties or obligations to agents and correlative rights to their recipients; and these attributions are true if they follow from the concept of what it is to be a rational agent in the ways indicated above. This point may also be put in terms of correspondence. The *PGC* and the moral judgments that follow from it are true in that they correspond to the concept of a rational agent as this is involved in the normative structure of action. For they indicate both what obligations must logically be admitted by every agent, on pain of his contradicting himself, and hence what obligations necessarily pertain to every agent. The concept of a rational agent is in part an empirical concept in the ways indicated above; it is not, like the concept of a triangle, an idealization whose dimensions are not found in any experience.

This correspondence, when more fully developed, indicates a somewhat more complex way in which the *PGC* and its entailed moral judgments may be held to be true not only analytically but also by virtue of correspondence. It was noted earlier that there is a contrast between moral judgments and factual empirical statements in that the latter, unlike the former, can have their truth tested by recourse to empirical facts to which they correspond or (if false) fail to correspond (1.2). The whole of my argument for the *PGC*, however, has undertaken to establish that the generic features of action provide objective, ineluctable contents for testing the truth or correctness of moral judgments, parallel to the objectivity and ineluctability of the contents that observable facts provide for testing empirical and scientific propositions. The generic features of action serve this function not by directly being correspondence-correlates for moral judgments but rather by setting, through the normative structure of action, certain requirements for moral judgments, which must conform to these features on pain of contradiction. For the generic features of action supply necessary premises from which moral judgments logically follow. As we have seen, it is necessarily true of every agent that he regards as good his particular purposes and the freedom and well-being necessary for all his purposive actions; that he hence also holds that he has rights to freedom and well-being; and that he must as a consequence accept certain 'ought'-judgments that logically imply the *PGC*. In this way, action and agency provide the objective content or subject matter that deductively tests the truth or correctness of moral judgments. For all moral judgments, to be true, must be deducible from the *PGC* (although we shall see that this deducibility may take various indirect forms), and the *PGC* is true because it follows from the normative implications of the generic features of action. Thus the problem of the independent variable for moral judgments is solved.

Because of this deductive relation, which underlies the way in which the *PGC* is analytically true in the sense discussed above, it may seem misleading to say that the *PGC* is also true by virtue of corresponding to the concept of an agent and to the generic features of action. If the relation is analogized to that which a theorem in a deductive system bears to the axioms and definitions, it would not be said that the theorem 'corresponds' to these primitives in the way an empirical statement corresponds to the facts that make it true. On the other hand, the concepts of action and agent from which the *PGC* is logically derived have objective empirical correlates in the actual and prospective actions and agents that constitute the subject matter of practical precepts. Consequently, the *PGC* also has these objective correlates, and it is true of them. In this respect the *PGC* is true by virtue of correspondence: it corresponds to what every agent logically must admit to be his duties, and hence it is true as stating the duties that necessarily pertain to every agent.

This basis of the *PGC*'s truth in the generic features of action must be differentiated from the claim sometimes made that moral judgments are true, or at least have their correctness tested, through being in accord with what perons are willing to accept on the basis of their self-interested inclinations or their disinterested ideals. For this basis lacks the invariance and necessity that the generic features of action provide; it would render conflicting moral judgments equally true or correct, as was seen in the above discussions of the Golden Rule. A similar difficulty marks the attempt to base the truth or correctness of moral judgments on their agreeing with the 'considered judgments' or 'qualified attitudes' of 'competent persons' (1.8). The potential relativism and circularity of these positions are avoided by the *PGC*'s derivation from the generic features of action.

3.19. Against the analyticity of the *PGC* the objection may be made that an analytic moral principle cannot serve as a guide to action or as an imperative. For what is analytic is based on an analysis of meaning; but from the fact that a word has a certain meaning nothing follows about what one ought to do, even if the word in question is 'action.' To put it otherwise, an analysis of meanings yields only indicatives about words or concepts, not imperatives or guides to action, so that there is no basis for presenting the *PGC* in the imperative mood or as a practical 'ought'-judgment.

To deal with this objection, it is important to relate correctly the position of the agent and that of the philosopher who analyzes what is involved in being an agent. The philosopher's analysis does, indeed, yield only indicatives, but among these indicatives are statements that point out that agents logically must claim or at least accept that they have certain rights, and such claims of rights can be reformulated as imperatives. The fact that the philosopher presents right-claims only in dialectical statements or indirect discourse—in such a statement as 'Every agent must hold that he has rights to freedom and well-being'— does not militate against the further fact that right-claims logically must, at least implicitly, be made or accepted in direct discourse or assertoric statements by agents, as in 'I have rights to freedom and well-being.' Hence, from the standpoint of the agent the conceptual analysis of his action shows that he logically must accept, as being made by himself, certain right-claims and hence certain 'ought'-judgments and imperatives (summed up in the *PGC*), even though, from the standpoint of the philosopher, the results of such analysis consist only in indicatives or in 'cognitive propositions.'

The agent cannot reject these right-claims and the consequent 'ought'-judgments on the ground that their attribution to him reflects merely the philosopher's linguistic usage or conventional meanings of words. To reject these attributions rationally, the agent would have to deny that he acts for purposes he regards as good and that he has rights to freedom and well-being. But such denials would fly in the face of the purposiveness that characterizes the agent's action and of the indispensability of freedom and well-being to his achieving his purposes. Hence, the agent must admit that he makes or accepts an affirmative, normative claim for his action. It is such normative claims or judgments by agents that conceptual analysis shows to be necessarily involved in action, and these entail the *PGC* in the way traced above. That philosophers are themselves agents and that the agents are assumed to be rational serves further to assimilate the philosopher's indicatives to the agent's imperatives.

3.20. A related argument against the action-guiding capacity of analytic moral principles or judgments is that since they are analytic they must be vacuous, having no substantive content: they are reducible to the form 'What is A is A.' Hence, they cannot tell us to do one thing rather than another. In order to guide action, a judgment or principle must be informative in that it tells us that some independently identifiable action is to be done or not done. If this independent identification of the action cannot be made—that is, if one cannot identify the action without already knowing that it has the moral predicate the judgment attributes to it, then one doesn't know *what* action it is that one ought or ought not to do. For example, an analytic moral judgment, such as 'Murder is wrong,' requires that one already know that the action in question is wrong, since 'murder' simply means wrongful killing. Hence, it amounts to saying that killing one ought not to do is something one ought not to do. But it doesn't enable one to identify *which* is the sort of killing one ought not to do. Hence, it cannot serve to guide one's action.[8]

The *PGC*'s subject-term does not signify an action but rather signifies the agent; its predicate-term signifies the obligations he incurs by virtue of being an agent. Even so, inasmuch as the *PGC* is analytic it is reducible to: 'A person who ought to act in accord with his recipients' generic rights . . . ought to act in accord with his recipients' generic rights.' And this is still of the form 'What is A is A.'

Despite having this form, the *PGC* is not vacuous. To see this, we must note the distinctions between explicitly and implicitly analytic statements and between logical and psychological vacuity. In an implicitly analytic statement, such as 'Every (Euclidean) triangle has angles that are equal to two right angles,' the predicate is deducible from the definition of the subject only through several intermediate steps, and this may be psychologically quite informative. In such statements one can identify the referent of the subject in terms, say, of concepts A and B without already being aware that the subject logically or implicitly also contains concepts X, Y, and Z. It follows from this that the *PGC* can give practical guidance, since it is only implicitly analytic. For, as we have seen, the referent of its subject-term, the agent, can be identified independently of our being aware that the moral predicate applies to him. This point holds also when the subject-term of a moral judgment signifies a kind of action. For if the judgment is only implicitly analytic, the kind of action the statement says is right or wrong can be identified independent of our being aware that the moral predicate applies to that kind of action. Thus, in specific reference to the *PGC*, we can know that a transaction is such that the recipient is coerced or harmed by it, independent of knowing that such a transaction is at least prima facie wrong; and yet its prima facie wrongness follows logically from the *PGC*, which is itself implicitly analytic by virtue of the concepts of 'action,' 'agent,' and 'reason,' as shown above.

It may be objected that on this view the *PGC* would not apply to all agents, that the word 'agent' would be equivocal as used in the *PGC* and in other, including opposed, moral principles and judgments, and indeed that there would not really be any moral principles that disagree with the *PGC*. For the very meaning of 'agent,' in the view just presented, includes that one is a person who ought to act in accord with his recipients' generic rights. But persons who deny the *PGC* would not agree to this meaning for 'agent.' Hence, when the *PGC* says that agents ought to act in accord with their recipients' generic rights and when other moral principles hold that it is not the case that agents ought to act in this way, the principles would really not be disagreeing with one another, since they would not be referring to the same persons as 'agents.'

This objection overlooks that 'agents' may be defined, and hence agents may be identified, in terms that at least explicitly are morally neutral, and hence without explicitly including in the definitions the *PGC*'s moral predicate. Thus both proponents and opponents of the *PGC* can agree that agents are persons who initiate or control their behaviors by their own unforced choice, knowing the proximate circumstances of their behavior and intending thereby to achieve certain preferred outcomes. Where proponents and opponents would differ is that the latter would not have followed out the logical implications of this definition of 'agents.' This would be, at least in important part, a failure of rationality.

3.21. A further objection against the analyticity of the *PGC* as a moral principle is the following. Any moral or other practical principle must be such that it is possible for the persons addressed by the principle both to obey it and to violate it. If both these alternatives are not available to the persons addressed, then there is no point in having or setting forth the principle. But it is logically impossible to violate an analytic moral principle. For a principle to be violated is for something (an action or a refraining from action) to occur that is the opposite of what the principle requires. But the opposite of what an analytic moral principle requires is self-contradictory, and what is self-contradictory cannot occur. Hence, violations of analytic moral principles cannot occur.[9]

In reply, it must be pointed out that there is a crucial ambiguity in the statement, 'the opposite of what an analytic moral principle requires is self-contradictory.' This statement is correct if by the 'what' in question is meant the *whole content* of the principle itself; for example, the negation of 'One ought to refrain from wrong killing' or of 'An agent ought to act in accord with his recipients' generic rights' is self-contradictory. But the statement is incorrect if by the 'what' is meant the *action* referred to in the principle; the opposite of refraining from wrong killing or from coercing one's recipient is not itself self-contradictory. Although, as we saw above, an agent who violates the *PGC* denies in effect that his recipient has the generic rights (3.3), the self-contradiction the agent incurs thereby pertains to his negative judgment, not to his action taken by itself. Hence, one can violate an analytic moral principle even though to deny the principle, or to affirm its opposite, is to contradict oneself.

It is important in this respect to be clear about the relation between a principle or rule and its violation. In the case of a rule of the form 'One ought not to do X' or 'Doing X is wrong,' its violation consists in doing X, not in bringing it about that doing X is not wrong. Hence, the violation of the rule is not affected by the relation between doing X and wrongness, since it consists only in doing X. But what makes a moral rule analytic is the relation between an agent or an action and his or its deontic predicate, and this relation is not affected by whether or not the action is performed. Thus, even in the case of an explicitly analytic moral rule like 'Wrong killing is wrong,' or 'Wrong killing ought not to be done,' its violation consists in wrong killing, not in bringing it about that wrong killing is not wrong. What is self-contradictory or logically impossible is that it not be the case that an agent who ought to perform some action ought to perform it, or that an action that is wrong be not wrong, not that the action be performed. But when one performs a wrong action one does not thereby make the action not wrong. Hence, the performance of a wrong action or the violation of an analytic moral rule is not a case of doing what is contradictory or logically impossible.

These considerations apply directly to the *PGC*. An agent who denies or refuses to accept the *PGC* contradicts himself because he holds that a right that belongs to him insofar as he fulfills a certain description, and that hence belongs to all persons who fulfill that description, does not belong to another person who fulfills that description. But this contradiction pertains to the content of his beliefs, which is a logical matter; it does not affect the fact that his action occurs, removing the right in question from the person to whom it rightfully belongs. His action does not make right or not wrong what is wrong—this would indeed be self-contradictory. But in performing his violative action, even if he says that his action is right, his violation consists in removing from someone a right that rightfully belongs to the latter, not in bringing it about that that right does not rightfully belong to him. To put it otherwise, the analyticity of a moral rule or principle essentially involves its normative, not its empirical, content, its rightness or wrongness, not the empirical facts that enter into it. To violate the rule or principle consists in bringing or refraining from bringing certain empirical facts into existence—for example, in assaulting or failing to rescue someone. But what is analytic about the rule or principle turns not on the existence of the facts, but on a certain moral predicate's pertaining to the facts.

Because of this relation of the moral predicate to its subject, the violation of an analytic moral principle may also be construed in another way. It may mean not that one performs an action the principle prohibits, or that one fails to perform an action the principle requires, but rather that one acts according to the denial or negation of the principle. This, however, would be to act according to two mutually exclusive moral predicates applied to the same action. Since the negation of an analytic moral principle is self-contradictory, to act according to the principle's negation is indeed impossible, for it would mean that one both performs and does or may not perform the same action. Thus, the negation of 'One ought to refrain from wrong killing' is, 'It is not the case that one ought to refrain from wrong killing.' Here, if one acts according to the predication of 'wrong' to the killing, then one definitely must refrain from the killing; but if one acts according to 'It is not the case that one ought to refrain from' that killing, then it is left open to one to perform that same killing. But it is logically impossible that one both refrain from and perform the same action, so that it is logically impossible to act according to the denial or negation of an analytic moral principle. Here, however, the violative action bears on the whole content of the principle's negation, and hence on its applying to the same action two mutually exclusive moral predicates that make two conflicting practical provisions concerning the same action. This is not the same as the previous case where the violative action consisted only in the action directly referred to in the principle. The fact that violations of an analytic moral principle cannot occur in the former sense does not remove that they can occur in the latter sense.

This consideration also applies to the *PGC*. It is logically impossible to violate it in the sense of acting according to its denial, for this denial amounts to saying that it is not the case that a person who ought to act in accord with his recipients' generic rights ought to act in accord with those rights. If someone were to act as this denial says, he would both have to refrain from interfering with his recipients' freedom and well-being and possibly not refrain from such interfering. But although violation of the *PGC* cannot occur in this sense, it can occur in the other sense indicated above, so that the *PGC*'s analyticity does not prevent it from being a practical moral principle.

3.22. It may also be objected that to regard moral principles and judgments as analytic and hence as logically necessary is to attribute to them a much more stringent modality than that found in natural science. But this is anomalous. As philosophers since Aristotle have emphasized, each discipline must seek only that degree of precision its subject matter admits of. Since the subject matter of ethics is human actions and institutions, which involve much more variation than the subject matter of the natural sciences (let alone mathematics), the moral principles and judgments that ethics propounds must be correspondingly variable and contingent.

In reply, it must be noted that there is another tradition (to which belong philosophers as otherwise different as Locke and Kant and also, possibly, Plato), which regards moral judgments as necessarily true. In one respect there is no irreconcilable disagreement between the two traditions, since the contingency Aristotle emphasizes pertains to the context where moral rules are applied to particular cases amid all the variable circumstances in which they are involved, whereas the necessity the other tradition emphasizes pertains rather to the ultimate principles themselves from which the particular judgments are derived. Thus with regard to Aristotle's own moral principle that moral virtue consists in a mean "determined by reason [hōrismenē logō] and as the man of practical wisdom would determine it,"[10] this principle surely has for Aristotle a more stringent modality than have the various attempts to determine the mean in particular cases. Correlatively, although the *PGC* has a necessary modality that also pertains to its derivative rules and that transcends the particularities of different times and places, the various applications of the rules to particular cases must take account of the variable historical circumstances that condition the possibilities of fulfilling the rules' requirements. Variabilities also arise in trying to ascertain whether and to what extent the cases have the specific characteristics referred to in the rules. But such ascertainment is itself a rational process controlled by objective features of the subject matter. It is thus distinct from the kind of relativism and hypotheticalness where the validity of moral rules is made to depend on the self-interested desires or the variable institutional backgrounds of the agents to whom the rules are addressed.

3.23. Still another objection to the analyticity of the *PGC* is that even if the freedom from self-contradiction that analyticity assures is the necessary and most basic condition of rational justification, this has no specific bearing on moral justification or rightness. To contradict oneself is to make an intellectual mistake, but this is different from making a moral mistake in the sense of doing what is morally wrong. The immoral person is not necessarily poor at logic or at figuring out how to avoid inconsistency; he is, rather, villainous and lacking in sympathy for others. Even if it could be shown that the range of actions that commit an agent to generic consistency and inconsistency coincides extensionally with the range of actions that are, respectively, morally right and wrong, this would not remove the fact that there is a significant intensional difference between these characterizations and criteria of action.

This objection may be amplified in a way suggested by Hume's critique of rationalist ethics.[11] In arguing that an agent who denies or violates the *PGC* both contradicts himself and does what is morally wrong, I seem to be presupposing this major premise: What is self-contradictory is immoral. But this premise, far from being self-evident, itself requires proof. Hence, the objection concludes, my argument that the *PGC* is analytic so that denial of it is self-contradictory has not yet shown that the *PGC* is the principle of moral rightness or obligation and that violation of it is morally wrong.

In reply, it must first be emphasized that such personal characteristics of moral agents as sympathy, kindness, and the like are indeed admirable both in themselves and as facilitating morally right action. Nevertheless, possession of such qualities is neither a necessary nor a sufficient condition of moral rightness. They differ in this regard from the quality or disposition of respect for other persons that is required by the *PGC*. The crucial difference is that such respect is directly connected with the *PGC* itself as its invariant part or concomitant, in contrast to such highly desirable but not essential qualities as sympathy and kindness. The main concern of a moral principle is with the criteria that ground or justify attributions of moral rightness and wrongness to actions and institutions, regardless of the variable psychological or other qualities that may characterize moral agents. So far as concerns the moral goodness of persons, consisting in certain specific traits of character, this is to be defined by reference to the morally right actions they habitually try to perform (cf. 5.18), so that the criterion of moral rightness is the logically prior consideration.

The central question raised by the above objection concerns the relation between the *PGC*'s content and its form. Its content is obviously morally relevant, in that the *PGC* is concerned with recipients' rights to freedom and well-being and hence to the necessary goods of all action. Why, then, isn't it sufficient for a moral principle to require this content? Why is it necessary, in addition, to introduce the formal component of consistency or, more strictly, the inconsistency that results from denying or violating the principle? If one person coerces or physically harms another, such as by assaulting him, don't we have, in this content, a sufficient basis for a moral judgment, in that one person is removing certain basic goods from another? What does consistency or analyticity add to this?

The answer to this question is that the formal consideration of consistency and inconsistency is indispensable for at least two reasons. First, as we have already seen, without the consideration of the logical inconsistency the agent incurs when he coerces or harms his recipients, the categorical obligatoriness of refraining from these actions cannot be established (as against merely being asserted). To establish this, it must be shown that no person can rightly evade or violate the requirement of refraining from the actions. For this, in turn, it must be shown that judgments which say that the actions are wrong are necessarily true, and the only way to establish this necessary truth is by showing that the denials of the judgments are self-contradictory. Second, without this formal consideration the crucial moral issue of what is the right distribution of goods cannot be adequately treated. When one person assaults another, he brings about a disparity in this transaction's specific distribution of freedom and well-being as between himself and his recipient. To ascertain that this disparity is morally wrong, a consideration other than that of contents is needed; for, after all, so far as concerns the contents of freedom and well-being, the agent adds some of these to himself while removing some of them from his recipient, so that the sum total of the contents may remain the same. And if it is said that what makes the action wrong is not its contents or effects themselves but rather the fact that these are made to befall a human person, there still remains the question of why such treatment of a human person is wrong. Answers which appeal simply to the concept of a human or a rational person do not answer this question, nor does an appeal to intuition.

To establish the moral wrongness of physical assault and other harms requires the principle that all persons have equal rights to freedom and well-being. To establish this distributive principle, in turn, the formal consideration of consistency is both sufficient and necessary, given the substantive background of the generic features and normative structure of action as presented above. That it is sufficient has, of course, been the point of the whole argument leading to the *PGC*. As we have seen, the agent must hold that he has rights to freedom and well-being because he is a prospective purposive agent; he hence must admit, on pain of logical inconsistency, that all prospective purposive agents have these rights. The consideration of contradiction or inconsistency here serves a distributive function, for it shows that the agent cannot justifiably withhold from any other person who is his recipient the rights he upholds for himself, since he logically must extend to every person fulfilling a certain description the predicate of the rights-judgment he applies to himself on the ground of his own fulfilling that description.

That the *PGC*'s consideration of consistency and inconsistency is necessary as well as sufficient for this distributive purpose is shown by the fact that without this consideration no way is provided for conclusively comparing the rights of persons with one another. But such conclusive comparison is required if equality of rights is to be established. Without relevant comparison, equality cannot be proved, and without conclusiveness, the comparison leaves the equality of rights as dispensable. But, as we have seen, in order to make relevant comparisons among persons with regard to their having the generic rights, it must be shown that being a prospective purposive agent is the quality that is decisively relevant as the sufficient condition for claiming these rights; and for this purpose it must be shown that the agent contradicts himself if he denies this decisiveness. Once this sufficient condition has been established, consistency must again be invoked in order to show conclusively that all prospective agents are equal in having the generic rights. Hence, the logical consideration of consistency is necessary for establishing what is the right distribution of rights and goods, which a person violates when he physically assaults another or otherwise inflicts a basic or specific harm.

The requiredness of the formal consideration of consistency and inconsistency for this distributive purpose can also be suggested inductively by noting the failure of the attempts to ground egalitarianism on empirical correlations without invoking this consideration (1.8). Other arguments for an egalitarian moral principle that do not appeal to inconsistency at crucial points are also unsuccessful. For example, it may be held to be a principle of reason that all persons ought to be treated alike or equally unless there is some good reason for treating them differently or unequally. This principle rests on the still more general principle that cases that are of the same kind ought to be treated in the same way, and being human is held to be such a kind. But not only is this latter principle doubtful of itself, despite its apparent similarity to some of the formal considerations used above; the principle also leaves unspecified what constitutes a 'good reason' for treating persons differently, that is, which subkinds are relevant to differential treatment. Very many differences, including merit, intelligence, sex, and color have been held to be thus relevant, so that the principle can result in drastic inegalitarianism. This result stems from the failure to show that only a certain equally distributed quality is decisively relevant to how persons ought to be treated, such that the denial of this relevance commits one to self-contradiction.

It may also be argued that all persons have equal rights because they are equal in worth or dignity or are equally ends in themselves or children of God. Such normative characterizations, however, reduplicate the doctrine to be justified, that all humans have basic equal rights. If one is doubtful about the latter, one will be at least equally doubtful about the characterizations invoked to justify it. Without the appeal to inconsistency, there is no logical necessity to accept this argument. Similar strictures apply against the attempts to derive egalitarian moral precepts from the concept of a 'human being' or a 'rational person' or even a 'rational agent.' Crucial questions are begged unless it is shown, in the way presented above, just how such concepts conclusively ground moral requirements. In particular, the moral equality of the persons signified by such concepts can be conclusively established only if it can be shown that the persons are equal with regard to the empirical qualities that are decisively relevant to their having rights, and only if the denial of their equally having these rights can be proved to be rationally unjustifiable. For these distributive purposes, as we have seen above, recourse must be had to the consideration of consistency.

Generic consistency in its very concept is a moral as well as a logical requirement, so that the extensional equivalence of the two requirements in the *PGC* is not merely coincidental. For the *PGC* bears not on consistency of beliefs or actions on the part of one person in isolation, but rather on consistency that is transactional and hence interpersonal in connection with the distribution of rights and goods. To be generically inconsistent is to uphold a disparity between the essential conditions of action that one necessarily claims for oneself and what one is willing to concede to others. It is to maintain for oneself the most general rights of action in a transaction with other persons, while denying these rights to the persons who are affected by one's action and who are relevantly similar to oneself. It is therefore to make exceptions in one's own favor with regard to the necessary conditions of purpose-fulfillment, and hence to be unfair to others. To violate the *PGC* is thus to do what is morally as well as logically wrong. Since the criterion of logical consistency provides the necessary condition of the correctness of all principles and judgments, a conclusive proof that violating the *PGC* is morally as well as logically wrong is given by the fact that agents who violate the *PGC* must contradict themselves within the context of interpersonal actions. For this context is central to all morality. This shows that when the logical form of consistency is imposed on the matter of the generic features and normative structure of action, the result of this combination is a principle that is at once logically and morally necessary. The supreme principle is thus ascertained by the use of reason.

3.24. There may still remain a problem about the relation between morality and generic interpersonal consistency. Even if it is acknowledged that the generic inconsistency prohibited by the *PGC* involves the combination of formal and material elements noted above, may not an agent exhibit such inconsistency in a way that favors others over himself? Consider, for example, the saint or hero who subordinates or even sacrifices his own goods to those of other persons. 'I'll go as a hostage instead of you'; 'You shall have the last seat in the lifeboat rather than I.' Here, insofar as the agent and his recipients are prospective purposive agents and he grounds his judgments on this quality, he may be thought to be contradicting himself. For he seems to be saying that his recipients have rights to freedom and well-being that he does not have even though he is relevantly similar to them with regard to the quality that grounds the having of these rights; or at least he seems to hold that he should act in accord with their generic rights but not in accord with his own. His inconsistency here, however, it may be thought, is in the reverse direction from that previously indicated, for he distributes freedom or well-being or both in a way which is disadvantageous to himself and advantageous to his recipients. But such inconsistency, with its accompanying actions, is surely not immoral; on the contrary, it represents the highest form of supererogatory morality. Doesn't this refute the thesis that an interpersonally inconsistent distribution of goods or rights is a morally wrong one?

To deal with this question we must look more closely at the relation between the saint's or hero's supereratory principle and the *PGC*. As we have seen in developing the *PGC*, it is inconsistent for the agent to act in accord with his own generic rights and not in accord with his recipients' generic rights. Now it might be thought that the supererogatory principle is the reverse of this and is hence equally inconsistent. Nevertheless, the saint or hero cannot rationally be interpreted as holding that he should act in accord with his recipients' generic rights and not in accord with his own generic rights. For him to act not in accord with his own generic rights, that is, for him to act in disaccord with or in violation of these rights of his, would mean that in acting he allows other persons to interfere with his freedom and well-being without his consent. Such a nonconsensual abdication of one's generic rights, however, would be not only pointless but impossible. For since his action is voluntary and purposive, this would mean that in some particular action he voluntarily permits himself to be treated involuntarily, or consents to have the necessary conditions of his action removed without his consent. But when a person performs heroic actions like those mentioned above, he consents to these deprivations of his life and liberty, so that they are not cases of his acting in violation of his own generic rights. On the contrary, he still acts in accord with his generic rights, for he still sees to it, so far as he can, that there is no interference with his freedom and well-being without his consent.

The saint or hero is also not saying that in acting as he does he acts in accord with his recipients' generic rights. It is indeed the case that he does not violate their generic rights and in this sense he acts in accord with them; but he also acts beyond what their rights require of him, which is why his action is supererogatory. For when the hero sacrifices his life or liberty for his recipients' sakes, it is not a question of their rights nor hence of his duties in the strict sense. The recipients do indeed have rights to life and liberty, but only in the sense that other persons ought to refrain from interfering with their life and liberty, or ought to assist them to preserve these if this can be done at no comparable cost to themselves, but not in the sense that another person ought to sacrifice his own life and liberty for the sake of theirs. Such sacrifice would involve that the agent sets up a disparity or inequality between himself and his recipients with regard to freedom and well-being in favor of his recipients; but what the PGC requires as a matter of strict duty is that the agent not set up such a disparity in favor of himself. The case of the saint or hero is thus different from that where a person can save someone else's life at no risk of his own (see 5.8 ff.). His self-sacrifice is an act of grace on his part, but not of strict duty, unlike what is required by the PGC and its derived rules and judgments. Hence the agent is not here being generically inconsistent.

Does the PGC, then, provide any basis for either approving or disapproving such supererogatory actions or for recognizing their moral merit? This basis is found in the fact that the PGC requires at least that the agent not distribute freedom or well-being in a way that is to his recipients' disadvantage by giving them less of it in some transaction than he takes for himself. For since it is necessarily true of the agent, so long as he is an agent, that he acts in accord with his own generic rights, the PGC's concern is that he should maintain the conditions of just distribution by not violating his recipients' generic rights. Since supererogatory actions provide overabundant assurance of this result, they are to this extent in conformity with the PGC. The saint or hero acts in the direction indicated by his recipients' generic rights, and he also acts in accord with their generic rights since he both does not interfere with their freedom and well-being without their consent and helps them to have freedom and well-being. But his action goes considerably beyond such noninterference and beyond their strict rights, because he helps them at the risk of losing his own freedom and well-being.

MOTIVATION AND RATIONALITY

3.25. A traditional problem for any doctrine that tries to ground morality on reason is that of accounting for the motivational or prescriptive force of moral judgments. This problem is held to arise from the consideration that in making a moral judgment a person does not merely describe a certain fact or indicate a certain logical relation; rather, he advocates or endorses that some action be performed, he intends to guide, influence, or motivate his hearers to act in some particular way, and in accepting the judgment for himself he has a motivation to perform or to refrain from performing the action as required by his judgment. But if, as Hume held, "reason of itself is utterly impotent"[12] in respect of influencing or guiding actions, it follows that reason alone cannot serve to ground any moral principle or judgment. This conclusion poses a problem for my above argument that purported to justify the *PGC* by showing that any agent who denied it would have to contradict himself; for the argument is an attempt to ground a moral principle on logical consistency and hence on deductive reason.

Without going into the meaning or merits of Hume's dictum on its own account, it must be noted that in the context of my argument the problem specifically arises in the following way. Motivational or prescriptive force is obviously present in several of the crucial steps leading to the justification of the *PGC*. When the agent says 'I have rights to freedom and well-being,' he makes or accepts the statement for his own self-interested reasons, or at least for reasons bearing on his pursuit of his own purposes, so that he here advocates or endorses that he have these rights. A similar motivational or prescriptive force may be attributed to the 'ought'-judgment entailed by this right-claim—'All other persons ought at least to refrain from interfering with my having freedom and well-being'—since this 'ought' too is upheld by the agent with a view to his own self-interest or at least to his being able to pursue his own purposes. The case is different, however, with the subsequent step where the agent's right-claim entails the generalization, 'All prospective purposive agents have rights to freedom and well-being.' For this generalized judgment is not set forth by the agent for his pursuit of his own purposes or for his own self-interested reasons; on the contrary, it imposes restrictions on his acting for these purposes or reasons. Hence, since he does not endorse the generalization for such reasons, in what way can its use of the expression 'have rights' be understood to carry for the agent the prescriptive or motivational force his individual right-claim carried for him? And since the PGC is derived by entailment from the generalized rights-judgment, the same question applies to it: Why will the agent uphold or accept the PGC if he has no motivation for doing so based on his own self-interest or, more generally, on his pursuit of his own purposes?

It may seem, then, that in the absence of such motivational or prescriptive force the PGC is not a moral or practical principle, regardless of its rational status as being impossible to deny without self-contradiction. It may also seem that the lack of acceptance or advocacy by the agent creates a crucial gap in my argument, since I am proceeding by a dialectically necessary method that throughout remains within the standpoint of the individual agent and what he must accept. It may also be held that the authoritative question of why one should be moral has not yet been answered, since my answer that acceptance of the PGC is required by reason (3.5) does not indicate any motivation for the agent.

In dealing with this problem, it is important to note its limitations. As we have seen, the PGC keeps the opposition to self-interest within careful bounds because it requires of the agent not that he sacrifice his freedom or well-being to that of other persons but rather that he refrain from removing freedom or well-being from other persons for his own self-interest, and that he assist other persons at no comparable cost to himself when they cannot have well-being by their own efforts. The PGC thus provides for a parity of freedom and well-being between the agent and his recipients. The question, then, is how, apart from an appeal to the agent's self-interest, the constraints the PGC imposes on the agent's actions are compatible with the PGC's having prescriptive force for him and with his having a corresponding motivation for accepting it.

3.26. As an initial answer to this question, it might be suggested that the PGC must have prescriptive force for the agent because it follows logically from his individual right-claim, which admittedly has prescriptive force for him. Now it is indeed important for the motivational basis of the PGC that it is derived from the agent's prescriptive right-claim. Moreover, as will be seen below, this answer is correct if it is properly interpreted. But, taken in the unqualified form just given, the answer is unsuccessful, because maintenance of illocutionary force (of which prescriptive force is a species) is not required for logical entailment. Thus, in such an argument as, 'If X is good, I'll buy it; X is good; therefore I'll buy it,' the force or use of 'good' in the first premise is not commendatory or prescriptive, while in the second premise it is; nevertheless the argument is valid. Hence, the fact that the *PGC* is entailed by the agent's prescriptive individual right-claim does not prove that the *PGC* must itself have prescriptive force for him. Indeed, the agent might hold that he advocates or endorses rights only when they are his own, so that regardless of his right-claim's entailing rights for other persons, he does not uphold the latter, since he has no motive for doing so.

It still remains the case, nevertheless, that there would be what I have previously called a kind of illocutionary equivocation (2.11) if the agent gave unqualified endorsement to his individual rights-claim and gave no endorsement at all or only a qualified endorsement to the generalized rights-judgment and the *PGC* that are entailed by it. The situation here is parallel to, although not identical with, the problem I noted above for the universal ethical egoist who gives unqualified endorsement to his acting for his own self-interest but only qualified endorsement to other persons' acting for their self-interest. The solution to this problem is likewise found in a consideration parallel to that adduced in the discussion of the universal egoist's dilemmas. It will be recalled that in competitive games each competitor believes both that his rivals ought to make certain moves and that he himself ought to prevent their making those moves. Both these 'oughts' were seen to be qualified ones in that they were upheld within the context or principle of the rules and objectives of the game with their requirements about certain moves and countermoves. Hence both 'oughts' have similar illocutionary force, since they give prescriptions whose endorsing character is qualified through their being derived from the same more general prescriptive principle.

This way of avoiding illocutionary equivocation also pertains to the agent's various rights-judgments and correlative 'oughts,' both those that uphold rights for himself and those that generalize these rights to other prospective agents. For all these rights-judgments are made within the context of the agent's overall acceptance of rationality in the sense indicated earlier. This is true even of his individual judgment wherein he claims for himself the rights to freedom and well-being; for, as we have seen, he is logically required to make or accept this judgment from within his own standpoint of purposive agency. To be sure, this step is dependent upon his valuing of his general purpose-fulfillment; but, as we have also seen, this valuing is itself a logical consequence of his engaging in purposive action. Thus there is no divorce between his commitment to rationality and his conative pursuit of his purposes. And on the same rational grounds he likewise endorses the generalized rights-judgment that all other prospective purposive agents also have rights to freedom and well-being, since this judgment follows logically from his individual right-claim. He accepts as prescriptive for himself all the rights- and 'ought'-judgments traced above because all of them are required by that minimal rationality that he unqualifiedly accepts. His endorsement of all these judgments is, then, qualified by this general context of rationality. Hence they all have the same prescriptive force for him, so that he avoids illocutionary ambiguity. At the same time, as was noted earlier, his acceptance of rationality, far from being an arbitrary 'commitment,' rests on the consideration that it is the only sure way of avoiding arbitrariness and attaining objectivity and truth (1.9).

This point may be further developed in the following way. As rational, the agent understands and accepts certain basic logical criteria, including especially the principle of contradiction. To say that the agent accepts these criteria is to say that he recognizes them as justificatory grounds for conclusions based on the criteria, so that insofar as he assents to any premises, he acknowledges the requirement that he also assent to certain conclusions when they follow from the premises according to these criteria. This is equivalent to saying that for the rational agent, his recognition that a conclusion is grounded according to such criteria carries prescriptive force; he endorses the conclusion as logically correct, valid, or justified. Hence, since the *PGC* logically follows from the agent's individual right-claim, the agent must assent to and endorse the *PGC*. The point is not that the *PGC*, to be entailed by the individual right-claim, must share the latter's prescriptiveness, but rather that the agent rationally must accept the *PGC* because it is entailed by another statement he accepts.

It may still be asked how this logical prescriptiveness is related to the prescriptiveness that was based on the agent's self-interested reasons. The latter are obviously practical; they are directly relevant to what the agent is prepared to claim and do with a view to pursuing his own purposes. But the former prescriptiveness, grounded on recognition and acceptance of logically valid arguments, is merely theoretical, although the context within which it occurs is the practical one of the generic features of action. There still remains, then, the question of how the logical prescriptiveness has any practical relevance in the sense of why any person would or should act according to its specific contents.

This point may also be put in terms of such last-ditch questions as,

'Why should I care if I contradict myself? Why should I be rational anyway?' Even if the agent's individual right-claim entails the judgment that all other persons also have rights to freedom and well-being, the agent's denial of or refusal to accept the latter judgment will at most make it impossible for him consistently to uphold his individual right-claim. But this inconsistency will not necessarily affect adversely his ability to maintain his freedom and well-being and hence to act in pursuit of his purposes; it bears not on the practical efficacy of his action but only on the logical justifiability of his judgments. Hence, it may be held that the *PGC* with its consideration of logical consistency provides only a reason for making certain judgments but not a reason for acting in accordance with them.

In addition to the general point that in asking 'Why?' one asks for a reason and to this extent accepts the criteria of rationality, this attempted divorce between reasons for judgment and reasons for action cannot be maintained. When a person makes a judgment that he ought to do X (where this 'ought' is more than prima facie), he judges that he has a conclusive reason for doing X. Insofar as he accepts the judgment with its reasons, he accepts that he has this reason for action, so that, in his own view, he has a conclusive reason for doing X. Now since the logical criterion of avoiding self-contradiction takes precedence over all other justificatory criteria (for logical consistency is the necessary condition of all justifications), an 'ought'-judgment about certain required actions whose conclusiveness is based on this criterion presents a conclusive reason not only for judging that such actions ought to be done but also for doing the actions. Hence, every agent has a conclusive reason both for judging that he ought to act as the *PGC* requires and for acting as the *PGC* requires.

This point is reinforced because of the centrality of justifying reasons in the structure of action. The very purposes for which the agent acts, and which he regards as good, constitute for him at least tentative justifying reasons for his actions. More directly, his holding that he has rights to freedom and well-being is based on justifying reasons consisting in the indispensability of these generic features to his pursuit of his purposes. But since the most basic criterion of justificatory reasons is the principle of contradiction, in that no reasons can be justified or correct if they are self-contradictory, it follows that the agent cannot have a justified position—he cannot adhere to the justificatory criteria to which his engaging in purposive action commits him—if he contradicts himself. Consequently, the agent must care about being rational and avoiding self-contradiction if he is to engage in action, as against going through motions that he emits with no control exerted by him for purposes he regards as good.

In dealing with the question of how the agent's adherence to rational criteria bears on the prescriptiveness of the *PGC*, it is important to distinguish between positive and normative interpretations of prescriptiveness. On the positive interpretation, what is prescriptive is a factual, empirical question of what some person, including the agent, accepts or is likely to accept either as theoretically valid or as practically required of him. The answers to this question are in part contingent; they depend on variable considerations of the agent's particular attitudes, conditioning, intelligence, and so forth. On the normative interpretation, however, what is prescriptive is a question of what the agent is logically required to accept either theoretically or practically or both. On this interpretation, even if as a matter of positive fact the agent ignores or flouts what is rationally justified, he nevertheless ought to uphold it and hence ought to regard it as being prescriptive for him, since its being rationally justified is tantamount to his being logically required to accept it. This 'ought,' it must be noted, is a rational, not a moral, 'ought.' Thus, when the agent recognizes that the generalized rights-statement and the *PGC* are entailed by the individual rights-statement that is positively prescriptive for him because of his own purposes or self-interested reasons, the generalized rights-statement and the *PGC* then become normatively prescriptive for him.

This distinction between positive and normative prescriptiveness is in part parallel to Hutcheson's distinction between 'exciting reasons' and 'justifying reasons'[13] and hence to the distinction between motivation and justification. It also goes back to Plato's and Aristotle's distinctions between rhetoric (concerned with persuasion) and dialectic (concerned with truth).[14] I am saying, in part, that the question whether the *PGC* is rationally justified is distinct from the question whether the agent is directly motivated or influenced to accept it. But I am also saying that by virtue of the *PGC*'s being rationally justified the rational agent is in fact motivated to accept it, since, being rational, he accepts what is rationally justified. And I am saying further that every agent ought to be motivated to accept the *PGC*, where the criterion of this 'ought' is initially not moral but rational or logical. The normative concept of prescriptiveness is hence a way of bringing justification and motivation together.

The *PGC* can also be made positively prescriptive for agents through laws and education. And the rationality on which its normative prescriptiveness rests may lead in a more direct way to its becoming positively prescriptive for agents, for the *PGC* does not require for its effectiveness a blunting or distorting of man's rational nature, as do opposed moral principles. The agent will advocate or endorse the *PGC*, he will regard it as prescriptive for himself, when his rationality is allowed to develop so that its criteria become effectively binding for him. In addition, the *PGC* can become self-reinforcing, for the social institutions based on it (to be discussed below) serve in turn to give it practical support.

It must also be noted that the *PGC*, because of its derivation, is in any case not open to the strictures of Hume and other critics of ethical rationalism. Their main targets were construals of moral principles as rationally self-evident or as justified solely through having certain logical properties, and their objection was that such construals cannot show how moral principles "have an influence on the actions and affections." The *PGC*, however, is not presented as self-evident, nor is it justified as a moral principle solely through its denial's being self-contradictory. Rather, an intrinsic part of the principle's justification rests on its having a necessary content referring to the freedom and well-being that every agent must regard as his rights. This content is a direct source of human motivations, and the principle is derived from the agent's judgments that directly reflect these motivations. Beginning from his statements that he acts for various purposes, which are the objects of his conative strivings, the argument has shown that every agent logically must accept certain value-judgments and prescriptive right-claims that in turn entail the *PGC*. Thus, the agent can reject the *PGC* only by surrendering the logical right to uphold these evaluative and prescriptive judgments, so that the principle's proximate logical basis is in judgments that express the purposive strivings necessarily characteristic of all agents. Because of this basis and content, the *PGC*'s derivation shows how reason can be practical; but 'reason' now includes not only logical form but also the conative content, itself ascertained by conceptual analysis, that in the argument is necessarily combined with this form.

3.27. Let us now consider a final objection bearing not on the *PGC*'s motivational force but rather on the relation between logical consistency and rationality. The objection is that avoidance of self-contradiction is not a necessary condition of all rational justification, since it may sometimes be rational to contradict oneself. A Machiavellian ruler, for example, may find it expedient to make mutually inconsistent statements when this advances his end of maximizing his power. Since a basic kind of rationality is the use of efficient means for achieving one's ends, such self-contradiction is rational. It may be further objected that under certain conditions self-contradiction is even morally right. For example, A says to B's friend, 'B is in this house'; shortly thereafter, when an armed gangster C comes looking for B in order to murder him, A says to C, 'B is not in this house.' Since A's statement to C prevents a murder and is intended to do so, A's self-contradiction is morally justified.

There are two replies to the Machiavellian case. One is that, so far as the ruler is aware, his own reasons for making mutually inconsistent statements are not themselves inconsistent or self-contradictory. He would not regard his reasons as justified or correct if they entailed or had as their effect that he would thereby both increase and fail to increase his power. Hence, the ruler implicitly accepts, as more authoritative for his action, the requirement of consistency in his reasons for action, even if at a lower level the statements he makes as instrumentally justified by these reasons are themselves inconsistent. Second, since the statements are intended by him to increase his power over other persons, there remains the question of the justification of this interpersonal end or purpose and hence of the transactions he initiates for its sake. If the purpose and transactions are such that they enmesh the ruler in inconsistency, then they cannot be rationally justified despite their contribution to his purpose of maximizing his power. Although the political applications of the *PGC* involve various complexities, some of which are discussed in chapter 5, the inconsistency of the Machiavellian ruler's purpose can be brought out by the consideration that it commits him to holding both that he has rights to freedom and well-being qua prospective purposive agent and that other prospective purposive agents do not have rights to freedom and well-being. Since any justificatory differences he adduces between them and himself must, if relevant, be justifiable through the *PGC*, the Machiavellian ruler necessarily fails the test of such justification and hence of rationality.

This point is also pertinent to the case of A's making mutually inconsistent statements in order to save B's life. When A says to C, 'B is not in this house,' A intentionally says what is false and intentionally contradicts himself; yet his saying this is rationally justified because he is trying to prevent a murder. It is important to note here that the *PGC*, through its generic content, provides for degrees of moral urgency. Murder is the most extreme case of an agent's acting in accord with his own generic rights while violating his recipient's rights and hence incurring a transactional generic inconsistency. For while claiming rights of freedom and well-being for himself qua prospective purposive agent, the murderer completely removes these rights from another prospective purposive agent. A's factual self-contradiction, then, is rationally justified because it helps to prevent this extreme transactional inconsistency and thus to maintain consistency, so that it is incurred in the service of the *PGC*.

To be sure, lying is itself a violation of the *PGC*, since A's lying to C enables A to maintain his own capabilities of purposive action while lowering those of C. Nevertheless, in the situation as described, A's contradicting himself by lying to C is subordinate, in respect of rational justification, to A's saving C's life by the action, and the reason for this is found in the generic content of the *PGC*. For the purposes or goods fulfilled by preventing a murder are more basic than those that would be fulfilled by telling the truth or by being propositionally consistent in this situation. Moreover, since A's lying is done for the sake of preventing a murder and is authorized by the *PGC*, this makes A relevantly different from C, so that A does not incur the inconsistency of upholding rights for himself while denying them to a relevantly similar person. This example makes clear the points stressed above: that the formal consistency requirement must be considered together with its generic content, and that the latter as well as the former is an application of reason.

The main phase of the project of this book is now completed: to show that determinate criteria of moral rightness are logically derived from the generic features of action. Every agent, by the fact of engaging in action, is logically committed to the acceptance of certain evaluative and deontic judgments and ultimately of a moral principle which requires that he respect in his recipients the same generic features of action, freedom and well-being, that as rational he necessarily claims as rights for himself. By virtue of this logical necessity, the *PGC* is rationally justified as a categorically obligatory moral principle.

4

DIRECT APPLICATIONS OF THE PRINCIPLE

Kinds of Applications and Principles

4.1. The arguments presented above have shown that the Principle of Generic Consistency satisfies the conditions for being the supreme principle of morality, in that it provides conclusive and determinate answers to the central questions of moral philosophy. But the principle must also undergo an a posteriori inquiry to ascertain whether it is adequate for explicating and evaluating all morally relevant actions and institutions in a consistent and conflict-resolving way. Such an inquiry is especially important because, as a complex principle combining rights of freedom and of well-being on the part of both agents and recipients, the *PGC* faces the problem of the inherent consistency of these combinations. And because the principle is maximally general in scope, whereas morality is ultimately a matter of how persons ought to act in particular situations, the practical moral significance of the principle emerges only in what it requires of persons in particular cases.

In tracing these applications, there is an important place for the inductive confrontation of the supreme principle with widely held beliefs and judgments about lower-level moral rules. Although these beliefs are by no means infallible and may conflict with one another, they provide valuable further tests for the principle insofar as they stem in varied measure from a historical and ongoing arena of discussion and debate that fosters reflective thought. It may, indeed, be contended that persons are far surer of their particular moral beliefs than they are of any supreme principle, including the *PGC*, and that accordingly they are far less willing to surrender or modify the beliefs. Even if this contention is true, there still remains the question of the justification of such an attitude. Since there is an essential difference between the *PGC* and other moral principles because of the way the former was derived, the justification of the attitude where it is directed to utilitarianism and other overly one-sided principles need not tell against the *PGC*.

Both because of the *PGC*'s own content and because the great variety of the subject matter of morality is found both within and outside various institutions, the *PGC*'s implications for particular actions are not all of a simple deductive kind. In general, its applications are of two different sorts, direct and indirect. In the direct applications, the *PGC*'s requirements are imposed upon the interpersonal actions of individual persons. According to these applications, actions are morally right and their agents fulfill their moral obligations if they act in accord with their recipients' generic rights, allowing the recipients to participate in their transactions with freedom and well-being. In the indirect applications, the *PGC*'s requirements are imposed upon various social rules that govern multiperson activities and institutions, and the requirements of these rules in turn are imposed upon the actions of individuals who participate in the activities and institutions in accordance with their governing rules. Thus, the *PGC* is here applied to the actions of individual persons only through the mediation of social rules. These rules are morally justified, and the persons who act according to them fulfill their moral obligations, when the rules conform to the *PGC*'s requirements that agents act in accord with the generic rights of their recipients as well as of themselves. Such conformity of the rules to the *PGC* may occur in different ways, which will be examined in due course.

There is a certain parallelism between the distinction of direct from indirect applications of the *PGC* and the distinction of act-utilitarianism from rule-utilitarianism. In act-utilitarianism, the Principle of Utility is applied directly to individual actions, whereas in rule-utilitarianism, the Principle of Utility is applied directly to rules that in turn are applied to actions, the rules being justified when they conform to the Principle of Utility. Nevertheless, there are several important differences. The applications of the Principle of Utility, whether in act- or in rule-utilitarianism, are only aggregative: they consist simply in maximizing utility, either directly in individual actions or indirectly through rules. This maximizing must be maintained with no independent concern for distributive considerations; hence, the requirements of distributive justice may be violated. The applications of the *PGC*, on the other hand, are of several different kinds, by virtue of the complexity of the *PGC* itself. But they put central emphasis on distributive considerations, on equality between agent and recipient with regard to the rights of freedom and well-being. Although in some contexts of application this equality must be maximized, in others it figures in quite different ways. A further difference is that the logical basis of the Principle of Utility itself and hence of its various applications is left indeterminate. The applications of the *PGC*, on the other hand, reflect throughout its inherently rational structure. To uphold violations of the *PGC* at any level is to contradict oneself.

4.2. I shall now compare the *PGC*'s applications somewhat further both with utilitarianism and with various deontological theories. Although the full understanding at least of the *PGC*'s side of these comparisons must await the more detailed working out of the applications I present below, it may be helpful at this stage to list some of the main points of contrast. Three differences deserve special emphasis. The first bears on the recipients, the persons to whom moral duties are owed. For utilitarianism, these recipients are all of mankind, or perhaps even all sentient beings indiscriminately, since its basic precept is simply that each person ought to maximize utility as far as possible. In a related way, when Kant's categorical imperative makes the test of the moral rightness of actions consist in whether their maxims can be universalized, this involves that the agent must consider not merely the specific recipient of his specific action, but rather the import of such an action's being performed by all persons fulfilling some relevant description (such as liars), and hence its being undergone by all persons complementary to that description (such as those lied to).[1] The *PGC*, in contrast, focuses on the specific duty owed by the agent to his particular recipient, whether it be keeping his promise, refraining from inflicting physical injury, helping to ward off danger, or any other. For the *PGC* requires that the agent act in accord with the generic rights of his recipients and not of all mankind; it is hence to the particular recipients of his actions that he owes noncoercion, nonharm, and aid. Although at some points the general tendencies and social contexts of actions must be considered, this is only to bring out more clearly their moral import for the particular recipients in each case.

This particularizing emphasis corresponds more closely to the nature of many moral duties as they actually confront the agent, including especially the requirements of distributive justice. Its central relevance is not affected by the traditional distinction between 'real' and 'personal' rights, where the former are rights of noninterference against all mankind.[2] For the universality that figures in this distinction bears on the agents who are the respondents of the rights, not on the recipients who are the subjects or holders of the rights. It is a matter of what every person ought to refrain from doing to some particular person, not of what some particular person ought to refrain from doing to all mankind. Thus, both in this distinction and in the *PGC* more generally it is still to the individual person or recipient that the agent has a duty. There may, of course, be cases where his actions affect the rights of many persons beyond his immediate environment (3.1). One of the ways in which this more extensive social dimension especially affects moral duties is when the agent must act in conformity with morally justified legal and other rules that set requirements for an agent not toward a particular recipient but toward more extensive groups of persons, especially when these have certain roles in accordance with various institutions. This dimension is provided for in the indirect or social applications of the *PGC*, without, however, erasing its difference from the agent's moral duties to particular recipients, including the requirements of distributive justice.

A second differentia of the *PGC* bears on the contents of moral duties. Formal deontological theories,[3] requiring simply that moral rules have such logical characteristics as consistency or fulfill such formal requirements as equality, either omit or tend to deemphasize the contents of these rules, the substantive features of the actions that agents ought to perform or refrain from performing. They hence leave obscure the relation of moral requirements to ongoing human purposive strivings. Material deontological theories do specify contents for moral duties, but these contents do not consist in or refer to axiological factors as such, factors of nonmoral goods or values that are ordinarily objects of desire and provide motives for action. The agent is required, for example, to keep his promise because it is a promise, not because of any good involved in or caused by the act of promise-keeping. Utilitarianism, on the other hand, does provide an axiological content for moral duties. But in many utilitarian theories, this content is put simply as the doing of good and avoidance of evil, with either no specification of what these goods and evils consist in or some very general ones, like pleasure or happiness, which are notoriously difficult to specify. Nor is there any guarantee that the good utilitarianism requires to be done to recipients will correspond to their own conceptions or desires as to what is good.

In contrast to these theories, the *PGC*, in requiring that every agent act in accord with the generic rights of his recipients, provides an axiological content for moral duties and specifies this in terms of the freedom and the well-being, including the drive toward purpose-fulfillment, that figure in all purposive actions. Each of these commits the agent to take favorable account of his recipient's wishes, since the recipient normally does not want to be coerced or to undergo deterioration of his abilities to have basic, nonsubtractive, and additive goods. Hence, the substantive content of moral duties as set forth by the *PGC* is in part relative to the recipient's wishes as well as having important invariant elements. In addition, where for utilitarianism, as for other teleological theories, the contents of moral duties depend on the total consequences either of particular actions or of the general performance of kinds of actions, for the *PGC* moral duties have a direct axiological content, since they require respect for the freedom and well-being of each individual recipient, so that once again the sustantive requirements of distributive justice have primacy.

A third difference of the *PGC* bears on the justificatory ground of moral duties. Both the *PGC* and utilitarianism include in this ground a reference to goods and evils. But utilitarianism leaves unclear just how this axiological content yields duties—how that which is good bears on that which ought to be done, either in particular cases or especially by way of maximization to achieve the 'general good.' There are familiar difficulties in Mill's argument from each individual's desiring his own happiness to the conclusion that the general happiness is desirable as the ultimate end and the criterion of right and wrong. Parallel difficulties arise for Sidgwick's argument that the egoist who holds his own happiness is good "from the point of view of the Universe" must admit that "*his* happiness cannot be a more important part of Good, taken universally, than the equal happiness of any other person." As Sidgwick pointed out, the egoist need not consider his own happiness from this universal point of view.[4]

The *PGC*, on the other hand, combines the axiological substantive content of moral duties with a formal consideration of consistency or mutuality. It is not only that the agent must act in accord with his recipient's rights to freedom and well-being; what gives this its justificatory basis is that the agent also, and necessarily, acts in accord with his own rights to freedom and well-being. According to the *PGC*, there must be an equality between agent and recipient in respect of being treated in accord with the rights each of them has to freedom and well-being. The agent's moral duty to his recipients can thus be explicated and justified in terms of the inconsistency he necessarily incurs if he infringes this distributive mutuality by violating his recipients' generic rights while acting in accord with his own generic rights. The *PGC*, unlike utilitarianism and material deontological theories, hence contains within itself the ground of its necessity; it is self-justifying. It requires not only that the agent apply a certain content to his recipients—that of respecting their freedom and well-being—but that he render it with a certain distributive form or proportion as between himself and his recipients. Since the agent necessarily applies this content to himself, and since his failure to apply it to his recipients results in self-contradiction, the agent cannot rationally or justifiably extricate himself from the *PGC*'s requirements, and it is this necessary logical rationality that provides the justificatory ground of moral duties (see especially 3.14).

Formalist deontological theories are similar to the *PGC* in providing for distributive justice by making formal considerations like consistency and equality basic to moral justification. In this, such theories also differ from utilitarianism. But formalist theories, unlike the *PGC*, omit the content that is also necessary to morality. They thus make it possible to argue that distributions fulfilling purely formal requirements are morally right regardless of the contents distributed, as when all persons are equally deprived of life, liberty, or property. The *PGC*, on the other hand, combines the formal distributive consideration of equality or mutuality with a substantive consideration consisting in the freedom and well-being that derive from the generic features of action; hence it does not incur these difficulties of pure formalism. All moral duties have a certain logically necessary form together with a certain content that is axiologically necessary within the context of action. Their primary structure is as follows: 'All other persons ought to do X for me because I am Q; therefore I ought to do X for them because they too are Q.' The content of 'do X' here is far from depending on the persons' arbitrary desires, for it consists in acting in accord with some component of the generic rights of one's recipients. And to be 'Q' is also not arbitrary, for it signifies having the quality of being a prospective purposive agent.

It is sometimes held that not all moral duties have the form of mutuality as between the agent and his recipients that the *PGC* makes central to moral rightness, as it is also held that justice is not the whole of morality or even of moral rightness or duty. Leaving aside for the present the vexed question of duties to oneself, I think that the mutuality of the *PGC*, combined as it is with substantive considerations, can be shown to encompass a far greater variety of moral duties than some of the traditional distinctions have recognized. Although the full detailing of this point must await the subsequent discussions, its general plausibility can be seen from the consideration that fair or just, and unfair or unjust, treatments of other persons do not occur only in a political or legal or even a broadly societal framework; they occur wherever one person acts on another person with or without positive regard for the other's rights to freedom and well-being.

Traditionally, the main concern of justice has been the relation or proportion of the distribution of goods or rights among persons. It is false that the concept of distributive justice necessarily implies a social or political distributing authority; what is essential is the distributive relation itself. The *PGC* shows how this relation is central to all morality, and it also shows how the agent, in acting toward his recipients, ought to distribute goods and rights in a certain relation as between himself and them. This distributive relation and operation thus have an important bearing on the whole structure of morality.

In addition to these three differences, the *PGC*, because of its derivation from the generic features of action, articulates the underlying structure of the whole area of moral rights and duties. Past moral philosophers have sought to systematize this area by means of such distinctions as those between perfect and imperfect duties, duties to oneself and to others, ethical and juridical legislation, and so forth. But within the crucial sphere of perfect duties, defined as those to which there correspond correlative rights of one's recipients, little systematization has been provided. It is with this sphere in its interpersonal dimension of duties to others that the *PGC* is primarily concerned (see also 5.17), and the principle's derivation shows the justification of this primacy. For the necessary conditions of action take precedence, within the whole sphere of practice, over all other practical goods, since, by definition, without these conditions no other such goods can be attained by action. Even if one person A can receive certain goods from some other person B without A's acting to attain them, B or someone else must have engaged in action in order to attain them; hence, he must have had and used the necessary conditions of action. Now the perfect duties with which the *PGC* primarily deals are derived from the rights of persons to these necessary conditions; the duties require that all agents respect these rights. It is for this reason that the *PGC*'s contents must take precedence over all other possible duties.

This derivation also provides the basis of logical systematization within the sphere of all perfect duties. As we have seen, the necessary conditions of action, based on the generic features of action, are voluntariness or freedom and purposiveness or well-being. Since the *PGC* requires that the agent act in accord with his recipients' rights to these conditions as well as his own rights to them, his duties logically fall into two broad classes: duties regarding freedom and duties regarding well-being. And since well-being in turn is of three kinds—basic, nonsubtractive, and additive—the duties regarding well-being are likewise of these three kinds. I shall subsequently show how the possible conflicts among these various duties can be resolved by considerations that are themselves based on the *PGC*'s form or content or derivation (5.20).

I shall now try to cover systematically the main applications of the *PGC*, starting with the direct applications. An initial warning must be given. The moral duties I shall derive from the *PGC* in its direct applications must be viewed, so far as the present context goes, only as prima facie, not yet as actual or conclusive duties. For each of them may be affected in various ways by the duties derived from the *PGC*'s indirect or institutional applications. I shall discuss below when and why the direct applications must yield priority of weight or requiredness to the indirect applications, and how the relative priorities are to be assessed. But it must be kept in mind throughout that the indirect as well as the direct applications reflect the rational necessity of the *PGC*, and that the principle's institutional requirements override its more direct interpersonal requirements only when this is needed to support and extend the *PGC*'s own protections of the generic rights for all persons.

Equality of Generic Rights

4.3. In requiring of every agent that he act in accord with the generic rights of his recipients as well as of himself, the *PGC* prescribes what I shall call an *Equality of Generic Rights*. With regard to freedom, this equality constitutes the principle of Equal Freedom; with regard to well-being, the principle of Common Good. In each case it is an equality between the agent and his recipients with regard to their severally having the necessary conditions of agency. Directly, this equality sets an obligation for the individual agent to respect in his actions the freedom and well-being of his recipients. Indirectly, the equality must be provided, restored, or reinforced by social rules and institutions in their impact on the persons subject to them. To violate the *PGC* is to establish an inequality or disparity in one's own favor with regard to the goods that are in various ways necessary for purposive action. It is to make, by one's action, an unequal distribution of freedom or well-being between oneself and other persons who are affected by one's action.

There are familiar ambiguities in normative ascriptions of equality: between absolute equality and proportional equality, between formal equality under general rules and substantive equality of treatment provided for in the contents of rules, between equality of opportunity and equality of result, between an equal right to X and a right to equal X, between being similar in having X and having the same amount of X, and so forth.[5] These ambiguities are exacerbated when the X that is to be equally distributed is as diffuse as the generic rights and when the freedom and well-being that are the objects of the rights are viewed not only occurrently but also dispositionally. I shall here deal with these ambiguities only in a preliminary way, leaving the main clarifications to the places where specific applications of the *PGC* are worked out.

The main point to be noted about the equality of generic rights is that it is transactional and institutional, bearing on the ways agents act toward their recipients and the ways institutions affect the persons subject to them. Since to act in accord with someone's generic rights is to respect and refrain from interfering with his freedom and well-being without his consent, and since the agent necessarily respects these in his own case, the generic rights of agent and recipient are effectively equal when the agent respects and refrains from interfering with his recipient's freedom and well-being. While the nature and kinds of such respect and noninterference must be spelled out, they involve that the agent at least refrains from coercing or harming his recipients. By interfering with these, on the other hand, he prevents his recipients from controlling their own participation in transactions or he removes from them or prevents their having certain goods that in one degree or another are necessarily connected with acting for the fulfillment of one's purposes. The equality of generic rights is effectively maintained in transactions primarily when such prevention and removal do not occur. It requires, then, at least mutual abstention from coercion and harm.

This relatively simple equality becomes more complicated in several ways. One way is through the distinction previously noted between occurrent and dispositional interpretations of freedom and well-being. The primary objects of the generic rights, that with which agents must at least refrain from interfering, are certain dispositions. Just as the agent holds that he has rights to the general abilities and conditions whereby he can participate freely and with well-being in transactions, so he must grant that his recipients also have rights to such abilities and conditions. The agent must hence at least refrain from interfering with his recipients in these respects. This requires that he not violate his recipients' autonomy by reducing their capacity to make their own effective choices about their conduct. It requires also that he not lower his recipients' capabilities for purpose-fulfilling action by advancing his own purposes at their expense through exploitative and other harmful policies. In a secondary but also important way, the objects of the equality prescribed by the *PGC* are occurrent particularizations of these dispositions. Just as the agent holds that he has rights to participate freely and with well-being in his particular transactions with his recipients, as a consequence of his generic right to freedom and well-being, so he must allow his recipients also to participate freely and with well-being. Thus the agent must respect not only his recipients' capacities for freedom and well-being but also their having these in their particular transactions.

These dispositional and occurrent requirements, which will be illustrated below in some detail, usually work together. For the recipient's having the general abilities and conditions for freedom and well-being tends both to foster and to be fostered by his participating freely and with well-being in particular transactions. This double relation is parallel to the way in which, according to Aristotle, the moral virtues both foster and are fostered by acting virtuously in particular cases.[6] Hence, in many of my discussions of the *PGC*'s applications, I shall deal with either occurrent or dispositional equalities without explicitly distinguishing them.

The equality of generic rights becomes further complicated when historical and institutional factors are considered that bear causally on the effective implementation of the rights. An agent may currently refrain from interfering with his recipient's freedom and well-being, but this noninterference may occur against a background of past interferences on a large scale. The background may be institutional as well as personal, consisting in social structures that operate to interfere with the freedom and well-being of sizable groups. Because of such interferences, some persons' current abilities to act or to protect their freedom and well-being from interference may be drastically inferior to those of others. The abilities in question are not genetic but proximate and circumstantial. The equality of generic rights is concerned primarily with equalizing these abilities. It does not require an absolute leveling with regard to economic or other results. But it does demand that these results have a certain kind of structure bearing on how persons are able to act toward one another, for it requires that each person have the effective capability of being protected from coercion or harm by others, and that all persons be able both to participate freely in decisions which affect their well-being and to have access to the means of advancing their well-being without violating the rights of others. Persons must respect one another; they must not exploit one another, nor should they ignore one another's needs for freedom and well-being.

As these considerations suggest, the transactional context of the equality of generic rights becomes diversified in various ways. At one extreme this equality is violated when an agent coerces or harms his recipient. At the other extreme, there are situations where one person does not act on another, so that no explicit transaction occurs, but the equality of generic rights is nonetheless violated because some persons have much less well-being than others, in that they have in markedly inferior degree the abilities and conditions required for warding off misfortunes and for engaging in successful action. Poverty is the most obvious but not the only example of such inferiority. It might be thought, then, that in such situations the transactional context is entirely absent. The rich may simply ignore the poor, allowing them to suffer and starve.

There are at least two ways, however, in which such relations of inequality are potentially transactional. First, since to be poor is by definition to have less command over various external goods and resources than is had by the rich, the poor are at least indirectly subject to the power and hence the actions of the rich so far as concerns the possession and utilization of resources. For they cannot compete on anything like even terms for such resources as food, shelter, medical care, higher education, and so forth. Second, to be poor is in general to be much less able to defend and improve one's well-being, and also to some extent one's freedom. Hence, the poor are much more vulnerable to coercion and harm by others, especially by the rich, so that the inequality of generic rights is here also potentially transactional.

In the light of these diversities, the *PGC's* requirements for the equality of generic rights take different forms. With regard to potentially transactional relations like those just mentioned, assistance must be given to the poor by those who are able to afford it. This assistance, which will usually operate through appropriate social institutions, must be aimed not only at alleviating the immediate hardships and shortages of poverty but also at helping the poor to develop for themselves the ability to procure goods and resources by their own efforts and thus to improve their capabilities for successful agency. What is of central importance here is not that wealth or property itself is to be equalized but rather that, beyond the minimum required for basic goods, persons have as nearly as possible equal chances for developing and utilizing their own capabilities for successful agency. Within the limits set by natural differences and indispensable familial relations, the provisions for such equality may operate in a variety of ways, ranging from direct expansion of relevant opportunities to structural changes aimed at removing or lessening the occurrence of the vulnerabilities that make such help necessary.

Such assistance, given to persons who cannot by their own efforts acquire well-being in the sense indicated above, is not a matter of charity to be begged for but rather a matter of right. If this is denied by agents who already have such well-being, they contradict themselves. For while they necessarily hold that they have rights to freedom and well-being on the ground of being prospective purposive agents, they deny that other prospective purposive agents have these rights.

The equality of generic rights as thus specified has determinate contents concerned with bringing all persons up to certain levels of adequacy as to their capabilities of purpose-fulfillment. Because of these contents, the concept of the equality of generic rights is exempt from the difficulty sometimes brought against purely formal conceptions of equality, where no provision is made for the level at which the contents are to be equalized. If what is wanted is such an equality as will keep persons from coercing or harming one another, then can't this be obtained by keeping everyone equally poor and helpless? Isn't leveling down at least as much of an equalizer as leveling up? Such leveling, however, would still leave a serious inequality of freedom and well-being between those who keep the others poor and helpless and their recipients. Since the former would be coercing the latter and would also be harming them by keeping them poor, this would violate the equality of the rights to freedom and well-being. The equality of generic rights hence requires, as a matter of content, such conditions as will tend to prevent some persons from being in a position to impose deficiencies of freedom and well-being on others. Moreover, since the generic rights are rights to the necessary conditions of agency, the equality of these rights is directed toward the purpose-fulfillment with which agency is concerned. The requirements of such equality are hence not fulfilled by a purely formal relation that takes no account of this direction of its contents.

Common Good and Duties regarding Basic Goods

4.4. Let us turn from these general considerations to examine the specific duties prescribed by the *PGC* in its direct applications with regard to the equality of generic rights; and first as these bear on well-being. The agent's obligation is at least to refrain from interfering with his recipient's having the abilities and conditions needed for action. Since the agent necessarily holds that he himself has rights to these abilities and conditions, which constitute his well-being, and since his well-being consists in his having basic, nonsubtractive, and additive goods viewed generically-dispositionally, the *PGC*'s requirement with regard to well-being may also be put as the principle of Common Good: every transaction must be for the good of the recipient as well as of the agent. The word 'common' is here used distributively: a good is common to two or more persons if it, or that kind of good, is had by each person. A transaction is for the common good of its participants if it respects the good of each participant. The good in question need not be of the same kind for each except in the general sense in which the goods are viewed generically-dispositionally as consisting in the abilities and conditions required for action.

Transactions may be for the common good of their participants in different ways. These differences reflect the variety that was suggested in the preceding section concerning the equality of generic rights. At one extreme, a transaction is for the common good if its agent simply refrains from inflicting harm on its recipient, for in such a transaction the agent at least leaves unchanged his recipient's level of goods. At the other extreme, a transaction is for the common good if its agent, while advancing his additive goods, enables his recipient also to increase his own level of additive goods. The common good which the *PGC* requires for each transaction involves primarily that the agent not adversely affect his recipient's having the basic, nonsubtractive, and additive goods, where these are viewed generically-dispositionally as comprising the preconditions of action and the further abilities and conditions needed for acting to maintain and increase one's level of purpose fulfillment. But we shall see that this negative requirement has positive components for action at both the individual and the institutional levels. This modest conception of a common good becomes diversified in many different ways in the sociopolitical order.

4.5. Since the basic goods are the necessary preconditions for engaging in purposive action, the distinction between the particular goods and the abilities or conditions required for having or maintaining the goods holds only partially in their case. I call the basic goods 'preconditions' because they are not directly constitutive of purposive action or, for the most part, of the purposes themselves, but rather are parts of its causal background or prerequisites. Thus life, physical integrity, health and its various contributing factors, general freedom, mental equilibrium, and the like are attributes of an individual without which he cannot act, either at all or beyond some minimum relative to his pursuing and achieving purposes. There are other parts of the causal background that are attributes not of individuals but of the physical and social environment, ranging from habitability of the land and natural resources to some modicum of order and peace. The abilities and conditions of a person for having or maintaining these basic goods include the basic goods themselves. To maintain life one must live, have health, and so forth. But one also needs other conditions, including other persons' abstaining from taking one's life and some pattern of social organization. The obligations of an agent with regard to the basic goods of other persons are at least to refrain from interfering with their having these goods, and the recipients correlatively have what I shall call 'basic rights.'

Such interference inflicts on its recipients what I shall similarly call 'basic harm,' since it prevents or at least tends to prevent the persons interfered with from having and using the necessary preconditions of action. Basic harms thus include killing, maiming, and other sorts of physical injury, such as depriving of food, clothing, and shelter. They also include brainwashing, terrorizing, and other forms of extreme psychological pressure that, by threatening to impose harmful actions like those just mentioned, tend to cause persons to lose confidence in their ability to act for the achievement of any of their purposes. The advances of modern technology have provided many further, though more long-range, means of basic harm, including polluting the environment and contaminating food with carcinogens and other lethal materials.

All such basic harms are prohibited by the *PGC*. Where, as in technological contexts, scientific knowledge is needed to ascertain and ward off the potential harmfulness of various substances and policies, the *PGC* requires that this knowledge be pursued and made available to the fullest possible extent called for by such need. To conceal such knowledge when one has it is to contribute to the harms in question. All such basic harms are shown to be disjustified or wrong by the consideration of generic consistency analyzed above. For in each sort of basic harm the agent, while holding that he has a right to well-being insofar as he is a prospective purposive agent, denies this right to other prospective purposive agents and hence in effect denies that they have this right. To do such evil, to inflict such harms, is thus to contradict oneself at the most important level of goods.

The generic content of the *PGC* is essential to this formal result. Suppose the agent were to try to avoid inconsistency by declaring, in effect, that he himself does not have rights to basic well-being; for example, directly after killing or physically maiming his recipient he kills or physically maims himself. Here he treats his recipient in the same way as he treats himself—he applies to his recipient the same rule ('Undergo deprivation of your basic well-being') as he applies to himself—so that he is being quite consistent. There are, nevertheless, two crucial considerations, each derived from the generic content of the *PGC*, that refute such a claim. First, the agent here acts freely or voluntarily, whereas he coerces his recipient. Since his recipient is also a prospective purposive agent, the agent contradicts himself in thus coercing his recipient, regardless of the fact that the agent also inflicts basic harm on himself. For while necessarily holding that he has a right to freedom insofar as he is a prospective purposive agent, he denies this right to his recipient who is also a prospective purposive agent. Second, as we have previously seen (2.10), so long as he is an agent who has purposes he pursues and regards as good, he cannot consistently hold that he lacks the right to well-being. Hence, he cannot use a rejection of this right for himself as his ground for infringing his recipient's right to well-being.

4.6. Despite its general prohibition of killing and other basic harms, the *PGC* permits and may even require these in circumstances of self-defense. Suppose Ames physically assaults Blake, who then defends himself by physically assaulting Ames. In a purely formal view, Ames and Blake are each disobeying the moral principle that requires persons to respect and not infringe one another's well-being. On the *PGC*'s substantive view, however, these two infractions are not on a par as being both unjustified. Since Ames inflicted or acted to inflict basic harm on Blake, and hence intended to violate a generic right of Blake while acting in accord with his own generic rights, Ames's intention was inconsistent and his action morally wrong. Blake's defensive response, however, was not similarly wrong, for it was directly an attempt not to inflict a basic harm, but rather to prevent such an infliction or to restore an equilibrium of mutual nonharm disrupted by Ames. Preventing the violation of a generic right is not on a par with the violation itself. Since the *PGC* prohibits inflicting basic harms, it also upholds the prevention of such infliction so far as possible.

The means used for this prevention may include, if necessary, basic harms as severe as those the assailant threatens to inflict. Killing to save one's own life or the life of another threatened person is hence justified, but only in circumstances where there is no other way of saving the threatened life.

It is to be noted in this example that although Blake in defending himself against Ames acts in disaccord with Ames's right to well-being while acting in accord with his own right—for Blake inflicts physical harm on Ames—Blake does not thereby incur inconsistency. As we have seen, the agent must give, as his sufficient reason justifying his having the generic rights, the description of himself as being a prospective purposive agent. Since his recipient also fulfills this description, the agent cannot avoid inconsistency if he violates the recipient's generic rights. But when such violation occurs, a more specific description becomes relevant, which Blake is justified in assigning to Ames: that he is a person who has initiated a physical assault and hence, contrary to the *PGC*, is violating his recipient's right to well-being. This description, in its first part, does not also pertain to Blake. Hence, Blake does not contradict himself in defending himself from Ames's assault by assaulting him. Blake would not, however, be justified in assigning to Ames such other, even true, descriptions that also fit Ames, but not Blake, as that Ames is black or a foreigner or a disbeliever in a certain religion. The reason Blake is not justified in using such other descriptions, but is justified in describing Ames only as an initiator of a physical assault and in using this to avoid inconsistency while repelling the assault, is that the *PGC*'s content makes this description relevant. Since the *PGC* requires that persons act in accord with one another's generic rights, a case where some person violates this requirement is crucial to the description that is relevant to how he ought to be treated, and this supersedes the generic description that entered into the original derivation of the *PGC*. Other descriptions, however, are irrelevant when they are unrelated to such violation. Thus, the *PGC* determines what are the relevant descriptions that must enter into any response to a direct violation of it.

I referred above to Blake's assaulting Ames in self-defense as an attempt, in part, to 'restore an equilibrium' disrupted by Ames's attack. This equilibrium is the equality of generic rights, or more specifically an equality of mutual non-harm, that was assumed to be the situation before Ames's attack. But it is not always realistic to describe the initial situation in terms of such equality. The status quo may be one of extreme inequality of basic well-being imposed on one group by another, such as conditions of slavery, starvation, or other severe oppression. If the oppressed group, rising up to revolt or to seize withheld food, has to inflict basic harm on some of the oppressors in order to succeed, such a disruption of the status quo would be justified, and the oppressors' restoration of the status quo would be unjustified. Since the status quo in such a situation violates the *PGC*, what is required is not maintenance or restoration of the status quo but rather its replacement. Thus, everything depends on the content of the status quo with respect to its impact especially on the equality of basic rights, so that a purely formal requirement of mutual respect for purposes or restorations of the status quo is morally insufficient.

This consideration about inflicting basic harm to disrupt an oppressive status quo has many political and other implications, but it is vitally important to be careful in asserting that or how they apply in particular cases. Because of its own direct content of basic harm, violence is justified only when there are no alternative means of remedying severe injustices regarding basic well-being, and only when it is directed at the agents who inflict the injustices. Random violence engaged in as a protest against injustice simply constitutes further injustice. Where a nation is engaged in a just war of defense against an aggressor nation, however, the latter's soldiers are included among the agents of injustice. Before there is recourse to violence, the availability of nonviolent means of remedying the basic injustices in question must be thoroughly explored. In general, such alternative means are provided in a constitutional democracy resting on the method of consent (5.11), so that there is no justification for the violence preached and practiced by 'urban guerrillas' or terrorists in such a state.

When it is quite clear that basic injustices cannot be remedied in nonviolent ways, only as much violence may be used as is needed to remove the injustice. There must be no glorification of violence or of its results as such; its use must be a matter of the utmost regret, as signalizing the breakdown of rational communication and argument and hence of the *PGC* in its primary application. On the other hand, acquiescence in such basic violations of the *PGC* as genocide or enslavement is itself morally wrong, and resistance must be mounted to prevent or remove the violations. In extreme cases even assassination is justified, but only when it is directed at the leading agents of the extreme injustices in question. Violence, except to avoid immediately impending serious harm, should be left to officers of the state (5.8.); for private individuals to engage in violence is justified only where the state is so corrupt in its procedures and substantive effects that no other remedy for extreme injustice is available.

In all such cases, the justifications are not utilitarian: it is not that violence is justified by the aggregative criterion of whether more good will result from its use than from its nonuse. It is rather that violence is justified by the distributive criterion of whether unjust attacks on basic well-being, and only on this, cannot otherwise be prevented, and only when the violence is directed at the attackers themselves. It is also of the utmost importance, however, to try to determine whether the contemplated violence will remove or exacerbate the injustices in question. Such considerations are 'consequentialist' in that their justificatory criterion includes reference to the violent action's probable consequences. But here also it is vitally important to distinguish between utilitarian and deontological consequentialism. For the deontological consequentialist, a violent action against other persons is justified not if its consequences (or the consequences of a general rule upholding such actions) will serve to achieve more good than will any alternative action, but rather if the action, directed against the perpetrator of a severe injustice, will remove or remedy that injustice without leading to worse injustices, and only if it is quite clear that the severe injustice cannot otherwise be removed. The criterion of such injustice is given by the *PGC*: actions or institutions are unjust where agents violate their recipients' basic rights, in that they impose on these recipients a severe inequality with regard to basic well-being, where this imposition is not itself designed to remove a previous imposition of such inequality.

To consider consequences by reference to this criterion is to recognize that the wrongness of actions may vary in degree, depending on the rights the actions violate, and that actions that are wrong when viewed without consideration of special excusing circumstances may nonetheless be required in order to prevent or remove worse wrongs. It is also true that rights are in part defined in terms of goods, and that rights and duties vary in degree of moral urgency according to the degree to which they affect well-being and hence the possibilities of purposive action (2.6, 9). Nevertheless, the criterion that the *PGC*'s consequentialism uses for ascertaining the rightness of an action refers not to the goods alone but to the entitlements to the goods of the parties affected, as ascertained by the consideration of equal rights to the conditions of agency. The question is how this equality of rights is to be maintained or restored. None of this is equivalent to utilitarian consequentialism that aims solely at maximizing goods regardless of the rights of the persons affected. The calculation that deontological consequentialism uses is not concerned simply with measuring amounts of goods and bads with a view to maximizing the former or minimizing the latter, without regard to their distribution; it is concerned rather with correcting or preventing unjust distributions of basic goods without incurring further or greater injustices.

Should there be any limits on the use of violence for the correction of basic injustices? It might be thought that if killing is permitted, then anything is permitted. But this would be a mistake. The person who is justifiably killed is still viewed as responsible for his actions and as capable of understanding the principle of morality embodied in the *PGC*. To treat someone as a wrongdoer is not to violate his rationality or even his rational autonomy in the strict sense (3.3); it is not to assume that he lacks the minimal rationality needed for understanding what is required by the *PGC*. This consideration indicates the limits on the use of violence. This use must not violate the criteria involved in being a rational agent who can understand and act in accordance with the principle of morality. Consequently, the *PGC* prohibits torture, brainwashing, and other techniques that disrupt the assumptions underlying the rational acceptance of the principle.

The Duty to Rescue

4.7. The duties of the agent with regard to the basic goods of other persons have thus far emerged as primarily negative: the agent must refrain from inflicting basic harms on other persons. Violent actions have been justified only as preventing or removing such inflictions. The duties the *PGC* sets for agents, however, also include certain positive actions. For with certain qualifications, to be noted below, whenever some person knows that unless he acts in certain ways other persons will suffer basic harms, and he is proximately able to act in these ways with no comparable cost to himself, it is his moral duty to act to prevent these harms. Just as the agent necessarily holds that he has a right to the basic goods that are necessary preconditions of action, so he must hold that other persons also have this basic right. Their having this right entails that he ought at least not to interfere with their having these goods; but under certain conditions, it also entails that he ought to assist them to have these goods or to act so as to prevent their loss. I shall first illustrate this point with a familiar example; then I shall discuss some of the main issues raised by it.

Suppose Carr, who is an excellent swimmer, is lolling in the sun on a deserted beach. On the edge of the beach near him is his motorboat, to which is attached a long, stout rope. Suddenly he becomes aware that another person, whom I shall call Davis, is struggling in the water some yards away. Carr knows that the water is about thirty feet deep at that point. Davis shouts for help; he is obviously in immediate danger of drowning. Carr sees that he could easily save Davis by swimming out to him, or at least by throwing him the rope from his boat. But Carr simply doesn't want to bother even though he is aware that Davis will probably drown unless he rescues him. Davis drowns.

It would be generally agreed that Carr ought to have gone to Davis's rescue. But why? The utilitarian answer that this action would tend to maximize utility overall puts the emphasis in the wrong place with regard both to the specific person to whom the duty is owed and the specific nature of the duty. Carr's duty is a duty specifically to Davis, a duty to save Davis's life, not a duty to contribute to an increase of the 'general happiness' or of goodness or utility in general. As for the Kantian answer that no one could will not to be helped in such circumstances, so that Carr's maxim not to help Davis involves Carr in a 'contradiction of the will,' this is more promising; it is, indeed, in line with the position advanced here that every agent necessarily regards himself as having a right to basic well-being and must, on pain of contradiction, acknowledge a similar right for others. But put as the proposition that no person can 'will' not to be helped by others when he needs help, the Kantian answer encounters Sidgwick's objection that such a proposition is not necessarily true and that, quite apart from one's wishes "in the actual moment of distress," a person might reject the general maxim of being helped by others if he were of a strongly independent spirit.[7] A similar criticism may apply to the Golden Rule as a reason for Carr's duty; in addition, the cogency of appealing to the Golden Rule here is weakened by the many kinds of cases in which the Rule may justify wrong actions (3.12, 15).

I shall now show how the *PGC* supplies the sufficient ground for Carr's duty to rescue Davis in that, given the duties of agents as these are prescribed by the *PGC*, this duty necessarily follows. Most directly, the *PGC* requires that an agent not only refrain from interfering with his recipients' freedom and well-being, but also that he assist them to have these necessary goods when they cannot have them by their own efforts and when he can give such assistance at no comparable cost to himself. By 'comparable cost' is meant that he is not required to risk his own life or other basic goods in order to save another person's life or other basic goods, and similarly with the other components of the necessary goods of action. To engage in such risk or to incur such cost would involve the possibility or actuality of losing his own life in order to save theirs, and this, rather than maintaining an equality of generic rights, would generate an inequality in his recipient's favor (3.24). In the situation as described, however, Carr can save Davis's life without risking his own. Hence, the *PGC* requires that he come to Davis's rescue. To put it somewhat more extensively: in failing to come to Davis's rescue, Carr drastically violates the equality of generic rights that the *PGC* prescribes for transactions between agents and their recipients. For Davis participates involuntarily and contrapurposively and indeed suffers basic harm in a transaction that is under Carr's control and in which Carr participates voluntarily and purposively. By his inaction, Carr lets Davis drown, thus imposing on him a maximally unfavorable inequality with regard to the rights of well-being.

4.8. For this account to be more fully understood, the following interrelated questions must be answered:

a. In what way is Carr an agent in the situation as described? The *PGC* imposes duties on agents; but to be an agent, Carr must perform an action. Since he is inactive, how can he be held to perform an action?

b. In what way does Carr act on Davis? Since Carr remains passive and inert in the face of Davis's peril, how can it be held that there is a transaction between Carr and Davis, wherein Carr is the agent and Davis the recipient?

In answer to question (*a*), it must be noted that for someone's behavior to be an action, it is not necessary that he engage in gross bodily movements, or indeed in any bodily movements at all. What is both necessary and sufficient is that he behave voluntarily and purposively, controlling his behavior in that he chooses to behave as he does for some purpose of his, knowing such proximate circumstances as the nature of his conduct and its probable outcome. In this sense, a person's refraining from some action may itself be a form of action. We may distinguish in this respect between nonaction and inaction. Nonaction is the simple absence of any action, as when a person is asleep or in a trance or is the victim of hallucinations, bodily seizures, or accidents such as slipping on ice, and so forth. In such behaviors, the person involved is not behaving voluntarily and purposively; he is not in control of his movements or nonmovements and is not behaving for any purpose of his own. Inaction, on the other hand, occurs when a person's refraining from a certain action is itself voluntary and purposive: the inactive person unforcedly chooses to refrain in order to achieve some purpose of his own; he is aware of the proximate circumstances of his omission and intentionally engages in it.

As is suggested by the reference to 'a certain action' in this account of inaction, the correct characterization of a person's behavior as a case of inaction is always relative to some specific positive action he fails to perform. At least two elements must hence be distinguished in inaction: (i) some action X that a person S fails to perform; (ii) the voluntary and purposive character of this failure. Now with respect to (i), X may be, but need not be, a bodily movement on the part of S; X may consist, for example, in recalling a piece of music or working out a simple arithmetical problem. With respect to (ii), the voluntary and purposive failure to perform X may itself consist in, or be accompanied or accomplished by, a bodily movement. For example, S may jam his hands into his pockets or stamp his foot down hard in order to prevent himself from performing X, regardless of whether or not X is itself a bodily movement. When S engages in such a bodily movement, we might say that he performs another action, Y, in order to prevent himself from performing X. On the other hand, S may be inactive with regard to X without performing another action Y; it is sufficient if his failure to perform X is itself voluntary and purposive.[8]

Now Carr's behavior in the situation as described above is a form of inaction and hence of action, since it is voluntary and purposive. He refrains from moving toward Davis because he chooses not to do so in order to maintain his position of easy comfort. He knows what he is doing and what its probable outcome will be: that Davis will drown. It is not that Carr merely does not choose to rescue or to move toward Davis; it is rather that he positively chooses not to rescue or to move toward Davis when he could have done so at little cost to himself.

This brings me to question (*b*): even if Carr in refraining from going to Davis's rescue performs an action so that Carr is then an agent, in what way does he thereby act on Davis or set up a transaction with Davis? To answer this question, we must note that in order for someone to be an agent in a transaction, it is not necessary that he initiate the transaction; it is sufficient if he controls its course and thereby crucially affects what happens to the other person, who is hence his recipient (3.1). Now in the present situation Carr plays a determining role in Davis's undergoing a basic harm: Carr, by his inaction, allows Davis to drown and hence is a causal factor in his drowning, since his intentional failure to come to Davis's rescue is a necessary and sufficient condition of the drowning. Davis would not have drowned had Carr come to his rescue; and in the circumstances as described, given Carr's failure to come to Davis's rescue, Davis's drowning necessarily followed. Since Davis's drowning is a basic harm to him, and the *PGC* prohibits agents from inflicting basic harms on their recipients and requires assistance to prevent such harms where possible, it follows that Carr's inaction is a violation of the *PGC*. To put it in the terms used previously: by his decision not to intervene Carr determines that Davis will participate in the situation in such a way as to suffer basic harm. Carr thus violates Davis's right to basic well-being by allowing Davis's lethal plight to continue to its conclusion when he could easily have saved him. Hence Davis is here Carr's recipient because Davis's basic well-being is drastically affected by what Carr voluntarily and purposively refrains from doing.

4.9. This account of Carr's causal relation to Davis's drowning raises further questions, especially about differentiating various alleged causes and effects:

c. If Carr's inaction is a causal factor in Davis's drowning, then how is this causal role related to such facts as (i) that Carr exerted no positive causal efficacy, no physical force, on Davis to make him drown, and (ii) that Davis would have drowned even if Carr had not been present at all? Fact (ii) surely indicates that Carr's being present and inactive is not a necessary condition of Davis's drowning. How, then, is Carr's inaction related to such undoubted causal factors as that Davis was a poor swimmer, had a severe cramp, and was involuntarily sinking and swallowing large amounts of water?

d. If Carr's inaction is a causal factor in Davis's drowning, then why isn't it also a causal factor in innumerable other events that would not have occurred if Carr had acted to prevent them?

These questions ask, respectively, how Carr's inaction as presumed causal factor in Davis's drowning is related to other undoubted causal factors, and how Davis's drowning as presumed partial effect of Carr's inaction is differentiated from other events that bear the same relation to Carr's inaction without in any plausible way being its even partial effects.

I shall deal with these questions by first expanding on (c.i). It objects that Carr's inaction cannot appropriately be regarded as a causal factor in Davis's drowning because only a positive event can cause another event to occur; the mere absence of an event, as in Carr's inaction, cannot be a cause. In this respect, the objection continues, we must distinguish between a person's causing something to occur and his merely permitting or not preventing its occurrence. In causing some event X to occur, one performs a positive action whose outcome is the occurrence of X; but in merely permitting or not preventing the occurrence of X, one does not perform any positive action: one merely refrains from acting. Even if this refraining is itself voluntary and purposive, it still has no positive causal relation to the occurrence of X, since X would have occurred even in the absence or the nonexistence of the person who thus refrains. Hence, while it is indeed true that Carr let Davis drown, this by no means entails that

Carr played a causal role in Davis's drowning, just as in letting Davis die, Carr does not kill Davis. But since the *PGC* prohibits that an agent inflict basic harm on his recipient, that is, that he positively act to cause his recipient to suffer basic harm, such as by killing him, it follows that to this extent at least, Carr has not violated the *PGC*. This objection is reinforced when we look at the situation morally. Carr's not going to Davis's rescue is shocking enough; but surely it would be an even greater atrocity if Carr had deliberately held Davis's head under water until he died. In the latter case Carr would have performed a positive action that brought about Davis's death quite directly, unlike Carr's passive, inactive role in the situation as originally described. If we distinguish, as surely we must, between Carr's degree of moral guilt in the two cases, it must be admitted that in the original situation Carr did not even partially cause Davis to die, even though he let him die.

The answer to this objection is that an event, and a fortiori a harmful event, may be caused by a person's inaction or other omission as well as by his positive action. A train wreck may be caused by a signalman's omitting to move a switch; a man's failure to reach a physician in time may cause him to die of appendicitis. In such cases, what is appropriately singled out as the cause of the event is the particular antecedent circumstance, an omission, that either makes the difference from the normal course of events (where 'normal' may have either a statistical or a normative interpretation) or is such that, if it had not occurred, the event would not have occurred.[9] If the signalman's pulling the switch is expected and required in the normal operation of the railroad line, and if the various trainmen drive their trains in the expectation that the switch will have been pulled, then his failure to pull it is the cause of the ensuing wreck. To be sure, the wreck also has a 'positive' cause: trainman A drove his train to place X at the same time as trainman B did. But here the 'cause' is synonymous, or nearly so, with the effect. The main point is that trainmen A and B in driving their trains to place X were following the normal course, sanctioned by the relevant rules, of relying on the signals, and this reliance normally avoids any wrecks, so that it is not the cause of the wreck in this case, although it may be a 'condition' of the wreck's occurring. The cause is the signalman's failure to do what he normally does, to move the switch in keeping with the relevant rules that are normally followed. For this failure made the difference between situations where wrecks do not occur and the present situation.

Carr's failure to come to Davis's rescue is the cause of the latter's drowning in a related way. As an omission, it is similar to the signalman's failure in that, like the signalman, Carr is subject to a valid prescriptive rule that he is blamable for disobeying. In the signalman's case, it is the rule about giving signals and moving switches; in Carr's case, it is the *PGC*'s requirement about helping persons to avoid basic harms and to have basic well-being. But unlike the case of the signalman, there may not be an ongoing rule-regulated system of expectations to which Carr's failure comes as an exception. Even if Carr and Davis live in a society in which, as a matter of empirical fact, persons are not expected to care for one another, Carr's inaction is still morally wrong. What makes it the cause of Davis's death is not that it departs from an ongoing system of expectations, but rather that Carr, as a rational agent, is aware of and is subject to the moral requirements of the *PGC*. It is against the background of these requirements that Carr's failure to rescue Davis counts as the cause of his death. This background is a normative moral one and not, as in the other cases cited, an empirical one.

In this regard, it must be remembered that the duties the *PGC* imposes on agents may be positive as well as negative. In prohibiting certain kinds of harmful inactions, as well as in requiring certain kinds of assistance, the principle requires performance of certain actions. If this positive component is not kept in view, so that the *PGC* is interpreted as requiring only that a person not do something, then, since Carr in failing to rescue Davis does not do something, it might be thought that he has not violated the principle. One way to see the incorrectness of this interpretation is to recall that the *PGC* imposes on every agent the duty to respect his recipients' well-being as well as his own (3.3, 4). Such respect requires a positive concern for the basic well-being of other persons where this basic well-being may be affected by one's action or inaction. The agent must not treat his recipients as mere means to his own purpose-fulfillment with no positive consideration for their own well-being. In ignoring Davis's plight, Carr fails to respect Davis's well-being; he allows a process to continue that he knows is drastically harmful to Davis and that he could reverse without any comparable cost to himself. In thus failing to respect Davis's well-being, Carr violates the *PGC*'s prohibition against inflicting basic harm.

It is indeed the case, as was noted in question (c.ii), that Davis would have drowned even if Carr had not been present. This does not, however, disprove that Carr's inaction was a necessary condition of Davis's drowning in the circumstances as they actually occurred. The concept of the 'necessary condition' of some event may be interpreted according to one or another of two different tendencies. The generalizing tendency thinks about the event as a member of a whole class of similar events, and about its conditions in terms of the whole general realm of physical possibility. The particularizing tendency thinks about the particular event as it actually occurred amid all its particular circumstances of time and place, and about its conditions in terms of the limited range of possibilities actually present and operative on that particular occasion.[10] The particularizing tendency is better suited to practical inquiry precisely because of its concern with the particular. Now when it is said that Carr's inaction in the face of Davis's peril was a necessary condition of Davis's drowning, the particularizing tendency is obviously followed. If Carr had not been inactive in that situation, Davis would not have drowned. To the generalizing tendency's objection that the drowning could have occurred even in Carr's absence or in spite of his actively trying to rescue Davis (Carr might have been a poor swimmer, or suffered a heart attack . . .), the reply is that these circumstances did not actually occur on the given occasion, nor were they likely to occur in view of Carr's actual swimming ability and excellent physical condition, so that they are irrelevant to the explanation of what actually did occur. Carr's inaction, given the actual circumstances, was part of the whole causal nexus that also included Davis's being a poor swimmer, suffering a severe cramp, and so forth. The actual event did not, however, include such quite different possibilities as that Davis was an excellent swimmer, suffered no cramp, but happened to be seized by a gripping hallucination that caused him to lose all control.

It may also be argued that the concept of inflicting harm or of interfering with someone's well-being does not apply to Carr's failure to rescue Davis, because such infliction or interference involves that the antecedent situation is one of well-being or at least of nonharm. Since Davis is already in a situation that is drastically harmful to him, Carr's inaction does not cause Davis to undergo a harm he would otherwise not have undergone. It is possible, however, to harm someone or interfere with his well-being by refusing him the help he needs in order to recover from an already bad situation. Such interference involves not that one turns an antecedent well-being into ill-being, but rather that one prevents the other person from attaining well-being through means that are under one's proximate control. One's refusal to help inflicts harm on the other person not necessarily by making his situation worse (although the dashing of hopes or expectations may indeed do this), but by permitting the existing harm to continue when it could have been stopped. Such permitting constitutes acquiescence in the harm; it hence violates Davis's right to have his basic well-being respected.

As was indicated above, the causal attribution of Davis's drowning to Carr requires the normative background of the *PGC*. Even though many other factors contributed to Davis's death, the *PGC* makes it appropriate and indeed mandatory to single out Carr's inaction as a dominant causal factor in Davis's drowning. For it is this inaction that directly violates the *PGC*'s basic requirement of nonharm and of respect for others' well-being; and since the *PGC* is the supreme principle of morality, it determines both what duties obtain in such a situation and hence what considerations are relevant in describing and accounting for an event where one person's basic well-being is affected by the action or inaction of another.

4.10. Let us now consider question (*d*). If Carr's inaction is a causal factor in Davis's drowning, then must it not also be regarded as a causal factor in an immense number of other events? A sea gull swoops down and catches a fish; a bunch of seaweed drifts out to sea; in distant Vladivostok a boy slips on ice and twists his ankle. Of all these events it is analytically true to say that they would not have occurred if Carr had intervened to prevent them, and that, given Carr's failure to intervene, the events necessarily occurred in accordance with the particular causal forces that were respectively at work. But it is quite implausible, to put it mildly, to hold that Carr's inaction even partially caused these and countless other events to occur. This question requires that we supply a differentiating ground to distinguish where someone's inaction is and is not a causal factor in events he fails to prevent.

There are two main answers to this question. One is that we must distinguish between events Carr is able to prevent, so that the particular antecedent circumstance that caused the event is under Carr's control, and events where this is not the case. Since Carr, being in the United States at the time, could not have intervened to prevent the Vladivostok incident and had no knowledge of it, his failure to prevent it is a case of nonaction, not inaction, and cannot be regarded as a causal factor in the event. The other answer is that since Carr is a rational purposive agent, his potential causal relation to Davis's drowning or not drowning is morally relevant to a correct description of his behavior in a way in which his potential causal relation is not morally relevant to such other events as the sea gull catching the fish and the seaweed drifting out to sea, events Carr was aware of and might have prevented. As a rational purposive agent, Carr necessarily holds that he has rights to freedom and well-being and he necessarily recognizes that all other prospective purposive agents also have these rights. Since Davis is a normal human being, he too is a prospective purposive agent. Hence, entirely apart from any feelings Carr may or may not have for Davis as a fellow human being, Carr's rational recognition that Davis has the same right to life as Carr claims for himself gives his potential causal relation to Davis's drowning or not drowning a moral relevance and urgency quite different from Carr's potential causal relation to the other events mentioned above. The latter relations impose no moral obligations on Carr; the former does in virtue of the relevant similarity between Carr and Davis as prospective purposive agents. In calling attention to this moral relevance, the *PGC* brings out an essential feature of Carr's potential causal relation to Davis's drowning.

This point also bears on the slippery slope objection that if Carr's inaction is a causal factor in Davis's undergoing a basic harm, then it is also a causal factor in many other persons' lacking goods that Carr's beneficence might have provided for them. For example, he is aware that the boy living next door would like to have a ten-speed bicycle, but although Carr has plenty of money and has considered the matter, he refrains from buying it for the boy. Isn't it analytically true here too that if Carr had bought him the bicycle, the boy would have it, and since Carr didn't buy it for him on some occasion when he considered the matter the boy fails to obtain it and suffers disappointment? The answer is that this is not relevant to the description of Carr's inaction as authorized by the *PGC*, because the principle does not impose the duty of positive beneficence in the sense of providing for others particular additive goods (5.18). It requires rather that persons refrain from inflicting basic or specific harms by their action or inaction, and that they help other persons to avoid such harms when they can do so at no comparable cost to themselves.

4.11. It may be objected to the above argument that when the duty to rescue Davis is imposed on Carr, this removes the latter's own right to freedom, which goes counter to the *PGC*. According to the *PGC* the agent ought to act in accord with the generic rights of his recipients *as well as of himself*. But how can Carr act in accord with his own right to freedom if he must also act in accord with Davis's right to well-being? In acting freely, he may choose not to rescue Davis; and if he must rescue Davis regardless of his own unforced choice in the matter, then he does not act freely. Hence, isn't the *PGC* subject to internal conflict on this point?

This objection may be further developed by noting that even if Davis has a right to life, he does not have a right to the means necessary for life when other persons already have rights over these means. Hence, Davis does not have a right that Carr or anyone else rescue him, a right Carr violates if he does not go to Davis's rescue. For this right of Davis would violate Carr's right to freedom. Carr's freedom is infinitely precious to him, and to put it into a calculus in which it is balanced against the good of some other person is to take away Carr's right, his absolute ownership, over his own movements and decisions. Each person is to be treated as an end in himself, not merely as a means; but to require Carr to come to Davis's rescue would be to use Carr as a means to Davis's well-being. The uniqueness and separateness of each individual preclude making him a means to some greater social good.[11]

In reply to this objection, it must be noted that the *PGC* requires that the agent adjust his own rights of freedom and well-being to the rights of his recipients. For the agent to act in accord with his own right to freedom is for him to see to it that without his consent there is no interference with his freedom—that is, with his control of his own behavior by his unforced choice (3.3). Such seeing to it implicitly characterizes him so long as he acts. The *PGC* requires, however, that the agent rationally consent to whatever interferences may be required in order to avoid his inflicting basic harms on other persons or his failing to prevent such harms when he can do so at no comparable cost to himself. The agent gives his rational consent when he recognizes the rational requirements imposed on him by the *PGC* and undertakes to act accordingly. As a rational agent, he accepts and shares in the *PGC*'s end of mutual respect for freedom and well-being between himself and his recipients. Hence, Carr is not treated merely as a means to Davis's well-being when he is required to act in accordance with the end he himself accepts as a rational agent. The right of freedom which the *PGC* ascribes to the agent as well as to his recipients does not, then, include the total absence of any duty on the part of the agent. The right requires, rather, an accommodation to the rights which his recipients also have to freedom and well-being.

It is arbitrary to hold that restrictions on freedom are justified only from considerations of freedom and not also from those of basic well-being, including life. Since every agent has a deep stake in his own basic well-being, he must hold that he has a right to it and that other persons also have this right. He must hence admit that he ought to refrain from interfering with their basic well-being, and where his inaction would interfere, that he ought positively to act to protect their well-being if he can do so without comparable harm to himself. To be sure, each person also has a right to freedom. But this right, like the right to well-being, is relative to the requirements of agency on the part of each person. Since if one is not alive one cannot act, and since a temporary loss of a small occurrent freedom like that of Carr in having to rescue Davis is far less consequential for his agency, Davis's right to life and to Carr's rescuing him takes priority over the freedom Carr may temporarily lose thereby. As a rational agent, moreover, Carr rationally consents to perform this action and hence does not lose any freedom.

It must also be noted that insofar as Carr's freedom to refrain from rescuing Davis is here weighed against Davis's life, this is not part of a utilitarian calculus. It is a question not of ascertaining how utility may be maximized overall without regard for its distribution, but rather of how Carr's brief exertion of himself compares with Davis's life so far as these are related to maintaining the requirements of agency on the part of each of these persons.

The duty to rescue, as I have dealt with it so far, is not yet a legal obligation; it does not involve coercion by other persons, including legal authorities. To be sure, such an ardent libertarian as John Stuart Mill held that a person "may rightfully be compelled to perform . . . certain acts of individual beneficence, such as saving a fellow creature's life."[12] I shall deal subsequently with the question of legal compulsion (5.13, 14). But, like all strict duties, the duty to rescue does carry with it subjection at least to severe censure for violators, with the possibility of legal sanctions to express and enforce this censure.

A related objection is that although in a broad sense of 'ought' Carr ought to have rescued Davis, this is only in the sense that it would be generous, beneficent, or praiseworthy of Carr to perform this action, not that he has a strict duty to do so. For my assertion that Carr has here a strict duty blurs the difference between justice and beneficence or supererogation—between what other persons have a right to demand of us and what they have no right to demand but is rather a favor, an act of grace whose bestowal should be at the option of the giver. If this distinction is overlooked in the present case, then, the objection continues, no sense is made of the difference between Carr's situation and that of a lifeguard who has a professional, contractually undertaken duty to save Davis by virtue of his job or office.

These distinctions are indeed important, but they do not apply in instances like that of Carr and Davis. To begin with, it is not the case that strict duties are found only in connection with contractually undertaken jobs or offices. 'My station and its duties' does not exhaust the area of strict duties unless 'station' is interpreted not in the narrow sense of a specific rule-governed status ranging from one's job or profession to one's membership in some specific community, but rather in the broad sense of one's status as a human being who is a prospective purposive agent. As we have seen, rights and strict duties are logically connected with being such an agent. This duty, moreover, pertains to Carr and not only to a professional lifeguard, because of the basic harm impending to Davis and because Carr is in a position to ward it off at no comparable cost to himself. It is these two characteristics that especially differentiate Carr's strict duty from acts of generosity or supererogation. Without these characteristics, Carr's inaction would not be a case of inflicting basic harm on Davis, which the *PGC* prohibits. Correlatively, Davis has a basic right to be rescued by Carr; because this is a generic right that belongs to Davis as a human being who is a prospective purposive agent, it is not only a right to some professional person's job-oriented action.

4.12. The general point that emerges from the above discussion is that the moral duties imposed by the *PGC* include positive actions to defend other persons' rights to basic goods when the actions are necessary for such defense without bringing comparable harm to their agents. Obviously the point of my prolonged consideration of the drowning case can be extended to cases of starvation, alerting the police to criminal attacks, and many other threats to basic goods. The duties in all such cases follow from the equality of generic rights that the *PGC* requires. Failure to fulfill these duties is rationally unjustifiable: the agent in such circumstances is involved in an unavoidable contradiction between his implicit judgment that he has a right to basic well-being insofar as he is prospective purposive agent and his denial that his recipient, who is also a prospective purposive agent, has this right. This point has important implications for social and political action in connection with such issues as starvation and health care. I shall deal with some of these below.

It must also be recognized that the duty to intervene in defense of other persons' rights to basic well-being has limits. The drowning case was obviously extreme in several respects. Davis was in immediate danger of losing his life; Carr knew this; there was something Carr could immediately do to save Davis; this action involved no significant cost to Carr. There are, then, at least four variables to consider:

(i) the kind or degree of harm impending to the recipient; (ii) the agent's knowledge of this harm; (iii) his ability to ward off the harm; (iv) the cost to the agent of doing so. The first variable bears on the duties of persons to prevent others from suffering harms that are less than basic. I shall consider this below (4.14). I have already mentioned the other variables, including that of comparable costs. Thus if Carr were a poor swimmer so that if he tried to swim to Davis he would probably drown himself, he would have no duty to swim out to Davis. He would still, however, have a duty to do whatever he could to help rescue Davis, such as shouting for help, looking for a rope or a plank, rushing to seek aid from other persons, and the like.

There is an important distinction that affects and cuts across all four of the variables listed above, especially the first and the third. Both the harm impending to the recipient and the agent's ability to ward off this harm may be regarded either as occurrent or as dispositional. If they are regarded as occurrent, consideration is given only to the directly impending harm and to what can be directly done to avoid it. But if they are regarded as dispositional, consideration is given to the longer-range causes and background conditions that do or may bring about the directly impending harm and to the longer-range action required to remove these causes and conditions. The duties emerging from this consideration require not the individual actions discussed above in the case of Carr, but much more elaborate institutional policies. This raises problems of a political nature (5.13).

Duties regarding Nonsubtractive Goods

4.13. A person has a nonsubtractive good when his status quo as to his possession of goods is maintained so that his level of purpose-fulfillment is not lowered through his being made to lose something he views as good. To cause someone to incur such loss is to inflict on him what I shall call 'specific harm.' The *PGC* requires that in certain respects the agent refrain from inflicting such harms. Since what persons regard as good includes the basic goods that are the necessary preconditions of actions, there is to this extent an overlap between basic goods and nonsubtractive goods, and between basic harms and specific harms. I shall here confine nonsubtractive goods and specific harms to those kinds that remain over and above basic goods and harms.

Persons, of course, regard as good an immense variety of objects and dispositions other than basic goods. This variety raises the following difficulty. If the *PGC* prohibits all specific harms, all interferences with nonsubtractive goods, then all frustrations or violations of anyone's purposes must be morally wrong. 'Harm' is a value-word meaning deprivation of good; so what constitutes harm varies with all the diverse criteria of good, including the wide variety of human purposes. The devout religionist's purposes are violated and he loses something he regards as good if he hears someone express irreligious opinions or sees someone playing ball on Sunday or reading pornographic literature; a suitor's purposes are violated and he is made to lose something he regards as good if he is spurned by his beloved; an artist is made to lose something he regards as good if the prize in an important competition goes to his rival; the patriot's purposes are violated and he loses something he regards as good if onlookers fail to salute the flag or continue talking while the flag is unfurled; and, among myriad other possibilities, some persons' purposes, including those of atheists, civil libertarians, dissidents, and revolutionaries, are violated by the opposites of the actions that offend the religionist, the suitor, the artist, and the patriot. Thus, if the PGC is interpreted as prohibiting all specific harms, this allows all sorts of arbitrary and mutually conflicting criteria to serve as the grounds for condemning actions as morally wrong.

In addition to this consideration, the suggested interpretation of the PGC would go counter to the equality of generic rights between the agent and his recipient. It would mean that although what it is morally right or morally wrong for the agent to do to his recipient is determined by rational criteria, no such limitation enters into the determination of the specific harms on the basis of which the recipient may rightly demand certain forbearances of the agent. According to the PGC, the agent must allow his recipient to participate purposively in their transaction, and such participation includes that the recipient not have his purpose-fulfillment lowered in the transaction by losing something that seems to him to be good. But if the criterion of 'good' and of 'purpose-fulfillment' here is allowed to vary indiscriminately with all the variable purposes of recipients, so that violation of any of these purposes convicts the agent of moral wrongdoing, then the agent's area of justified freedom and purpose-fulfillment would be restricted to a much greater degree than would that of his recipients. The agent would have to adjust his own purposes so as to defer to any even arbitrary purposive whims of the recipients in order to avoid 'harming' them.

The removal of this disparity requires a way of distinguishing between arbitrary and nonarbitrary criteria of the harm that consists in having one's level of purpose-fulfillment lowered, where the infliction of the nonarbitrary harms is morally wrong. This problem is similar to that confronting the expositors of Mill's principle of liberty, which sets forth 'harm to others' as the only justification for restricting a person's freedom, where such harm, too, is deemed morally wrong.[13] The expositors have offered various distinctions in the attempt to avoid having to admit arbitrary or benighted conceptions of 'harm.' These distinctions have been suggestive, but they have also been open to serious objections. For example, the basis of the distinction between arbitrary and nonarbitrary criteria of harm is not to be found in the difference between physical assault and nonphysical damages; for theft, promise-breaking, libel, and so forth inflict harms in a nonarbitrary sense and are correctly regarded as morally wrong. Nor can the sphere of nonarbitrary harms be demarcated by the criterion of whether all persons would resent the harms in question, for slaves might be conditioned not to resent even physical assaults on them, and the subjects of a dictator might be brainwashed into not resenting his lies and oppressions. Somewhat more promising is the idea that conduct that inflicts merely arbitrary harm has nonrationally grounded moral beliefs as the necessary and sufficient conditions of its being deemed harmful. The point is that if there is to be a nonarbitrary basis for regarding conduct as harmful, then one must be able to adduce considerations that are independent of the belief that the conduct is harmful or morally wrong.[14] Nevertheless, this attempted grounding of the distinction is unsuccessful, for it includes too much as nonarbitrarily harmful and as morally wrong conduct. For example, if a girl informs her ardent suitor that she no longer wants to see him or if one person hurts another's feelings by criticizing his clothes or his writing, such action may adversely affect its recipient independent of his false moral beliefs; yet the action need not be morally wrong.

4.14. It seems, then, that if a criterion of what is harmful is not arbitrary, as when it is confined to physical injury, then it includes too little, while if it also includes nonphysical damages, then it becomes arbitrary and includes too much. The basis of this arbitrariness is that the criterion of the harmful is made to depend on contingent beliefs or attitudes that can vary indiscriminately with all the highly diverse values different persons may uphold. To find a nonarbitrary criterion, we must hence look to values every person must uphold insofar as he is a prospective purposive agent: we must look to the very conditions of purposive action. As has already been seen, it is undeniable that the harmful includes whatever·adversely affects the necessary preconditions of one's action, as by removing one's life, freedom of movement, physical integrity, or mental equilibrium; I have called these 'basic harms.' They are nonarbitrarily harmful because, amid the diverse values different persons may have, as actual or prospective agents they objectively need the basic goods that are attacked in such ways. Now in the case of nonsubtractive goods there are further objective, although less serious, injuries.

It will be recalled that I distinguished above between goods and the capabilities of action required for having them (2.4). The nonsubtractive goods, viewed occurrently, consist in not losing what one regards as good; but amid the immense variety of what one so regards, the nonsubtractive capabilities of action required for avoiding such losses are much more constant and are of a much more general order than those goods themselves. They have this greater generality because they are second-order goods and abilities: they consist in retaining undiminished one's capabilities for particular actions, including one's abilities to act for the purpose of retaining one's first-order goods or maintaining one's level of purpose-fulfillment, regardless of what one's particular purposes and goods may be. And it is when actions universally tend to attack or diminish these capabilities that they inflict nonarbitrary harms in the sphere of nonsubtractive goods, over and above the basic harms that come from having one's basic goods attacked.

A person who has the nonsubtractive capabilities of action can act more confidently in pursuit of his various purposes. His flanks, so to speak, are not under attack as he undertakes to move ahead; his ability to maintain both his level of particular goods and his capacity for particular actions is not being affected adversely while he is trying to act. Examples of ways of undergoing such adversity include being lied to, cheated, stolen from, defamed, insulted, suffering broken promises, and having one's privacy violated, as well as being subjected to dangerous, degrading, or excessively debilitating conditions of physical labor or housing or other strategic situations of life when resources are available for improvement. To interfere with someone's nonsubtractive capabilities of action is to affect them adversely as they bear on maintaining the resources with which he acts. Such interference hence violates what I shall call his 'nonsubtractive rights.'

When the nonsubtractive goods whose loss constitutes harm and lowered purpose-fulfillment are viewed at the generic range of capabilities of action, interferences are to be considered harmful with regard to such goods only when they would universally tend to affect adversely anyone's nonsubtractive capabilities of action, including his ability to avoid losing particular goods and to maintain undiminished his capabilities for particular actions. Idiosyncratic or other specialized tendencies must be ruled out. Further, the tendency to cause such adversity must be ascertainable by empirical methods publicly available to every intellectually normal person, and its being such an effect must not be the result of beliefs whose validity is not thus ascertainable. This recourse to empirical methods is in keeping with the *PGC*'s grounding in inductive as well as deductive rationality.

Empirical considerations hence enter this criterion of harmfulness in two ways. When it is said that conduct of type X adversely affects its recipient's capacity for purpose-fulfilling actions and hence is nonarbitrarily harmful to that recipient, this affecting is a causal relation and must be open to empirical test. Hence, if the recipient says that the adverse effect occurs only by threatening his immortal soul, or can be ascertained only by unique methods of spiritual intuition, this does not satisfy the criterion. But even if the adverse affecting in question is empirically ascertainable, it must not itself be the result of nonempirical beliefs of the sort just mentioned. If Jones becomes thoroughly dejected by Kane's conduct, and this in fact causes Jones's capacity for purpose-fulfilling action to be reduced, this will not count as genuine harm on the present criterion if Jones's dejection is the result of his belief that conduct like Kane's condemns its practitioner to eternal damnation.

Three further qualifications must be indicated. First, when the deleterious effect on any recipient's capacity for action is made the criterion of specific harmfulness and hence of morally wrong actions, those recipients must be excluded who have already suffered such drastic lowering of their capacity for purpose-fulfillment that it would not be appreciably reduced by further adversities. Slaves and terrorized persons are examples of such recipients. Since they are the victims of actions or institutions that are morally wrong according to the *PGC*, the effects of this moral wrongness should not be allowed to serve as further criteria of the morally right or wrong; for this would be to sanction rather than reject the previous wrongs. Second, just as the effects of wrong institutions must be excluded, so the workings of institutions that are morally right because justified by the *PGC* must also be excluded from the harms the *PGC* prohibits as morally wrong. Thus, in my above examples of the suitor and the artist, it may indeed be the case that the former's nonsubtractive capabilities of action are drastically reduced by his beloved's rejection of him, and the artist's by his loss in the competition. But quite apart from the question whether such reduction always or universally tends to result from the respective transactions, it must be noted that each of these transactions occurs within a certain institution and in accordance with its rules: courtship and marriage in the first case, artistic and other competitions in the second. Each of these institutions with its rules is justified by the *PGC*, as will be shown in chapter 5. Hence, the lowered capabilities of action that may result from the justified workings of these institutions are not harms whose infliction is morally wrong.

Third, the effects bearing on capacity for purpose-fulfilling action must include tendencies as well as actual effects. For an action-type to be harmful according to the proposed criterion, each of its tokens need not cause a lowering of its recipient's capacity for purpose-fulfillment. It is sufficient if such an action's empirically ascertainable tendency, and hence its usual effect, is to produce such decreased capacity so long as it would have this effect on any recipient who has not previously experienced drastic decrease and who does not have special nonempirical beliefs that cause him to undergo the decrease. Thus, for example, to steal a small sum of money may in some particular case have no direct effect on the victim's capacity for purpose-fulfilling action, but the usual tendency of such action is to have an adverse effect on its recipients because it tends to diminish their purchasing power. The tendency of other actions to cause parallel adversities may be exhibited in such specific areas as the abilities to plan for the future, to have knowledge of facts relevant to one's projected action, to utilize one's resources to fulfill one's wants, and so forth.

The word 'tendency' has figured prominently in utilitarian theories where the rightness of an action is determined by the overall consequences not of that action or kind of action alone but of everyone's performing that kind of action. Reference to tendencies, however, need not be confined to such generalized consequences in rule-utilitarian theories, nor even to any other form of utilitarianism. For example, W. D. Ross puts his deontological theory of prima facie duties in terms of an action's "tendency to be our duty . . . . Tendency to be one's duty may be called a parti-resultant attribute, i.e., one which belongs to an act in virtue of some one component in its nature."[15] In general, to say that X tends to Y is to indicate that there is a certain positive relation between X and Y. The relation may be logical or causal. My use of 'tendency,' like that of utilitarians, is causal, but otherwise it is closer to Ross's use. A kind of action X tends to lower its recipient's capacity for purpose-fulfilling action if, viewed by itself in abstraction from other variable circumstances, such an action would produce such an effect. Because such actions are not usually accompanied by circumstances that remove such an effect, it can also be said of this tendency that actions of kind X usually lower their recipients' capacities for purpose-fulfilling action.

There are thus two important differences from the utilitarians' use of 'tendency.' First, where the utilitarians focus on the consequences of general performance of actions of kind X ('What would happen if everyone did that?'), I focus on the performance of such a particular action by itself in abstraction from other variable circumstances, so that the action is considered in terms of the effects each individual action of that kind usually has. For example, there is a difference between considering, on the one hand, the consequences of all persons' stealing from one another and, on the other, the usual consequences of stealing as a kind of action, where each action-token is taken to have the characteristics and hence the consequences of the kind. There is a difference between considering the consequences of everyone's stealing and the usual consequences of any one person's stealing when it is not assumed that all persons steal. Second, where for the utilitarians the generalized consequences of such an action determine whether the action is right or wrong by the criterion of whether it would tend to maximize utility overall, for the PGC the tendency determines rightness or wrongness by the criterion of whether such an action raises or lowers the capabilities for purpose-fulfilling action on the part of its individual recipients.

Actions that lower these capabilities and thus inflict specific harms violate the equality of generic rights prescribed by the PGC, in that they are forms of exploitation. By such actions the agent exercises and advances his own capacity for action by lowering his recipients' capacity; he obtains additive goods by making his recipients lose basic or nonsubtractive goods; he gains at their expense; he uses them as mere means to his own ends. All such actions are rationally unjustifiable in that the agent claims a nonsubtractive right to participate purposively and without lowered well-being insofar as he is a prospective purposive agent, while he denies this right to his recipients although they too are prospective purposive agents.

The above account also explains how there are degrees of moral wrongdoing, and it indicates an order that ought to be observed with regard to the moral preferability or nonpreferability of actions. One kind of action X is more wrong than another kind Y if X is more harmful than Y, in that X tends to lower its recipient's capacity for action more than does Y, where he has a right that such capacity not be lowered. Thus, the basic harms are more wrong than the specific harms, and among the latter physical assault is usually more wrong than lying or promise-breaking. This order derives from the generic content of the *PGC*. Since the *PGC*'s prohibition of violating the generic rights of one's recipients is derived from the agent's claim that he has rights to the necessary conditions of action, one violation is more wrong than another if it interferes with a more necessary condition of action. For it is these conditions that determine, with regard to content, the moral rightness or wrongness of actions.

This point also bears on the question of actions supporting the nonsubtractive goods of other persons. In addition to the positive duty discussed above to rescue and prevent other basic harms, does a person have a positive duty to prevent others from suffering the specific harms of lowered capabilities of action? Since such harms have a less serious and immediate impact on their victims' well-being, there is less urgency about them. Still, the degree of seriousness may vary within this group; in addition, the victims may vary in their ability to avoid such harms or to recover from their effects. In general, the more serious the harm and the less able its recipient is to ward it off, the greater is the obligation of another person to prevent it if he can do so without suffering comparable harm himself. Thus, if A hears B telling C a seemingly harmless white lie, A has little duty to warn C of this; but if C is a poor widow whom B is about to defraud of her meager life's savings, then A has an urgent duty to warn C of this and to act further to prevent such loss. It must also be kept in mind, however, that in a state based on the *PGC* there are laws that prohibit and punish such fraud (5.8), so that the preventive action need not be taken by A alone, unlike the immediacy and urgency of Carr's rescuing Davis from drowning.

The duty to perform such preventive actions is derivable from the *PGC* in a way parallel to the duty to rescue. The *PGC* prohibits inflicting specific harms on other persons, and it requires that one assist others to avoid such harms when the others cannot avoid them on their own and when one thereby incurs no comparable cost. Hence, if A is aware of the impending fraud and can prevent it at no comparable cost to himself, then by failing to warn C he participates in the harmful action. In the case of the seemingly harmless white lie, on the other hand, A's warning C might well bring to A greater disadvantage in the way of hostility than the disadvantage undergone by C.

4.15. Questions may be raised about the specific harms and nonsubtractive rights as I have defined them. Even if the harms usually or even always tend to lower their recipients' capacity for action, is this the primary point in their being morally wrong? Indeed, may there not be actions that tend to lower their recipients' capacity for action but are not morally wrong, and may there not also be actions that do not tend to lower their recipients' capacity for action yet are morally wrong? The first of this group of questions bears particularly on such an action as promise-breaking. The objection is that in promising, the agent puts himself under a specific obligation to his recipient precisely by virtue of having promised, and what directly is morally wrong in breaking the promise is the agent's failure to fulfill this obligation.

Hence, if as my account maintains, what makes promise-breaking wrong is its tendency to lower its recipient's capacity for action, this reason fails to differentiate promise-breaking from actions that do not involve failure to fulfill a self-imposed obligation but that also tend to lower their recipients' capacity for action. Compare, for example, two possible cases where Norton, a farmer who already has a tractor, purchases the only other available tractor in the area, leaving Owens, another farmer, with no tractor. This purchase by Norton tends to lower Owens's capacity for action, since it will make his farming operations much less efficient than they would otherwise be and than he would want them to be. In the one case, however, Norton has promised Owens that he would not purchase the tractor; in the other case, he has made no such promise. Two points follow from this difference. One is that, in the absence of his making a promise, Norton has not done something morally wrong even though his action has tended to lower Owens's capacity for action. The other is that Norton's breaking his promise is a moral wrong done to Owens that is quite distinct from the fact that Norton has acted so as to lower Owens's capacity for action. But, the objection concludes, if what is wrong in promise-breaking is simply its tendency to lower the promisee's capacity for action, then these two different cases of Norton's purchasing the tractor would not be morally distinguishable.

My answer to this objection is that breaking the promise constitutes an additional lowering of the promisee's capacity for action, in the ways indicated above. There is indeed an obligation to keep a promise that is distinct from other obligations to refrain from harming someone by lowering his capacity for action. But the promissory obligation would not be a moral one if it lacked a certain sort of content, if what was promised had no positive bearing on the promisee's own purposes, on what he viewed as good. Promise-breaking is wrong because the promiser, for his own purposes, intentionally raises the promisee's expectations in regard to the latter's values or purpose-fulfillment and then, by breaking his promise, derives for himself an additive good at the promisee's expense, so that the latter suffers a specific harm in basing his own projected action on a false expectation and on misplaced confidence.

A second part of the objection was that a person may cause another to have a lower capacity for action without thereby doing what is morally wrong. This objection holds, however, only if the action is performed within an institution that is itself justifiable through the *PGC*. The above case of Norton's buying the tractor (where he has not promised that he will not do so) falls within an institution of commercial transactions, whose justifiability requires separate discussion. But it is at least plausible that Norton's monopolizing the supply of tractors is morally wrong precisely because of the wide disparity it generates between himself and Owens with regard to their respective capacities for action and purpose-fulfillment.

The third part of the objection was that actions may be morally wrong without lowering their recipients' capacity for action. This can be seen in such cases as where one breaks one's promise to a person whose capacity for action is already minimal, such as a paraplegic or a dying person. In reply, it must be pointed out that the paraplegic is still capable of action and hence of purpose-fulfillment through action: he can think, choose (although within narrower limits), and plan. To this extent, to break one's promise to him is to lower his capacity for action in the way indicated above.

As for the promise made to a dying person and broken after his death, this is indeed a marginal situation. If living persons know of the promise and rely on its being kept, they would be auxiliary promisees and it would be their related capabilities of action that the promise-breaking would tend to lower. If the promise was made and known only to the person who subsequently died, much depends on the relation of the promise's content to the capabilities for action of other persons. For example, if Pratt promises Quinn that he will look after his children, he presumably thinks that Quinn's children will need looking after, and this bearing on their nurture or on the development of their capabilities of action gives Pratt's promise its main obligatory force. But even if there is no such direct bearing on anyone's capabilities of action, breaking the promise is still wrong. It may lead or tend to lead the promiser to break his promise in other cases, so that the action-capabilities of other, living persons will be adversely affected. Moreover, a person ought to be honorable and trustworthy, both as a duty to himself and because of the bearing of such qualities on his general observance of the *PGC* (5.19).

We saw above that basic harms, while generally prohibited by the

PGC, may rightly be inflicted on other persons to prevent their inflicting or continuing to inflict such harm on oneself. A parallel situation obtains with regard to the specific harms, but with several qualifications. One person may not lie to or steal from another in order to prevent him from lying to or stealing from oneself, for such wrong actions can be prevented without engaging in similar actions. Such specific harms may be inflicted, however, if there is no other way to prevent greater wrongful harm. We have already seen this in the case of lying to prevent a murder (3.27). Similarly, one may steal in order to prevent oneself or one's family from starving, but not in order to obtain amenities that go beyond basic goods.

In political and other contexts, there is the Machiavellian doctrine that the end justifies the means, so that lying and promise-breaking should be engaged in where needed to maintain one's power. Are there any cases where this is acceptable? Surely not where the end is one's own aggrandizement, or that of one's firm or corporation, despite the approval of contemporary Machiavellians. On the other hand, the Boston Tea Party was a case of stealing and destroying property, and it was justified as a means of protest against deprivation of important political rights of the method of consent (5.11). When these rights, bearing on extensive freedoms required for the possibility of successful action, take precedence over property rights, it should be only as a temporary expedient with a view to securing the former rights. In relations between nations, similarly, lying and promise-breaking should not be engaged in except in desperate circumstances where such actions are necessary to prevent subjugation by an unjust aggressor. In all such cases, what justifies inflicting the specific harms is not the maximizing of good but only the need for avoiding much greater violations of the equality of generic rights.

Duties regarding Additive Goods

4.16. Additive goods are part of a prospective agent's well-being when they are viewed generically-dispositionally. In this view, they consist in the means or conditions that enable any person to increase his capabilities of purpose-fulfilling action and hence to achieve more of his goals. Such additive goods differ from basic and nonsubtractive goods because of their positive vector. They are dynamic rather than static, concerned not with maintaining the necessary preconditions and capabilities of one's action but with augmenting and developing these capabilities. Thereby one is able to gain and utilize opportunities for improving one's lot by one's own productive work. As a result, one can fulfill a wider range of purposes in a mutually reinforcing way. A main (though not the sole) justification of property rights by the *PGC* derives from the double consideration that they retrospectively result from such work and that they prospectively facilitate the means and opportunities for engaging in it. This justification is an application of the agent's acting in accord with his own rights to freedom and to additive well-being; but it indicates as well that the right to property is limited by the *PGC*'s requirement that agents also act in accord with their recipients' rights to well-being. Concepts like efficiency and maximizing are especially pertinent in this context of additive goods. They apply to the well-being of the prospective agent insofar as he may have plans and purposes which in turn lead to further plans and purposes as part of a complete life, where this well-being consists in having the relevant additive abilities.

The *PGC* requires, as part of its protection of the right to well-being, that agents respect the additive goods or abilities of their recipients. The derivation of this obligation is parallel to the derivations discussed above of obligations regarding basic and nonsubtractive goods. Since the rational agent views as a necessary good his well-being in that component of it which consists in his having the conditions of increasing his capabilities of purpose-fulfilling action, he holds that he has rights to these conditions insofar as he is a prospective purposive agent. I shall call them 'additive rights.' Hence he must grant, on pain of contradiction, that all other prospective agents, including his recipients, also have these rights and that he has a correlative obligation to refrain from interfering with their having such conditions. To interfere with someone in this way is to inflict on him specific harms. Such harms are parallel to those discussed above in connection with nonsubtractive goods and are likewise prohibited by the *PGC*. In certain circumstances, when prospective agents are unable to provide for their additive well-being through their own efforts, the agent's obligation extends to assisting them to have such well-being, although this obligation normally pertains to appropriate social institutions.

Central to all additive goods viewed as dispositions or abilities is the prospective agent's sense of his own worth. We have seen that every agent regards his particular purposes as worth pursuing and hence attributes value to them. When such evaluative purposiveness is more than incidental and transient, the agent has an abiding self-esteem in that he views the worth of his goals as reflecting his own worth as a rational person whose life, freedom, and well-being are worthy of protection and development. Without such self-esteem, his ability to achieve further goals becomes problematic, and with it his prospects of taking satisfaction in what he accomplishes thereby.[16]

The *PGC* requires that this self-regard include a social dimension in two directions. The agent's self-esteem must be reflected in a corresponding esteem for him on the part of other persons, and he must himself have a corresponding esteem for other persons. None of these relations requires invidious comparisons among persons, especially if they fulfill the other duties of the *PGC*. Just as the agent's self-esteem is reflected by his awareness of himself as acting for purposes worth pursuing without necessarily comparing these with other persons' pursuits or purposes, so too with his relations to other persons. Recognition of the great diversity of goals or values and of effectiveness in achieving them is quite compatible with such a noncomparative basis of self-esteem. The auto mechanic's efficiency at repairing motors differs from the accountant's efficiency in tracing deficits without affecting the more general value each puts on himself as a purposive agent. Regardless of such diversities, the *PGC* requires a general respect for all other prospective purposive agents with regard not only to the external effects of their agency but also, and primarily, to the factors of rational personhood and aspiration that support and generate these effects (3.3).

In consequence of such respect, each person must refrain from feeling or exhibiting contempt toward others; persons must not be insulted, belittled, or patronized, nor must they be discriminated against on grounds of race, religion, or nationality. Put positively, the duties of such respect require that persons have toward one another an attitude of mutual acceptance and toleration, including acquiescence in diversity so long as this falls within the limits set by the *PGC*'s duties regarding basic and nonsubtractive goods. The duties of respect also require a readiness to be considerate of one another's needs and to help one another in ways that are mutually supportive. Thus, although esteem or respect is directly not an action but rather an attitude or disposition, it is proximately related to actions both in its possible effects and as resulting from actions. Failure to fulfill these duties constitutes violation of the additive rights of one's recipients in one of the most central phases of such rights.

Closely related to the agent's sense of his own worth are various virtues of character. These are additive goods because they serve to ground and reinforce the agent's self-esteem and because, as deep-seated enduring dispositions that underlie and help to motivate actions, they contribute to his effectiveness in acting to fulfill his purposes. They may be summarized under three of the traditional four cardinal virtues. Courage is the disposition to have and to act from a sound estimation of what is and is not to be feared; it includes the ability to appraise and confront dangers, fortitude and perseverance in the face of adversity, determination in overcoming obstacles rather than taking the easy way out. Temperance is the state of character whereby one guides one's conduct judiciously with regard to controlling one's appetites and inclinations; it enables the agent to maintain a proper balance between lust or gluttony and abstemiousness or asceticism in matters bearing on his physical and mental health, and to uphold his self-respect as a rational person in contrast to being only an animal. Prudence is the proximate ability not only to calculate the most efficient means for achieving one's particular ends but also to distinguish among both particular and more general ends themselves, to ascertain which of one's possible ends are most worth pursuing in the light of one's overall capacities and deepest aspirations; it therefore includes both self-knowledge and knowledge of one's natural and social environment, as well as the proximate ability and tendency to bring these to bear on one's actions and projects. Just as all three of these virtues (or groups of virtues) are acquired by regular perform- ance of the corresponding actions, so they contribute to a certain practical stability on the part of the agent whereby he is not deflected from his actions and projects by each new stimulus or by passing, temporary fancies or by insufficiently sifted fears or inclinations. A person who has these virtues is not a mere passive recipient or victim of external causes but rather, as a regular matter, controls his own behavior by his informed, unforced choices and plans.

As so far depicted, these self-regarding virtues are not moral but prudential.[17] To be moral virtues, in that sense in which 'moral' is opposed to 'immoral' as well as to 'nonmoral,' they must be guided by or at least be subordinate to the other-regarding virtue of justice as this is embodied in the *PGC*. To paraphrase Kant, none of the prudential virtues is unqualifiedly good, for a person who acts according to them may incur generic inconsistency in that they may be used for immoral purposes. It cannot directly be said, then, that the agent has a moral duty to develop these virtues in himself. His moral duty in this regard, rather, is in large part to refrain from actions that hinder the development of the prudential virtues in other persons. Such actions may take a variety of forms: promoting a climate of fear and oppression; encouraging the spread of physically or mentally harmful practices such as excessive use of alcohol, tobacco, drugs, or pornography; contributing to misinformation, ignorance, and super- stition, especially as these bear on persons' ability to act effectively in pursuit of their purposes. By such actions the agent violates his recipients' rights to additive well-being as this is found in their having the prudential virtues. He also has the positive duty to assist, so far as he can, the development of these virtues in other persons, while respecting their freedom. This assistance, as provided by the individual agent, takes such forms as setting an example of the practice of the virtues in his own actions and supporting a social and educational milieu in which these virtues are respected and fostered.

It is in such indirect ways and for such other-directed reasons that the agent has a moral duty to develop in himself and to practice the prudential virtues on his own. For he cannot contribute to other persons' having these additive goods of character unless he himself has them and acts according to them. As was noted above, moreover, his practice of these virtues must be guided by the *PGC*; when so guided, his having the prudential virtues will also contribute to his own effectiveness as a moral agent. To acquire the broad knowledge on which prudence is based requires the use of reason; and when reason is applied to the necessary conditions of action, the *PGC* can itself become known more fully and, with it, the conditions for its effective implementation. In these ways the prudential virtues of the agent also become his moral virtues whose development in himself is his moral duty required by the *PGC*. Although the *PGC* directly requires certain kinds of actions rather then virtues, it also requires that the agent act in such ways that he develops the moral and prudential virtues in himself, because of the assistance such development provides for his fulfillment of the various moral duties of action prescribed by the *PGC*.

There are also certain more general conditions that contribute to the development of self-esteem and of the prudential virtues and that enable persons to develop in other ways their general capabilities for fulfilling their purposes through action. These conditions include freedom, knowledge, education, wealth, and income. The first three of these are obviously closely connected. Not only is knowledge of oneself and of one's natural and social environments central to the virtue of prudence; in addition, the voluntariness of action requires that the agent have knowledge of relevant circumstances. Both the acquisition and the practical use of such knowledge also require freedom in the sense of the unhindered exercise of one's mental powers; for although knowledge presupposes norms or criteria that must guide these powers, the recognition and application of the norms must not be fettered by any irrelevant restrictions. And more generally, as is clear from the whole central emphasis on freedom as a generic feature of action, without a person's control of his behavior through his unforced choice, he cannot act to attain his purposes. For the achievement of both knowledge and freedom, education is a prime means.

The relation between any person's capabilities of action and the conditions for equal opportunity to develop and increase these capabilities is in part an empirical, causal matter. To ascertain the conditions is easiest when one confines oneself to basic goods, but it becomes progressively more difficult as one advances from this minimum to the means by which the full range of persons' problem-solving, purpose-achieving abilities can be effectively developed. Three sorts of difficulties of ascertainment may be especially indicated. One concerns the relation of various means both to one another and to the projected end. There are problems in finding out how, for example, the acquisition of formal education is related to the acquisition of wealth and income, how each of these is related to the development of self-esteem, and how all of these bear on increasing one's general capacities for purpose-fulfillment. A second, closely connected difficulty concerns the comparative development of these additive goods among persons. It is difficult to determine how persons are to have equal means, or equal access to means, of acquiring education, income, self-esteem, and other additive goods, and how their equality with regard to one of these is related to their equality with regard to the others.[18] Third, there is the difficulty of ascertaining these means-end relations amid the diversities of different groups in different social structures. The agent must at least refrain from interfering with his recipients' additive goods; but his ability to fulfill this obligation varies with his resources. For example, the ability of parents thus to refrain and also to fulfill their nurturing obligations is conditioned by the kind of society in which they live and by their place in that society. The difference between an impoverished peasant and a wealthy landowner provides a graphic but by no means unique illustration of the point.

In view of such difficulties, caution is needed in discussing some of the specific contents and interrelations of additive goods viewed as the means of improving persons' capabilities for purpose-fulfilling action. Nevertheless, the general considerations presented above are sound; as they have suggested, the additive goods serve as means to purpose-fulfillment not only or mainly in a narrowly instrumental way but also through being direct components of persons' dignity and effectiveness as agents.

4.17. The *PGC*'s equality of generic rights includes equal additive rights, but these are equal rights to additive well-being viewed dispositionally, not equal rights to particular additive goods. Thus all prospective purposive agents have equal rights to acquire and have self-esteem, the prudential virtues, freedom, knowledge, and education, but this does not entail that the various particular goods that different agents may achieve by the use of these components of additive well-being must also themselves be equally distributed. It is one thing to fulfill particular purposes, another thing to have the means of such fulfillment. To be sure, the latter is in part for the sake of the former, and if persons never or rarely fulfilled their particular purposes, their possession of the general means or conditions would be highly doubtful. In addition to the broader scope of the general conditions, however, the distinction between them and particular additive goods is important from the standpoint of moral rights and duties. Whereas fulfillment of one's particular purposes is usually the function of the agent himself, to acquire the means or conditions of such fulfillment requires in various ways the assistance of other persons and institutions. It is to such assistance that one has additive rights, although even here the individual can and must participate actively by making his own progressive contributions.

This distinction between particular goods and the general means of obtaining them applies especially to wealth and income. In one respect, because of the directness of their relation to particular purchasable additive goods, wealth and income are themselves such particular goods: they are direct aids to or elements in purpose-fulfilling action. What the *PGC*'s equality of additive rights requires concerning wealth and income, however, is not that these, as particular goods, be distributed equally, but rather that the means of acquiring them be distributed equally so far as possible. As against giving money, for example, the emphasis falls rather on developing for each person the means that enable him to obtain money for himself through his own agency as applied in productive work. The main obligation for contributing to such development, as with the development of education more generally, falls not on individuals but on appropriate social institutions, beginning with the family but continuing to broader supportive frameworks.

This conception of the equality of generic rights as applied to wealth and income is quite similar to traditional ideas of equality of opportunity, where 'opportunity' consists in proximate potentialities for fulfilling one's purposes. There are also traditional objections against equality of opportunity as an ideal of social morality. It is held that genuine equality of opportunity is impossible because of genetic and environmental differences among persons. It is also held that such equality is in any case an unworthy ideal because the context of 'opportunity' is one of competition wherein persons seek to outdo one another in a scrambling rat race. The force of the latter objection, however, so far as it applies against the *PGC*'s equality of additive rights, is considerably mitigated by the fact that the principle also defends and makes prior the equalities of basic and of nonsubtractive rights. This priority entails that the equality of opportunity is limited as to the results for which opportunities are to be provided: they may not include, for example, opportunities for killing or enslaving other persons or for depriving them of other basic or nonsubtractive goods. More generally, the *PGC* requires that the competing agents fulfill the negative and also, where necessary, the positive duties involved in mutuality of respect for generic rights. The equality of additive rights also requires that whatever the genetic differences among persons or the diversities imposed by familial environments, arrangements must be made to compensate persons for the more severe handicaps imposed by those contexts. In this way, the competition will at least be made more equitable.

Many agents are not aware of the contribution that specific additive goods such as education may make to their general well-being. As agents, however, they value as a necessary good the well-being that enables them to achieve their purposes, and the right they implicitly claim to this general well-being becomes specified as they acquire greater knowledge of its various means or conditions. The derivation of the obligations of agents regarding additive goods thus proceeds from the conditions required for each person's development of his capabilities of action to the actions or omissions whereby other persons either assist or do not interfere with this development. The basis of these obligations is not utilitarian. One important difference is that the obligations are not concerned with maximizing utility or purpose-fulfillment overall regardless of the rights or goods of individuals, but rather with each individual's equal opportunity to develop and maximize his own capacities for purpose-fulfillment as contributing to the enhancement of his own life.

It is important to distinguish between the individual and the social dimensions of these obligations. There must be social institutions that assist persons to attain various important additive goods; the fuller justification of this, and the nature of the corresponding obligations, will be discussed in the next chapter (5.13). But so far as concerns individuals other than parents acting apart from or in supplement to such institutions, their obligations with regard to additive goods, except those bearing on self-esteem discussed above, are largely negative. The agent must refrain equally in each case from interfering with his recipients' acquiring the means for increasing their capabilities of action. This obligation bears on equal opportunity for development: it is a matter of not restricting any person's chances for such growth. This negativity does not, however, leave the rights to additive goods unsupported. Their fulfillment is in important respects a matter of self-development on the part of each person, once parental and societal nurturing has done its part and the general requirements bearing on self-esteem are fulfilled. If other persons refrain from putting obstacles in the way and there are the requisite assisting social institutions, each person can proceed to promote and develop his own capacities for purpose-fulfillment. This is in part an empirical hypothesis related to such psychological concepts as 'self-actualization' that attempt to characterize human abilities of 'growth' and 'creativity.' It also reflects the Deweyan doctrine of the continuum of means and ends, in that the process of attaining and protecting the necessary goods of freedom and well-being for each prospective agent must embody so far as possible his own progressive use of these goods.[19]

Although persons differ in their capacities for purpose-fulfilling actions and in their abilities to develop these capacities, their differences in intelligence and in effort do not derive exclusively from causes over which they have no control. The hard determinist thesis is as little to be credited here as in connection with the general causation of choices. The concept of a person is not to be resolved solely into a locus of forces impinging from without, as if the person himself made no contribution to what he is, does, and becomes, so that he does not deserve anything for this contribution and for its beneficial effects on the well-being of other persons. On the contrary, each person is himself a source of his own energizing activity; unlike Cartesian inert matter, he can develop himself from his own internal resources to whose structure and contents he can make his own effective contributions.

Apart from the active participation of each person in the development of his capacities for purpose-fulfillment, the primary obligations with regard to a person's attaining additive goods stem from and operate within the context of the appropriate institutions. These include supportive families, enlightening schools open to all, unfettered and abundant communications media, a pluralistic, nonhierarchical social structure, a libertarian political system with a related legal system, and widely diffused property and opportunities for obtaining property. Individual persons, however, have corresponding obligations to give enlightened support to such institutions, including the mutual respect that helps to make them effective.

Some of the obligations bearing on additive goods are close to those bearing on nonsubtractive goods. This is not surprising, because the conditions needed to maintain capabilities of action merge into those needed to increase them. There is, nevertheless, a difference of emphasis. For example, to break a promise involves the double harm that it tends to lower the promisee's capability of action because of the false expectation on which he may have to act, and that it prevents him from improving his relevant capability of action as involved in the promise made to him that he agreed to accept. When Long breaks his promise to Miller to give him ten dollars, Miller is worse off than he was before the promise (because he now has a disappointed expectation and a false belief on which he bases his plans); and he has also lost a means of being better off. His level of purpose-fulfillment has been lowered and has also been prevented from being raised.

DUTIES REGARDING FREEDOM

4.18. Thus far, I have been discussing the various parts of the *PGC*'s requirement that the agent act in accord with his recipient's right to well-being. I turn now to consider the applications of the other main component of the principle, the recipient's right to freedom. Just as well-being consists in both having and exercising certain capabilities of action bearing on purpose-fulfillment, so too freedom is not only occurrent but also dispositional: it consists not only in exercising control over one's behavior by one's unforced choice in particular situations, but also in having the long-range effective ability to exercise such control. Both occurrent and dispositional freedom require that one not be interfered with by other persons in doing what one unforcedly chooses to do; but in the one case the noninterference pertains only to the particular action, whereas in the other it is more temporally extensive. For the most part these two aspects work together, but at some points occurrent freedom may come into conflict with maintaining long-range freedom. I shall hence deal primarily with the right to occurrent freedom that the *PGC* requires that the agent accord to his recipients in particular transactions, postponing for later the consideration of conflicts.

Since, as we have seen, the agent necessarily holds that he has a right to freedom, to participate voluntarily in transactions in which he is involved, on the ground of being a prospective purposive agent, he must admit that his recipients, who are prospective purposive agents, also have the right to freedom or voluntariness of participation in transactions in which they are involved with him. The recipients' right to freedom is structurally similar to but not identical with the freedom of agents. Just as the agent controls by his unforced choice whether or not he will perform or initiate some action affecting his recipient, so the latter has the right to control by his unforced choice whether or not he will undergo the agent's performance or initiative. In each case one's unforced choice is to be the necessary and sufficient condition of one's participating in the transaction, so that one is not interfered with by others regarding this participation. The recipient has the right to determine for himself whether he will participate, so that his participation must be subject to his own unforced consent, and hence to his own reasons and autonomy. The *PGC* is thus a principle of Equal Freedom in that it requires that both the agent and his recipient participate freely in the transactions in which they are involved. It is necessarily the case that the agent participates freely in the particular transaction. But whether the recipient also participates freely depends upon the agent, since he can and should refrain from acting on the recipient unless and until the latter gives his unforced consent. The agent hence has the duty to respect his recipient's freedom. If the agent violates this requirement by coercing or deceiving his recipients, then he contradicts himself and hence lacks rational justification for his actions, unless there are further considerations, themselves derived from the *PGC*, that justify such violation.

There may be degrees of freedom. The agent may act with varying degrees of knowledge of relevant circumstances; he may be subject to more or less external pressure or emotional tension; the alternatives between which he chooses may be more or less desirable to him, more or less restricted, and so forth. Parallel considerations apply to the recipient. Hence, the equality of freedom as between agent and recipient can be only approximate. What is required of the agent, however, is that he not knowingly or intentionally lower his recipient's degree of voluntariness by removing or weakening the latter's informed control over his own participation in the transaction, and hence his own rational autonomy.

The better to understand this duty regarding freedom, we must look more closely at the relation between freedom and well-being. In one respect, freedom is such a general concept that many and perhaps all elements of well-being may also be viewed as aspects of freedom. The basis of this coalescence is that freedom, especially in its negative form of 'freedom from,' may be conceived universally as the absence of certain conditions, especially adverse ones. The structure of this view is thus that if some W is a part of well-being, then to have W is to be free from non-W or from deprivation of W. For example, adequate food, an essential component of basic well-being, may be presented as involving freedom from starvation and malnutrition; life, physical integrity, security of property and contract, self-esteem, knowledge, and education may be interpreted, respectively, as freedom from death-threats, physical assault, theft, promise-breaking, insult, ignorance, and miseducation or forced indoctrination. A similar point applies if freedom is construed in its positive form as 'freedom to,' where this is the power or ability to do what is needed in order to have some component of well-being. On this construal, to do or have W, especially where 'W' is viewed dynamically, is to be free to do, acquire, or maintain W. For example, to have food is to be free to eat when hungry; to have life and property is to be free to live, to use money, and so forth.

The trouble with such conceptualizations is that they tend to obscure the specific contribution of freedom as an independent value. They focus on the objects or purposes of freedom rather than on freedom itself; on what one is free from or free to do rather than on what being free consists in. The importance of the objects or purposes cannot be gainsaid, but these are adequately covered in the consideration of the right to well-being. Insofar, however, as the right to freedom comprises something more or other than this, the above coalescences of freedom and well-being serve to conceal it.

This concealment may be further encouraged by the fact that interferences with well-being are also usually interferences with freedom. For when recipients are subjected to basic or specific harms, ranging from deadly physical assault to libel or insult, this is done against their will, without their giving unforced consent. Nevertheless, this very point indicates the crucial difference between freedom and well-being, and between interferences with each of these. Amid their considerable extensional equivalence, interferences with freedom and with well-being differ conceptually in the ways indicated earlier with regard to voluntariness and purposiveness as generic features of action (1.12). To interfere with someone's freedom is to interfere with his control of his behavior, including his participation in transactions; such interference hence affects the procedural aspect of the behavior. To interfere with someone's well-being, on the other hand, is to interfere with the objects or goods at which his behavior is aimed; it hence affects the substantive or purposive aspect of his behavior. This contrast holds even where well-being is interpreted, as here, so that it consists in having the general abilities and conditions required for maintaining and obtaining goods. For the emphasis still falls on the relation of the general abilities to all the objects or purposes that for any prospective agent are goods required for or attainable by action. Thus although killing, libeling, and insulting are interferences both with well-being and with freedom, they have the former aspect as removing or diminishing certain goods required for action, but they have the latter aspect insofar as they are inflicted through violence, coercion, deception, or other procedures whereby the recipient participates in the transactions. Such actions interfere with their recipient's freedom and rational autonomy in that he does not give his unforced, informed consent. As we shall see below, this conceptual difference between interferences with freedom and with well-being is reinforced by the fact that some interferences with freedom do not interfere with well-being, and conversely.

There are two especially important variables regarding interferences with freedom as a specific condition distinct from well-being. One involves the modes or processes of interference, of which three broad kinds may be distinguished: violence, coercion, and deception. In violence a recipient is acted on with direct physical or psychological compulsion and with no consent or opportunity for consent on his part. In coercion the recipient gives his consent, but it is forced in a way parallel to forced choice (1.11): the agent sets compulsory undesirable alternatives between which the recipient must choose, with the realistic, enforceable threat of inflicting the worse alternative if the other is not chosen or consented to. In deception the recipient gives his unforced consent, but only as a result of falsehoods or misrepresentations intentionally presented by the agent. Examples of these three modes of interference are, respectively, robbery with assault and battery, a holdup by a gunman, and fraud; or, again respectively, rape, forced prostitution (or 'white slavery'), and seduction.

Although these three kinds of interference with freedom are mutually exclusive, they are not exhaustive unless the respective concepts are considerably broadened. Various forms of constraint, pressure, and prevention fall between these rubrics; for example, there are many ways of acting on recipients without their consent that do not involve the violent compulsion referred to above, such as deft pickpocketing or a stolen kiss. Whatever their varieties, this whole spectrum of interferences with the freedom of recipients is prohibited by the *PGC* unless there are mitigating circumstances, to be indicated below.

It must also be emphasized that these modes of interfering with freedom are confined to effects produced by individual agents on their recipients, as these effects bear on the procedures relevant to freedom as a specific condition. A person's freedom may be interfered with in at least two other ways. One stems from factors internal to the person himself, including both those over which he may have no control (including various sorts of physical or mental illness) and those that are self-induced, including willful ignorance, self-deception, obsessive submission to some dominating passion, anarchic subjection to conflicting, unordered desires, and other lapses from the prudential virtues that prevent the person from controlling his behavior by his own unforced, informed choices. The other kind of interference derives from large-scale social or institutional forces that may not operate directly through violence, coercion, or deception, as these were defined above, but rather by setting limits on the alternatives available for one's effective choice. In the former case, when a person's inability to control his behavior by his unforced, informed choice derives from self-induced causes, he is nevertheless still subject to the requirements the *PGC* imposes on agents. For it is within his power, as a rational prospective agent, to avoid getting into the condition of this proximate inability; it is still subject to his indirectly dispositional choice and control (see 1.11). In the latter, institutional case, effective choice and hence freedom of action may still operate within the alternatives that are left open by the social forces in question; these alternatives may even include actions in opposition to those forces. But if it is maintained, as in Marx's economic determinism, that no alternatives are left open for choice, that even the capitalist's choices are entirely forced by his role in the productive process, this view is subject to strictures parallel to those advanced earlier against hard determinism (1.11).

Let us now consider a second variable regarding interferences with freedom. This bears on their duration or extent: the interferences, as well as the freedoms themselves, may be occurrent or dispositional. In occurrent freedom a person controls his behavior in a particular case at a particular time, and occurrent interference removes this control without necessarily affecting his ability to exercise control over others of his behaviors. In dispositional freedom a person has longer-range control over his behavior, and dispositional interference removes this longer-range control. The structure of the recipient's dispositional freedom is: If at any time in the future A were to initiate a transaction affecting some other person B, B would be effectively able to control by his unforced choice or voluntary consent whether he would participate in the transaction. For example, a person's freedom of movement is occurrently interfered with, in a way slightly akin to coercion, if a locked door prevents him from leaving a building; but the interference is only momentary if another, adjacent door is left unlocked. Occurrent interference may thus leave available many other alternatives between which the person may still effectively choose. On the other hand, a person's freedom of movement is dispositionally interfered with if he is imprisoned; here few or no alternatives as to his physical movements are left available for his effective choice, and a whole host of other behaviors dependent on his having freedom of movement are debarred to him. This is even more drastically the case if a person is enslaved. For even if the slave has considerable occurrent freedom of movement, he has lost control over his behavior in a deeper sense; for as a self or person to whom his choices would otherwise belong, he is now the property of another and must hence do as the latter chooses, not as he himself chooses. Thus both in imprisonment and in slavery dispositional freedom is lost.

It is important to emphasize the difference between losses of occurrent and dispositional freedom. Some extreme libertarians characterize all such losses indiscriminately as 'enslavement'; every tax, every restriction is viewed as menacing 'freedom' viewed globally, and hence as wrong. But this ignores the different durations and different availability of alternatives both as to freedom and as to well-being. The *PGC* does indeed prohibit in general interferences with freedom. But, as we have seen, it also requires interferences with the freedom of agents insofar as it imposes duties on them and hence limits the alternatives among which they may rightly choose. These restrictions are required by justice, as components of the equality of generic rights whose violation commits the agent to self-contradiction. Where the agent is rational in the ways that enter into the *PGC*, he will not view these duties as restrictions on his freedom, as forms of violence, coercion, or deception, for he will give his unforced and informed consent to them. Nevertheless, they are still restrictions. But since they leave available to the agent many alternatives that do not involve coercing or harming his recipients, he still has a broad range of justified freedom.

In addition to the two variables of the modes and the extent of interference with freedom, a third variable may be distinguished. This bears on the degree of importance of the objects or purposes to which the behaviors interfered with are directed; and it serves to indicate again the close connection between freedom and well-being. Since the agent controls his behavior with a view to various purposes, interference with this control will seem more or less important to him according as the purposes to which his actions or behaviors were directed are more or less important. This relation was already indicated earlier in my discussion of coercion or forced choice as involving the imposition of undesirable alternatives between which a person must choose. For example, if someone is prevented from eating his favorite apple pie, this would be less serious than if he is prevented from eating at all. Each of these, whether it operates by violence, coercion, deception, or in some other way, is an interference with freedom in that it curtails its recipient's effective ability to control his behavior by his unforced choice. But it is the right to well-being that is directly involved in the consideration of the vastly different degrees of importance of the objects of the behaviors interfered with. What pertains specifically to the right to freedom, however, is the aspect of prevention, constraint, or interference itself. Hence, I shall deal first with this aspect, although the relation to the purposes interfered with will be tacitly assumed. Subsequently I shall indicate how the latter relation affects the justification of various interferences with freedom.

4.19. The right to freedom, as the right to control one's participation in transactions by one's unforced choice, may be distinguished in certain respects according as it pertains to the agent or to the recipient. Agents are of course also recipients, and conversely; but they can be distinguished conceptually according to their diverse roles in transactions (3.1), and the freedom needed for acting may be similarly distinguished from the freedom involved in undergoing someone else's action. The aspects of freedom that pertain to agents and to recipients have many features in common, so that I shall for the most part consider them together as the control of one's behavior or one's participation in transactions by one's unforced choice. In the agent's freedom, however, this control consists in initiating and directing his behavior for the achievement of his purposes, while in the recipient's freedom the control is in the first instance passive or reactive: it involves seeing to it that he is let alone unless and until he unforcedly consents to be involved in transactions whose initial control rests with the agent. The agent's freedom or control thus largely consists in his having the unhindered powers or abilities required for achieving the purposes to which he directs his behavior. As such, this freedom, even as procedural, is a component both of additive and of basic well-being; in the latter case, as noninterference by others with the agent's initiation of his behavior, it is one of the essential preconditions of action. In both cases the agent's freedom is a necessary condition of his agency as such, although there are different degrees of this necessity.

Freedom is not, however, a necessary condition of being a recipient; recipients may undergo violence, coercion, deception, and other nonconsensual procedures. As was indicated above, the recipient's right to freedom is in the first instance a right to be let alone by others until and unless he unforcedly consents to undergo their action. It thus includes having a sphere of personal autonomy and privacy. The agent too has this right insofar as it is he, and not someone else, who controls for his own reasons his engaging in action, both as an actual and as a prospective agent. It follows from this right to freedom that, within the limits set by the rights to well-being discussed above, all prospective agents have rights to a vast area of protected actions of their own, including physical movement, speech and other forms of expression, assembly, religion, and sexual conduct. And they also have rights to a vast area of nonperformance of actions on the part of other persons, in that others must refrain from imposing on them such actions as killing, physical maiming, libeling, and so forth. The area of the latter restraints coincides in large part with the area of the rights to well-being discussed above. But there remains the conceptual distinction between the procedural right of freedom and the substantive right of well-being. There is also the question of the limits on the right to freedom. Before discussing these, the concept of this right must be further analyzed.

As we have seen, the recipient's voluntariness or freedom, as a procedural feature of his participation in transactions, is marked by consent, whereby he responds or reacts at least relatively favorably to something proposed or initiated by some other person or group; he agrees to accept the proposal. The right to freedom, taken by itself, involves that the recipient's voluntary consent is the necessary and sufficient condition of a transaction's being morally justified, so that the agent must refrain from acting on his recipient unless such consent is given. The indication of consent may be verbal or nonverbal, but in any case, if consent is to count as making the recipient's participation voluntary or free, it must conform to the general conditions of voluntariness discussed earlier. I shall now present some of the main conditions with specific reference to the recipient's rights and the agent's duties.

To begin with, just as the agent's choice must not be forced if his action is to be voluntary, so the recipient's consent must not be forced if his participation in the transaction is to be voluntary. In general, the conditions of forced consent are similar to those of forced choice (1.11); in both cases these conditions may vary in degree. In the strongest kind of forced consent, the recipient is confronted with two undesirable alternatives that someone else has set for him with the intention of causing him to accept or agree to one alternative by threatening that, in case of noncompliance, he will undergo the other, worse alternative regardless of any dissent on his part, where each of the alternatives goes outside the regular course of events and impends only because of the threatener. Whereas in forced choice there is a sense in which either of the undesirable alternatives may be chosen, in forced consent only one of the undesirable alternatives is presented for consent; if this consent is withheld, then the other alternative is forthcoming without any consent on the part of the recipient. The following is an example:

> A woman's right to control her own body is the basis for two new cases against involuntary sterilization which the A.C.L.U. has undertaken in South Carolina and California. The A.C.L.U. Foundation has brought suit against Dr. Clovis Pierce and officials of Aiken County (S.C.) hospital for coercing two women to be sterilized. . . .
>
> In the South Carolina case, the first plaintiff, Jane Doe (a pseudonym to protect her privacy) alleges that Dr. Pierce informed her that she must submit to sterilization following the delivery of her fourth child. If she did not agree, Dr. Pierce would refuse to attend her or her child during or after labor, would deny her access to Aiken County Hospital, and would see that her assistance from the Department of Social Services (D.S.S.) was terminated. Faced with the imminent birth of her baby, Jane Doe was forced to consent to sterilization.[20]

It must be noted that consent would not be forced in the sense relevant here if the alternatives with which the threatening agent confronted the recipient were regarded by the latter as desirable relative to her present situation. Each alternative must constitute a lowering of her present level of purpose-fulfillment; it must be a loss by comparison with what she would otherwise have or normally expect. Thus, even if in the above situation the choice with which Dr. Pierce confronted Jane Doe is described not as being between two 'bad' things (being sterilized or losing the physician's services), but rather as being between two 'good' things (not being sterilized or retaining the physician's services), this would not change the forcedness of her consent. For since the alternatives are presented as exclusive and exhaustive, the 'good' alternative of not being sterilized includes the 'bad' situation of losing the physician's services, and the other 'good' alternative of retaining the physician's services includes the 'bad' situation of being sterilized. Unlike the 'costs' exacted in regular commercial transactions, where to obtain 'goods' one must pay 'prices' (and hence incur something 'bad'), each of the full alternatives confronting Jane Doe still constitutes a drastic loss for her by comparison with her situation before Dr. Pierce's threat; and each goes outside the normal or usual level of costs or losses that would obtain in the absence of Dr. Pierce's imposition of the alternatives. Because he subjected Jane Doe to this coercion, his action was morally wrong. The case would be different if he had tried to win her unforced, informed consent by presenting the reasons for her not having more children, in a discussion or dialogue in which her own consideration of reasons would be a central factor. Such an approach would have respected her rational autonomy as a prospective purposive agent.

A second requirement consent must fulfill if it is to be voluntary is that the recipient must have knowledge of relevant circumstances. As in the above example, this knowledge must be provided by the agent where necessary. Thus, if the agent withholds such knowledge or, what is even more serious, if he deceives his recipient about relevant circumstances, the latter's consent to the transaction is not voluntary. Since such deception tends to decrease the recipient's capacity for action by lowering his ability to cope with the content of the further transaction directed at him by the agent, an important disparity is thereby created between the levels of effectiveness with which the agent and the recipient respectively participate in the transaction. A third related requirement is that the recipient must be in an emotionally calm state of mind. This is parallel to the whole set of 'internal' factors, including reflexes and disease, that may operate as causes that decisively contribute, in ways beyond a person's control, to the occurrence of some behavior and that debar that behavior from being an action (1.11). Contractual and other transactions that satisfy these three conditions on the part of the parties concerned fulfill the *PGC*'s requirement that agents act in accord with their recipients' right to freedom, and are to this extent morally right in the sense of permissible. The agent has the duty to refrain from acting on his recipients unless and until they give their consent characterized by these three features of unforcedness, knowledge, and calm.

4.20. This duty of the agent is only prima facie, not conclusive, because the requirement of the recipient's voluntary consent may be overridden by other considerations. It must be emphasized that these overriding considerations themselves derive from the *PGC*. The reason for the overriding, and hence for the prima facie character of the agent's duty regarding freedom as so far stated, is that the *PGC*, as a complex moral principle, comprises other requirements in addition to freedom. The criteria for interrelating these requirements will be presented at appropriate points and will be summarized in synoptic fashion below (5.21).

One kind of overriding of the requirement of the recipient's voluntary consent, to be discussed more fully in the next chapter, occurs when a transaction is in accordance with social rules that are justified by the *PGC*. Standard examples of this are where a judge sentences a defendant to prison, an umpire declares a batter out, a storekeeper is forced out of business by a competitor, a suitor is spurned by his beloved, and the like. Such transactions proceed according to the rules of the institutions of law, baseball, business, and marriage respectively, and insofar as the rules are justified by the *PGC*, so too are the transactions, even in the absence of consent to the particular transaction. It must be noted, however, that in these cases the degrees of undesirableness, compulsoriness, and threat may vary greatly.

A second kind of overriding of the consent requirement is found when the occurrent or overt consent in question is replaced by a dispositional or tacit consent. To see this, we must note that although the voluntary consent required if transactions are to be morally right includes the recipient's knowing relevant circumstances, there are cases where his lack of such knowledge is not caused by the agent. In such cases, the lack may not remove the voluntariness of the recipient's consent and hence the rightness of the transaction, especially if a distinction is recognized between occurrent and dispositional consent. For a recipient to give dispositional consent means that he would have unforcedly acquiesced in a transaction if he had been aware of the relevant circumstances and had been in an emotionally calm state of mind. To begin with a trivial case, suppose X greets Y, who has been absent-mindedly walking by and has failed to recognize X. On a strictly occurrent interpretation of 'control' and 'consent,' it would have to be said that X made Y participate involuntarily in the greeting-transaction initiated by X, since Y was made the recipient of a greeting without exercising any control over the matter and without giving consent. But presumably Y would have acquiesced in or been favorably disposed to receive the greeting if he had been aware of X's presence. When this presumption is justified, Y has dispositionally consented to X's greeting, and X has not violated the requirement that the recipient voluntarily consent. A similar point applies in such a case as where a speeding automobile is bearing down on Y, who is strolling absentmindedly in the middle of the road, and X brusquely pushes him out of the way, thereby saving Y from severe injury or death. Here, too, Y gives dispositional consent: he would have consented to X's pushing him out of the way if he had been aware of the circumstances.

Apart from such obvious cases, two problems arise for the notion of dispositional consent in relation to the requirement of knowledge on the part of the recipient. First, the appeal to dispositional consent may be used in a paternalistic way to justify acting on recipients without regard for their actual desires or beliefs or occurrent consent (or dissent). Such agents may contend that their recipients would have consented to the transaction if they had had the relevant knowledge, so that their failure to give occurrent consent is simply a result of their being victims of propagandistic manipulation or benighted customs. If, however, the requirement of knowledge is extended so far that it can be met only by a small intellectual elite, very few persons would qualify as agents, and very few of persons's behaviors would be actions. Such an extension would conflict with the universality of the *PGC* as a principle addressed to and capable of being understood and accepted by all rational agents, in the minimal sense in which 'rational' has been defined above. The extension would derogate from the autonomy of all such agents as capable of recognizing and acting according to rational criteria. The extension would also obscure the fact that the knowledge needed for action is knowledge of proximate, particular circumstances, which ordinarily does not require any special expertise, although deeper, more general knowledge may sometimes also be helpful. In areas bearing on basic or specific well-being where expert knowledge is needed, the *PGC* requires that such knowledge be communicated and made available to all those whose well-being would be affected by it. Without such communication, in controversial matters appeal to dispositional consent while disregarding occurrent consent is illegitimate. None of this, however, affects the rational consent given by agents who accept the requirements of the *PGC*.

A second difficulty, however, is that even if the knowledge requirement for voluntary consent is not unduly extended, and the relevant knowledge is duly communicated, a recipient may still not give his even dispositional consent to transactions that are for his well-being, because he is proximately incapable of having or assimilating this knowledge for reasons not stemming from the agent but rather from certain unusual aspects of the recipient's own situation or background. In the cases cited above, the knowledge in question dealt with relatively simple empirical facts whose comprehension was within the powers of the recipient. The premise of the cases was that a person may be presumed to consent to something that is clearly for his own well-being, along a spectrum ranging from social amenities to the avoidance of physical injury or death. There are many cases, however, where this presumption is false. In such cases the recipient's freedom of participation in transactions may stand in opposition to his well-being. We have already seen the basis of this opposition in the conceptual difference between freedom and well-being as, respectively, procedural and substantive conditions of participation in transactions. Because of this difference, the *PGC*'s freedom requirement may conflict with the well-being requirement. For agents may respect the freedom of recipients in transactions whose outcome lowers the latter's well-being, so that it is possible for agents to fulfill the freedom requirement while violating the well-being requirement. Conversely, certain outcomes desired by recipients, or goods related to their capabilities of action, may be attained in different ways, some of which do not respect the recipients' freedom, so that agents may fulfill the *PGC*'s well-being requirement while violating the freedom requirement.

It is important, however, to distinguish two kinds of cases where the *PGC*'s freedom requirement is not fulfilled. In one, this requirement is overridden by the *PGC*'s requirement regarding well-being. In the other, the freedom requirement is not so much overridden as inapplicable. The reason for this inapplicability is the kind of situation mentioned above, where it is impossible to fulfill one or another of the conditions required for the recipient to give his voluntary consent to participate in a transaction, this impossibility stemming not from the agent but from the recipient himself. An assumption of the freedom requirement is that the recipient can have knowledge of relevant circumstances and can bring this knowledge to bear on deciding whether to consent to some proposed transaction. Another assumption is that the recipient can have the emotional calm needed for assaying the alternatives. Where these assumptions are false, the freedom requirement becomes inapplicable. In such cases the recipient would be incapable of giving even dispositional consent to a transaction that is for his well-being, despite the ready availability of the relevant knowledge. Because of this inability, transactions in which the recipient is forced to participate would not violate the *PGC*'s freedom requirement, and the way would be left open for the well-being requirement to be decisive by itself. The freedom requirement would not have been fulfilled, but only because it was inapplicable in the situation in question.

Cases of such inapplicability may in turn be of two main sorts. In one, the recipient, from causes not deriving from the agent, does not fulfill the knowledge condition for voluntary consent; in the other, he does not fulfill the emotional condition. With regard to both conditions he is unable to give even dispositional consent.

Let us first consider a case where the *PGC*'s freedom requirement is inapplicable because the recipient does not fulfill the knowledge condition for voluntary (including dispositional) consent. A Christian Scientist, on deeply felt religious grounds, may refuse to consent to a blood transfusion even though it is needed to save his life. Here it may be said that he does not know certain relevant facts; but the knowledge in question, as it relates to the whole web of his religious beliefs, is far more complex than the simple awarenesses mentioned earlier, and it may be difficult or impossible for him, because of his religious commitment, to assimilate whatever knowledge would serve to refute or even cast doubt on his beliefs. In the absence of his having such knowledge, he would not give his voluntary consent to a blood transfusion, so that the idea of dispositional consent, and with it the *PGC*'s freedom requirement, has no application in his case.

Because of this inapplicability, the *PGC* escapes what would otherwise be a serious dilemma. According to the freedom requirement a transaction is morally wrong if its recipient does not voluntarily consent to it, while according to the well-being requirement a transaction is morally wrong if it interferes with the recipient's basic well-being. It may be contended that the latter requirement would not be violated in the present case because if the Christian Scientist is allowed to die, there will have been here no transaction initiated or controlled by agents. But, as we saw earlier, to let some person die or undergo some other basic harm when one could prevent it at no comparable cost to oneself is to inflict on him a basic harm and hence to violate his right to basic well-being (4.7 ff.). It might seem, then, that the *PGC* is caught in a dilemma: if a blood transfusion is forced on the Christian Scientist, then the requirement of freedom is violated; but if a blood transfusion is not forced on him, then he is allowed to bleed to death, so that the requirement of well-being is violated. The *PGC* escapes this dilemma, however, insofar as the freedom requirement is inapplicable because of the Christian Scientist's inability to have the relevant knowledge and hence to give his informed consent.

In such a situation, the requirement bearing on well-being must alone be fulfilled.

A related way of avoiding this dilemma is to appeal to a version of the dictum that 'ought' implies 'can.' If the agent ought to refrain from giving the Christian Scientist a blood transfusion until the latter gives his informed consent, then if he is not capable of such informed consent (from causes not stemming from the agent), it is no longer the case, at least on this ground, that the agent ought to refrain from giving the transfusion. Since the requirement of voluntariness cannot be fulfilled here, there is no conflict between it and the requirement of well-being, so that the latter requirement would alone be applicable. It might be objected that the 'ought-can' dictum applies only when it is the same person whose obligations and abilities are in question, whereas in the present case the purported obligations are those of the agent while the abilities are those of the recipient. This restriction, however, does not hold universally. The dictum's 'can' refers to any environing conditions that limit an agent's ability to fulfill some obligation. Thus, the Christian Scientist's inability to give informed consent is also a limitation on the agent's ability to fulfill his obligation to refrain until the former has given his informed consent. The agent may, then, give the blood transfusion even in the absence of consent; yet the requirement of freedom of participation is not thereby violated. It must be added, however, that this nonfulfillment of the freedom requirement should be at best temporary. As will be shown more fully below, because the *PGC*'s substantive concern is that all persons have the generic goods of action, where it is conclusively established that some person is unwilling or unable to accept or consent to what is needed for his having these goods, there is no point in forcing him to have them.

A similar account applies to the other condition listed above that consent must fulfill if it is to be voluntary, that the recipient be in an emotionally calm state of mind. If he goes berserk or becomes intensely angry or agitated, then his acquiescence (or failure to acquiesce) in some transaction cannot be considered voluntary. Hence, agents have the obligation to refrain from driving their recipients into such a condition, for the latter do not voluntarily participate in such transactions and are at least temporarily debarred from other voluntary participation. But if a person who is already in such an extreme emotional state threatens to inflict grave harm on himself and cannot be returned to a calm state, at least in the particular situation, then the requirement that he give voluntary consent becomes inapplicable, and it is not violated if some other person forcibly restrains him, for the sake of the latter's well-being. With regard to this emotional requirement, as with the preceding cognitive one, however, it is important not to extend it so far that it can be satisfied only by states of mind which attain some ideal psychological condition.

4.21. Thus far, I have been considering cases where the *PGC's* freedom requirement, although not fulfilled, is not violated because it is inapplicable. Let us now turn to cases where the freedom requirement is applicable but may nonetheless be at least temporarily overridden because it conflicts with the *PGC's* requirement regarding well-being. What does the *PGC* require in cases where persons fulfill the cognitive and emotional conditions for voluntary consent and yet refuse to consent to interferences with their self-destructive or other projects whereby they intend to inflict basic harms on themselves? Such projects include suicide, selling oneself into slavery, ingesting harmful drugs, and the like. It may be contended that the conditions of voluntary consent are never fulfilled in such cases, that only abysmal ignorance or deep emotional trauma can lead persons to extreme measures like these. While this is true in many cases, it would be difficult to prove that it is true in all. Where it is not true, there would seem to be an irreconcilable conflict between the *PGC's* requirements of freedom and well-being as rights of recipients that agents must respect. And, in the case of selling oneself into slavery, there would also be a conflict between the rights to occurrent and dispositional freedom. In selling himself into slavery, a person would occurrently control by his unforced choice his participating in a selling transaction aimed at his surrendering all his future control over his participations in transactions. He would hence have used his occurrent freedom to surrender his dispositional freedom.

Two important qualifications must be noted. First, I have here been talking of 'self-harm' as if only the intending actor would be harmed by his projected action. Although there is a long and familiar line of discussion that disputes the very possibility of this, I here accept that there may be purely self-harming projects so long as rather stringent empirical criteria are fulfilled. One such criterion is that the self-harming person must not lose control of his behavior in such a way as to endanger others, as often results from excessive use of alcohol or drugs. Another criterion is that the would-be self-harmer must have no dependents on whom his project would inflict loss of economic or other support. If there were such dependents, then the issue would not concern only the individual's right to freedom as against his own right to basic well-being, for the basic well-being of other persons would also be involved as his recipients, and, as we have seen, this sets limits on the individual's freedom. In addition, other persons' interests would be adversely affected if they were expected to provide support for the self-harmer after he had succeeded in incapacitating himself.

A second qualification is that in the present context I am not asking what the state or its laws should do about preventing persons from harming themselves; my present question is not one of legal or criminal paternalism. I am asking rather what informed individual persons should do in this regard. Although to some extent the two questions and their respective answers overlap, I have not yet dealt with the *PGC*'s justification of laws and government, including their coercive relation to their recipients. Because of the central importance of basic harm for morality, the individual agent cannot rightly evade the question of what should be done when persons near him voluntarily refuse to consent to interference with their projects of inflicting such harms on themselves.

As a first step, the *PGC* justifies and indeed requires deep concern on the part of other persons over the projects in question, because of its requirement that persons intervene where they can to prevent basic harm to others. Since this requirement is mainly confined to basic harms, it does not justify wholesale interference in the lives of others; it does not apply to projects that may lead only to decreased physical or mental efficiency, such as eating excessive amounts of candy or pursuing pornography. Persons must be left free to live their lives as they please and to make and perhaps profit from their own mistakes, although the possible social costs of remedying the mistakes justify extensive educational measures, in accord with the right to additive well-being (4.16). As a second step, the *PGC* justifies at least temporary interference with the projected basic harms in order to ascertain whether the conditions of voluntariness have indeed been met by the would-be actor, so that the freedom requirement is applicable. Although such ascertainment may be difficult, there are at least surface indicia of calmness and informedness that can be used. So long as these indicia are not found, interference with the would-be actor would be justified until he can be brought to a point where he is capable of voluntary participation. It is to be expected that at this point many intending self-harmers would give up their intentions.

As a third step, however, when it is clear that the conditions of voluntariness have been met by the projected self-harmer, further interference with him must be discontinued. The basis for dealing with this issue is found in the consideration that both the freedom and the well-being requirements set by the *PGC* for the participation of recipients in transactions derive from the generic features of action. The point of the requirements is to assure that all prospective purposive agents, and not only actual agents, are able to enjoy the generic goods or emoluments of action, having freedom by controlling their own participation in transactions and having their well-being respected. But a necessary condition of such enjoyment is that persons intend to have and maintain their freedom and their basic well-being. If they firmly intend to surrender one or both of these, even after becoming intellectually and emotionally clear about the consequences of this surrender for all their future actions, then the necessary coindition is not fulfilled. Thus, if interference with them is continued, they will not be able to act; and if interference with them is not continued so that they go ahead with their self-destruction, they will also not be able to act. Consequently, the justification for further interference with their freedom to engage in such actions is removed. It must also be kept in mind, however, that the would-be self-harmer does not violate his own generic rights, since it is not the case that he allows other persons to interfere with his freedom or well-being without his consent. In addition, self-destructive actions may vary in the immediacy of their removing the possibility of action; ingesting heroin or LSD is a slower method of suicide than shooting oneself.

These requirements of the *PGC* also involve more general social considerations. Consider the case where a person intends to give up his freedom, as by selling himself into slavery. If his contracting is interfered with, then he is made to participate involuntarily or unfreely in the particular interfering transaction; if his contracting is not interfered with, then he loses his effective ability for subsequent voluntary or free participation. Because this latter loss of dispositional freedom is so much more extensive and serious than the former loss of occurrent freedom, the *PGC*, being concerned with freedom as a generic right, requires that the envisaged contract be interfered with at least until it has been ascertained that the intending seller has met the conditions of voluntariness.

But since freedom, like life itself, is a necessary good to all prospective purposive agents, such a case requires consideration of questions like the following: What is the motive of the would-be slave? What is the nature of the psychological conditions and the social order that would permit or foster his having this motive? Persons may indeed become so desperate for basic goods or for warding off basic harms that they come to regard their enslavement as a welcome solution. But this then requires a critique of social institutions. In the longer run, as I shall show in the next chapter, the *PGC* requires that there be institutional arrangements that help to assure for all persons the rights of freedom and well-being and hence minimize the circumstances that lead some persons to try to surrender one or both of these rights of action by inflicting basic harms on themselves.

4.22. The concept of freedom, especially as applied to recipients, involves such complexities that some further remarks are needed to avoid misunderstanding of the *PGC*'s duties regarding freedom. It is important not to confuse the requirement that the agent not act on other persons without their unforced consent and a certain kind of 'utilitarian' requirement of positive beneficence, that the agent act according to the desires or wishes of his recipients. Since these desires might well be limitless and since they might conflict both among themselves and with the agent's desires, the latter requirement would make right action impossible. The *PGC* does not, however, provide that the desires of potential recipients are sufficient conditions of obligatory actions; it provides rather that the consent of the recipients is a necessary condition of permissible actions. To be sure, the recipient's unforced consent should be both the necessary and the sufficient condition of his participation in transactions. But this involves that the transaction is already initiated and controlled by the agent through his own unforced choice; it hence does not involve that the agent should be forced to initiate the transaction because the recipient wants him to. The consent of the recipient that is required if the transaction is to be morally right is reactive; it is hence not coextensive with the whole range of the potential recipient's desires, nor does it justify or require having the agent undertake the action in the first place.

In addition to this distinction, it is important to bear in mind the distinction between nonaction and action. The latter is voluntary and purposive, the former not. Although inaction too is voluntary and purposive, inaction does not constitute acting on other persons unless the latter suffer basic or other serious harm thereby (4.9, 10). If these distinctions are overlooked, the way is opened to various absurdities. For according to the *PGC* a person ought not to act on another person without the latter's unforced consent. Now take anything X that any person B may want A to do for him. If A does not do X, then according to the 'utilitarian' view, A acts; and he acts on B, since he affects some purpose or desire of B; and he acts on B without the latter's consent, since B does not accept that A fail to do X. Hence, A does what is morally wrong whenever he fails to do whatever someone else wants him to do. This absurd consequence is avoided when the *PGC* is correctly interpreted in accordance with the above distinctions.

It is also important not to confuse the roles of the agent and the recipient. Suppose Rice accosts Shaw and demands his watch, threatening to punch him in the nose if he does not comply. Shaw refuses to comply. Now Rice does not consent to this refusal; a fortiori he does not give his unforced consent. In refusing to hand over his watch, has Shaw violated the *PGC*'s requirement that the agent act on his recipient only with the latter's consent? Obviously not, for Shaw is not here an agent. To suppose that he is would be to commit the fallacy of thinking that the relation of agent and recipient is symmetrical; that is, that if Rice (the agent) acts on Shaw (the recipient), then it logically follows that in reacting in some way to Rice's action Shaw also acts on Rice. On this view, even if Shaw refuses to consent to Rice's action toward him, this very refusal would itself constitute an action of Shaw on Rice. And since Rice does not consent to this action, it would follow that Shaw's refusal to hand over his watch violates the *PGC*.

The relation of 'acting on,' however, is not symmetrical. The crucial and irreducible difference between an agent and a recipient in situations like the foregoing is that the agent controls whether the transaction will occur and what its nature will be: it is he who intentionally accosts the other, threatens him, and so forth. The recipient, on the other hand, does not control the occurrence or nature of the transaction; rather, he reacts to the agent's initiation or control of the transaction's occurrence, as by being affected in some way and perhaps also by consenting or dissenting. Hence, since controlling the occurrence or nature of a transaction and reacting thereto are distinct, the recipient is not himself an agent in a transaction like the above. Since the *PGC* requires that the agent act in accord with the recipient's right to freedom, and since the recipient is not himself, in the transaction in question, an agent, it follows that the recipient does not violate the *PGC* when he dissents from the agent's action and hence does something the latter may not voluntarily agree to or accept.

When reference is made here to a 'transaction,' it is important to distinguish two possible interpretations. In one broad interpretation, 'transaction' includes the whole sequence from the agent's intending that he deal in some way with the recipient to the final outcome in whatever happens to the recipient in the situation. In the other, narrow interpretation, 'transaction' includes only the agent's intending that he deal in some way with the recipient and the steps taken by the agent himself in pursuance of his intention; it does not include all that may happen to the recipient, which may fall outside the agent's intention or control; specifically, it excludes whatever the recipient may intentionally do in reacting to the steps taken by the agent. Now, when it is said that the agent controls the occurrence and nature of the transaction, this is universally true only when 'transaction' is given its narrow interpretation. For the agent controls whether he will form his intention and act on it; but he does not necessarily control, in all relevant respects, how the recipient will react, except where the action is one of gross physical violence, ranging from shooting to other ways of ensuring complete passivity on the part of the recipient. Short of these, the recipient's reactions may range from exultant acceptance to vehement opposition.

There remains, then, this distinction: the agent is the person who controls the occurrence and nature of the transaction in the narrow sense in that he forms a certain intention toward someone else and takes steps to execute it, and he also controls how he will deal with the recipient, as by coercing or attempting to coerce him or letting him make his own unforced decision; the recipient, on the other hand, does not control the occurrence and nature of this transaction, in that he does not intentionally take such steps, but he reacts to or is affected by what the agent does. Such reaction, however, is not itself an action; it may be completely passive and involuntary; and in any case it is a response to a transaction whose occurrence and nature are controlled by someone else.

This distinction between agent and recipient obtains even when the latter, in reacting to the agent's initiative, behaves voluntarily and purposively within a limited context into which he has been placed involuntarily and contrapurposively. Suppose Tracy kidnaps Upton, who resists, shouts, and bangs on the inside of the car trunk in which he has been abducted. It may be contended that these movements by Upton are voluntary and purposive actions; hence, since he is here participating voluntarily and purposively in the transaction initiated by Tracy, the latter has not violated the PGC. This, of course, is absurd. Upton's movements are at most cases of forced choice in response to violence. Even if he is subsequently able to engage in actions like kicking and screaming—actions that are under his control and are attempts to retain certain basic, nonsubtractive, or additive goods—this does not remove the fact that he was forced in the first place to participate in that transaction involuntarily. And since he is still being kept imprisoned, the initial transaction is still being enforced on him against his will. Hence, Tracy's kidnapping of Upton is a violation of the *PGC*.

The general point is that although the *PGC*'s requirements about transactions refer to transactions in the narrow sense, this sense still comprises the whole sequence from the agent's acting on his intention toward the recipient (here the *PGC*'s requirement is that the recipient voluntarily consent) to the outcome intended and controlled by the agent in what happens to the recipient (here the *PGC*'s requirement is that the recipient's basic, nonsubtractive, and additive goods not be interfered with). It is indeed true that at some point within or subsequent to this sequence as the agent intends it, the recipient may be able to behave voluntarily and purposively in ways not intended by the agent. But this does not affect the moral character of the intended sequence itself as it is adjudged by the *PGC*'s requirements, which bear on what the agent himself controls with a view to achieving his own purposes.

There are cases where the distinction between agent and recipient is less sharp (see 3.1). The recipient may himself be active to some degree in precipitating and not only in reacting to the transaction; he may in various ways have caused or influenced the agent to form the intention he did.[21] Suppose, in my above example, Shaw had flaunted his watch in a poor neighborhood, or had boasted about it. In such a case, didn't he contribute to the situation that led Rice to accost him, and isn't he to some extent an agent in their transaction? The answer must to some extent be affirmative. To this extent, Shaw is himself in violation of the *PGC*'s requirements concerning voluntariness and nonsubtractive goods, if his flaunting or boasting is forced on Rice or if he has reason to believe that Rice will experience thereby extreme pangs of envy or desire or will suffer pronounced loss of self-esteem. This does not, however, excuse, let alone justify, Rice's threat against Shaw. And it must be recognized that the recipient often does not exhibit such antecedent precipitating conduct.

4.23. In the light of the above discussion, what, according to the *PGC*, should be the limits on the freedom of the individual? In answering this question, it must be kept in mind that I have so far dealt only with moral limits without specific reference to legal enforcement; I shall consider the latter in the following chapter (5.16). These moral limits, however, provide for enforcement by individuals or groups in some (though not in all) cases.

In general, the *PGC* limits the freedom of agents only where they coerce or harm other persons, that is, where the agents violate the rights of their recipients to freedom and well-being. An agent should be free to perform any action, to engage in any transaction, if and only if his recipients are left free, through their voluntary consent, to participate or not participate in that transaction and if and only if he does not inflict basic or specific harm on them. We have seen that 'harm' has been given a determinate set of criteria as comprising deprivation or reduction of basic, nonsubtractive, or additive well-being. The harms in question include those inflicted by inaction as well as by action, such as when one lets someone drown when one could have rescued him at no comparable cost or risk to oneself, so that in such cases one should not be free to refrain from acting.

The exceptions to this general criterion have been of two kinds. First, the limitation on the freedom to coerce and harm other persons is removed when coercion and harm are needed in order to prevent these persons from inflicting harm on persons other than themselves or from violating the freedom of others; in such cases the reactive harm may not be more severe than is needed for this preventive purpose. Second, persons' freedom may be restricted to prevent them from inflicting basic harm on themselves or from giving up their own dispositional freedom. In such cases, the limitation on the freedom to coerce other persons is removed because the coercion is needed for the sake of these other persons' own freedom or well-being. As we have seen, however, coercion or interference with freedom for this purpose should at best be temporary. Freedom is a basic good; it has its own independent value as a necessary condition of action; and it should be limited only where needed to prevent or remedy interferences with other persons' necessary conditions of action.

5

INDIRECT APPLICATIONS OF THE PRINCIPLE

SOCIAL RULES AND INSTITUTIONS

5.1. In the indirect applications of the Principle of Generic Consistency, its requirements are imposed in the first instance not on individual agents and their actions but rather on certain social rules—rules of social activities, associations, or institutions. The requirements of these rules, in turn, are imposed on the actions of individuals. Because such actions occur within or involve reference to the structured context of rule-governed activities and institutions, the morally justified requirements the actions must fulfill are not directly those of the *PGC* but rather those of the social rules that govern the activities and institutions. Since, however, these social rules must themselves in various ways conform to the *PGC*, the actions are indirectly in accordance with the *PGC*. Hence the *PGC* still remains the supreme moral principle: it serves directly or indirectly as the criterion of all morally right actions and institutions.

If the *PGC* is inherently rational in that to deny or violate it is to contradict oneself, then what rational justification can there be for any agent to act toward other persons in accordance with the social rules rather than directly in accordance with the *PGC* and its generic or specific rules? This question is made all the more pressing by the fact that social rules may require that agents violate the *PGC*'s direct applications, for the rules may make it obligatory or at least permissible that agents coerce or harm their recipients. How can this be morally right or rationally justified in view of all the considerations adduced in the preceding chapters for the *PGC*'s requirements of noncoercion and nonharm? From the conviction that no justification is possible here stem such positions as extreme individualism, libertarianism, and anarchism. The errors of these positions are paralleled by certain versions of utilitarianism and of the Golden Rule. All these doctrines seek to apply their respective moral principles directly to such rule-governed actions as those whereby a judge sentences a criminal to prison or an umpire declares a batter out. They thereby incur serious difficulties: to justify such actions that in various degrees coerce and harm their recipients, the doctrines have recourse to the vagaries of utilitarian calculations or, alternatively, to the presumed desires of other persons besides those directly affected. The failure of these attempted justifications stems from the fact that they overlook the crucial intermediate role of the social rules and institutions in accordance with which the agents in question directly perform their respective actions and which provide the direct justifications of the actions. To understand how and why such actions can and must be justified, we must hence ask how the respective specific social rules and institutions can themselves be justified.

To answer this question we must first consider the general justification of there being social rules. Many morally relevant situations are not bilateral but multilateral, comprising not a simple relation between agent and recipient but more complex interactions among many persons. These interactions may involve conflicts between the freedom or well-being not merely of an individual agent and his recipient but of larger numbers of persons. Social rules are means of regulating such conflicts as well as other aspects of the interactions. Especially important among human interactions are different structured ways in which persons associate with one another as members of various specific groups, associations, and institutions of different sizes organized for various purposes. Each mode of association has its requirements, stemming from the purposes for which persons engage in it, concerning how persons are to act in their respective roles within the association; and social rules specify what these requirements are, determining different roles and permissible, mandatory, and prohibited ways of acting within each role, as well as setting rewards for certain fulfillments of the requirements and sanctions for violations. These sanctions include penalties that may in various ways coerce or harm the participants in these several activities. If there were no requirements, the associations would not fulfill their purposes; if there were no sanctions for violating the requirements, the latter would be ineffectual and the associations would cease to exist. In particular, since conflicts of purpose or interest may arise among persons in the various associations, rules are needed to resolve the conflicts in standard, predictable ways. Without this, the associations as structured groupings would not survive. The moral justification of the social rules thus resolves itself in part into the moral justification of the social interactions, activities, and associations they serve to regulate.

273

Since the social rules determine right and wrong ways of acting in accordance with various roles, the rules exert certain constraints on the persons who fulfill the roles. These constraints mean that the voluntariness and purposiveness of participation that the *PGC* directly requires agents to accord their recipients are replaced, so far as concerns the recipients in transactions, by the requirements of the relevant social rules. Insofar as the agents themselves are addressed by moral precepts that require them to act in accordance with the social rules, it still remains the case that their actions are voluntary and purposive. But once they come under the direction of the social rules, their conduct as well as that of their recipients becomes subject to the requirements of the rules. The treatment of the batter in a baseball game cannot be made to depend on his occurrent consent or on his not losing in the transaction; if the umpire declares him out, he is out. The same point holds for the treatment of the defendant in a trial; if the judge sentences him to prison, he is sentenced. Even if the batter and the defendant do not consent to be treated in this way, and their nonsubtractive or additive goods are interfered with, they are nonetheless treated rightly in accordance with the relevant rules. Thus the social rules, and persons acting according to the rules, may coerce recipients and inflict basic and specific harms on them. The umpire, the judge, and the other officials come under comparable constraints.

5.2. The associations regulated by social rules include various institutions. Now some of the direct applications of the *PGC* also deal with institutions. For example, the specific rules that prohibit lying, fraud, promise-breaking, and stealing concern actions that presuppose or occur within institutions of linguistic communication, buying and selling, promising, and property. The rules of these institutions, however, unlike the social rules now being considered, do not permit or require any actions opposed to the *PGC*'s direct applications. It is hence important to see how what I am calling the social rules differ from these other rules of institutions. For this purpose, institutions and their kinds must be briefly considered.

In general, an institution is a relatively stable, standardized arrangement for pursuing or participating in some purposive function or activity that is socially approved on the ground (whether justified or unjustified) of its value for a society. Because it is standardized, an institution is constituted by rules that define what persons are required to do if they are to participate in the respective activities or functions; and these requirements are the obligations persons have qua such participants. There is an important distinction, however, between *functional* and *organizational* institutions. A functional institution consists in the purposive standardized activity itself with its rules and requirements, while the organizational institution includes also structured groupings of persons associated for pursuing and especially for regulating the standardized activity and enforcing the rules. Many functional institutions have accompanying organizational institutions: education has schools and colleges, religion has churches, athletics has various professional leagues, and so forth. Indeed, the latter member of each pair is sometimes referred to as 'organized education,' 'organized religion,' 'organized athletics,' and the like, and it is sometimes asked whether a given (organizational) institution has lost its function. On the other hand, some institutions are solely functional: for example, promising and truth-telling have no directly corresponding organizational institution. To be sure, organized legal institutions may undertake to punish such of their abuses as breach of promise and fraud; but such enforcement pertains not to the regular or ordinary standardized activities of the functional institution but only to certain of their specialized contexts.

In the light of this distinction, we may further distinguish three different aspects of certain actions or kinds of actions: (*a*) the actions (or action-types) themselves; (*b*) their being standardly required, prohibited, or permitted by institutional rules constituting functional institutions; (*c*) the enforcement of these requirements by organizational institutions. The important question for present purposes concerns how these actions, rules, and enforcements are related to the *PGC*. Certain transactions, such as murder and slavery, are prohibited by the *PGC* as morally wrong regardless of whether they or their negations are standardly required by institutional social rules or enforced by organizational institutions. 'Murder' here refers not to any killing of other humans or, vacuously, to killing that is morally wrong; it refers rather to killing of innocent humans that has as its reason or nature only such factors as the gain, gratification, or desires of the killer, whether an individual or a group. Similarly, 'slavery' here refers not to any deprivation of liberty but only to such deprivations as make one person the property of another person for the latter's gratification or gain. The moral wrongness of murder and slavery as thus specified emerges directly from the *PGC*, since the actions of murdering and enslaving inflict basic harms on their recipients in ways that violate the equality of generic rights.

There are, however, cases where one person's depriving another of life or of liberty is not prohibited by the *PGC* as morally wrong, such as when the deprivations are inflicted in a just war or by imprisonment for such crimes as murder. Since in such cases the recipients undergo basic harms just as do the recipients of murder and enslavement, why are these deprivations not also morally wrong? An important part of the answer is that in such cases, unlike the preceding ones, the deprivations are inflicted by agents of organizational institutions enforcing institutional social rules. This is only part of the answer, however, because institutions with their social rules may themselves be prohibited by the *PGC* as morally wrong; consider, for example, the agents of tyrannical governments or the enforcers of fugitive slave laws. The answer hence requires, in addition, that the institutions and their rules must be in conformity with the *PGC*, and that such conformity takes precedence over the direct harmfulness of the corresponding actions. I shall hence have to show how this conformity and precedence are to be established.

In addition to cases of the above two sorts, there are intermediate cases where the moral rightness or wrongness of an action is directly determinable from its relation to the *PGC* although the action occurs within or involves reference to a functional institution with its rules. In this class fall actions like lying and breaking of promises. These do not seem to be specifiable apart from functional institutions and their rules concerned with the use of language for interpersonal communication of information and for making promises. Such institutions, however, are solely functional, not also organizational; they are not normally supported by agents of organizational institutions enforcing institutional social rules. The reasons for this include the fact that such functional institutions, unlike more specific ones, are so pervasive and so indispensable to human action and association that they cannot be delimited or supervised by determinate organizational institutions.

There is also another important difference, reflecting the same absence of institutional enforcement rules. Whereas such actions in accordance with institutional rules as killing in war or sentencing to prison require, for the *PGC's* moral justification of them, a reference not only to the rules and institutions but also to antecedent morally wrong actions by their recipients, the case is otherwise with actions in accordance with such functional institutional rules as those of truth-telling and promise-keeping. For such actions do not need for their moral justification a reference to antecedent actions that violate the *PGC*. On the contrary, the actions of telling the truth when asked and keeping one's promises are directly in conformity with the *PGC*; the institutional rules that require them serve primarily to define the nature of the actions rather than to justify them. Such rules simply specify the *PGC's* prohibitions of coercion and of basic and specific harms as actions done by individuals to individuals. Hence, the fact that the actions presuppose or occur within functional institutions of linguistic communication, promising, and the like does not remove the directness of the *PGC*'s application to the actions. The justification of the actions and the disjustification of their opposites can be directly inferred from the *PGC* without an intermediate justificatory reference to the institutions themselves. In telling someone the truth or in keeping one's promise to him one normally advances the recipient's well-being and fulfills rather than frustrates his purposes, and one's recipient unforcedly consents; these characteristics of the transactions are sufficient to justify such actions. Further justificatory recourse to institutions, especially to organizational ones, is not needed. Thus, where the rules of some functional institutions prescribe actions to which the *PGC* is directly applied, these are distinct from the social rules of organizational institutions that prescribe actions to which the *PGC* is only indirectly applied. For in the latter cases it is the social rules and not the actions that must directly conform to the *PGC*'s requirements; the actions, in turn, may themselves go counter to these requirements.

5.3. The above considerations provide a partial answer to the question of when and why the social rules may take precedence over the *PGC*'s direct applications in setting requirements for conduct. Man's existential situation is in important respects interactive and associative; hence, social rules are needed that are concerned specifically with such associative relations. Because of this specific concern the rules, once certain justificatory requirements are fulfilled, take precedence in the relevant social contexts over the *PGC*'s direct applications, because the latter deal primarily with transactions among individuals that do not fall within contexts structured according to these rules. The social rules are also concerned with transactions of agents toward their recipients, but the agents now act in their corporate or social roles, not in their individual capacities.

This diversity of roles helps to explain why the social rules, with their authorizing of coercion and harm, do not involve their agents in inconsistency even though the agents, while acting in accord with their own generic rights, may not act in accord with the generic rights of their recipients. It will be recalled that in the direct applications of the *PGC* an important basis of its inherent rationality is that there is no relevant difference between agent and recipient, in that each has the generic quality of being a prospective agent who wants to fulfill his purposes (2.19; 3.2). It is on the ground of having this quality that the agent rationally claims the rights of freedom and well-being; and it is because his recipients are similar to him in also having this quality that the agent must admit, on pain of self-contradiction, that his recipients have the same generic rights as he necessarily claims for himself. The self-contradiction would not occur if the agent could rationally argue that he is relevantly different from his recipients in that respect in which he claims generic rights for himself.

We have now reached the point where it is possible to show how such rational justification of relevant differences must proceed. When actions fall under specific social rules that are themselves morally justified, the relevant qualities that ground rights are determined by the specific roles persons have in accordance with the rules. The rules justify differentiations of role that in turn justify differentiations of treatment. Thus an umpire or a judge, a pitcher or a prosecutor, or any other agent does not contradict himself when he acts coercively toward batters, defendants, or other appropriate recipients or when he interferes with their nonsubtractive or additive goods in ways stemming from his specific rule-based roles. For the quality by virtue of which the umpire or the judge, as such, rationally claims the right to act in this way is not a quality that is also had by the batter or the defendant, as such: it is no longer the generic quality of being a prospective purposive agent but the more specific quality of being an umpire, or a judge, and so forth.

These considerations about the function of social rules in relation to the activities of groups, associations, and institutions provide a necessary part of the justification of the rules; but the justification is not yet sufficient. For social rules and the activities and associations they regulate may be morally wrong. To supply the missing elements, we must first note a distinction between general and specific objects of justification. It is one thing to ask for the justification of humans' associating according to rules in general; it is quite another to ask for the justification of specific modes of association and rules. To take an analogous case, it is one thing to ask for the justification of any person's acting in general; it is another to ask for the justification of his acting in one way rather than another. The former, general pole in each case is 'natural' in the sense that to be human is to engage in action and in association, and this is not subject to justification because it is not normally under the control of human persons. Thus it would be as pointless to ask whether the *PGC* justifies there being any social rules or institutions in general as it would be to seek from the *PGC* (or any other moral principle) a justification for persons' performing actions at all. What is under the control of persons is their specific ways of acting and associating, and it is to these that questions of justification are relevant. For alternatives are possible with regard to specific modes of associative action. Humans may associate with one another as governors and governed, as masters and slaves, as employers and employees, as husbands and wives, and in countless other ways, and they may compete or cooperate according to many different rules. The question, then, is: Which of these specific associations, activities, and rules are morally justified, and why?

If the PGC is to provide the justification of the social rules and activities, it must also fulfill a further condition in addition to this specificity. As we have seen, the social rules may permit or require that agents acting in accordance with them coerce or harm their recipients. The PGC's justification of the rules must hence show how a principle that prohibits that individual agents coerce or harm their recipients may nevertheless authorize such coercion and harm; how a principle that requires an equality of generic rights as between agents and their recipients may also justify an inequality among agents and recipients in relation to the objects of those same rights.

A historical analogy may be helpful. The relation between the PGC and the social rules is parallel in certain respects to the relation traditionally upheld between 'natural law' and 'human' or 'positive law,' where the former was conceived to embody the basic principles of morality. In each case the relation is one of derivation or at least of conformity, in that human laws or social rules are not legitimate or justified unless they are derived from or are in conformity with natural law and the PGC, respectively. The crucial question, however, concerns the precise nature of this derivation or conformity. In the classic formulation of Thomas Aquinas, there are only two morally right modes of derivation: human laws must be derivable from natural law either by deduction or by specification. In the first way human law's prohibition of murder is derived from natural law's prohibition of inflicting evil on other persons; in the second way human law's specification of a determinate penalty for evildoing is derived from natural law's prescription that evildoers be punished.[1] The trouble with this simple way of relating natural law to human law is that it does not serve to explain the seeming conflicts between the two kinds of law. For example, Aquinas holds that the preservation of human life is a precept of natural law, but he also holds that human law may legitimately prescribe capital punishment. The relation between these precepts is surely not a deductive one, nor is it a relation of specification. And although the latter precept may be held to be derivable from some other precept of natural law, there still remains the problem of conflicts unless ways are provided of modifying its precepts. The same difficulty is found in connection with familiar lists of 'natural rights.' According to the Declaration of Independence, the unalienable rights of man include life, liberty, and the pursuit of happiness; yet Jefferson accepted the legitimacy of capital punishment, imprisonment, and military conscription. If no qualifications are introduced, two complementary things must be said about the relation between the ideal rights and the actual laws: not only is the relation between these not one of deduction, but they appear to conflict with one another unless modifying considerations are provided.

The same problem is found in the relation between the *PGC* and the various social rules. Since the *PGC* prohibits coercive and harmful actions, while the social rules permit and may even require various kinds of coercion and harm, it follows that if the social rules are not to be in conflict with the *PGC*, their relation to it cannot be one of simple deduction or specification. The *PGC* must serve to justify not only the rules that are obviously in accord with it (such as prohibitions of murder or assault) but also those rules that, while they are morally justified, appear to conflict with the *PGC*, such as rules prescribing punishment and various other adversities.[2] The relation of the *PGC* to the former rules may indeed be one of deduction, but its relation to the latter rules must be more complex.

In this connection, two extreme positions on moral rules and obligations must be avoided. The extreme individualist and the extreme institutionalist hold, respectively, that all justified moral obligations directly derive only from the generic rules about transactions between individuals as such and only from the requirements of social institutions. Indeed, for one kind of extreme institutionalist 'morality' itself is but one institution among many others and its requirements can correctly claim no primacy among various other sorts of institutional rules. Now it is indeed true that there are and have been different 'positive' or 'conventional' moralities in the sense of informal systems of social regulation. But it is also true that these moralities can themselves be evaluated in respect of their moral rightness. This might be interpreted as meaning simply that one code of positive morality is used to evaluate another. Such an interpretation, however, would still leave open the question which of those positive moralities is morally right or justified. What this shows is that the normative concept of morality in the sense of moral rightness is distinct from the positive concept of morality as what is upheld as right by the rules of one or another institution of positive morality. It is to the former concept and not to the latter that appeal is made when the question concerns the moral evaluation and justification of institutions, including those of the various positive moralities. Consequently, the extreme institutionalist position that all justified moral obligations and rules derive only from the requirements of social institutions is mistaken. Before the institutions can be regarded as providing the ground of morally justified rules, the institutions must themselves be shown to be morally justified.

The extreme institutionalist moves from the true premise that there are no 'bare' or 'isolated' individuals existing outside all institutional contexts to the false conclusion that all justified moral obligations derive from the rules set by such contexts. This conclusion overlooks the fact that actions are the central subject matter of all morality and that the *PGC*, as the principle of moral rightness, is rationally derived from the generic features of all action. Because of this rationality and universality, the morality whose supreme principle is the *PGC* is not merely one institution among others; it is rather that which provides rationally justified evaluations of the rightness of all other institutions as well as of all actions. The moral obligation to respect the generic rights of other persons does not need, for its justification, any rules of institutions, because it logically follows from the generic features of all agency, including the claim necessarily upheld by every agent that he has rights to the necessary goods of action. Since, moreover, persons to whom even the social or institutional rules are addressed are agents whose conduct is characterized by the generic features of action, whatever justification the rules may have must ultimately derive from the generic moral rules that follow from those features. Thus, although the extreme individualist position is mistaken that the generic moral rules directly constitute the whole of moral rightness, the generic rights of individuals supply the ground for the authority of institutions to set morally justified rules and obligations. The freedom and the well-being components of the *PGC*'s requirement that agents respect the generic rights of their recipients serve, when suitably qualified, to provide the moral justifications of social rules.

To understand these justifications, we must note that some human activities and associations are extensions of freedom, in that persons unforcedly choose or agree to participate in them and to obey their rules, or at least their rules are arrived at by procedures that provide for the consensual participation of all the persons subject to them. Other activities and associations are such that while all their participants may not unforcedly agree to them, they and their rules serve to protect and extend well-being, especially basic well-being. These two kinds of rules and activities are justified, respectively, by the voluntaristic or libertarian and purposive or well-being components of the *PGC*. I shall call these two sorts of justification *procedural* and *instrumental*, respectively, since the former rules and activities are engaged in through procedures of voluntary agreement and the latter are instrumental toward the well-being that underlies the purposiveness of human action. Each of these sorts of justification is not only an indirect application of the *PGC* but also an application of reason. The procedural and the instrumental justifications are deductive specifications, respectively, of the voluntaristic and the purposive components of the *PGC* in relation to social rules and institutions. The instrumental justifications, in addition, involve at various points the use of inductive reasoning in the form of means-end calculation.

Each of these two modes of justification has complexities both in themselves and in their relation to one another and to their basis in the *PGC*. These complexities leave unchanged what I referred to above as the primary logical structure of moral duties (4.2). This structure is still mutualist and involves consistency: 'All other persons ought to do X in relation to me because I am Q; therefore I ought to do X in relation to them because they too are Q.' Here, however, 'do X' consists directly not in acting in accord with the generic rights of one's individual recipients but rather in acting in accord with social rules justified by the *PGC*. The latter mode of action, however, is a specification of the former, so far as concerns the justification of the rules. For to act in accord with social rules that are procedurally justified is to act in accord with persons' rights to freedom, since it involves allowing persons to participate in institutions and activities that are freely accepted by their members or that proceed by voluntary consent. And to act in accord with social rules that are instrumentally justified is to act in accord with persons' rights to well-being, since it involves obeying laws that protect and support persons' basic and other important goods. Both modes of action in accord with justified social rules include the moral duty of fairness, since both require not only that each person accept the respective rules but also that he accept the particular applications of the rules to himself when he comes under their specific provisions.

OPTIONAL-PROCEDURAL JUSTIFICATION OF SOCIAL RULES: VOLUNTARY ASSOCIATIONS

5.4. The libertarian or voluntaristic component of the *PGC* requires that the agent act in accord with his recipients' right to freedom, so that he must refrain from involving persons in transactions unless they unforcedly consent to this; once their consent is given, the transactions are prima facie morally right. The procedural justification of social rules and groups applies this requirement by providing that the rules as well as the activities and groups or associations they regulate are prima facie morally right in the sense of being permissible and that they ground morally justified duties when the persons who are subject to the rules and who participate in the associations and activities either freely consent to the rules or have certain other consensual procedures universally available to them. The consensual procedures provided for in such justifications take two different forms and have two different kinds of objects or subject matters, which I shall call *optional* and *necessary*.

The optional-procedural justification takes this form: if there are to be specific social rules and associations, then all their members must voluntarily consent to them. Here the antecedent is morally optional in that it is left to the free or voluntary consent of individuals to determine both whether there is to be some particular association with its rules and who is to belong to it and be bound by its rules. The consequent is necessary as a condition of the moral rightness of the antecedent, which is itself not morally necessary.

In the necessary-procedural justification, on the other hand, the antecedent as well as the consequent is morally necessary. The necessary procedural justification takes this form: if there is to be a political association or state having legal rules or laws, obedience to which is obligatory for all members of the society, then its constitution must provide for the method of consent to determine the contents of its specific laws, including the legislators who decide these contents and the executives who administer them. Here the antecedent is itself morally necessary in that it is not open to individuals' voluntary consent to determine whether there is to be a state governed by laws, obedience to which is obligatory. The consequent is morally necessary as a condition of the antecedent; and just as in the optional-procedural justification the consequent indicates that if social rules and associations are to be morally right then their existence and contents must be subject to consensual procedures consisting in the free choices of their individual participants, so in the necessary-procedural justification the consequent indicates that if the state with its specific laws is to be morally right then its constitution must provide that the laws be determined by the method of consent. But unlike the associations and rules dealt with in the optional-procedural justification, obedience to the state and its specific laws is obligatory for all members of the society. The necessary-procedural justification thus involves a double, simultaneous necessity: there must be states having specific laws and officials, and there must be a certain kind of procedure whereby these laws and officials are determined or designated. With possible exceptions to be discussed below, these political objects are not morally justified in the absence of the procedures. But because of the necessity of there being these objects, the procedures must themselves be present; use of them is not optional or contingent on persons' desires to have or belong to the political association, as in the case of the optional-procedural justification.

A related contrast between the two kinds of procedural justifications may be put as follows. In the optional justifications, the consensual procedures operate externally to the associations and rules in that they exist independently of the associations and determine whether the associations are to exist and what their rules are to be. In the necessary justification, on the other hand, the consensual procedures operate internally to the political association in that they do not exist independently of the state but are circumscribed by the necessity that there be such an association, since they are modes of political action. The procedures determine, within the necessary context of the state, what its specific laws shall be and who shall make and execute these laws.

The necessity I have ascribed to the state is a morally normative matter in that, as we shall see, the *PGC* determines that there ought to be states as well as what kind of constitutional structure they ought to have. This is why both the antecedent and the consequent of the necessary-procedural justification are morally necessary. Despite this necessity, the justification provides for and indeed requires consensual freedom for each individual; but this is a freedom to participate within the state in the particular electoral and other political procedures that enter into the determination of who shall govern the state and what its specific laws shall be. The freedom does not extend to determining whether there should be a state at all and what kind of basic constitution it should have.

5.5. Let us first consider the optional-procedural justification. This provides that if there are to be groups or associations regulated by rules that persons are morally obligated to obey, then these persons must freely consent to belong to the associations and to accept their rules. The validating conditions of this consent are the same as in the direct applications of the *PGC*: unforcedness, knowledge of relevant circumstances, and a certain degree of emotional calm. I shall refer to groups that are procedurally justified in this optional way as *voluntary associations*. Such associations are both results of freedom and extensions of freedom, since they enable their members to participate in collective, rule-governed activities of their own unforced choosing. The social rules that are justified in this way are, in turn, applied to the particular actions of persons within the activities and associations governed by the rules, in that the actions to be morally right must conform to the rules, so that the agents are morally obligated to obey them.

As we have already noted, even when an association has an optional-procedural justification and is hence voluntary, its rules may impose conditions or constraints on its members by way of penalties and other measures that may be opposed to their particular desires or choices. I previously illustrated this by the example of the rulings of the umpire in a baseball game, but the same point holds for other, more pressing voluntary associations. Within the framework of voluntariness, then, there may be rule-governed effects that are coercive, hence going counter to the voluntariness directly prescribed by the *PGC*. This coerciveness is justified by the voluntary consent to the rules that provides their procedural justification; for since they entail duties on the part of the persons subject to the rules, the justification of the rules is also the justification of the corresponding duties. Thus voluntary acceptance of social rules justifies the requirement that persons even involuntarily obey particular applications of the rules.

The transactions whereby persons consent to participate in an association with its activities and rules may be of different sorts. In some cases there may not literally be a clear distinction between agents and recipients, since all the participants may spontaneously agree or give their optional consent to undertake some joint activity. An example is an informally arranged baseball game. Even in such cases, however, the participants are reciprocally one another's agents and recipients in that they accept one another's proposals to participate in the game. A similar relation is found in contractual arrangements or groupings where persons agree to exchange goods with one another, including labor for pay. In other cases a division may be found between agents and recipients. The agents are the leaders or exponents of the association, including persons who suggest, advise, urge, or at least hold out the possibility of participation on the part of other persons. The former persons are agents in the transaction in that they either have taken the initiative or at least have controlled whether the other persons' participation in the association or activity is voluntary or involuntary, purposive or contrapurposive. In all these cases the obligations imposed by the rules of the activity or association are morally justified insofar as the participants voluntarily or optionally consent to participate and hence to be subject to the rules. These obligations include the duties related to the jobs or offices persons undertake through contractual agreements.

In an important respect, then, these obligations or constraints are self-imposed by the participants: by voluntarily consenting to the rules, each participant voluntarily accepts the compulsions required by the rules in all cases to which they apply, including his own. Hence no contradiction is incurred by any of the participants if in some particular case governed by social rules, while operating as an agent and hence freely, he fails to act in accord with his recipients' right to occurrent freedom. For when he coerces or harms his recipients in accordance with the relevant social rules he is acting toward them in accordance with rules they have voluntarily accepted. The *PGC* here applies to this second-order level of the voluntary acceptance of the rules, not directly to the first-order level of the impact of the rules on the participants in a particular transaction. This point may also be put, then, by saying that the agent still acts in accord with his recipients' right to freedom, since in coercing or harming them as provided by the rules he still sees to it that they are at least not interfered with in their participation in activities or associations whose rules they have freely accepted.

The prima facie moral rightness or justification that associations with their rules receive through being voluntarily consented to is logically necessary. It is not that the association's constitutive rules are themselves logically necessary or that acceptance of them or participation in the activities they regulate is logically necessary. Rather, it is logically necessary both that social rules that are optionally-procedurally justified by the *PGC* are prima facie morally right in the sense of permissible and that persons have a prima facie right to participate in such procedurally justified activities. It would be self-contradictory to deny (a) 'All persons have a prima facie right to participate in activities or associations whose rules they have freely accepted.' For, as we have seen, it is self-contradictory to deny (b) 'All prospective purposive agents have a right to freedom.' But (a) is a specification of (b), since for persons to participate in procedurally justified activities or associations is for them to use their freedom within the limits imposed by the *PGC*. Hence, since denial of (b) is self-contradictory for any agent, so too is denial of (a). For the same reason, it would be inconsistent of any agent to accept (b) and deny (*a*). The arguments that established (*b*) also show that it would be self-contradictory for any person to hold that he has a right either to prevent persons from participating in such optional procedurally justified activities or to coerce them into participating. Thus, just as in individual transactions the voluntary consent of the recipient renders the agent's action toward him prima facie morally right, so in associations and social activities the voluntary consent of the participants makes them and their rules prima facie morally right.

If any participant refuses to accept an adverse impact of procedurally justified rules on himself or on others, or if he violates any of the rules, then he contradicts himself. For in agreeing to participate in the activity, he has accepted the need for obeying the rules: 'I and all the other participants ought to obey the rules.' But in violating one of the rules he says, in effect: 'I have a right not to obey the rule,' or 'It is not the case that I ought to obey the rule.' This point applies not only to the direct participants but also to such persons as umpires or other officials who are charged with applying the rules to the participants in particular cases. This charge is made by second-order rules; but since these rules are also in part constitutive of the association or activity, there would be a contradiction if one agreed to participate in accordance with the second-order rules by serving in some such capacity as judge or umpire, and if one then proceeded to violate or repudiate these rules. This obligation on the part of persons who apply the rules to particular cases includes the requirement of fairness. The first-order rules set forth sufficient conditions for the participants' receiving certain treatment by way of penalties and rewards. If the judge, umpire, or other official makes an unfair ruling, that is, if he does not apply the rules impartially in cases the rules hold to be similar, then he is saying that a sufficient condition for a certain treatment of a participant is not sufficient, that what is right in one case is not right in a relevantly similar case, where the relevance of the similarity is determined by the rules.

It is especially in this context that the idea of justice as consisting in distribution according to merit has application. Criteria of merit differ widely. But when persons form an association for various purposes, merit consists in contribution to achievement of these purposes, as defined and measured by the association's explicit or implicit rules. According to these rules, then, it is just for A, or A has a right, to receive twice as much of the relevant rewards as B if A contributes twice as much to achievement of the association's purposes. This is an application of the Principle of Proportionality (2.22), where this principle is subordinate to the *PGC* in certain of its optional-procedural applications.

The possibility of such proportional numerical measurement depends, of course, on the nature and purposes of the association. In a stock company where the contributions are in money, measurement is relatively easy; but on a scientific team where the contributions involve supplying and testing theories, measurement may be much more complex. Nevertheless, in each context justice requires that the relevant rewards—money in the one case, honor or recognition in the other—be proportioned according to merit in contributing to the purposes for which the respective groups are formed. This requirement may be outweighed, however, by the consideration of contractual agreements freely entered into, where the rewards are fixed by such agreements.

5.6. Voluntary associations may be differentiated according to several variables, including not only their purposes and the explicitness or implicitness of their structuring according to rules, but also the degree of voluntariness of entry into and exit from the association or group, the duration of membership in the group, the ability of its members to change the rules while continuing to be members, and the impact of the association and its activities and rules on the well-being of the participants, especially as regards the severity of its sanctions. As these variables indicate, the fixity and purposive scope of various associations and rules are matters of degree. At one extreme are casual groupings formed for brief minimal purposes, such as baseball teams assembled at a picnic. At the other extreme may be placed familial relationships, although with some qualifications bearing not only on the size of the group but also on the consensual participation of children. The *PGC* justifies preferential familial rights and duties by the special force of the purposes for which each partner voluntarily enters the union. Like the different roles found in other voluntary associations, this preferential status does not violate the *PGC*'s equality of generic rights, because every prospective purposive agent is still left free to pursue and enter into such a marital relation, and because he is not coerced or harmed by such relations on the part of others.

Between the extremes of temporary, casual associations for minimal goals and enduring, intimate associations for maximal purposes of self-expression and emotional and physical union there is a vast array of other voluntary associations that depart in varying degrees from each extreme. The contents of the rules of such associations may vary in optionality. For although membership in voluntary associations depends on the optional consent of the participants, the purposes of the associations may be such that they require more or less fixity in the rules. An informal baseball game among picnicking families, for example, may vary the traditional rules by allowing four instead of three strikes for children and by reducing the number of bases from three to two. But in a scientific society certain of its rules must conform to relatively invariant scientific criteria, including rules of evidence and hence of logical inference.

Among the various kinds of complex human groupings, there is much unrealism in the distinction sometimes drawn between 'public' and 'private' associations, with the former being classed as 'compulsory' and the latter as 'voluntary.' Although the state is the supreme public association, membership in which is not voluntary but compulsory, it is false to assert that the modern state has a monopoly of legitimate coerciveness and that all other associations are private and have voluntary memberships. Insofar as membership in various professional organizations, labor unions, and other interest groups is a necessary condition of earning a livelihood, such membership may reflect a kind of forced choice on the part of persons who want to pursue the relevant profession, trade, or business.[3] The justification of such organizations and rules may hence be based more on their contribution to well-being than on their being procedurally justified, especially when they monopolize their respective kinds of activity and refuse entry to new members. It should also be noted, however, that labor unions in particular may extend the area of freedom by making more alternatives available for choice by the workers. Through such associations the alternatives, bearing on wages, working conditions, and other important matters, may be subjected in part to control by the organized workers as well as by their employers.

For optional-procedural justifications to provide more than prima facie moral rightness, the groups and activities they justify must satisfy the further requirements set by the PGC. Although the members of some group voluntarily accept its conditions, these may involve coercing nonmembers; hence, they are not morally right. For example, the voluntary agreement of all the members of a bank-robbing gang, including their acceptance of various job-related duties such as gunman and getaway man, does not excuse the coercive and harmful impact of the gang on its victims outside the gang. In addition, as with the direct applications of the PGC's freedom component, so too with the procedural justifications, the component of well-being must be taken into account. Consider, for example, social rules that establish institutions like slavery or 'games' like the gladiatorial contests of ancient Rome. Consent of all the parties would give these rules a procedural justification, but they would still be morally wrong in the final analysis. Such wrongness might be explicated by further appeal to the requirements of procedural justifications, on the ground that the consent the victims give to such institutions and activities is not voluntary but forced. This, however, raises the question of the nature and range of the alternatives open to the consenting parties. If one side has few alternatives available to it and those hardly desirable, then its consent would be forced in a way or to a degree not found on the other side. A similar point applies to less dramatic contractual economic arrangements that affect the livelihood or economic well-being of the parties, where there are serious inequalities of bargaining power among the contractors arising from differences of wealth.

These considerations indicate that for optional-procedural justifications to establish more than prima facie rightness, the relation among the contracting or consenting parties must fulfill the *PGC*'s central requirement of the equality of generic rights, in its component of well-being as well as its component of freedom. This equality requires that persons not be harmed in transactions in ways that adversely affect their capacities for action. Both the background and the contents of agreements and contracts must fulfill this requirement. Thus, if disadvantaged persons have suffered such incapacitating harms, as evidenced by their poverty and its effects in poor health, wretched living conditions, and insecurity, then arrangements and contracts whose terms reflect these adversely unequal positions are to this extent not morally right. Similar considerations show that contracts to give up one's dispositional freedom or basic well-being cannot be morally right. Even if all the precautions indicated above for the voluntariness of consent are fulfilled (4.21), such contracts reflect a moral failure of social institutions.

Static-Instrumental Justification of Social Rules: The Minimal State

5.7. On a purely libertarian or voluntaristic criterion of moral rightness and justice, optional-procedural considerations, through contracts and other voluntary agreements, are necessary and sufficient for all justifications of social rules. As we have seen, however, such considerations may not make adequate provision for rules that protect each person's right to well-being. This difficulty is not removed if a voluntary association is formed for the purpose of protecting basic well-being from attack by other persons.[4] For, though each person would presumably agree to belong to an association whose rules prohibit interferences with his own well-being, there is no guarantee that only one such association would be formed in each territorial region, or that stronger persons would agree to remain in the association when they believed they could better advance their well-being by leaving it. But by the purely libertarian doctrine where the justification of social rules is made to depend solely on the contingent agreement or consent of each associate, the stronger individuals who quit the association (perhaps to form a rival one) would no longer be subject to its rules and requirements; hence, so far as concerns the rules, they would do no wrong in interfering with the well-being of other persons by inflicting serious harm on them, so that the rights of the latter to well-being would be left unprotected.

It might still be contended that an appeal to unanimous voluntary consent is sufficient to ground such protective social rules. For, as we have seen, the rational agent must hold that all prospective purposive agents have the generic rights; hence he will give voluntary consent to any social rules that serve to protect these rights. This argument is sound, and it shows that such social rules have a consensual basis. The argument leaves open, however, the question of the relation between the rational and the empirical agent, with their respective 'wills' and 'consents.' There is a familiar ambiguity here: the rational self wills and does only what is right; but since the objects of his will include rules of some sort resembling the criminal law with its coercive sanctions, which are applied to persons who have done wrong, another, empirical self must also be at work. Hence, even if every rational agent gives voluntary consent to the *PGC*, the fact that coercive rules of the criminal law and other sanctions are needed shows that the voluntary consent of actual agents, some of whom may violate the rational rules of morality, is not sufficient to ground these rules. For such violators may not consent to the rules. We are now dealing with the context where, given that the *PGC* and its derivative rules upholding the generic rights are rationally justified, we must consider what is to be done to protect these rights for all prospective purposive agents in actual or possible empirical situations. For this purpose, recourse must be had to what I shall call the instrumental justification of social rules.

The instrumental justification derives from the *PGC*'s purposive generic rule that requires that the agent act in accord with his recipients' right to well-being, so that he must at least refrain from harming them in ways connected with their capacities for action. The instrumental justification applies this requirement to social rules: the rules and the activities and associations they regulate are morally right and ground morally justified obligations when they serve to prevent such harms and to protect persons' rights to well-being. Since the *PGC* requires that there be an equality of generic rights and hence mutuality of nonharm among persons, social rules are instrumentally justified when they maintain or bring about this equality. More generally, then, such social rules are justified as contributing to the existence or reinforcement of a social order in which the *PGC* is more fully observed.

Although freedom is included among the generic rights, the instrumental justification of social rules is distinct from the procedural justification whereby social rules are justified when they derive from or express the free consent of the persons subject to them. It is one thing for rules to be expressions or effects of freedom; it is another for rules to serve to restore or protect freedom, and in this way to operate as causal conditions of freedom. The latter relation, unlike the former, is included together with other generic rights in the *PGC*'s instrumental justification of social rules.

We may distinguish two main phases of this justification. One phase is *static*. It assumes that persons are already equal in their effective possession of the generic rights at least as to occurrent noninterference with basic or other important goods, and it holds that social rules are justified when they protect or restore this occurrent equality. The rules of the criminal law are justified in this way, and so too are any laws of society or of the state that may be required for fostering or expediting such protection and restoration. The other phase of the instrumental justification is *dynamic*. It recognizes that persons are dispositionally unequal in their actual ability to attain and protect their generic rights, especially their rights to basic well-being, and it provides that social rules are justified when they serve to remove this inequality. Thus, where the static phase tries to restore an occurrent antecedent status quo, the dynamic phase tries to move toward a new situation in which a previously nonexistent dispositional equality is attained or more closely approximated. Social rules supporting the various components of well-being, but especially basic well-being, are justified in this dynamic way. In all cases, social rules are instrumentally justified by the *PGC* insofar as they are required to bring about, statically or dynamically, the occurrent or dispositional equality of generic rights prescribed by the *PGC*. This requiredness may be more or less strong; social rules may also contribute to promoting or stabilizing a social order in which the *PGC*'s requirements are more effectively achieved.

Nearly all political philosophers have found in the criminal-law function mentioned above a primary justification for the existence of political society with its coercive laws. The present distinction between two kinds or aspects of instrumental justification through the *PGC*, however, provides a unifying perspective that departs from certain strands of traditional thought on this subject. Beginning with Aristotle, political and legal thinkers have distinguished between 'distributive' and 'retributive' (or 'rectificatory') justice as two quite different branches of justice.[5] Distributive justice is conceived as determining who should receive what goods or what burdens on the basis of such criteria as merit, ability, work, or need, while retributive justice assigns penalties for various crimes and delicts. Of special importance for this distinction are the facts that retributive justice, unlike distributive justice, presupposes that there has been wrongdoing so that it connotes guilt on the part of the persons subject to it, and that it determines penalties without any 'respect of persons' in that it considers only the nature of the crime committed and not any of the personal qualities or needs of the criminal. Thus, although both distributive and retributive justice may be held to come under the general formula of justice as "rendering to each person his due," both the presuppositions of the 'rendering' and the criteria of the 'due' are drastically different in the two cases.

Utilitarianism provides one way of bridging the gap between these two kinds of justice, but it has notorious pitfalls, some of which I shall discuss further below. The *PGC* provides another way, which avoids these pitfalls. For it makes the equality of generic rights central to both retributive and distributive justice as the criterion of 'due' referred to in the general formula. It thereby serves to relate both kinds of justice to the necessary conditions of human action, while at the same time it makes intelligible the distinction between them by reference to different aspects of these conditions and of corresponding reactions or 'renderings' in rules and institutions. Both kinds of justice have the function of maintaining or protecting the supreme principle of moral rightness consisting in the equality of generic rights that the *PGC* makes mandatory for actions and institutions; thus both kinds of justice are instrumental to securing this equality. Retributive justice is the static phase of this instrumentality: it fulfills this function by correcting occurrent interferences with basic and other important goods that disrupt an occurrent equality of noninterference with generic rights. Distributive justice, on the other hand, has two branches: regular and redistributive. The regular branch is the one dealt with in nearly all the applications of the *PGC* so far considered; it fulfills the above function by providing for the various mutualist duties of agents both outside and within voluntary associations. The redistributive branch is the dynamic phase of the instrumentality for securing the equality of generic rights. It fulfills this function by removing dispositional inequalities of well-being that have institutional sources.

In a broad sense, then, both retributive and redistributive justice are corrective and distributive in that both undertake, at least in part, to correct situations that are morally wrong (in that they violate the equality of generic rights) either by distributing penalties to persons who deserve them because of their criminal actions or by redistributing components of well-being. The morally wrong situation that retributive justice corrects, however, carries a connotation of personal guilt in that some particular person (or persons) has intentionally inflicted an occurrent disruption of an antecedent, narrowly circumscribed equality of generic rights; retributive justice, as static, seeks to restore this equality. The situation corrected by redistributive justice, on the other hand, although it too is morally wrong in that it dispositionally violates the equality of generic rights, does not carry a connotation of personal guilt because the situation is a social, dispositional one involving multitudes of persons whose comparative possession of well-being has, at least in part, a much broader historical and institutional base. Redistributive justice, as dynamic, seeks to move toward a previously nonexistent equality.

5.8. Let us first consider the static phase, that of retributive justice. As was already mentioned, the rules of the criminal law are instrumentally justified in that they serve to uphold in certain ways the rights of all persons to such basic goods as life, liberty, and physical integrity, as well as such other important goods as reputation and privacy. To uphold these rights is to maintain the equality of generic rights; for if one person voluntarily and purposively kills, kidnaps, physically assaults, or defames another, then in that transaction the former sets up an occurrent inequality between himself and his recipient with regard to necessary preconditions or other important goods of action. The criminal law provides punishments that rectify this inequality and also serve to protect the equality of rights whereby such harmful actions are eschewed. For any one person to be protected in his rights to these basic or other goods, other persons must be prevented from infringing them. The criminal law consists in rules that prohibit and provide for preventing such infringements. The institutional arrangements for establishing these prohibitory rules constitute the minimal state. The rules are publicly promulgated in advance by state authorities explicitly designated for this purpose; to enforce the rules and to rectify violations of them there is a system of publicly indicated penalties, including loss of property or of liberty; there are policemen to apprehend and arrest violators of the rules and courts to try and sentence offenders.

The criminal law as thus explicated bears two relations to the *PGC*. Its content is largely even if not entirely the same as that of the most basic part of the *PGC*, prohibiting the infringement of life, freedom, and other basic goods, as well as of such nonsubtractive goods as privacy and reputation. In this respect, denial of the obligatoriness of the rules of the criminal law involves self-contradiction in the same way as does denial of the *PGC*. And the public promulgation of these rules also brings the basic part of the *PGC* to public notice as being obligatory. On the other hand, the criminal law adds to the *PGC* the enforcement provisions noted above, including the threat and application of punishment for violators. In this regard, to say that the criminal law is required to bring about the equality of generic rights prescribed by the *PGC* is, in part, to make an empirical, contingent statement. The relation of requirement in this part is not logical but causal: the functioning of the criminal law is a necessary means to the end of persons' obeying the *PGC*. Nevertheless, as will be shown more fully below, self-contradiction is incurred by denial of the obligatoriness of the criminal law not only in its content but also in its enforcement aspect.

Although the justification of the rules of the criminal law is instrumental, the end toward which they are instrumental is the *PGC*, with its predominantly distributive emphasis on the equality of generic rights. If adequate account is not taken of this latter point, the justification is faced with problems that traditionally beset utilitarian and other consequentialist theories. Since an instrumental justification of social rules views them as means to some end, it seems to hold that the end justifies the means and thus to open the door to a calculus in which the rights of individual persons dealt with in the rules are subordinated to the end. Thus the justification of the criminal law, by providing for enforcement of the *PGC*'s requirements through the threat and application of punishment, might seem to uphold making some persons suffer various harms for the protection of others and hence using the former as mere means for benefiting the latter. The instrumental justification might also seem to oppose the specificity of criminal punishment, both as to its recipients and as to its amount. If some persons' being punished is justified by the end of protecting the generic rights of other persons, why must the punishment be inflicted on the criminals and not on innocent persons whose being punished will have the same preventive or deterrent effect? And why may not the punishment even for slight offenses against generic rights be made very severe if this will serve more effectively to protect the rights?

The instrumental justification of the criminal law through the *PGC* does not incur these difficulties. First, the end in question is not the aggregative utilitarian one of the maximizing of utility. Such an aggregative end indeed permits and even requires the submerging of rights and of distributive considerations in general. In the overall theory of the *PGC*, on the other hand, the end to which the criminal law is instrumental is the distributive one of the occurrent equality of generic rights: persons must be equally free in relation to one another, and transactions between them must respect the well-being of each of the participants. This distributive end must be departed from either not at all or only in such a way as to restore or reinstate an equality that has been previously disrupted by a voluntary action of one of the participants.

Second, when X is said to be 'instrumental' to some end Y, this can have two different meanings. In one, the means or instrument is external to the end in that it need have none of the distinctive characteristics of the end. In the other, the means or instrument is internal to the end; it is instrumental to the end not only causally but also conceptually in that its features are also constitutive of the end. It serves as an instrument to the end by enforcing, reinforcing, reinstating, or in some other way bringing about a certain result, while at the same time it embodies distinctive characteristics of the result. For example, if a lecture on some scientific or philosophical topic is delivered simply or mainly in order to earn money, the lecture, as means or instrument, is external to the end: spreading enlightenment or understanding on scientific or philosophical topics is conceptually distinct from earning money, since each can be done without the other. If, on the other hand, the lecture is delivered for the purpose of improving its hearers' understanding of the topics with which it deals, the lecture, as means or instrument, is internal to the end: the very process of presenting the relevant intellectual considerations exhibits and conforms to the same intellectual criteria as constitute the end of improving the understanding of the subject matter.

It is in this internal way that the rules of the criminal law are instrumental to the *PGC*. The *PGC* requires that there be an equal distribution of the rights to well-being between the agent and his recipients. If the agent inflicts a basic or other serious harm on some recipient, he violates this equality in a quite specific way, and the punishment prescribed by the criminal law is justified as a way of restoring the equality by redressing the previously disturbed balance. Penalties are to be inflicted on wrongdoers in proportion to the seriousness of their crimes. This is an application of the Principle of Proportionality (2.22), although the penalties that are its contents are not rights but rather certain removals of rights. Such apportioning, however, should not be construed mechanically as requiring an exact equality or even identity between the crime and its punishment, so that, for example, the rapist is himself to be raped or the killer killed. The point, rather, derives from the background of the application of the criminal law which, at the risk of some oversimplification, may be put schematically as follows. At the outset, both A and B are persons equal in respect of basic well-being in the specific sense that neither is actually depriving the other or any third parties of basic or other important goods such as life, physical integrity, or good reputation. This means, in particular, that there is an occurrent equality of mutual restraint as between A and other persons in that each observes toward the others the restraints on his conduct that the *PGC* prescribes for agents with regard to the basic well-being of their recipients, and that are embodied in the substantive rules of the criminal law. Then A disturbs this equality by removing X units of basic or other important well-being from B. The size of X will vary according as the well-being removed from B consists in his life, his other physical integrity, his property, and so forth. A not only removes X units from B; he also adds a comparable number of units to his own stock of well-being. For while A benefits from other persons' observing toward himself the aforementioned restraints on their conduct, he disrupts the equality of mutual restraint by lifting the prescribed restraints on his own conduct; he hence derives a certain degree of additional satisfaction. The amount of the latter is roughly proportional to the amount A has removed from B. The punishment prescribed by the criminal law, in accordance with the Principle of Proportionality, removes from A this additional satisfaction; it thus restores the original equality and prevents him from profiting through his violation of the mutual restraints prescribed by the *PGC*.

These references to 'X units of basic well-being' and to 'added units' of satisfaction or well-being are, of course, quite artificial. They are intended to refer only to the fact that crimes vary in seriousness according to their impact on the basic well-being of their victims. But this need not be taken to mean that such seriousness is measurable by exact units or that it is relative to the variable psychological disposi-

tions of different victims. If nothing else, the requirements of standardization as embodied in rules, as well as the general regularities of
human experience, are sufficient guides to what must be done to
redress the previously disturbed balance without having to allow for
the minutiae of possible individual variations. In this way, the rules of
the criminal law are instrumentally justified by their serving to restore
the *PGC*'s equality of generic rights to basic and other important
well-being; the rules thus embody the same distributive emphasis as
is found in the *PGC* itself.

It must also be kept in mind that the rules of the criminal law are
concerned only with the static equality of generic rights, in that, with
respect to their being instrumentally justified by the *PGC*, the
assumption is that persons are already equal as to their mutual
occurrent restraint from removing basic and other important goods. It
is hence no objection to this account that since persons are not in fact
equal in their total well-being, the description of the function of
punishment as restoring an antecedently existing equality rests on a
false conception of how things actually are. The equality of rights
with which the criminal law is concerned is strictly limited in its scope:
it extends not to all goods but only to the aforesaid mutuality of
occurrent noninterference. And it is with the restoration of this
equality that the punishment provided by the criminal law is concerned.

Because the rules of the criminal law are instrumentally justified in
this distributive way, there must be equality of all persons before the
law. It is illegitimate to single out any persons for punishment or for
protection on any grounds not directly constitutive of the *PGC*'s
equality of generic rights. Since the *PGC* requires that all persons
equally have these rights, all persons' generic rights to basic and other
important goods must be protected equally, and punishment is to be
meted out only to the persons who deserve it through having
voluntarily and purposively violated the occurrent equality of rights
to basic goods and the other important goods noted above by inflicting
basic and other serious harms on other persons. It follows that it is
illegitimate to punish innocent persons, and that justified punishment
consists not in using some persons as mere means by inflicting harm
on them for the benefit of other persons, but rather in restoring the
occurrent equality of generic rights that some persons have voluntarily
infringed. It also follows that the criminal law should not extend to
actions that do not inflict basic or other serious harms on other
persons. Nor does it justify, let alone require, vindictiveness or cruelty
in punishing; indeed, these are strictly prohibited.

It follows further that punishment and the whole apparatus of the criminal law are necessary evils, required for restoring an antecedently infringed equality of generic rights that is a good for the reasons elaborated above. The equalizing function of punishment is not a good in itself; it would be far better if the evil of inflicting basic and other harms had not occurred, so that its rectification was unnecessary. The need for such rectification also serves to emphasize that persons who inflict such harms are to be condemned and their misdeeds deplored. What requires rectification in this area is wrong, and punishment as inflicted by the state conveys the community's solemn public expression of disapproval. At the same time, the punishment serves to acknowledge that the criminal is a person who is responsible for his actions as a member of the moral community.

5.9. Although the rules of the criminal law are internally instrumental to the *PGC* in this way, they also bear a causal relation to the *PGC*. For within the limits of the conceptual relation whereby punishment is intended to restore the *PGC*'s equality of generic rights, the punishment and the rules that provide for it are also justified as having a deterrent effect. By calling to public notice the punishment and the threat thereof, the rules are intended to bring it about that persons refrain from inflicting on others the basic and other serious harms the *PGC* prohibits. Thus the *PGC*'s relation to criminal punishment is both backward-looking and forward-looking, but the latter relation is subordinate to the former. Punishment is justified in part by its helping to bring about that persons abide by the *PGC*; but this justification obtains only insofar as punishment is justified by its serving to restore the *PGC*'s equality of generic rights through being inflicted only on persons who infringed the equality. That the rules of the criminal law have this double relation to the *PGC*, both conceptual and causal, in the order indicated, is no more anomalous than that a similar double relation can be found in my earlier example of a lecture.

The above points also bear on the 'public' character of the criminal law. If the whole justification of the basic rules of the criminal law is instrumental, consisting in their subserving persons' basic and other important purposes regardless of whether any particular recipients of the rules consent to them, why should it not be open to any person to make and enforce these rules? Why should the specific legal-political apparatus of the minimal state be required for this? The answer to this question comprises several parts, some of which go back at least to Locke.[6] First, as was indicated above in my discussion of the duty to relieve distress, each person has the duty to prevent basic harm from befalling some other person if he can do so without injury to himself. Second, however, the grave importance of basic harms, the threat they pose to any stable transactions among persons that are to fulfill the requirements of the *PGC*, requires that there be public rules prohibiting the infliction of such harms and publicly designated officials whose duty it is to promulgate and enforce the rules and to administer sanctions for their violation. These tasks require not only functional but also organizational institutions. To leave fulfillment of the tasks to random individuals, including the recipients of the harms or their relatives and friends, would remove not only the stability the prohibiting rules must have because of the gravity of basic harms, but also the uniformity of the sanctions attached to them that is required by justice.

By virtue of their instrumental relation to the *PGC*, the rules of the criminal law have a stringent logical status. Since any agent's denial of the *PGC* and hence of its obligatoriness is self-contradictory, it is also self-contradictory for any agent to deny the obligatoriness of these rules where their content is largely the same as the most basic part of the *PGC*. And insofar as enforcement of the rules through punishment is causally required for protecting the *PGC*'s equality of generic rights in the way indicated, the obligatoriness of the enforcement must also rationally be granted. The basis of the obligation to obey the law, then, is not simply that it is the law but rather that the law is instrumentally justified by the *PGC*. Hence, indirectly, the obligation to obey the law is a rational obligation, in that to violate the law is to contradict oneself.

The rules of the criminal law thus have a more stringent logical status than social rules that are only procedurally justified by the *PGC*. It would indeed be self-contradictory to deny that the latter rules are morally right in the sense of permissible, since they are expressions of the freedom whose exercise the *PGC* holds to be permissible. Hence, it is morally wrong to interfere with persons' engaging in any procedurally justified activity so long as the limits imposed by the *PGC* are observed. And once one has joined such a voluntary association and accepted its rules, it is morally obligatory to obey the rules. But the contents of the rules are not morally obligatory apart from the voluntary consent of the persons subject to them. It would not be self-contradictory to deny the obligatoriness of these contents, nor is it morally wrong to refrain from participating in some voluntary association and accepting its rules if one has not agreed to do so. The reason for this difference between procedurally and instrumentally justified social rules is that the latter, unlike the former, are required for restoring and maintaining the equality of generic rights. Since this equality is obligatory, the rules that protect it are also obligatory.[7]

5.10. The criminal law, together with the minimal state that administers it, diverges in two ways from the procedural justification of social rules through voluntary consent, and also from the PGC's requirement in its direct applications that recipients participate freely or voluntarily in transactions. First, criminals who are punished in accordance with the criminal law are recipients in transactions whose agents are policemen and judges; but the position now is that it is not required that these recipients participate voluntarily in the transactions, nor purposively, since they may be made to lose various goods and even to suffer basic harms. Second, whether there is to be a minimal state with its criminal law in the sense of a body of enforceable rules is not subject to the voluntary or optional consent of the persons who must obey it. Now if the upholders, promulgators, or enforcers of the criminal law are viewed as its agents, then the other persons who, together with the former, must obey this law are the recipients in the promulgating transaction; and the position now is that, in seeming contrariety to the PGC, it is not required that the recipients participate voluntarily in the transaction. How, then, can these nonvoluntary aspects of the criminal law be reconciled with the requirements of the PGC?

To deal with the first point, the requirement that criminals be coerced and harmed is reconciled with the PGC's requirements by a consideration similar to that indicated above in connection with all social rules (5.3), although, of course, the coercions and harms are more drastic. Once a set of social rules is justified by the PGC, whether procedurally or instrumentally, transactions that occur in accordance with these rules must be regulated directly by the rules rather than by the PGC. Hence, criminals must be treated in the ways provided by the enforcement provisions of the PGC, and their voluntary and purposive participation is no longer required. Indeed, if a criminal were to bribe a policeman or a judge, so that both parties participated voluntarily and purposively in their immediate transaction, it would still be wrong. For the transaction, although conforming to the PGC in its direct application, would violate the criminal law that is justified by the PGC. This justification and its corresponding requirements take precedence over the PGC's direct applications because the former serve to rectify serious infringements of the *PGC*'s equality of generic rights and thereby help to maintain this equality for a whole society. The bribing transaction would disrupt the uniformity of the application of the social rules required by the *PGC* and hence would violate an indirect application of the *PGC* itself; it would constitute and abet an unfair evasion of this application by the criminal and the persons he bribes. It must be noted that this consideration about a 'whole society' is still distributive, not aggregative.

This justification of the criminal law also explains why a judge who acts in accordance with the law does not contradict himself in sentencing a criminal to be punished, even though he here coerces and harms the criminal. The judge here claims for himself the right to participate voluntarily and purposively in the transaction while he denies this right to the criminal. There is no inconsistency in this claim and denial because, although both the judge and the criminal are prospective purposive agents, the *PGC* authorizes the attribution to the judge of a more specific quality as relevant to his right-claim. This is the quality of being a judge who acts in accordance with the rules of the criminal law; and the criminal does not have this quality. The *PGC* authorizes this more specific description because the rules of the criminal law are justified by the *PGC*. It is not arbitrary to appeal to this more specific description as relevant to the judge's right-claim, for since the *PGC* is rationally justified, the subordinate rules it in turn justifies are also rationally justified.

This brings me to the second point raised above, the lack of provision for voluntary consent to the minimal state and the criminal law itself. To deal with this, we must consider further why the instrumental justification of the criminal law is sufficient without any procedural justification. Since the criminal law directly embodies and enforces basic aspects of the *PGC*'s generic rules, its obligatoriness can no more be contingent on persons' optional consent than can that of the generic rules themselves. Persons' basic well-being and their equality of generic rights are defended by the criminal law; and that this equality is inherently right and must be upheld, and that each prospective agent values his well-being and wants it to be defended from attack by other persons, are not subject to optional decisions as are the purposes pursued in voluntary associations. The protection of each person's equal right to basic well-being is a necessary condition of the observance of moral rightness as determined by the *PGC*. But if some person's obligation to obey the rules of the criminal law, which provides such protection, were contingent on his optional consent, this would mean that the necessary condition of the observance of moral rightness would not be a necessary condition after all, since its fulfillment would not be obligatory in the absence of such consent.

Nevertheless, there is a place for consent at the basis of the minimal state and the criminal law with its instrumental justification. This consent, however, is not empirical, optional, or contingent but rational and necessary. As we have seen, it is by recourse to what must be admitted by rational agents that the argument for the *PGC* is made. This is one way the use of the dialectically necessary method is indispensable. Since such agents logically must consent to accept the rules of the criminal law, these rules and the minimal state have a consensual basis. It is important, however, to distinguish this basis from that which constitutes the optional-procedural justification of social rules and institutions. As critics of contractualist theories of the state have long pointed out, the consent that grounds the state cannot be assimilated to, let alone identified with, the empirical, optional consents that ground voluntary associations with their contingent goals. It is rather that all rational agents logically must accept the criminal law and the state that enforces it as being instrumentally justified by the *PGC*.

This rational basis shows how the agent's legal obligation—his necessary obedience to the law—is compatible with his preservation of his own autonomy. For the rational agent views the law not as something imposed on him from without but rather as something he imposes on himself, since he recognizes that the law fulfills the same criteria by virtue of which he himself is a rational agent who accepts the *PGC* as justified. In this way his actions in conformity with the criminal law are voluntary despite the constraints it places on those actions. This is parallel to the way the rational agent who accepts the procedurally justified rules of voluntary associations acts voluntarily even when a particular application of the rules forces him to be treated contrary to his desires or interests. In each case the agent controls his respective behaviors by his unforced choice; his choice here is unforced because, despite the constraints just noted, it is based on his rational acceptance of the rules as justified.

For the criminal, however, the coerciveness of the criminal law may well appear as a case of forced choice: "Obey the law or suffer punishment!" (see 1.11). In such a case his behavior in conformity with the law would not be strictly voluntary. On the other hand, his conduct in violation of the law may well be voluntary in that, disregarding the law's punitive provisions, he would control his behavior by his unforced choice with a view to attaining his objectives. While infringing the generic rights of his victims, he would still be acting in accord with his own generic rights in that he would maintain his freedom and well-being so that they are not interfered with by other persons without his consent. Another consideration also shows how the criminal law's coerciveness is consistent with voluntariness on the part of the criminal. For, unlike the forced choice presented by the gunman, the law's requirements are set forth not as threats but as embodying correct reasons he can share with all other persons, including the promulgators of the law (see 1.10).[8] To this extent, the assumption of the persons who address the precepts of the law to him is that he can control his behavior by his unforced choice in acceptance of these reasons. Insofar, however, as the criminal rejects the reasons, his behavior in conformity with the law would for him be based on a forced choice. But this fact would not constitute a violation of the *PGC*'s direct generic rule that agents respect their recipients' freedom because, as we have seen, the principle itself requires that this direct application be overridden by the static-instrumental justification of the criminal law in cases where the two conflict.

Necessary-Procedural Justification of Social Rules: The Method of Consent

5.11. In the optional-procedural justification of voluntary associations and their rules, it must be left to the optional consent of each person to determine whether he will belong to the association and be subject to its rules. Whether such associations and their rules are to exist at all depends on the optional consents or choices of their members. In the static-instrumental justification of the minimal state with its criminal laws, as we have just seen, each rational person gives his rational consent to these, because such consent is rationally necessitated by their instrumental relation to the *PGC*. But it is not left to the optional consent of persons to determine, individually or collectively, either whether they shall accept the criminal law and to this extent belong to a minimal state, or whether such a state shall exist. Although emigration from one's state must indeed be permitted, it will probably be from one state to another, not to a completely nonpolitical condition; but in any case, acceptance of and obedience to the criminal law is mandatory for all.

This contrast between the optionality of voluntary associations and the rational necessity of the minimal state carries over to other political objects, but in a somewhat more complex way. Although the central content of the criminal law is the same as the most basic part of the *PGC*, such identity does not directly characterize other laws that the fuller state may need to have, concerning which there may be many legitimate conflicts of interest and differences of opinion. These laws may range from rules of the road and other provisions for public goods to requirements that promote various other components of well-being for particular groups in the society. All such laws must be in accordance with the *PGC*'s equality of generic rights; but once the requirements of the criminal law are met, this accordance may be more or less stringent, in that the contents of some laws are more directly derivative from the *PGC* than others. In the case of the rules of the road, the rules may be of different kinds because everyone's right to well-being is fulfilled simply by the safety and predictability secured by there being such rules; in the case of legislation protecting the environment, other aspects of well-being are fostered, and still others where the economic deprivations of the poor are relieved.

In the next section I shall deal more fully with some of the main substantive issues. But even apart from the specific contents of different laws, they all have a claim to obedience because, among multitudes of persons living together, there must be uniform rules. Without the standardization these rules provide there will be disorder and unpredictability, and conflicts of interest will be unresolved or resolved only by force. To this extent, all laws as such, and the fuller or supportive state in which they operate, are instrumentally justified by the *PGC* in that they provide a general context of order that serves to protect and extend well-being. To this extent, also, obedience to the laws is obligatory for all the members of a society: the laws are coercive (although not necessarily coercing) in that their claim to obedience is backed by a threat of punishment for noncompliance. The laws and the supportive state or political society that they constitute and regulate are thus in a different position from voluntary associations and their rules, whose existence and acceptance by individuals depend only on their optional consents. The existence of a supportive state and the obligatoriness of obeying its laws, as such, cannot be made to depend on varied optional consents, because this would remove the uniformity and predictability that are among the main justifications for having laws and hence for the obligatoriness of obeying them.

Because the laws are coercive, and the officials who make, interpret, and enforce them have great power, it is a matter of crucial importance what procedures are used to designate these officials and thereby to determine what specific laws the state may have. The obligatoriness of obeying the laws may be overridden not only if their

contents violate the requirements of the *PGC* but also if the procedures for determining the laws violate these requirements. To see what
these procedural requirements are, we must note the problem they
confront. As we have seen, the existence of the state and its institution
of law, as such, cannot be made to depend on optional, variable
consents or decisions of individuals; it must depend, rather, like the
minimal state and its criminal law, on rational consent through the
arguments of the *PGC*. If, however, the specific laws and officials of
the state are also held to be determined by such rational consent, this
would obscure the difference between the moral invariability of the
general requiredness of the state and law and the moral variability of
having some specific officials and laws as against others. For determining these officials and laws, then, the *PGC* requires that the
voluntary consents of the persons subject to them must be invoked as
fully as possible; in this way as much freedom can be preserved as is
compatible with the moral necessity of having states and laws.

But how can this compatibility be attained? If obedience to the
specific laws and officials is made to depend on the voluntary or
optional consent of each individual, will this not lead to anarchy and
hence the removal of order and predicability? The *PGC*'s solution of
this problem consists in making mandatory a certain kind of constitution for the state. This constitution provides for a decision procedure
that depends on certain freedoms for all members of the society. The
procedure requires that the use and availability of these freedoms
must be decisive in determining the specific laws and officials of the
state. Thus, while the constitution is mandatory and hence is not itself
subject to optional consent by individuals, it provides that such
consent must be used as fully as possible within the political process
itself for determining the laws and officials.

The solution, then, may be summarized as combining constitutional
or structural mandatoriness with procedural consensualness or voluntariness. The consensual procedures are provided for and operate
within the mandatory constitutional structure. At the same time
obedience to the officials and laws determined by these consensual
procedures is itself mandatory. Thus, four levels of political objects
may be distinguished : (1) the minimal state with the criminal law, (2)
the supportive state with its need for other laws and officials, (3) its
constitutional structure providing for certain consensual decision-
procedures, (4) the specific laws and officials determined by the use of
these procedures. Obedience to all four of these objects is mandatory,
although at the third, procedural level there is maximal provision for
voluntariness, and there may be various sublevels within it. Fulfill-

ment of the requirements of the third, constitutional level is a necessary, and usually a sufficient, condition of the mandatoriness of the fourth level.

This four-level structure stands in contrast to traditional theories that tried to base political obligation on the consent of the governed. These theories did not, for the most part, distinguish between optional and rational consent, that is, between consent that is fully at the option of each individual according to his own variable desires or opinions, and consent that is fully determined by rational arguments. Although we shall see that the political method of consent provides a way of bringing together these two modes of consent, they are conceptually distinct. As a consequence of failing to distinguish them, the traditional theories also failed to distinguish between the status of voluntary associations and the political society or state, and they failed to show how a morally mandatory constitutional structure can be combined with consensual procedures in a way that safeguards both moral necessity and freedom. As a futher consequence, the traditional theories are always in danger of eventuating either in anarchy or in a reactive kind of absolutism or tyranny in which all the voluntaristic safeguards intended by their consensual basis are lost.

It is because the political objects of the consensual procedures just referred to are necessary or mandatory, in that obedience to the state with its laws and officials is normally obligatory for all its members, that I call the justification of these objects through the procedures used to determine them 'necessary-procedural.' This stands in contrast to the 'optional-procedural' justification of voluntary associations and their rules. The consensual procedures are in each case necessary to justify obedience to or acceptance of their respective objects. But whereas in the optional justifications their objects, the voluntary associations, have no independent moral necessity or requiredness, in the necessary justifications their objects are morally necessary or required simultaneously with the procedures. These procedures must exist in part because their objects must exist, whereas in the case of the optional justifications the objects must exist only because and insofar as the procedures exist and have been used. The constitutional structure of the state, in turn, determines what the former procedures shall be. And the *PGC*, finally, determines what should be this constitutional structure.

5.12. The main point of this constitutional determination by the *PGC* consists in the equal distribution of the civil liberties. As we saw earlier, the *PGC* requires that each person be left free to engage in any action or transaction according to his unforced choice so long as he does not coerce or harm other persons (4.23). This requirement sets an important limit on the legitimate powers of the state: it must not interfere with the freedom of the individual except to prevent his coercing or harming others. Thus an immense array of kinds of action must be exempted from governmental control. As we have seen, this prohibition of coercion and harm by individuals and groups is consistent with the coercive controls that are legitimately exerted in voluntary associations and in the minimal state; and we shall also see this with regard to the supportive state's own protections of well-being, to be further discussed below.

Now the actions and transactions that the *PGC* thus requires to be left equally free for each person include the objects of the civil liberties, especially the actions of speaking, publishing, and assembling and associating with others. These are called 'civil liberties' for two interconnected reasons, bearing on two different relations these liberties must have to the state. On the one hand, they are 'passive' in that they must be protected by the state as rights of persons. On the other hand, they are 'active' in that the actions that are their objects function in the political process to help determine who shall govern in the state. In both relations, the *PGC* requires that the civil liberties pertain equally to each prospective purposive agent (except criminals): each person has an equal right to participate freely and actively in the political process and to be protected by the state in that participation. Insofar as there are diverse states, this equal right pertains to each citizen, and each person has a right to be a citizen of a state having the civil liberties. These liberties of expression and association also extend to contexts of individual and social activity other than the political process.

The availability and use of the civil liberties in the political process constitutes what I shall call the *method of consent*. With possible qualifications to be discussed in the next section, this method is a necessary and sufficient condition of all morally justified political and legal obligation that goes beyond the minimal state; that is, specific laws and political arrangements over and above the criminal law discussed earlier have a morally justifiable claim to be obeyed by each person in the state if and only if these laws and arrangements have resulted from the method of consent. This method consists in maintaining, as a matter of constitutional requirement, a system of civil liberties whereby each person is able, if he chooses, to discuss, criticize, and vote for or against the government and to work actively with other persons in groups of various sizes to further his political objectives, including the redress of his socially based grievances. In this way each person has the right to participate actively in the political process. The method of consent thus directly comprises not determinate acts of consent occurring in individuals, but institutional arrangements for effectively implementing the equal rights to the civil liberties for all individuals in the state who are prospective purposive agents. Government by consent means that the particular holders of political authority are not independent variables so far as their authority is concerned but are dependent on the votes of the electorate, consisting of all adult, noncriminal members of the society, each having one and only one equal vote. This entails that the government, as a matter of constitutional requirement, is regularly subjected to an egalitarian electoral process that passes judgment on it and may transfer its authority to other hands. The equal right of dissent is thus a basic part of the method of consent. The process culminates in an election, but it also includes free discussion and criticism of the government's policies and competition for votes among different parties. The election, which may be viewed as the culmination of this competition, determines who is to occupy government office in the subsequent period. The government's right to govern depends finally on its winning the election by the required majority or plurality of votes.

Unlike other varieties of political consent, the method of consent, without incurring the difficulties of anarchy or tyranny, provides the necessary basis of morally justified political obligation for all persons in the society in which the method is operative, not only for those whose side wins the election but also for those whose side loses, as well as for those who abstain altogether from voting or participating actively in the political process. The method provides this comprehensive basis of obligation because it is itself directly justified by the *PGC*, which grounds all morally justified obligations. The *PGC* requires that all persons have equal rights to freedom, and, as we have seen, these include equal rights to the civil liberties and to participation in the political process. Because of the vital importance of this process for well-being, these liberties are especially important among the freedom rights upheld by the *PGC*. With regard to participation in the political process there is to be no discrimination among prospective purposive agents on any criteria other than criminality. Since the method of consent consists in institutional arrangements for implementing and exercising these equal rights, it is itself morally justified as a fair procedure. It therefore imposes within its specific sphere the general obligations imposed by the *PGC*. These obligations include not only obedience to the minimal state with its criminal law but also acceptance of the results of the method of consent when the method is applied to determine the officials who shall give effect to the criminal law as well as other officials, laws, and policies of the state.

Possession of the civil liberties together with the effective capacity for participating in the method of consent is required for the dignity and rational autonomy of every prospective purposive agent. It is an important component of the self-esteem and sense of one's own worth that we saw earlier is central to the additive rights of each person (4.16). If the civil liberties are denied to any persons, whether in the political or in any other context, the denier is caught in a contradiction. For he is then in the position of denying to other persons an important right of freedom he claims for himself even though his recipients fulfill the same condition on which he rationally bases his own claim. Politically, he brings it about that they are always political recipients, never political agents. In setting up this inequality between himself and other persons he reduces them to a position of tutelage or subservience in political or other areas whose subject matter is of crucial importance to them. Such a position, resulting from an unjust distribution of the civil liberties, is incompatible with the equality of generic rights required by the *PGC*, and the persons who impose it lack rational justification for their actions.

The method of consent itself may hence be held to rest on a kind of hypothetical or dispositional rational consent given by each rational person. If persons are rational in the ways that enter into the *PGC*, each of them will consent to the method of consent as the procedure for reaching binding decisions on matters of public policy over and above the criminal law. Or, to put it still more strongly, the method of consent imposes obligatory decisions on such matters if and only if each rational person would consent to accept it. Since all such rational persons necessarily would so consent, because of the method's connection with the *PGC*, they are rationally committed to accept the method and its results.

Of central importance are the limits that restrict the justifiable contents of the laws and policies emanating from the method of consent. The method cannot rightly transgress the constitution which, through the *PGC*, provides its justification as a procedure whose results are binding. As we have seen, this constitution must require that there be equal freedom to participate in the political process for all members of the society, so that the civil liberties must be equally preserved for all. Hence, laws violating these liberties are invalid.

Similarly, since the method of consent is justified through the *PGC*, the laws or policies that result from it cannot rightly allow criminal acts, including murder and enslavement, against any persons. Inflicting basic harms can be justified only as punishment for crimes. More generally, the method of consent must respect the equal right to freedom on the part of all persons, so that it must make maximal possible provision for individual freedom in the sense of letting persons control their own lives. Any restrictions the method's results impose on freedom must be justifiable through the *PGC*.

It is sometimes held that there is a sharp distinction between individual freedom and political freedom as found in a democracy. Political freedom consists in persons' controlling the government under which they live through active participation in the political process, whereas individual freedom consists in the absence of external control over persons' actions. These are said to be distinct, since a democratic government established through active popular participation and election may institute extensive controls over persons' actions. When, however, a government derives its authority through the method of consent, there are, as we have seen, sharp limits on the restrictions it can rightly impose on individual freedom. These limits exempt from government control not only such actions relevant to political participation as speech and assembly, but also all other actions to the extent to which restrictions on them are not justifiable through the *PGC*.

A related problem for the method of consent is that the equality of political participation that it makes possible may be more formal than real. In particular, differences of economic power may strongly influence the degree of effectiveness with which different persons and groups participate in the political process. Hence, with a view to the equality of generic rights, it is a matter of great importance what steps are to be taken to ensure that other serious harms are not inflicted by those who are superior in economic or other power on those who are inferior in these respects, and that the opportunities available to the latter for attaining well-being are more nearly equalized. In the following section I discuss certain primary aspects of this question. It must be emphasized, however, that these difficulties do not remove the considerations indicated above about the value and indeed the necessity of the method of consent for human dignity and as a morally justified political decision-procedure. This justification includes the ability the method makes available to less advantaged groups for publicizing their grievances and pressing their claims.

DYNAMIC-INSTRUMENTAL JUSTIFICATION OF SOCIAL RULES: THE SUPPORTIVE STATE

5.13. In the static phase of the *PGC*'s instrumental justification of social rules, it is assumed that to begin with persons are occurrently equal in their effective possession of rights at least to basic goods in that they mutually refrain from seriously harmful actions, so that the rules of the criminal law are required simply to protect these rights and to redress the balance when it is disturbed. In the dynamic phase, on the other hand, it is recognized that there is a dispositional inequality of effective rights to well-being. Many persons may lack adequate food, housing, necessary medical care, and other basic goods, and they may also lack the capacities to assure that they will continue to have these goods as needed; they may be subjected to degrading conditions of dependence, danger, and disease in their situations of life and work; they may also not have the means to increase their capabilities of purpose-fulfilling action, such as adequate education and income. Insofar as persons who labor under such economic and other handicaps and privations cannot remedy these lacks through their own efforts and are not provided with the means of remedy by others, they do not have effective rights to well-being. In their case, by comparison with persons who have such effective rights, the *PGC*'s requirement of the equality of generic rights is violated. This violation is at least potentially transactional in the sense indicated earlier (4.3). Even if the inferior position of those who lack effective rights to well-being is not directly the result of exploitative and other harmful actions by other persons, their position makes them vulnerable to such actions. Their life chances are sharply reduced by the social environment that maintains this unequal distribution of well-being. Such maintenance operates at least by permitting different persons to have drastically unequal starts in life because of the economic status into which they are born. Although, as was noted above, persons are not simply the passive products of external forces, their capacities for self-development require an initial basis in familial and societal nurturing. If the appropriate background is absent, children born into poverty generally face serious disadvantages with regard to well-being.

Social rules are dynamically-instrumentally justified when they serve to remove or at least reduce this inequality of effective rights. In their bearing on the distribution of wealth, the aim of these rules is for the most part meliorative rather than conservative or revolutionary. As such, they fall between two extremes. A certain libertarian extreme would defend the existing distribution of wealth insofar as it has resulted from voluntary or contractual arrangements that ensue on an initial, presumably just acquisition. The other, egalitarian extreme proposes a drastic redistribution to be guided solely by the aim of maximally benefiting those who are least advantaged. The former extreme does not recognize the independent right to well-being, including additive goods, on the part of those whose initial position in life subjects them to serious disadvantages. The latter extreme does not recognize the independent right to freedom as applied in the production of valued commodities and the consequent earning of income. Thus the two extremes overlook, respectively, the claims of severe economic need and the claims of desert as based on voluntary effort and accomplishment. The retort that all effort is a product of forces beyond the agent's control ignores that persons with similar advantaged socioeconomic backgrounds may differ drastically in the ways they voluntarily marshal the resources available to them. On the other hand, the retort that voluntary exchanges and autonomous effort provide sufficient justifications for all distributions of wealth ignores the extent to which unfavorable familial and social back-grounds severely handicap both the exertion of effort and the possibility of successful agency.[9]

In contrast to these extremes, the *PGC* recognizes the claims of both freedom and well-being. The aim of the social rules it justifies dynamically-instrumentally is neither to distribute or redistribute wealth with no regard for contribution or effort nor to maintain the existing distribution unchanged while ignoring the disadvantages that unfavorable economic and social backgrounds impose on persons' capabilities for attaining additive and even basic well-being. Rather, the aim of the *PGC*'s social rules, in their bearing on economic distribution, is the double one of permitting the free exertion of productive effort to reap its rewards and of providing compensating goods to those who are disadvantaged in the ways indicated above. The point of this latter aim, in keeping with the *PGC*'s concern for the conditions of agency, is not to reinforce or increase dependence but rather to give support that enables persons to attain the conditions whereby they can control their own lives and effectively pursue and sustain their own purposes without being subjected to domination and harms from others. Thereby they will have their generic rights respected while respecting the generic rights of others, and they will be able to make their own contribution by productive work. It must be recognized, however, that such moderately equalizing and hence redistributive conditions must often include political as well as economic changes whereby productive work is made available. It is a matter not only of developing personal skills and other additive goods but also of fostering an economic environment in which there are sufficient employment opportunities for utilizing these skills. The possibilities of such fostering are, of course, limited by the resources actually available in a given society; but when possible and needed, there must be help from other societies.

The rules that serve this equalizing function must have three kinds of contents. First, they must provide for supplying basic goods, such as food and housing, to those persons who cannot obtain them by their own efforts. Second, they must try to rectify inequalities of additive well-being by improving the capabilities for productive work of persons who are deficient in this respect. Education is a prime means of such improvement, but also important is whatever strengthens family life and enables parents to give constructive, intelligent, loving nurture to their children. The wider diffusion of such means is a prime component of increasing equality of opportunity. Third, the rules must provide for various public goods that, while helping all the members of the society, serve to increase the opportunities for productive employment.

These contents of the rules are recognizably derivative from the *PGC*'s equality of generic rights. The rules are to be instrumental toward promoting equality of well-being in the internal, conceptual sense of 'instrumental' discussed above in connection with the criminal law (5.8); for the rules themselves embody the egalitarianism of the end. Thus there can be no question of such utilitarian instrumentalism as would allow the enslavement or impoverishment of some persons in order to maximize freedom or well-being overall.

There still remains the question of how the equalizing rules are to be applied and made effective. This is a question of external instrumentalities, of the causal factors that are most likely to bring it about that the rules achieve their equalizing ends. Since this is an empirical causal question, the answer must be in terms of various probabilities. There are two chief alternatives: the effectuating agency may be either the voluntary activity of individuals or groups or the coercive activity of the state. The latter alternative is more likely to achieve the desired end. Thus the duty to make the arrangements for applying the equalizing rules should pertain in the first instance to the state when members of the whole society governed by it have the required resources or means. The social rules in question should be democratically enacted laws of the state prescribing to state officials, who are ultimately responsible to the democratic electorate, that they make the necessary arrangements, and also prescribing to individual citizens that they contribute to these arrangements by paying taxes in proportion to their ability.

Social rules are required here because, unlike the drowning case considered before (4.7), the need for such arrangements is recurrent and affects sizable numbers of persons. The *PGC*'s prescription that persons suffering from economic deprivation be helped hence cannot be addressed simply to individual agents; an association of persons is required for this purpose. This association, moreover, is to be the political one of the state with its coercive laws. Like the problems that evoke the criminal law, if the needs in question are recurrent and pressing they should not be left to the vicissitudes of private charity. Voluntary associations for providing needed food and other basic goods, unlike voluntary associations for punishing criminals, would indeed be helpful; the nonuniformity of the resulting provisions above a certain minimum, being ameliorative rather than punitive, would not violate the recipients' rights to well-being. But it is plausible to hold that the primary responsibility must rest with the state, because only the state has the ability to assure that three required aspects of these arrangements are forthcoming. First, as was already mentioned, the arrangements must be securely provided as needed; hence, if they are left only to the optional decisions of willing private persons, sufficient funds may not be given. Second, the benefits of these arrangements must be equitably and impartially distributed to the persons who need them, without discrimination based on the variable preferences of potential providers. Third, the duty to contribute to such arrangements through taxes must also be equitably distributed to all the persons who have the required economic resources, in proportion to their ability. To leave the fulfillment of this duty solely to voluntary associations would allow many persons to shirk their duty. In this way, the state has a further moral basis as being instrumental to the redistributive justice required by the *PGC*.

There are traditional objections, many of which go back at least to Herbert Spencer, against making the supplying of food and other components of well-being a legally prescribed duty.[10] These objections are to be dealt with in ways similar to those presented above in connection with the duty to rescue (4.11). The present sociopolitical context also makes it possible to give a further related reply. Persons are not treated as mere means, nor is their rationally justifiable freedom violated, when they are taxed in order to help other persons who are starving or otherwise suffering from economic privation. For the principle underlying the taxation of the affluent to help the needy is concerned with protecting equally the rights of all persons, including the affluent. The *PGC*'s requirement that agents act in accord with the rights of their recipients entails that all prospective purposive agents must refrain from harming one another and that in certain circumstances they must help one another if they can. Hence, limitations on their freedom to abstain from such help are rationally justified. The facts that only some persons may actually be threatened with harm or need help at a particular time, and that only some other persons may be in a position to inflict harm or to give help, do not alter the universality of the *PGC*'s provision for the protection of rights. Such protection is not only occurrent but also dispositional and a matter of principle; it manifests an impartial concern for any and all persons whose rights may need protection. Hence, the *PGC*'s requirement for taxing the affluent involves treating all persons as ends, not merely as means.

This point also bears on the objection that the above economic and social rights, including the right to be given food and the other goods needed for alleviating severe economic handicaps, cannot be 'human' rights because they do not meet the test of universality.[11] According to this test, for a moral right to be a human one it must be a right of all persons against all persons: all persons must have the strict duty of acting in accord with the right, and all persons must have the strict right to be treated in the appropriate way. Thus all persons must be both the agents and the recipients of the modes of action required by the right. This test is passed by the rights to life and to freedom of movement: everyone has the duty to refrain from killing other persons and from interfering with their movements, and everyone has the right to have his life and his freedom of movement respected by other persons. But in the case of the right to be relieved from starvation or severe economic deprivation, it is objected that only some persons have the right: those who are threatened by starvation or deprivation; and only some persons have the duty: those who are able to prevent or relieve this starvation or deprivation by giving aid.

The answer to this objection need not concede that this right, like other economic and social rights, is universal only in a 'weaker' sense, in that while all persons have the right to be rescued from starvation or deprivation, only some persons have the correlative duty. Within the limits of practicability, all persons have the right and all have the duty. For all persons come under the protection and the requirements of the *PGC* insofar as they are prospective purposive agents. Hence, all the generic rights upheld by the *PGC* have the universality required for being human rights.

It is, indeed, logically impossible that each person be at the same time both the rescuer and the rescued, both the affluent provider and the deprived pauper. Nevertheless, the fact that some prospective purposive agent may not at some time need to be rescued from deprivation or be able to rescue others from deprivation does not remove the facts that he has the right to be rescued when he has the need and that he has the duty to rescue when he has the ability and when other relevant conditions are met. As we have seen, this duty stems, in the way indicated earlier, from the claim he necessarily makes or accepts that he has the generic rights by virtue of being a prospective purposive agent. The universality of a right is not a matter of everyone's actually having the related need, nor is it a matter of everyone's actually fulfilling the correlative duty, let alone of his doing so at all times. Nor is it even a matter of everyone's always being able to fulfill the duty. It is rather a matter of everyone's always having, as a matter of principle, the right to be treated in the appropriate way when he has the need, and the duty to act in accord with the right when the circumstances arise that require such action and when he then has the ability to do so, this ability including consideration of cost to himself.

When it is said that the right to be relieved from economic deprivation and the correlative duty pertain to all persons insofar as they are prospective purposive agents, this does not violate the condition that for human rights to be had one must only be human, as against fulfilling some more restrictive description. As was indicated earlier, all normal humans are prospective purposive agents; the point of introducing this description is only to call attention to the aspect of being human that most directly generates the rights to freedom and well-being. In this regard the right in question differs from rights that pertain to persons not simply by virtue of being prospective purposive agents but only in some more restricted capacity, such as being teachers as against students, umpires as against batters, or judges as against defendants. The universality of human rights derives from their direct connection with the necessary conditions of action, as against the more restrictive objects with which nongeneric rights are connected. And since both the affluent and the economically deprived are prospective purposive agents, the latter's right to be helped by the former is a human right.

5.14. In addition to legal provisions that serve to secure certain minimal levels of well-being and to foster additive well-being for the poor and other deprived groups as means to the equality of generic rights, there should also be laws that promote public goods and help to facilitate the general increase of wealth and productive capacity for the whole society. Public goods are beneficial commodities, such as unpolluted air, public roads, courts for resolving civil disputes, and protection against fire that are 'common' goods in the distributive sense specified above (4.4), since their benefits necessarily accrue to each and all members of a territorially circumscribed society. Laws that promote such goods and tax persons to support them are justified to the extent that the goods contribute to the equal right to well-being, including the right to the additive goods whereby persons' capabilities for purpose-fulfilling action are increased.

A similar but not identical justification pertains to the state's helping to facilitate the general increase of wealth for the whole society. Research, exploration, new industry, and free development of productive capacities must be encouraged for this purpose, within the limits posed by the requirements of public goods. This is a maximizing aggregative aim of social and legal policy, and it may be asked how this aim is derivable from the *PGC*'s distributive emphasis. As was pointed out in my contrast of the *PGC* with the principle of utility (4.2), whereas the latter principle focuses on maximizing utility overall without any independent concern for distributive considerations, the *PGC*'s primary emphasis is on distributive justice as epitomized in the equality of generic rights. It must also be kept in mind, however, that this emphasis includes a substantive concern for freedom and well-being, including the drive for purpose-fulfillment and for increasing the related capabilities.

The justification of the maximizing of goods derives from its being instrumental to the effective implementation of this equality. For the more national wealth there is in a whole society having the democratic institutions of the method of consent previously discussed, the more likely it is that persons at the lower end of the scale will have a share sufficient to enable them to prevent occurrent and dispositional violations of their generic rights. It is not only that the poor will be better off, but also that their being better off will further the distributive end of maintaining an equality of generic rights whereby the freedom and well-being of the poorer as well as the richer are equally protected in the ways analyzed above. The expansion of productive capacity in the society will foster this result not only by making available a greater supply of goods but also by providing greater opportunities for productive and more remunerative labor for all members of the society.

That the maximization of wealth will have this distributive result is an empirical hypothesis. Its likelihood of being true is affected by many considerations, including the actual possibilities of further economic growth. It also requires the other conditions noted above, including a democratic constitutional structure, universal education, and combinations among workers. It requires, in addition, rectifications of past injustices whose present effects handicap groups with a history of deprivations in their efforts to obtain additive goods. But given that these conditions are met, increases in productive capacity are likely to facilitate the equality of generic rights, and this is the prime justification of the legal provisions for encouraging the increases.

The ultimate purpose of all the social rules that are dynamically-instrumentally justified is to foster in persons and in institutions the general fulfillment of the *PGC*'s requirement that there be mutual respect for the freedom and well-being of all persons. For this purpose there must be not only institutional arrangements like those discussed above but also policies that focus on development of certain important personal qualities. These are of two kinds, with each of which a certain kind of education can be correlated. One kind consists in self-esteem and the various prudential virtues discussed earlier (4.16). The other kind is the moral virtue of justice, consisting in the recognition of the generic rights of all other persons and the disposition to act in accord with these rights. Correlated with the first kind is education that aims to develop the prudential virtues in each child to the fullest extent of his abilities. Correlated with the second kind is moral education, both formal and informal, that aims to develop in each person a respect for the generic rights of others, including an understanding of why they have these rights and how the rights should be implemented, as well as a practical will to act in accordance with this understanding. Both these modes of education should be embodied not only in public institutions of formal education but also in other political and social institutions of the whole society that both foster and are fostered by the respective prudential and moral virtues.

5.15. The above discussion has had a double emphasis. It has assigned certain functions to the state through the dynamic-instrumental justification that laws and policies have when they protect and foster the *PGC*'s equality of generic rights. But it has also provided, through the necessary-procedural justification of these laws, that the state officials who are to make the laws and implement these policies are to be subject to the democratic electoral process of the method of consent. May not there be a conflict between these two emphases, the one substantive, the other procedural? What assurance is there that the electorate that votes for officials will uphold the dynamic-instrumental supportive policies required by the *PGC*? Since these policies are instrumentally justified in the way indicated above, why should they be subjected to the vicissitudes of shifting electoral majorities through the method of consent, and why do they need the additional justification that such majorities and procedures supply?

These questions raise familiar problems of democratic theory, bearing as they do on the relation between democratic methods and libertarian-egalitarian results. Ultimately the problems may be traced back to the relation between freedom and well-being as, respectively, procedural and substantive necessary goods of action; for, as we have seen, these may conflict when agents use their freedom in ways opposed even to their own well-being. Since the issue concerns the reasons for making the rationally justified policies of the supportive state dependent for their obligatoriness on the democratic procedures of the method of consent, we must consider the issue in the light of the various contexts in which consensual procedures are required for grounding political obligation.

In traditional theories of the consensual or contractual basis of political obligation three different kinds of political objects have been held to require the optional empirical consent of their subjects as the ground of the obligatoriness of obeying them. Such consent has been invoked as providing the justificatory answer to the following questions: first, whether there should be any state and government at all; second, what kind of constitution it should have, including especially what basic decision procedures it should have for designating governmental officials and making laws; third, who should be these officials actually in political authority, and what laws the state should actually have. I have argued that the first two of these objects, consisting respectively in the minimal state and the method of consent, should not be dependent on empirical, optional consent for their obligatoriness or authority, but only on rational consent, because, as intrinsic parts or logical consequences of the *PGC*, they share its inherently rational justification. Why, then, shouldn't this also be the case for the equalizing, redistributive laws of the supportive state that constitute part of the third political object listed above? Aren't they justified by the *PGC* in the same way as the criminal law and the method of consent?

There are three interrelated answers to this question. First, to determine the specific contents and justifications of the laws and officials of the supportive state is a far more circumstantial and continuing process than to determine the structures of the minimal state and the method of consent. The latter are the general constitutional frameworks of the society, and the general considerations of the *PGC* in its institutional applications are sufficient to deal with their contents and justifications. The supportive state, on the other hand, is concerned with more ongoing, particular problems of redistributive justice, and there are many different permissible alternatives concerning how these are to be dealt with. These alternatives bear on such issues as the extent to which support should be given, what should be the kinds of support, and how they should be related (expenditures for public education and their relation to expenditures for food, clothing, and other needs; giving of money as against goods in kind), the point at which support should yield to self-help, and the relation of each of these to more general economic conditions and policies in the society. These are complex issues whose appropriate solutions, beyond very general aspects, are not derivable from the *PGC*, and they involve conflicts of opinion and interest in the society whose just treatment requires the more circumstantial, detailed inquiry and discussion that the method of consent makes possible.

A second answer to the above question is that the method of consent itself has as its content provisions for empirical, optional consent. It is important not to confuse these two points: (*a*) the justification of the method of consent is the rational consent deriving from the *PGC*; (*b*) the method of consent requires that the optional, empirical consents of the members of the society, using the civil liberties, are to determine specific laws, policies, and officials. Both (*a*) and (*b*) are true, and they indicate the different consensual bases of the constitution and the specific laws (other than criminal law). The constitution, resting on rational consent, requires that empirical consent be decisive at every subsequent stage.

A third answer deals more directly with the moral issue of the possibility that democratic majorities operating by the method of consent may fail to endorse the redistributive justice of the supportive state. In extreme cases, the great urgency of preventing starvation and other basic harms among the people of some society may justify non-democratic methods where the people's condition makes it difficult or impossible to use the democratic process for this end. On the other hand, the public moral education that the method of consent and the civil liberties foster in a democracy makes it much more likely that the outcome will support the equal right of all persons to basic goods. It must be noted that in a state that rests on the method of consent there is not a complete disconnection between the rational consent on which rests the *PGC* together with the constitutional structure, and the optional, empirical consent of the democratic electorate. The two kinds of consent do not inhabit different worlds, like Kant's phenomena and noumena. Rather, the rationality that is dispositionally present in every prospective purposive agent and that leads him to accept the *PGC*, and with it the democratic constitution of the method of consent, will also tend to lead him to uphold the redistributive justice of the supportive state, if he is given suitable means of public communication and information, means that are themselves intrinsic parts of the method of consent.

Because of the connection of the method of consent with human dignity, the method's political freedom must not be lightly dismissed whenever some aspect of well-being, even for all or most members of a society, may be more effectively achieved without it. Only when it is clear, on the grounds of the most adequate available empirical evidence, that the most pressing rights of basic well-being cannot otherwise be assured, is a departure from the method of consent justified. And in such cases the aim must be to establish or reestablish, at the earliest possible time, the method as the dominant procedure for making laws and designating officials.

5.16. It must nevertheless be recognized that the connection between the democratic procedures of the method of consent and the requirements of distributive justice is not logical but contingent. Despite its rational basis, majoritarian empirical consent may support morally wrong laws and policies. Famous examples are the fugitive slave laws, the prohibition amendment, the segregation laws of the Southern United States, censorship laws, and statutes forbidding the teaching of evolutionary theory in public schools. In addition, policies of duly elected officials may be unfair in ways that likewise violate the *PGC*. In such cases, further use must be made of the procedures of the method of consent to rectify these injustices. When and only when such use proves fruitless, civil disobedience may be justified. Such disobedience should usually consist in violating the specific law or policy that is held to be unjust, although this may not always be possible. The disobedience should be nonviolent; it should operate not as a kind of power play but rather as a public, principled appeal to the same rational considerations that underlie the method of consent and hence the *PGC* itself. The aim should be to bring to the public's attention the specific way these rational requirements are violated by the law or policy protested against.

It is important to note that civil disobedience is not justified whenever someone believes, even quite conscientiously, that a law or policy is morally wrong. He must be able to provide at least the outlines of a rational justification of his belief, and the rationality of this justification must pass the tests that underlie the *PGC*. The offended racist or the militarist intent on subjugating other nations thus cannot, as such, engage in justified civil disobedience. And since there is usually widespread disagreement over such issues as whether the law is in fact morally wrong and whether it is a valid law in terms of the constitutional structure in both its procedural and its substantive requirements, persons who consider engaging in civil disobedience must focus explicit attention on such issues and urge their thorough sifting. It is also incumbent both on the relevant governmental officials and on the electorate at large to give careful consideration to the arguments of civil disobedients and to recognize and make due allowances for the seriousness of their moral concern.

In states that do not rest on the method of consent, civil disobedience may be a more precarious undertaking. In extreme cases of severely repressive regimes, violence may be justified. Nevertheless, even in such states the fullest possible consideration should be given to using civil disobedience as a way of focusing principled attention on the moral violations in question.

The issue of civil disobedience also bears closely on the issue of the justified limits of legal or governmental interference with individual freedom. The two issues are not coextensive and do not always have the same answers, for civil disobedience may be justified on grounds other than that a law or policy unjustly interferes with individual freedom, and such interferences do not always justify civil disobedience. But the two issues are related because each bears on the just use and limits of political authority.

When, then, is governmental or legal interference with individual freedom justified? The answer to this question is in part a restriction and in part an extension of the moral limits on individual freedom discussed earlier (4.23). It is important to distinguish these two questions, for although the legal limits on individual freedom are also moral ones so long as they derive from the *PGC*, the moral limits proper derive from the *PGC*'s direct applications only and do not, as such, make use of the coercive force embodied in the legal limitations on freedom. The latter must be more restricted than the moral limits proper. For the criminal law and the *PGC* in its direct applications do not prohibit entirely the same actions. Both prohibit the infliction of basic and other serious harms, as these have been defined above; but the legal prohibition, unlike that of the *PGC* in its direct applications, should not in general extend to the specific harms of interfering with nonsubtractive and additive well-being. The reason for this difference is that the harms in question, such as lying, promise-breaking, and insulting, are usually less important in their impact on their recipients' well-being and hence do not justify marshaling the state's coercive legal resources to combat or correct them. In view of this, it is morally better that persons voluntarily refrain from such harms than that they refrain only under the coercion of law, and moral education can be used to help develop the appropriate critical judgment and conditions of character.

These considerations also apply, although with some qualifications, to specific harms against the additive good of temperance and against related nonsubtractive goods. We have already seen that a variety of self-harming actions, ranging from smoking to suicide, must in final analysis not be interfered with (4.21). What, however, of related actions affecting other persons, including the sale of tobacco, liquor, hard drugs, and pornography, public nudity, and the public performance of sexual intercourse and excretion? The harm apparently done by such actions varies along two dimensions, one physical, the other affecting persons' dignity as rational agents superior to animals in their ability to control their behaviors and appetites. The physical harms, however, are to be viewed on the same basis as self-harms; the sale of the kinds of harmful items listed above should not be prohibited so long as relevant knowledge about them is made available and their effects are not burdensome to other persons. But when the harmful effects of various actions cannot be confined to the immediate participants, legal regulation and even prohibition may be justified. This is the case with the kinds of public performances mentioned above, because of their shocking offensiveness against the criteria that differentiate humans from beasts, and hence against nonsubtractive and additive well-being. It is also highly important, however, that these criteria not be extended from the physical displays mentioned above to offenses against more particularized codes of conduct, such as eating pork in the sight of Moslems or selling pornographic literature. Private actions are even less subject to restriction in this regard.

The legal limits on individual freedom must also, however, be more extensive than the moral limits of the *PGC*'s direct applications, because the objects of the former include also various actions bearing on indirect applications of the *PGC*. These justified legal limits are of two interrelated kinds. One consists in the requirement that all the laws, not only the criminal law, be obeyed so long as they do not violate the *PGC* in the ways discussed above in connection with civil disobedience. These laws include various provisions for the operation of the method of consent, including the protection of the civil liberties. Individual persons or groups must not be free to violate the civil liberties of others. The laws also include the requirements of the supportive state; these requirements impose limits on individual freedom with regard to regulations pertaining both to public goods and to other ways of equalizing the right to well-being. For example, freedom of contract must be restricted where it operates to subject workers to unduly low wages or dangerous or degrading working conditions, and discrimination in employment on grounds of race, religion, or sex must be prohibited regardless of whether it emanates from employers or from workers and their unions. The freedom to discriminate in the availability of public accommodations must also be restricted.

A second kind of justified legal limitation on individual freedom consists in the requirement of paying taxes needed to maintain the various state functions, including those required by the supportive state. The functions include providing public education and other public goods needed for equal rights to well-being, as well as the modes mentioned above of facilitating the general increase of wealth in order to promote the equality of generic rights. Taxation for these purposes interferes with the freedom of the persons taxed to use their money as they choose; but, like the other restrictions on individual freedom, it is justified by the *PGC* in ways indicated above. It must be emphasized that neither kind of justified legal limitation on freedom extends to purely aggregative goals of maximizing the general welfare without consideration of their distributive impact on the equality of generic rights. Measures that simply increase the wealth of the rich, for example, cannot justify legal limitations on freedom if they cannot be shown demonstrably to further equalize at least the opportunities of the poor.

For the reasons mentioned earlier, the justified legal limits on individual freedom must exclude interferences with the civil liberties, especially the freedoms of expression and association. These have a privileged position because of their central connection not only with the democratic state's method of consent but also with the rational autonomy on which rests all morally right action. Freedom of expression may be legally limited, however, on two counts. One is when speech directly threatens basic or other serious harm, such as falsely shouting "Fire!" in a crowded theater. The other is when it is used wrongly to attack the dignity or rational autonomy of its recipient. Such wrongful attacks include slander, where falsehoods harmful to the recipient's reputation are knowingly uttered, and violations of privacy, where one reveals intimate details about another person's life against his wishes.

The allegation of harmfulness, however, cannot be rightly invoked when participation in the method of consent is involved. That one's statements endanger national security is not a legitimate basis for restricting or punishing them where the statements consist not in revealing military secrets required for a just war but in expressing and urging views about the justice of one policy as against another. Legal restriction of such expression is unjustified, for since the legitimate authority of the laws and government officials derives from the method of consent with its provisions for freedom of expression, this authority cannot rightly be used to inhibit such freedom.

In discussing these familiar issues of the justified limits on freedom, I have been traversing the same ground covered more extensively in Mill's essay *On Liberty*. The main differences are that 'harm' has here been given a more determinate set of criteria (see 4.13,14) and that Mill's primary emphasis is aggregative rather than distributive: his utilitarian principle requires that the general welfare be maximized and that harm be minimized. This entails that when one person's action harms another, "the question whether the general welfare will or will not be promoted by interfering with it, becomes open to discussion."[12] Mill's principle hence makes the extent of justified freedom a matter of utilitarian calculation, of weighing the overall beneficial and harmful consequences of permitting and prohibiting various sorts of vaguely 'harmful' actions. Despite Mill's own strongly libertarian intentions, the implications of this aggregative approach especially for the civil liberties are very serious, since it provides copious bases for restricting these liberties in order to secure all sorts of benefits or prevent all sorts of harms. The approach fails to give adequate recognition to the facts that freedom is a basic good and that the equal right to freedom has an inherently rational justification transcending the variable considerations of utilitarian calculation.

In the *PGC*, on the other hand, the central point is that each person has rights to freedom and well-being. The primary emphasis is thus distributive rather than aggregative: to determine whether an action should be legally interfered with requires a consideration not of whether such interference will or will not promote the general welfare but rather of the equality of generic rights. With regard to actions of an individual agent toward his recipients, this involves consideration of whether he violates such of their rights to freedom and well-being as have been specified above; the freedom to commit such violations must be legally prohibited. With regard to actions bearing on the requirements of the method of consent and the supportive state, the equality of generic rights involves consideration of whether the requirements of this equality justify legal interferences with individual freedom. Thus it must be the distributive rather than the aggregative consequences of legally interfering with individual freedom that are decisive: the bearing of such interference on justice as determined by the *PGC*'s equality of generic rights. It must also be kept in mind, however, that such consideration of consequences must observe the limitations of the internal instrumentalism of the criminal law and the supportive state (5.8,12). The relevant laws must themselves embody the equality of generic rights, so that there can be no question of enslaving or impoverishing some persons in order to increase the well-being of others. Central to this consideration must be the recognition that the human rights protected by the supportive state are universal, regardless of who may be the particular beneficiaries of some of its specific laws.

The Completeness of the Principle

5.17. One of the conditions of the *PGC*'s being the supreme principle of morality is that it must be adequate for establishing the moral rightness or wrongness of all morally relevant actions and institutions. Amid the complexities of the direct and indirect applications traced above, one central point has been that the *PGC*, from its very concept, is concerned with what I have called strict duties, which are also traditionally called 'perfect duties'—that is, "duties in virtue of which a correlative right resides in some person or persons."[13] Now these duties as developed by the *PGC* are the most important part of morality, even if not the whole of it. Whatever else may be demanded of moral rules and principles, they cannot be held to fulfill even their minimal point if they do not require that persons be protected in their rights to the necessary conditions of action. For without such requirements, any other requirements or provisions of a morality would be building without a foundation; the goods, interests, utilities, or duties with which it concerned itself would not include those that must be presupposed by all the others in the actions, institutions, or states of character with which they deal. An initial question, then, is whether the *PGC* has been shown to apply to all such strict duties. A related, criteriological question is whether, even if it does apply to them all, the grounds or criteria it provides for applying to them, for justifying or disjustifying them, are the correct ones.

Neither of these questions is purely factual, for the range of what one regards as perfect or strict duties is itself a function of one's moral principles or overall moral position. For example, St. Augustine held that 'true justice' cannot be found in a pagan state because the pagans' justice "takes man away from the true God and subjects him to impure demons."[14] Thus, for Augustine no genuine moral duties would have been established in the absence of a theological criterion. More generally, the wide variety of distributive and substantive criteria that have been upheld (1.1) shows that one cannot appeal to a consensus to determine the answers to these questions. In the face of this diversity, however, I have tried to show that the duties derived from the *PGC* are rationally justified in that it is self-contradictory to deny or violate them, in part because they have a necessary content consisting in the essential conditions of action. And I have also tried to show that this consideration of rational justification does not merely express a 'commitment' that is on a level with rival commitments to some religion or ideology or the like, but that it bears definitively on what is justifiable or correct.

In addition to this general consideration, the basis on which an affirmative answer to both the above questions can be suggested is that all the duties presented here have been shown to derive directly or indirectly from the rights of all persons to the goods that are the necessary conditions of action. The list of duties, then, is exhaustive at least in its general outlines if the list of goods for which the duties are required is exhaustive, consisting in freedom and well-being, with the latter divided into basic, nonsubtractive, and additive goods. There are pure deontological theories that deny that duties and rights can be derived from or are required for any goods at all; but I have indicated why I think this is a mistake (2.9; 4.2). On the other hand, the duties I have discussed regarding the various kinds of goods can undoubtedly be augmented. I have sought to list the most important ones under each rubric, but there are other such duties. They would, however, be seen to derive from the same principle and its divisions as those explicitly mentioned. In addition, the duties falling under justified social rules have been sketched here only in general terms; much more needs to be said about such duties in the legal, political, and economic spheres, which I reserve for the sequel to this work.

Among the possibly strict duties I have not discussed are what may be called 'reactive' duties, such as reparation and gratitude. If Alden inflicts some specific harm on Benson, such as by insulting or cheating him, then Alden owes it to Benson to make amends; if Cohen does something helpful for Drake, such as saving him from drowning or returning his lost watch, then Drake owes it to Cohen to express gratitude. These, then, are not 'original' duties, but arise from preceding actions that violate a duty or contribute to another's well-being. The ground for holding according to the *PGC* that reparation is a duty is in general the same as in the case of punishment (5.8): an antecedent occurrent equality of generic rights, which the *PGC* requires, has been disrupted, and reparation is required in order to restore that equality. The criminal law is reserved for the rectification of basic and other serious harms because of their greater importance in relation both to agency and to the stability of the social order.

As for gratitude, it should first be noted that the duty is not one of feeling grateful, since this may not be within the power of the person benefited (though he can try), but rather one of expressing gratitude in words or deeds or both for some favor one has received from another. The most direct justification for this duty is that it serves to promote a social order in which the *PGC* will be more readily observed, so that it has an instrumental justification. In addition, in situations like those described above, Drake owes Cohen gratitude because, from an initial equality of generic rights between them involving mutuality of noninterference, Cohen has voluntarily interfered with his own freedom and well-being (since he has at that point given up at least his ability to do other things) in order to prevent a loss of well-being for Drake or to obtain an increase of well-being for him. In either case Cohen has contributed to Drake's capabilities of action in a more or less extensive way by voluntarily exerting his own capabilities and hence intervening in the objects of his own generic rights. This contribution alters the antecedent equality of generic rights in Drake's favor, and Drake owes it to Cohen to try to redress the balance at least by expressing gratitude. The amount of redress—that is, of gratitude expressed—should be proportional to either or both of the two variables, Cohen's exertion and Drake's benefiting. Thus it is the importance of maintaining the kind of balance involved in the *PGC*'s equality of generic rights that imposes on the person benefited the duty of expressing gratitude to his benefactor.

5.18. Even if the *PGC* can be shown to justify all 'perfect duties,' and even if these are the most important part of morality, as I have argued above, the objection may still be made that this is only a part of morality: to confine morality to strict duties and rights in the ways analyzed above is to construe it entirely on the model of law and juridical relations. But what of the whole sphere of the supererogatory? What of the personal virtues and moral goodness? What of duties to oneself? Unless the PGC can be shown to deal adequately with these, its claim to completeness as a moral principle cannot be accepted without serious qualifications.

Supererogatory actions are those it is good but not obligatory to perform. They range from heroic and saintly actions that demand great sacrifices to much more ordinary actions of disinterested kindness, generosity, and graciousness. By definition, such actions cannot be shown to be required by the PGC. I have already indicated how the PGC provides for the meritoriousness of saintly and heroic actions (3.24). The more moderate kinds of supererogatory actions have in part a similar basis of merit: they are in the direction required by the PGC but go beyond its requirements. The PGC requires that the agent not distribute the necessary goods of freedom and well-being in a way that is disadvantageous to his recipients. The moderate kinds of supererogatory actions give overabundant assurance of this, since they distribute, in ways that are advantageous to their recipients, emoluments that may go beyond these necessary goods. In addition, such actions have a justification of the kind we saw above in the case of gratitude: if persons engage in such actions, then not only do they not violate one another's generic rights, but they conduce to social relations of a quality that tends to make persons more inclined to support these rights for all.

The complex concept of positive beneficence is appropriately discussed within the sphere of the supererogatory. The PGC does not set for the individual agent a strict duty of positive beneficence in the sense of intentionally increasing the particular additive goods of other persons. If this were a strict duty, as in some versions of utilitarianism, it would impose unremitting toil on agents. It is important in this respect not to confuse positive beneficence with refraining from or preventing maleficence or harm or helping persons to have well-being in the senses in which 'harm' and 'well-being' have been elucidated above. To prevent other persons from losing basic, nonsubtractive, or additive well-being or to assist them to have these is not the same as to increase their stock of additive goods to the point where the persons become blissful. Persons in general have no strict right to be made blissful by others, although, of course, to try to produce such bliss is permissible and even praiseworthy.

'Positive beneficence' may also have another meaning: to work actively to protect the generic rights of those persons who are least able to protect them for themselves. Such work directly supports the rights not of everyone equally but of those persons whose differential needs, status, and abilities make them most vulnerable to attacks on their rights to freedom and well-being. The end that justifies positive beneficence of this distributive-differential kind is the *PGC*'s equality of generic rights, and it is indeed a strict duty. We saw earlier, however, that this duty is limited by the condition that the agent must be able to perform the action in question at no comparable cost to himself (3.24; 4.7). When this cost is paid or exceeded, the action is supererogatory. Now, there are indeed idealistic and public-spirited persons who try to make the equality of generic rights more generally operative in their society and in the world by combating extreme violations of it inflicted on large groups of persons, by actively advocating and working to effect countermeasures that remove the violations and to stabilize these countermeasures in laws and institutions. Much of the social moral progress in the modern era has come from persons who have engaged in such effective advocacy.

Two different views may be held as to the moral status of such socially beneficent action. One is that the masses of persons in need of large-scale help do not have a strict right that any particular person provide the necessary assistance; they cannot correctly demand this of anyone in particular, so that no one in particular has the correlative strict duty, and the assisting actions are supererogatory. A second view is that such action is a strict duty of particular persons: those who are so fortunate that they do not have to worry about their own generic rights and are in a position to provide the needed assistance. In this view, there is no important difference, save that of greater diffusion of need and of required actions, between Carr's strict duty to rescue Davis from drowning and the obligations of the more fortunate members of a society toward those who are least fortunate. For the justification of this view, in turn, appeal might be made either simply to the *PGC* or to a further argument that the more fortunate persons in a society do not deserve their good fortune, since it derives from the 'natural lottery' that makes an arbitrary distribution of advantages and disadvantages. Although this latter argument undeniably contains some truth, when pushed to an extreme it incurs the difficulty that it takes inadequate account of what persons can accomplish through their own voluntary actions. It assumes a determinism whereby all the causes of a person's behavior are external to him, so that nothing is to be attributed to his own control through his own unforced choice.[15]

The *PGC* by itself provides sufficient ground for the conclusion that positive beneficence of the differential-distributive kind is a strict duty of those who are most fortunate. For their being most fortunate entails that they can engage in such action at no comparable cost to themselves. This answer is further suggested by the dictum that a person who is affluent and well-meaning but inactive is 'part of the problem,' in that his informed failure to work for the generic rights of impoverished groups helps to maintain their continued impoverishment. It must also be emphasized, however, that this work may take various forms, that the members of such groups should also try on their own to take relevant initiatives toward improvement of group abilities, and that they should utilize the legitimate opportunities provided by democratic institutions. The method of consent and the supportive state are important instrumentalities for this purpose.

The virtues are another segment of morality that are not objects of strict duties. We saw earlier that although prudential virtues are not the same as moral ones, persons have various moral duties to foster the development of the prudential virtues both in other persons and in themselves (4.16). Now it is one thing to have a duty to try to develop a virtue; it is another thing to have a duty to act from a virtue. Moral virtues are not the same as morally right actions; they are deep-seated traits of character whereby persons not only do what is morally right in the sense of obligatory but do it habitually, with knowledge that it is right and because it is right. This 'because' refers to the choice and motivation of the agent. In certain cases, from circumstances beyond his control a virtuous person may fail to do what is right; but he at least conscientiously tries. The concept of virtue hence includes the concept of the related action: the courageous person tends to perform courageous actions, the just person just actions, and so forth. The virtue adds to the action not only the dispositional regularity of habitualness but also the 'internal' aspects of knowledge, choice, and motive or reason in the sense of ground. Persons can be praised or blamed not only for their actions but also for having or not having relevant motives.

Two kinds of moral virtue may be distinguished. One kind is the 'internal' side of the *PGC*'s strict duties. Although the *PGC* requires the actions of these duties, it does not in the same way require the corresponding virtues: it requires just and fair actions, but not the virtues of justice and fairness. The reason for this is that the virtues, being long-range dispositions acquired in part by the habitual performance of right actions, cannot be had in the same direct way in which actions are performed, so that a command to have them is not directly fulfillable. On the other hand, the *PGC* shows that these virtues are good to have precisely because persons who have them are much more likely to do what the *PGC* requires. Moreover, in requiring that one regularly act in accord with the generic rights of one's recipients as well as of oneself, the *PGC* prescribes for the rational agent precisely that habitualness and motivation that tends to inculcate the corresponding virtues. In this way, the *PGC* is concerned with moral character as well as action. The awareness of the rightness of the actions, and hence of the goodness of the corresponding character, derives from the rational basis of the *PGC*, assent to which is within reach of every rational agent. It is because the moral virtues are in this indirect way under the agent's control that he can be praised or blamed for having or not having them.

In addition to the virtues that correspond to the *PGC's* strict duties, there are also virtues that correspond to the various sorts of supererogatory actions, ranging from heroic courage to ordinary sorts of kindness, generosity, and graciousness. The merits of such virtues are shown by the *PGC* in a way parallel to that of the strict duties, with the addition of the specific justifications that we have seen the *PGC* provides for the corresponding actions.

5.19. What of duties to oneself? An initial basis for considering these is that it seems anomalous for someone's duties to be grounded only on the freedom and well-being of other persons but not also on his own freedom and well-being. If A has a duty to refrain from harming B, then why doesn't B also have a duty to refrain from harming B, and A from harming A? The point of this question is not removed by the *PGC's* provision that the agent is to act in accord with his own generic rights as well as those of his recipients. For there is no distinct requirement or duty here that the agent act in accord with his own generic rights since, as we have seen, this is something he necessarily does in his particular actions. But for the agent to do this means that he necessarily sees to it that other persons do not interfere with his freedom and well-being without his consent. Thus the bearing of the agent's generic rights is here other-directed: it is a matter of other persons' not violating his rights without his consent, and thus of other persons' fulfilling their duties to him. This, however, is distinct from any duties the agent may have to himself with regard to his own freedom and well-being, although it is related to his having the prudential virtues.

The very idea of there being duties to oneself incurs important objections. First, if there are such duties and they are strict ones, then, like other strict duties, the person who upholds them believes that strong pressure and even coercion is justified to enforce them. Applied to duties to oneself, this would justify a large degree of paternalism; and when the coercion is applied by the person who has the correlative right, it would entail self-coercion. Second, if a person has duties to himself, then, because of the correlativity of duties and rights, he also has rights against himself. But any right-holder can always give up his right and thereby release the respondent of the right from his duty. On the other hand, no person can release himself from a duty. Hence, the notion of duties to oneself is contradictory, since it implies that a person both can and cannot release himself from his duties to himself. Third, if someone violates a duty to himself, then, if this is like other violations of duty, it follows that a person both gains and loses the same thing by the very same action. For insofar as he is the person to whom the duty is owed, he loses something; but insofar as he is the violator of the duty, he gains that something. Fourth, a duty to not harm oneself or to act for one's own interests or happiness would be nugatory; for the point of a duty is to curb what one is naturally inclined to do, but one's natural inclinations are already against self-harm and for one's own interests or happiness. Fifth, duties to oneself, or the self-regarding virtues with which they may in part be equated, cannot be moral duties or virtues on the social definition of 'moral' that has been accepted here.[16]

Despite these important arguments, there are two ways in which duties to oneself, including the duty to inculcate in oneself various self-regarding virtues, can be derived from the *PGC*. The first way, briefly indicated above in connection with the prudential virtues (4.16), may be further developed as follows. If A has a duty to do X, and if his doing Y is necessary or highly conducive to his doing X, then A has a duty to do Y if doing Y is in his power and if it does not involve his violating any of his other duties. Now since every agent has the moral duty to obey the *PGC*, if there are any personal, self-regarding qualities or prudential virtues that he can inculcate in himself and that are such that his having them is necessary or highly conducive to his obeying the *PGC*, then it is his duty to inculcate in himself such qualities. There are indeed such qualities. For if the agent leads a personally intemperate, fearful, self-brutalizing, dissolute, and unintelligent life, if he is slothful, ignorant, improvident, and lacking in self-respect, then he is less likely to respect other persons and to be able to fulfill adequately his strict duties to them. Hence, he has a duty to avoid such a life and to inculcate in himself the opposite qualities that are conducive to his fulfilling the *PGC*'s requirements: such prudential qualities as being self-respecting, self-aware, temperate, courageous, provident, and well informed.

Are these duties of the agent to himself? It may be argued that they are only duties regarding himself but not duties to himself, since their point is to enable the agent to fulfill his duties to his recipients. Even if this is the case, it still shows that the meritoriousness of various self-regarding virtues can be justified by the *PGC*. In this connection, the fourth argument given above against duties to oneself, that persons are naturally inclined to do what is for their self-interest, is not true if the 'what' refers to means as well as ends. The various good qualities that enable a person to fulfill his duties to others are also advantageous for certain aspects of his own self-interest (although these aspects may be turned in different directions so far as concerns his relations to other persons); but their self-inculcation often goes counter to his immediate natural inclinations. Hence, the agent's inculcating such qualities in himself remains his duty despite its advancing certain aspects of his own self-interest.

That he should try to attain such qualities is also a duty to himself. For his duty to obey the *PGC* is not only a duty to his recipients; it is also a duty to which he is rationally committed insofar as he is a rational agent and person. As we saw above in connection with the agent's autonomy, the *PGC* is not merely a requirement imposed on the rational agent from without; it is also imposed on him by himself, since he recognizes that it fulfills the same standards or criteria by virtue of which he himself is rational (3.3; 5.10). Hence, the agent's obedience to the *PGC* is a duty to himself qua rational agent. Since this is a strict duty, it follows that qua rational agent he also has a right against himself: a right that the *PGC* be obeyed by himself. But, as against the second argument given above against duties to oneself, the rational agent cannot give up this right and thereby release himself from his duty to obey the *PGC*. For his having both the duty and the right does not derive from some contingent or optional decision, desire, or transaction of his; it derives rather from the rational aspect of himself whose criteria are independent of his decisions or desires. And the necessity of his accepting these criteria is similarly independent. It is because of these independent, necessary criteria of rationality that the rational agent has the duties to himself both to obey the *PGC* and to try to inculcate in himself the self-regarding virtues that are necessary or strongly conducive to this obedience. And it is also because of these criteria that the rational agent cannot, while remaining rational, give up either his rights or his duties in this area.

A second, more analogical way in which duties to oneself may be justified by the *PGC* is derived from the unity of criteria that can be found in other-regarding and self-regarding virtues and vices and the corresponding actions. The *PGC* is directly concerned with other-regarding actions whereby a person is unjust or unfair to others, failing to respect them or degrading or demeaning them; it prescribes the opposite actions and, as we have seen, the inculcation of the corresponding virtues. Now the criteria underlying such virtues and vices, or closely similar criteria, are also applied in the sphere of self-regarding actions and qualities. Examples of these criteria can be found in expressions where it is said that a person who wastes his life on drugs or drink is being 'unfair to himself'; a person who squanders his talents 'does not do himself justice'; a person who is excessively timid 'demeans himself'; a girl who exposes her naked body to leering males 'degrades herself.' These expressions, with their reflexive structure, suggest that there is a certain unity in the criteria for being unjust to oneself and to others, for degrading oneself and degrading others. If there were not such unity of criteria, it is difficult to see how such specific expressions as those just cited could be used in both the personal and the interpersonal spheres.

The application of these criteria to the purely personal sphere may occur in at least two ways. According to each, when it is said that a person demeans himself or is unfair to himself, it is assumed that he is acting on himself—that he is both agent and recipient. One way such self-action may embody this combination is through the distinction between the person as immediate agent and the same person as long-term recipient. Qua agent, he is the person directly acting at that moment; but qua recipient, he is not only this momentary person but also the person who will undergo various effects of that present action. This distinction is a familiar one. The man who, guzzling his fifth martini, says to himself, 'I'll regret this later,' views himself as recipient of his own action and implicitly (qua subsequent recipient) criticizes himself (qua present agent). Now the *PGC* requires of every agent that he act in accord with his recipients' rights to freedom and well-being. Applied to the case of action on oneself, this becomes the requirement that the immediate agent take favorable account of his own freedom and well-being as the long-term recipient of his actions. He must, then, be fair to himself in this longer-range perspective. His present self has these duties to his future self; hence, he has duties to himself.

This argument may be construed so far as having only a quantitative reference, involving the distinction between short-range and long-range desires. But what if a person's long-range desires are as wanton, gluttonous, and otherwise degraded as his short-range ones? The question of personal morality concerns quality as well as quantity. When it is said that someone degrades himself, the reference is not primarily to his acting against his long-range interests but rather to the quality of the interests exhibited by his action, whether short-range or long-range. This qualitative consideration may be elucidated according to two familiar further models, each of which views the person not as divided between present and future selves but as differentiated among diverse interests, aspects, or 'parts' of his total psyche.

One model is egalitarian: it holds that there should be an equilibrium among such of a person's interests or aspects as his desire for physical pleasure, his intellectual powers, his mingling sociably with his fellows, and the like. In this equilibrium, each of these aspects is in harmony with the others, no one of them dominating to the detriment of the rest. The other model is hierarchical: it holds that one of these aspects should control and organize the others, as 'lower' selves. This controlling aspect is often 'reason,' but it may be the will to power, religious faith, or some one of the many other interests or concerns that have figured among the various substantive criteria of moral rightness and as competitors of reason. According to the first of these models, a person is unfair to himself when one of his parts or aspects disturbs the equilibrium by dominating the others in his conduct; according to the second model, it is when his lower self controls his higher self. When it is said that a person degrades himself, however, only the second model is usually invoked.

Although these attempts to split up the psyche incur well-known difficulties, they have an important point in calling attention to the various aspects of an individual's overall personality and to the impact of one of these aspects on the others. The *PGC* applies analogically, though not literally, to such impacts. According to the first model, it says to any aspect that is acting on the others that it should take due account of these others' generic rights, so that the freedom and well-being of the intellect should not overpower, for example, one's physical well-being, and conversely. According to the second model, the *PGC* requires that reason, in the sense of the capacity of the person to recognize and act according to the criteria of deductive and inductive rationality, should acquire relevant knowledge about the total self, and that this knowledge should be decisive in organizing the psyche. From Plato to Freud, philosophers and psychologists have in different ways elaborated on and endorsed this model.

According to each model, the *PGC* sets for each person duties to himself, since it holds that he ought to arrange the various parts of his total personality in the ways required by the respective models. Each of these kinds of requirement uses analogically the same criteria as are used to criticize interpersonal relations where one person is said to be unfair or unjust to another or to degrade or demean him. For just as in such social relations the agent acts on his recipients in ways that fail to take due account of their freedom and well-being, so too when duties to oneself are violated according to each of the above models, one aspect of the person acts on other aspects in ways that fail to take due account of the freedom and well-being of these others.

Conflicts of Duties

5.20. Even if the PGC is a complete moral principle in that it supplies justificatory grounds bearing on all morally relevant subject matters, there remains the question of its consistency. Are the requirements and other provisions it justifies always compatible with one another, or may conflicting requirements be derived from it? And since at least apparent conflicts of moral duties or requirements are found in the moral sphere, is the PGC able to resolve these?

The question of conflicts thus has two interrelated aspects. One is initially extrasystemic; it concerns the conflicting duties, or at least conflicting judgments about duties, that arise for persons independent of the PGC, as well as the conflicting values that the same or different persons uphold and that often underlie the conflicts of duties (1.6). The question is whether and how the PGC can resolve such conflicts. The other question is intrasystemic; it concerns the conflicts that arise within the whole system of the PGC itself, including both its own content and its various applications. There seem to be abundant bases for such conflicts because of the multiplicity of considerations that enter into and derive from the PGC. Thus the principle provides for rights both to freedom and to well-being, and for each of these as pertaining both to each agent and to all his recipients; within the right to well-being it provides for three different kinds of goods that may be viewed either occurrently or dispositionally; it also provides for two kinds of applications, direct and indirect, bearing respectively on individual transactions and on group interactions; within the indirect applications it provides both for procedural and for instrumental justifications, with the former in turn divided into optional and necessary kinds and the latter into static and dynamic varieties, the dynamic again being divided into aggregative and distributive-differential provisions. And in addition to all these, the PGC also gives justifications, as we have seen, for supererogatory actions, for various virtues, and for duties to oneself. In view of these multiple and seemingly opposed considerations, how can the system of the *PGC* avoid the inconsistency of giving conflicting directives for action?

The first point to be made about this complexity is that it reflects the complex structure of morality itself. Any attempt to deny this complexity by trying to derive all moral requirements in one simple way from one simple principle, as act-utilitarianism aims to do, incurs the difficulties intuitionists and others have pointed out. On the other hand, if, as with the intuitionists, moral requirements are left as an unrelated jumble, then structure is denied altogether to morality. But, in addition to permitting unresolved conflicts and thus inconsistencies, this ignores the common features that underlie the moral realm, including especially its grounding in human actions with their pursuits of purposes that seem good to their agents, and the consequent unifying moral criterion of the equality of generic rights. In the above analyses of the *PGC* and of its applications I have tried to take account of both these aspects of morality, its complexity and its underlying unity of structure. The unity that a moral philosophy propounds, then, must itself be complex, but in a systematic way such that certain rational orders of priority and posteriority can be found within the varieties of moral requirements and other provisions. If such a rational ordering of the complexities cannot be established, then the realm of the moral is left at that point with the arbitrariness generated by an exclusive or primary reliance on the contingent and variable choices and preferences of different persons as the bases of moral duties and judgments. It must also be emphasized, however, that at some points the inability to establish priorities among conflicting moral alternatives may itself have a rational basis in that the choice among them is in fact morally indifferent, as shown by the *PGC*.

Such priorities entail that in certain circumstances the requirements of some moral rules justified by the *PGC* must be overridden by the requirements of other rules that are also justified by the *PGC*. This overriding does not, however, remove the categoricalness either of the principle or of its derivative rules. As we have seen, for a moral principle or rule to be categorical its requirements may not be normatively overridden by any nonmoral considerations, including the agent's variable self-interested desires or social institutions that may lack moral justification. Overriding by such considerations does not occur when a duty derived from one moral rule is overridden by a duty derived from another moral rule, as is the case with the rules justified by the *PGC*. Categoricalness pertains primarily to the *PGC* itself, and derivatively to each of the moral rules it justifies insofar as it is not overridden by another such rule. Hence the importance of ascertaining priorities.

The overriding of one moral duty by another is also not antithetical to the logical necessity that characterizes the rules requiring the performance of all moral duties through their derivation from the *PGC*. The main reason for this is that the *PGC* is a material as well as a formal principle, and as a material principle it is concerned with the necessary goods of action. Insofar as some goods are more necessary for action than others, the duty to respect persons' having the former goods takes precedence over the duty to respect their having the latter goods when the two duties conflict. It may be contended that there is no conflict here because only the former duty is a 'real' or 'conclusive' duty; but this does not remove the fact that the latter too is a duty required by the *PGC*. Similarly, one duty may override another because the person to whom the latter duty is normally owed has voluntarily done something that causes him to lose the correlative right and instead makes it necessary that he be acted on in accordance with the former duty. Such overriding may also be interpreted as meaning that the latter duty is in such circumstances not a duty at all. But again, short of incorporating the exclusion of all invalidating or excepting circumstances into the descriptions of various duties, the fact remains that these are duties so long as such circumstances do not occur. These considerations, to be discussed more fully below, show that the logical rigor of the *PGC* and its derivative moral rules is compatible with an ordering whereby some moral duties are overridden by others. In particular, logical inconsistency is avoided in such overriding both because the prevention of an inconsistency is not itself inconsistent and because the relevant similarity between agent and recipient is altered by giving to one of these a different description, whose relevance is itself justified by the *PGC* in either its direct or its institutional applications. We have seen this in the cases of defending oneself against unjustified assault and oppression (4.6), lying to prevent a murder (3.27), and fulfilling different roles in justified social institutions (5.3,10).

In holding that a rational ordering of priority and posteriority must be sought among moral duties and rules, my position resembles John Rawls's important conception of a 'lexicographical' arrangement of principles in a serial order, "which requires us to satisfy the first principle in the ordering before we can move on to the second, the second before we consider the third, and so on."[17] A significant difference, however, is that Rawls's ordering is not derived from any of his principles, including his first principle of equal freedom; instead, the specific ordering he presents is based on considerations external to the principles, consisting in presumed reasons or motives persons have for choosing the principles from an 'original position' characterized by equal liberty and complete ignorance of their personal qualities. The choices Rawls presents on this basis, however, are somewhat speculative in more ways than one; they seem to reflect certain preferences of Western liberalism rather than providing a rational basis or justification of such liberalism. This is particularly the case for the choice of equal liberty over economic security as the primary principle, although Rawls indicates significant qualifications of this priority, at least in the short run.[18]

The ordering of moral requirements that I present here as the basis for resolving conflicts among moral rules prescribing duties stems from the *PGC*, just as do the rules and duties themselves. I have already given many examples of such conflict-resolution in the course of deriving the various rules. Thus in the following conflicts between alternatives justified by the *PGC*, it has been shown that and why the alternative listed first must in each case give way to the alternative listed second: when the rule against such specific harms as lying conflicts with the rule against letting a basic harm like murder occur when one could prevent it (3.27; 4.14,15); when the rule against killing human persons conflicts with the agent's acting in accord with his own generic rights where he is threatened with being killed by someone else (4.6); when one person's right to occurrent freedom conflicts with another person's right to basic well-being (4.11); when a person's right to occurrent freedom conflicts with his own right to basic well-being (4.20); when a person's right to basic well-being conflicts potentially over the long run with his own right to dispositional freedom (4.21); when a person's right to participate voluntarily or freely in transactions conflicts with his duty to obey procedurally justified social rules to which he has voluntarily or freely consented (5.5); when the rules against killing and restricting dispositional freedom of movement conflict with justified social rules requiring killing in war and punishment for crimes (4.6; 5.8); when social rules or arrangements of voluntary associations conflict with the right to well-being (5.6); when the right to occurrent freedom conflicts with the obligation to obey the criminal law (5.10); when the right to retain one's property conflicts with laws of the supportive state providing for taxation to prevent basic harms such as starvation and to promote public goods (5.13,14); when the results of the method of consent, which has a necessary-procedural justification, conflict in extreme cases with the effective implementation of policies relieving starvation and other basic harms, policies that have a dynamic-instrumental justification (5.15); and when these results conflict with other important rights so that civil disobedience is justified (5.16).

5.21. I shall now restate and amplify somewhat the criteria that serve to resolve these and other conflicts of duties. In so doing I shall not repeat the specific explications already presented of the various duties and their problem areas. I shall also not repeat the reasons why distributive considerations have priority over aggregative ones (4.2; 5.14). As was indicated above, the criteria for conflict-resolution reflect the fact that the *PGC* is both a formal and a material principle: formal in its requirement of consistency, material in that the consistency must be between the agent's necessary claim that he has rights to the necessary conditions of action and his judgment (and corresponding action) about his recipient's rights to these same conditions. The rational pursuit of this generic consistency requires consideration of both the constitutive and the causal aspects of the consistency-preserving transactions wherein the agent acts in accord with the generic rights of his recipients as well as of himself. The criteria for the resolution of conflicts are thus applications of either deductive or inductive rationality, the latter especially in the form of means-end calculation whereby one infers which of various alternatives will lead most efficiently to the desired end of mutually successful action. But the contents of this calculation must themselves be subject to the restrictions imposed by the *PGC*.

The following criteria derive in the following order from these considerations.

a. Prevention or Removal of Inconsistency. If one person or group violates or is about to violate the generic rights of another and thereby incurs transactional inconsistency, action to prevent or remove the inconsistency may be justified. Whether the action should always be undertaken depends on such circumstances as the feasibility and importance for subsequent action of removing the inconsistency; this may be very slight in the case of some lies, and very great in the case of basic harms (see 4.14). Thus, although the *PGC* prohibits coercion and basic harm, it authorizes and even requires these as punishment and for prevention or correction of antecedent basic harm. The authorized coercion and harm should be imposed only on the violators, it should not exceed in severity the antecedent violations it is designed to correct, and there must be the maximal possible ascertainment that the violations have occurred or are about to occur.

The authorized, reactive coercion and harm may occur in individual contexts where A, to prevent B from killing C or A, has to inflict on B coercion or harm sufficient to prevent him from doing this, or where a starved or enslaved person reacts against his oppressors. It may also occur in social institutional contexts that are instrumentally justified. One form of this is where A's basic harm against B, which involves A in severe transactional inconsistency, is legally punished by inflicting basic harms on A, thereby restoring the equilibrium he has disrupted so that his inconsistency is canceled out. When possible, the legal intervention should be used to prevent and remedy basic harms, rather than intervention by individuals. Such prevention of inconsistency in institutional contexts may also take an extreme form when nation D, whose institutions are in consonance with the *PGC*, is militarily attacked by nation E in an aggressive war. Here, to prevent the large-scale, multiple inconsistency such war represents, nation D has the right to defend itself militarily against nation E. On the other hand, aggressive war is itself a violation of the *PGC*, and the citizens of a nation that engages in it are justified in refusing to support the war and in trying to stop it.

b. Degrees of Necessity for Action. Since every agent has the duty to respect his recipients' rights to the goods that are necessary conditions of action, one duty takes precedence over another if the good that is the object of the former duty is more necessary for the possibility of action, and if the right to that good cannot be protected without violating the latter duty. Thus whereas criterion (*a*) deals mainly with duties bearing on goods of the same degree of importance, criterion (*b*) deals with goods of different degrees, but mainly within the same general context of preventing transactional inconsistency. For example, A's duty to prevent B from murdering or enslaving C overrides A's duty not to lie to B as well as A's duty to keep his promise to F. For the same reason, the criminal law, with its prohibition of basic and other serious harms, takes precedence over and sets limits for the procedurally justified rules of voluntary associations, so that these rules may not require or permit basic or other serious harms. In such ways the duty to respect the right to particular occurrent freedoms is overridden by the duty to respect the right to basic well-being, where these conflict. But the right to freedom still preserves its independent status as a necessary good of action, and it must be respected so long as the right to basic well-being is not infringed thereby.

It must be emphasized that this criterion of degrees of necessity for action is concerned with preventing violations of rights, not with increasing amounts of goods, including particular additive goods. The point is not, as with some versions of utilitarianism, that if X is thought to be a greater good or value than Y, then the duty to respect some person's Y may be overridden by the purpose of increasing some other person's X. For example, A may not lie to or steal from B in order to make C very happy. For the criterion to apply, X must be a generic right, and the aim must be not to increase indiscriminately the goods that are the objects of X (such as wealth or self-esteem) at the expense of some other person's possession of goods deemed less important, but rather to prevent X from being lost or violated.

c. Institutional Requirements. When many persons interact in a complex society, there must be rules governing their interactions, in some cases because persons voluntarily agree to such rules for particular individual or group purposes, in other cases to prevent serious coercion and harm of some persons by others, including the disorder and unpredictability that result from lack of uniform rules. In the case of procedurally justified rules, their requirements override in particular cases the duty not to coerce one's recipients so long as the latter continue voluntarily to accept the rules. These rules also include the special weight to be given to family relationships (5.6). In the case of laws of the supportive state, their requirements, imposing taxes for the protections of generic rights indicated above (5.13 ff.), may coerce and harm the persons taxed. But these requirements override the duties to refrain from occurrently coercing or harming these persons only when the following conditions are fulfilled: the requirements are necessary to prevent undeserved coercion and serious harm; they do not go beyond what is needed for such protection; the taxational coercions and harms imposed are slight by comparison with the harm they remove; they are imposed by the procedures of the method of consent.

It must be emphasized that this comparative criterion is different from that sometimes upheld by utilitarians. The purview is not that of trying to maximize utility for a society as a whole regardless of the costs borne by some of its members. Rather, it is that of imposing relatively slight costs on some persons only in order to prevent far greater costs from having to be borne by other persons, so that an equality of generic rights for all persons may be more nearly approached. As with the criterion of the degree of necessity for action, the right to freedom must be respected here as far as possible, so that the democratic electoral process must be used to impose the necessary taxes. At this point, too, the duty of public advocacy (5.18) becomes especially important.

These three criteria for resolving conflicts of duties are not in all respects mutually exclusive. They constitute different considerations that must be appealed to in different situations of conflicting duties. When a transactional inconsistency occurs or impends, the questions of degrees of necessity for action and of institutional requirements may not arise. But if they do, their criteria are to be invoked in the order indicated, subsequent to the criterion of preventing or removing the transactional inconsistency. The reason for this order is that the three criteria are successively less direct ways of fulfilling the *PGC's* central requirement that agents must act in accord with the generic rights of their recipients. Although it was noted above that the *PGC's* institutional applications take priority over its direct applications where they conflict (5.3), I have here included this priority within the first criterion listed above as well as the third. It should also be noted that the second criterion sometimes may be applicable when the first is not explicitly involved, such as when A has to break his promise to meet B in order to rescue C from drowning. Even here, however, if A failed to rescue C when he could do so at no comparable cost to himself he would incur a severe transactional inconsistency, so that his breaking his promise serves to prevent such inconsistency on his own part. Nevertheless, as both the second and third criteria make clear, conflicts of moral duties do not arise only when one duty has already been violated, as in the first criterion; they may arise also from the needs to prevent subsequent violations and to satisfy institutional requirements.

The three criteria for resolving conflicts of duties have many further ramifications in both the individual and the social spheres. But amid the various conflicts, it is important to keep in mind that the *PGC's* standard or central requirement is the equality of generic rights and hence mutual respect for freedom and well-being among all prospective purposive agents. Departures from this mutual respect are justified only where they are required either to prevent or rectify antecedent departures, or to avoid greater departures, or to comply with social rules that themselves reflect such respect in the ways indicated above. When such justifications are not to be found, the moral rules that directly follow from the *PGC* as its direct applications set actual or conclusive duties.

5.22. All three of the criteria for resolving conflicts of duties raise further questions. Among them are questions about extrasystemic conflicts, where the duties and ordering required by the *PGC* conflict with other conceptions of comparative duties and values. Reference to these other conceptions also reflects some additional problems about the completeness of the *PGC*.

Such questions arise especially with regard to the criterion of degrees of necessity for action. It may be objected that the criterion is too conservative or quietistic, that one duty X may override another duty Y even if X bears on a good that is less necessary for action than Y. The most famous example of this is perhaps where freedom is in conflict with life, as in Patrick Henry's "Give me liberty or give me death!" This may be interpreted as entailing that the duty to maintain freedom takes priority over the duty to maintain life itself. Other examples are where one prefers one's sacred honor to life itself, where one holds that it is better to be a starving Socrates than a well-fed pig, where (as with Marx) one chooses the life of a harassed, perpetually insecure revolutionary over the life of a contented bourgeois conformist, and where (as with Kant) one prefers the avoidance of lying to preventing a murder by telling a lie.

Related to these diverse orderings of goods is the more general contention that the *PGC*, with its focus on the necessary conditions of action, ignores the many kinds of values, whether morally relevant or not, that stem from human concerns other than those of practical agency. There is a whole array of human situations and outlooks whose orientation is quite different from that of practical well-being, such as those of the aesthete and artist, the religionist, the intellectual, the libertine, and so forth. For such persons, the focus is not on action but on contemplation, worship, thought, or pleasure. Thus, although the specific comparative ordering wherein basic well-being is rated as the most important good is inescapable when the requirements of action supply the criterion of measurement, it is objected that a different ordering emerges when aesthetic contemplation, for example, is made the decisive criterion. This is why some persons prefer to starve in garrets for the sake of painting or to give money to museums rather than to organizations for helping victims of famine. The upshot of this contention is that the *PGC* is not conclusive as to what all persons ought to do, so that the principle does not have the categoricalness or supreme and universal practical authoritativeness I have claimed for it. For insofar as duties are based on nonpractical values like those just mentioned, the duties derive not from the generic features of action but from concerns other than action, and the ordering of duties must hence be based on criteria other than their degrees of necessity for action.

In answer to these objections, it must first be noted that in this book action' is used in a sense that includes the activities of the artist, the intellectual, the religionist, and so forth. For all of these are voluntary and purposive behaviors. Hence, they· all fall under the generic features of action and necessarily incur the right-claims and 'ought'- judgments that follow from these. As we have seen, amid the myriad different answers to the substantive question of what interests are worth pursuing (1.1), there is one kind of answer whose rational justification is invariant because it is based on the objective necessary conditions for the pursuit of any and all interests. All such pursuits are purposive actions, and it is from the freedom and well-being that are the necessary conditions of all purposive actions that the duties of the *PGC* are derived. Hence, the requirements of the *PGC* can rationally be evaded by no agents, regardless of their diverse values, so that the *PGC* is categorically obligatory for every aspect of human transac- tions and interactions.

The moral judgments based on the *PGC* and its various applications do not, in general, limit the freedom of the respective agents to pursue their purposes according to their own respective scales of values so long as they do not coerce or harm other persons. Thus the *PGC* does not prohibit the artist from living a life of poverty for the sake of his painting. The principle requires a temporary interference only when his life or health is so directly threatened that a question legitimately arises about whether his behavior fulfills the cognitive and emotional conditions of voluntariness (4.20,21). The principle does, however, prohibit him from inflicting such harms on other persons; but this is a different matter. The principle also requires that taxes be levied to avert serious harms from those who cannot protect their own generic rights; but this still leaves affluent persons free to support museums and the like from their surplus. The *PGC*, then, does not remove the plurality of specific values or purposes that different agents pursue, but it requires that the necessary conditions of all such pursuits be provided for so far as possible.

It must also be noted that persons' diverse orderings of various goods have no direct bearing on the issue of the ordering of moral duties in cases of conflict. For the question of what moral duties one has to other persons is not the same as the question of what values each person may uphold for himself. The criterion of degrees of necessity for action applies only to the former question, not the latter, because, as we have seen, action is the common factor in all pursuits of values, so that what is needed for action provides the basis of all moral duties. Thus A's duty to relieve the suffering of starving B takes precedence over A's duty (if any) to buy philosophical books for C or even for B. If B insists that he would rather be a starving philosopher than a well-fed banker, or that he would rather starve than go without philosophical books, this is indeed within his freedom of choice, but it has nothing to do with A's moral duty to B unless he voluntarily rejects A's offer of food. Similar considerations apply to the preference for liberty or sacred honor over life itself. Such questions bear on the vitally important issue of what kind of life is fit for a human being. The *PGC* as a whole has been concerned with this as the moral issue of how persons ought to treat one another. It has also been considered as a somewhat more individual matter in terms of the prudential virtues and the rational autonomy of duties to oneself (4.16; 5.19). With regard to the alternatives listed above, however, it is A's moral duty to save both B's life and his liberty if he can, and even to save B's life where this may involve B's living without liberty, at least temporarily, unless B voluntarily rejects this choice (4.21). In this connection it is also important to keep in mind the distinctions between occurrent and dispositional freedom and between the different objects of freedom, for these bear on the relative importance of the freedoms that may conflict with other goods. Within the limits set by the *PGC*, persons should be free to live according to their own scales of values.

Broader questions of social morality are also raised by these diversities of basic evaluations. For example, should food be sent to a starving nation where this will serve to bolster a despotic regime? In such a situation, the conflict between the duty to sustain basic well-being and the duty to assist freedom is usually illusory. It is not the despots who are starving, and their violations of political freedom, far from being necessary to avert starvation, often underlie the unjust distributions of food that result in starvation for the many amid overabundance for the few.[19] Thus the sending of food must be coupled with provisions for control of its distribution by the persons who actually need it. By such control, liberty as well as life is fostered.

What should be done, however, where the forced choice between losing life and losing liberty befalls some nation or community because of the threats of another state? History is replete with tragic examples of this at least from Masada to the consequences of Munich for Czechoslovakia in 1938. The tragedy is exacerbated when the aggressor state demands that certain victims be singled out for death among the members of the threatened community. The *PGC*'s equality of generic rights prohibits, however, that some innocent persons be intentionally killed or otherwise basically harmed or sacrificed in order to prevent or mitigate harm to others when there remains the possibility of choosing to inflict neither harm. The members of the threatened community must hence face the aggressor together.

What choice should they make? Obviously the alternatives must be carefully considered. It is sometimes the case that the choice between life and liberty is here also more apparent than real, when the aggressor's record shows that he intends to remove freedom only as a preliminary to removing life. Here, then, resistance is the only justified course, so that if possible both life and liberty may be saved. This course must also be followed if life will be preserved but only at the expense of total enslavement. Since action is impossible with the loss of either life or freedom, vigorous efforts must be mounted to prevent either loss. Much also depends, however, on the nature of the threatened freedom. If it is occurrent, then subsequent freedoms may still be retained, so that the shorter-range freedom should be surrendered in preference to death. If, on the other hand, the threatened freedom is dispositional or long-range, there remains the further question of whether there are possibilities of regaining it by subsequent action. If there are, then life again must be chosen, but only with the fullest resolve to fight for freedom at the earliest available opportunity. These tragic implications of the criterion of degrees of necessity for action must thus be viewed in terms not only of the surrender of lesser degrees but also of the retention of the possibility of action.

The criterion of degrees of necessity also involves genuine moral conflicts of social policy in less critical circumstances. The PGC has been seen to justify levying taxes in the supportive state for the purpose of relieving economic deprivation and fostering equality of opportunity. But the divergent assessments of the relative importance of values may also be invoked in connection with public support of different goods. For example, should taxes be used to subsidize art museums and symphony orchestras as well as to relieve economic deprivation? If this can be justified by the PGC it will be on the ground that such amenities are akin to the 'public goods' dealt with above (5.14). Such a view is implausible unless adequate arrangements are made to assure that the amenities actually become common goods in the distributive sense, as when orchestras perform in public parks. In such cases the aesthetic and other goods may serve as aids to additive well-being, in that the broader cultural horizons they make available help persons not only to pursue their purposes with added vigor but also to have a deeper insight into the kind of life they want to lead and the purposes they regard as worth pursuing . In this way the PGC's focus on the whole range of freedom and well-being provides a perspective that is not narrowly 'utilitarian.' But aesthetic and similar values must not be publicly supported at the expense of basic well-being.

The *PGC's* central requirement of the equality of generic rights also raises the general question of the extent to which social equality should be fostered. There is a traditional conflict between freedom and equality, the former eventuating not only in economic inequality but also in many kinds of class differentiations, while the latter avoids these by reducing the freedom from which they emerge. The *PGC's* concepts of common good and equal freedom have been attempts to retain what is rationally justified from each of these poles. It has sought not to produce an economic or social levelling but rather to foster human relations and institutions in which persons have the ability to maintain their own freedom and well-being while respecting the equal rights of others. Because the *PGC's* emphasis is on the generic abilities of action, it is not directly concerned with social equality in the sense of removing all invidious distinctions, although the need for self-esteem among these abilities indicates a limiting point of such distinctions. But this limit is compatible with the fullest freedom for each person so long as he does not inflict the coercions and harms prohibited by the *PGC* (4.23; 5.16).

5.23. Let us now consider some of the other conflicts that may arise within the *PGC* itself. Since the principle requires that an agent act in accord with his recipients' generic rights as well as his own, there may be conflicts both between the agent and his recipients and between the respective rights.

a. A first possible source of conflict bears on the *PGC's* requirement that the agent A act in accord with the right to freedom of his recipient R as well as in accord with A's own right to freedom. What if A is threatened by another agent B that unless A coerces or does violence to R by forcing R to do or undergo something against his will, A will be similarly coerced by B? In such a situation it seems that if A acts in accord with R's right to freedom, then he will not act in accord with his own right to freedom. It is to be noted, however, that A would here be operating under forced choice, so that his behavior would not be free or voluntary in the sense indicated above (1.11). In this situation A would not be an agent; instead, he would be the recipient of B's threatening action. Hence, the *PGC* would now be properly addressed not to A but to B. It is B who intends to violate the *PGC*, which shows the moral wrongness of his intended action. The conflict between A's and R's rights to freedom arises not within the *PGC* but only from a threatened violation of it.

A moral principle should, however, give guidance for morally imperfect worlds in which the principle is violated. Does A have a right to coerce R in order to avoid being coerced by B? In the situation as thus abstractly described, the answer is no, and the *PGC* shows why this is so. Insofar as A can control his conduct he ought to refrain from coercing or inflicting violence on his recipients. If the violence or coercion threatened by B involves basic or other serious harm to A or R, then A ought, if at all possible, to appeal to the authorities to enforce the criminal law, which, as we have seen, contains and enforces the most basic part of the *PGC*. If this is not possible, he should try to prevent B from carrying out his threat.

b. What should A do if, in order to act in accord with his own right to basic well-being, he must violate R's right to basic well-being? Suppose, for example, the only way for A to see to it, so far as he can, that he preserves his own life is for him to act to destroy R's life: the life raft will hold only one of them, or the would-be assassin has only one bullet left with which he will murder one of them (he doesn't care which), and so forth. In such crisis situations, as in (*a*), A is confronted with forced choices that make his behavior not fully voluntary. Since the *PGC* is concerned primarily with the voluntary actions of agents, such situations depart from its assumptions that A necessarily acts in accord with his own right to basic well-being and that he can determine by his own unforced choice how he will act toward R with regard to R's basic well-being. Nevertheless, insofar as A is an agent in such situations, the *PGC* applies to him; it shows that he has no right to take R's life in the described circumstances.

Such situations are different from those where A can save R's life without endangering his own life (4.7). They are also different from situations where A can save R's life only by endangering or losing his own. The difference is that in the present case A is assumed to be already in a situation where his own life is directly threatened, whereas in the other case it is a question of A's voluntarily putting himself into a situation where he will have to lose his life if he is to save R's life. As we have seen, A has no duty to put himself into such a situation (3.24; 4.12), unless doing so is part of his assigned role in a justified institution (such as the police or the military). This is distinct, however, from the point that once A is in such a situation through circumstances beyond his control he has no right to make R lose his life in order to save his own life.

c. In addition to conflicts between A and R that, as in (*b*), involve the same level of basic well-being for both persons, there may be conflicts between A and R regarding different levels of well-being. What should A do if, in order to act in accord with his own right to basic well-being, he has to violate R's right to nonsubtractive well-being, or if, in order to act in accord with his own right to nonsubtractive well-being, he has to violate R's right to basic well-being? For example, in order to save his life A has to break his promise to R or lie to R; or in order to save R's life A must let himself be robbed. Here the criterion of degrees of necessity for action applies; since life is more necessary for action than being told the truth, having promises kept, or retaining one's money, A should give priority to his own life in the first case and to R's life in the second.

d. What should A do if, in order to act in accord with his own right to freedom, he has to violate R's right to one of the levels of well-being, or if, in order to act in accord with his own right to well-being in one of its levels, he has to violate R's right to freedom? For example, in order to avoid being imprisoned A has to kill R or lie to R. It makes an important difference whether R here is the aggressor threatening A with imprisonment (as with B above under [*a*]) or whether R is an innocent bystander. A may be justified in killing R if this is the only way to prevent R from imprisoning him, but R is here guilty of seriously violating the *PGC*. On the other hand, where R is an innocent bystander and someone else, B, is the aggressor against A, the criterion of degrees of necessity for actions applies. A has no right to kill R in order to avoid being imprisoned, but he may lie to him.

Thus far I have been dealing with conflicts between an agent and his one recipient. An action may, however, have several recipients, and their generic rights may conflict. These rights may have as their objects goods that are either on the same level or on different levels.

e. What should A do if, in order to act in accord with a basic right of one of his recipients, R, he has to violate a basic right of his other recipient, S? For example, in order to save R from drowning A has to let S drown, or in order to give starving R enough food to pull him through A has to deny food to starving S. In such tragic situations there may be no solution other than to urge A to do all that he can to save both persons. But let us consider a possible qualification in connection with the next case.

f. What should A do if, in order to act in accord with a nonsubtractive right of one of his recipients, R, he has to violate a nonsubtractive right of his other recipient, S? For example, in order to avoid lying to R (who has asked him whether S has had an abortion), A would have to break his promise to S (whom he has promised that he will not reveal that she has had an abortion). In such a case further considerations, including those of special relations among the parties, would help to determine the answer. If, for example, A is S's husband while R is a comparative stranger, A's duty to S outweighs his duty to R

(5.6). Indeed, A may simply not reply to R's question. On the other hand, if R is a physician concerned for S's health, then A should probably seek a release from his promise to S or, if this is impossible, he should perhaps break his promise for the sake of S's health, but only if it is quite clear that S's health will otherwise be severely endangered, so that S's dispositional consent may be assumed. Similarly, in the case of two recipients facing basic harms under (e) above, if one of them is a member of A's immediate family, his duty to that person comes first, because of the deeper, more intimate purposes subserved by the family as compared with other forms of association.

g. What should A do if, in order to act in accord with a basic right of R, he has to violate a nonsubtractive right of S? For example, in order to prevent R from being murdered, he has to lie to S. Here, as we have seen, the criterion of degrees of necessity for action obtains; the lesser evil must be preferred to the greater. Not all conflicts between basic and nonsubtractive rights, however, have such immediacy and exhaustiveness of alternatives. Consider such famous examples as where A, to keep his family from starving, has to steal a loaf of bread from S, or where A, to obtain money for a desperately needed operation for his wife, has to steal from his employer. The 'has to' in such cases has been modified by social progress; but in situations where no alternatives are available so that the 'has to' is literally true, the right course would still be indicated by the criterion of degrees of necessity for action. But the availability of alternatives must first be explored as fully as circumstances permit.

h. What should A do if he is confronted with a choice between harming one person and harming twelve? The answer depends in part on whether the harms are on the same level or on different levels. In saying that he is 'confronted,' it is assumed that his choice is forced by external circumstances beyond his control; hence, his degree of agency is limited. If his own previous actions have produced the harmful situation where he must now choose—as, for example, if he has been driving his car too fast and must now choose between hitting one pedestrian or twelve—his duty is to avoid driving too fast in the first place. But, given his initial fault, he should hit the one pedestrian if this is the only way to avoid hitting the twelve. But whenever possible, nonharmful alternatives must be chosen; and, if basic harm must be done through one's own fault, whenever possible one must accept the harm for oneself rather than violate the basic rights of others.

It must again be emphasized that this quantitative consideration is different from that sometimes upheld by utilitarians. The difference is that inflicting basic harms on one person or group is not justified or excused by the end of increasing the particular additive goods of other persons or groups so long as the result is to maximize utility overall. The *PGC* requires that the generic rights of each person be respected so far as possible, and this possibility is adversely affected in physical circumstances like the one just mentioned, but not where violation of someone's rights will lead to greater particular additive goods for others. If, however, a person is confronted with a choice between harming one person and harming twelve where the harms are on different levels—for example, he must break his promise to twelve persons in order to save one from drowning—then he must break his promise to the twelve. Here again the criterion of degrees of necessity for action applies.

What I have tried to establish here is that the *PGC*, as the supreme principle of morality, serves to unify the whole realm of morally right judgments and rules both in individual and in institutional contexts. As a principle of distributive justice requiring equality of generic rights as between agents and recipients, the *PGC* is able to resolve conflicts of moral duties and values through considerations based on its being both a formal and a material principle. All justified moral rules and judgments derive from the *PGC* in either its direct or its indirect applications, and all share in its inherently rational structure.

Some Concluding Reflections

5.24. The project of this book is now completed. I have tried to show that the requirements of the *PGC* and the steps leading to its justification cannot rationally be evaded by any prospective agent. Hence, if I have succeeded in my aim, the moral skeptic is refuted in his position that there can be no rational justification of a supreme, substantial moral principle. In this concluding section I shall examine some of the more general bearings of the whole argument.

The logical structure of the argument for the *PGC* raises a number of interconnected problems. First, there are problems about logical gaps and circularity. The argument proceeds from a morally neutral 'is' to a normatively moral 'ought'; it proceeds from a general concept of action that fits all moral and other practical precepts to a more specific activist concept of action; and it proceeds from a conceptually narrow practical base to a morally complex conclusion in which concepts like autonomy, dignity, and honorableness are used. Since the whole argument purports to be deductive, how can these conceptually enriched conclusions be explained?

I have already dealt in some detail with the main lines of the argument's derivation of 'ought' from 'is,' especially the crucial point where the agent, on pain of inconsistency, must hold or accept that he has the generic rights on the basis of holding or accepting that his freedom and well-being are necessary goods (2.10; 3.5,9), this latter judgment being based ultimately on his factual statement that he acts for purposes. But the problem may also be dealt with in a more specific form, in terms of the following consideration. Since the argument for the *PGC* has been primarily deductive, its egalitarian-universalist moral conclusion must be implicit in the premises. It is indeed the case that in truth-functional logic, through such rules as addition, the consequent may contain terms and propositions not contained in the antecedent. Even here, however, although rules are not the same as premises, the consequent logically follows only because of what is contained in the rules and premises taken together. In any case, the deductive argument for the *PGC*, proceeding largely through conceptual analysis, has not made use of the distinctive rules of truth-functional logic; hence, it still remains that the conclusion must be implicit in the premises. But doesn't this mean that the argument for the *PGC* is in some respect circular?

This question may be amplified in the following way. In considering the moral and other practical precepts from which the relevant concept of action and agency was to be derived, as a way of getting at the subject matter of morality and deducing the *PGC* therefrom, I emphasized that the precepts were not to be restricted to any one kind of morality as against any other. On the contrary, the starting point or premise of the argument was to be morally neutral in that the relevant concept of action and of the agent was to be common to all moralities (1.9). The *PGC*, however, is a moral principle that takes a distinctive moral position and hence is itself not morally neutral. If, then, the argument leading to the *PGC* is deductive, how can the principle be logically derived from premises (about moral precepts and action) that are themselves morally general and neutral? It seems, then, that the argument for the *PGC* faces the following difficulty. If the argument is deductively valid, then it must be circular; moreover, its starting point cannot be morally neutral. If, on the other hand, its starting point is morally neutral, then its morally nonneutral conclusion cannot follow deductively from its premises; hence, the argument is not logically or deductively valid.

In the face of this difficulty, one might be tempted to concede that my starting point in the generic features of action is not morally neutral. For by the very fact that the argument begins from the generic features common to all action and agency, it excludes the distinctive, exclusivist emphases of particularist and elitist moralities, and hence the specific differences that characterize some actions and agents as against others—for example, superior intelligence or will to power. But it is precisely these specific differential features that are given priority in particularist moralities. Hence, by beginning from the generic features common to all action, I pave the way to an egalitarian-universalist moral principle in which the specific differences and exclusiveness exalted in particularist moral principles are overridden or ignored. In this way, then, it may be contended that the premise or beginning point of the argument is not morally neutral, and it is for this reason that the argument for the *PGC* can be deductively valid and arrive at a morally nonneutral principle. The argument, thus, is circular.

In replying to this contention, I shall not go into the familiar distinction between explicit and implicit circularity, the latter consisting in the relation where the conclusion is not known to be logically 'contained' in the premises except through a considerable sequence of intermediate steps (see 3.20). The more direct reply is that to begin from the generic features common to all action and agency is to avoid arbitrariness and question-begging about which morality is right or correct, precisely because the generic features are found in the actions prescribed by all moralities and other practical precepts. If, on the other hand, one were to begin from a specific kind of action and agency upheld in one morality as against another, such as in that characterized by Aristotle's exaltation of superior intelligence or Nietzsche's apotheosis of the will to power, such a beginning point would be arbitrary and question-begging. For the question would still remain of why the exclusivist claims of such moralists should be given pride of place as against those of their rivals, including either other exclusivists or various egalitarians. Each of these opposed moralities has its own principles and criteria of goods and of distribution; but the question is, What justifies these criteria as against their rivals? Arguments can, of course, be given in support of each of these divergent criteria; but unlike the moral neutrality of the generic features of action, these arguments cannot appeal to the rational necessities of what is universally involved in the subject matter of all moralities as against the particularist choices on which restrictive moralities ultimately rest. A generic starting point, on the other hand, is morally neutral and rationally justified precisely because it includes what is common to and necessarily connected with all moralities and hence does not beg the question of the rightness of any one morality as against the others.

Because action is the necessary and universal subject matter of all moral and other practical precepts, it comprises what all moralities and moral philosophers must agree on, regardless of their divergent views about which actions are morally right. Consequently, all moralists and other agents must, on pain of contradiction, accept what logically follows from this universal concept and context of action. To accept this concept and context as one's starting point is not to make a dispensable 'commitment,' akin to other persons' commitments to religion, art, law, or other values, contexts, or institutions, including one or another specific morality. Rather, the acceptance of the concept and context of action is a necessity not subject to any choice or decision on the part of any agent. It is impossible to refrain intentionally from committing oneself to the context of the generic features of action, for any such refraining would itself exhibit those features. Hence, because of this acceptance, the moral 'ought' that is derived within that context is prescriptive at least in the sense that the agent is logically committed to accepting it and acting in accordance with it. Nevertheless, the derivation is not circular, because the derived 'ought' reflects not a dispensable choice or commitment but rather a necessity not subject to any choice or decision on the part of the agent. The objector hence cannot say, 'You've reached a commitment or prescription in the conclusion only because you've already chosen to put the commitment or prescription into your premise'; for the latter commitment in the premise is not one that the deriver has chosen or has put into the premise. Rather, the commitment is there in the nature of the case, and all he is doing is recognizing it; but he cannot evade it. It is therefore a significant result to have shown that from a morally neutral analysis of action there logically follows an egalitarian-universalist principle of morality.

It should also be noted that the argument for the *PGC* achieves its egalitarian conclusion without positing universal ignorance or complete equality or making other false or contrarational assumptions designed to ward off partiality or inequality. In contrast to such artificial constructs, I have begun from what is rationally necessary to the whole context of action, and from agents as they really are, acting freely for their respective purposes with knowledge of the proximate circumstances of their actions, including their particular qualities. What has been required of them is that they not definitively accept any specific moral principle prior to rational argument, and that they have and use deductive and inductive rationality. Impartiality is morally imposed on these agents not by artificially stripping them of all particular knowledge or inequality but rather by showing that their actions logically involve them in right-claims and 'ought'-judgments that are such that, to avoid self-contradiction, they must accept that their recipients equally have the same rights. The argument is thus rationally necessary without paying the price of beginning from contrarational assumptions.

Similar considerations apply to the other apparent logical gaps mentioned above. Since the concept of action from which the argument begins must be common to all moralities, including quietistic and obscurantist ones, how can there logically follow from it a moral principle that requires intelligent activism? And since the basis of the argument is conceptually narrow in that it is concerned with what is required for having the necessary conditions of action, how can there logically follow from it conceptually enriched moral conclusions that use such deontological concepts as human dignity, autonomy, and honor? The answer to these questions is that these results are logically achieved by applying the concept of reason to the premises in question. All agents, including those who uphold quietistic and obscurantist principles, must want to achieve their purposes, and for this they need freedom and well-being. These necessary goods, being the general conditions of all action, may enable their possessors to achieve many kinds of purposes other than those at which they originally aimed; hence, the rational analysis of action can serve as a learning process for agents. This is not, of course, to say or predict that every agent does or will engage in such learning. But the analysis of what is required for action enables the agent to vary both his purposes and his conceptions of the available means, through becoming aware of the components of the freedom and well-being that are variously required for action. The argument for the *PGC* eventuates in intelligent activism only in the sense that it shows what persons must have and do in order to achieve their purposes in a way that takes account both of the varying extents or time ranges of such achievement and of the rationally grounded equal rights of other persons to such purposive action. The free, cognitive, and conative features of purposive action thus carry through to all stages of the argument.

The logical derivation of deontological moral concepts like human dignity, honor, and autonomy has a similar rational ground. We begin from the agent as concerned simply with acting to achieve his purposes, whatever they may be. Because of the necessity of freedom and well-being for all such achievements, he must hold it as a matter of the utmost urgency that he has rights to them, and, by virtue of the subsequent argument, he must recognize that other persons' having these rights is equally necessary and urgent for them. This recognition

358

requires him to admit, as a matter of logical necessity, that he has certain obligations toward other persons, including that he must respect them and acknowledge their autonomy as well as his own (3.3). He must also recognize that, as rationally autonomous persons equipped with rights equal to his own, having their own purposes and the general abilities required for reflecting on them and controlling their behavior in the light of this reflection, all persons have human dignity. The agent must act with honor toward them because this is required by the duties he rationally knows that he has toward them. He must also respect himself and acknowledge that he has certain duties toward himself, not only because this is required for the fulfillment of his purposes and his moral obligations toward others, but also because of his rational autonomy as accepting and acting in accordance with rational criteria.

5.25. Since these criteria are ultimately those of deductive and inductive logic, it follows that in deriving the *PGC* from reason I have held that in the justificatory sequence logical principles are prior to and determinative of moral principles. Inductive rationality, moreover, is exhibited in or begins in part from empirical knowledge, and it also figures to some extent in empirical science. I seem to be committed, therefore, to the position that morality needs justification from deductive logic and empirical science, whereas these latter do not, in turn, need any justification from morality.

These priorities and justificatory relations may be questioned. That empirical science needs justification from morality is suggested by such considerations as that empirical science requires various personal and social moral traits and conditions, including honesty, truthfulness, freedom of inquiry, public communication of results, and willingness to subject one's ideas to public scrutiny, to follow the evidence wherever it may lead, and to subordinate one's own selfish desires to impartial acceptance of the facts. Deductive logic also has such moral involvements; for even if its criteria are morally neutral, their applications in public discourse have moral requirements. For there is an ethics of rational discussion: such discussion requires, in addition to the moral traits listed above, a certain commitment to justice in the sense of mutuality or equality of consideration. By 'discussion' is meant not a didactic, let alone a rhetorical or propagandistic relation, but rather a cooperative process where truth is genuinely sought by all the participants. Such discussion, including that conducted by logicians and scientists, is impossible unless one regards one's interlocutors as capable of grasping the subject matter under discussion and of making their own contributions to the give and take of ideas as a cooperative endeavor. It requires that one accord one's interlocutors the same attentive consideration one wants them to accord oneself, that one respect their right to contribute as one wants them to respect one's own.

In view of these moral aspects of the intellectual enterprise, it may be contended that the correct conception of the justificatory situation is not the unilinear one from deductive and inductive logic to morality assumed in this book, but rather a circular or spiral one in which morality provides a justificatory ground for logic and science as much as they provide justification for morality. This may be the point intended in Piaget's striking statement, "logic is the morality of thought just as morality is the logic of action."[20]

Even if such circularity obtains, it is not vicious. For the aspect of deduction and induction invoked in justifying the principle of morality is not the same as the aspect the principle justifies. It is the rules or criteria of deduction and induction that enter into the justification of the *PGC*; but what morality justifies is not these rules or criteria themselves but rather the way they are used and applied both in relations of interpersonal communication and in one's personal participation in intellectual operations. The 'syntactics' and 'semantics' of deductive and inductive rationality are the ultimate justificans of morality, while it is the 'pragmatics' of such rationality that morality justifies.[21] This is not to say that the rules or criteria of deduction and induction may not themselves need to be justified, and even justified pragmatically; but this justification does not in turn come from morality.

The justification of the *PGC* through deductive and inductive rationality does not violate the autonomy of morality properly understood. On one view of autonomy, the claim that some field F is autonomous means that F has its own internal principles and criteria of justification, so that there is no need to go 'outside' F to ascertain its principles or to justify them. In this view, the whole endeavor is misguided whereby one seeks to justify an entire F, including its principles, by more general considerations that are not confined specifically to F. Such 'heteronomy' is held to ignore the fact that the justification of anything can proceed only within some F, by assuming or understanding its principles and criteria; but the whole of F itself, including its ultimate principles, is not similarly susceptible to any justification. Instead, one must simply look and see what F consists in; one must study its own distinctive structure and contents to ascertain its principles and criteria. These are autonomous, neither needing nor admitting any 'external' justification. There is an irreducible plurality of Fs, each having its own principles, and each must be understood in its own unique terms.

This pluralistic view incurs two interrelated kinds of difficulty. One arises from the scope of the Fs. The view seems to confine itself to established, recognized 'institutions,' such as morality, art, natural science, knowledge in general, mathematics, religion, and perhaps also politics, law, economic relations, and so forth. But why should only such established institutions be accorded this autonomy? What of the practices of tribal medicine men and various other sorts of superstition? What of the practice of killing deformed children or of institutions like slavery, suttee, and the *jus primae noctis* associated with feudalism? Surely these can be evaluated and criticized on moral, epistemic, and other grounds. Such criticism, however, is disavowed by the pluralistic view, so that its insistence on accepting each F for what it is requires an immense conservatism.

A second difficulty arises from the conflicts within various Fs. Permissiveness and tolerance are indeed possible and even desirable in such an F as religion, despite, or perhaps because of, the variety of religions; and it is important to differentiate religious statements from scientific ones. But what of the conflicts within morality, law, and other such Fs? Must the morality of apartheid be accepted equally with the morality of racial nondiscrimination, and the law of totalitarian repression equally with the law of civil liberties? Unless 'morality' and 'law' are question-beggingly confined to certain favored alternatives, critical justificatory questions arise in these Fs; and these questions cannot be answered simply by reiterating the principles or criteria of each F. Choices must be made among them, and the guidance of these choices requires considerations that go beyond these Fs themselves. It requires a critical, justificatory examination of their various principles or criteria.

If, then, morality is not a single homogeneous field in the way envisaged by the pluralistic view, its autonomy is nevertheless not infringed when one appeals to rational criteria to resolve conflicts within morality and to justify its supreme principle. For rationality is internal to morality, not external to it. Moral judgments appeal to reasons and lay claim to justification or correctness. Hence, to evaluate them by consideration of the ultimate criteria of rational justification is to use and respect their own internal structure. That the same criteria are also applicable to other fields does not remove the autonomy of morality. It shows rather that morality is part of the whole vast area of rationality. On the other hand, the distinctiveness and practical supremacy of morality are preserved because the general, ultimate criteria of rationality are here applied to the generic features that distinctively characterize purposive action with its conativeness and its consequent evaluations and right-claims.

In this application, reason becomes practical in two ways. First, the rational form of deduction and consistency is imposed on the contents of action. Second, the logical consequence of this imposition is that reason, through its criterion of logical necessity, shows what is justified and what is unjustified in the moral judgments that purport to guide actions.

5.26. Consider the following statement, which I shall call 'J': 'A certain moral principle, the *PGC*, is rationally justifiable.' Is J a statement in 'metaethics' or in 'normative ethics'? It seems to be both. It is metaethical because it says something about the logical status and structure of the moral principle. It is also normatively ethical because it says that the content of the principle is morally right or correct by virtue of being rationally justifiable. Thus the argument for the *PGC* shows that in important (though not in all) respects there is no valid distinction between metaethics and normative ethics because metaethical statements have specific normative ethical implications, and normative ethical statements, when traced back to their ultimate grounds, rest on specific metaethical doctrines about the meanings of moral terms and the methods of supporting moral judgments.[22]

It may be objected that a valid distinction still remains in the present case, because 'rationally justifiable' is ambiguous as between 'morally justifiable' and 'logically justifiable.' J is a statement in normative ethics only if 'rationally justifiable' means the former, and it is a statement in metaethics only if 'rationally justifiable' means the latter. The difference between the two meanings entails that J cannot, without ambiguity, be both a normative ethical and a metaethical statement.

This objection focuses on a question I have dealt with at various points above (3.23,26). As we have seen, the *PGC* is logically justifiable or correct because any agent who denies or violates it contradicts himself; hence, he logically must admit that it is necessarily true. But what is thus admitted entails that the moral obligations the *PGC* sets for the agent are indeed his obligations. The *PGC* cannot, of course, force him to meet or live up to his obligations, but this is a different matter. So long as any agent accepts the canons of logical rightness, he logically must accept the *PGC* as setting genuine justified moral obligations for himself. But what the agent must thus accept is normatively ethical: that he has certain moral obligations or duties. This is a substantial, normative moral requirement. Hence, by virtue of stating that the *PGC* is logically justifiable, J is a statement in metaethics; but because what it states to be thus justifiable is that every agent has certain moral obligations, J is also a statement in normative ethics. The normative bindingness of the *PGC* can be evaded by any person only if he ceases to be even a prospective agent or ceases to be rational in the minimal deductive and inductive senses indicated above. Not only would either cessation carry a prohibitive price, but it would completely remove the ceasing person from the realm of morality as well as of action in general.

Viewed in terms of metaethics, my ethical theory is a modified naturalism. It is naturalistic in that it holds that moral judgments have truth-value as corresponding to pervasive facts about agents. It is a modified naturalism in two respects. First, as we have seen, the facts that make moral judgments true, while they include the empirical phenomena of agency with its voluntariness and purposiveness, include also facts about what agents logically must admit or accept as derived from the normative structure of action (3.18).

Second, the content of the theory is prescriptive. It construes moral judgments not only as being made true by facts about agents, but also, because of the derivation of these facts from the normative structure of action, as setting practical requirements that agents logically must accept. This prescriptiveness stems ultimately from the conativeness of purposive action. Because of this conativeness, agents regard their purposes as good and claim rights to the necessary conditions of their fulfillment. Thus both the right-claims and the correlative 'ought'-judgments have prescriptive force for agents, who advocate or endorse the actions to which the 'oughts' are attached. This advocacy, however, is not antithetical to the judgments' having truth-value. For they are true when they correspond to the normative structure of action. The judgments figure in logical relations of consistency and inconsistency; and it is the inconsistency of denying or refusing to accept certain of these judgments that renders them necessarily true when they are stated in indicative form. But the inconsistency of such denial stems from action and its normative structure. Thus my theory can be naturalistic in attributing truth to moral judgments even though the contents of the judgments have important prescriptive elements.

Because the *PGC* has been shown in this way to be necessarily true, the theory presented here offers a refutation of a famous tenet of noncognitivist metaethics: that persons may agree completely about empirical facts and logical rules and still disagree on issues of moral principle.[23] If persons are rational in the deductive and inductive senses previously indicated, then if they agree on empirical facts they logically must agree on the *PGC* and on its applications as traced above.

In one respect, however, the noncognitivists were right in their insistence that mere observation of facts and logical inference are insufficient to establish a moral principle as correct. For such establishment requires the conativeness whereby agents pursue purposes they regard as good; and this conativeness is not, or at least is not exclusively, a 'cognitive' matter. Without such conativeness, the concepts of goods and of rights would not enter the justificatory sequence. But the awareness of this conativeness and of its normative implications becomes available to the moral philosopher both empirically and through the conceptual analysis of action, which analysis is a form of deductive reasoning. Hence, as before, the prescriptive and other noncognitive elements of value and morality are subsumed under and are used by the cognitive elements of deductive and inductive rationality.

5.27. From the concept of action and its generic features, then, the supreme principle of morality has been logically derived, together with its manifold applications. The ascertainment of the contents of this concept and of the various logical connections is the work of reason, so that reason and its criteria provide the ultimate justificans of the supreme principle of morality. It is this that also explains, in the final analysis, why the *PGC* and its derivative moral rules can attain, in a substantial, nonvacuous way, a degree of necessity or stringency superior to that found in the laws of the natural sciences. For there is a unity of subject and object in morality that is not found in any of the natural sciences, including psychology insofar as it is an empirical discipline. Morality sets rational requirements for rational agents; hence, the whole enterprise is under the control of reason in the ways traced above. The rational agents for whom moral requirements are set are not in principle different from the rational persons who ascertain what these requirements are, despite the greater degree of analytical precision that distinguishes the philosopher from the nonphilosopher.

This unity of subject and object in morality must be distinguished from Locke's contention that moral knowledge can be certain because its objects are 'mixed modes' made by the mind itself.[24] For according to Locke, such modes do not represent anything beyond themselves, which is why they can be completely known by the mind that made them. This point is compatible with a view of the 'objects' of morality as completely conventional and even arbitrary constructs, so that moral rules would not necessarily impose obligations on persons who do not accept the constructs. My point, on the contrary, is that the generic features of action constitute objective independent variables from which true moral judgments are derived and to which they correspond. These features, unlike Locke's moral mixed modes, are not arbitrary or conventional, because they pertain to all actions, so that the requirements that follow from them are binding on all agents. The awareness of the necessity and universality of these features and the ascertainment of their logical consequences are works of reason. Since these consequences include moral requirements that are addressed to rational agents, the requirements are logically necessary not only as being derived by conceptual analysis from the generic features of action, but also as setting obligations for agents who can themselves grasp their necessity.

In this regard, morality is also unlike empirical psychology, where the independent variables are modes of behavior or of feeling for which the science sets no requirements, and which are not necessarily the same as the intellectual and empirical procedures that study them. This nonidentity is still more obvious in the relation between the knowing subject and the known objects in the other natural sciences. It is indeed the case that the persons for whom moral requirements are set are emotional and conative beings as well as rational ones, so that they do not automatically fulfill the requirements set by reason. This is why the implications of action constitute requirements or duties and not mere descriptions of spontaneously rational conduct. Nevertheless, rational agents in fulfilling moral requirements can control relevant aspects of their emotional and conative conditions in ways bearing on their actions. Thus, since the PGC follows from what it is to be a rational agent, the independent variable determining the content of the moral principle is the same as the persons for whom the principle sets requirements. It is because of its central focus in reason that the principle of morality can attain the status of a substantial necessary truth that sets overriding requirements for all agents.

NOTES

Preface

1 (p. xii) "Categorial Consistency in Ethics," *Philosophical Quarterly* 17 (1967): 289–99; "The Non-Trivializability of Universalizability," *Australasian Journal of Philosophy* 47 (1969): 123–31; "Must One Play the Moral Language Game?" *American Philosophical Quarterly* 7 (1970): 107–18; "Some Comments on Categorial Consistency," *Philosophical Quarterly* 20 (1970): 380–84; "Obligation: Political, Legal, Moral," in *Nomos XII: Political and Legal Obligation*, ed. J. R. Pennock and J. W. Chapman (New York: Atherton, 1970), pp. 55–88; "Civil Disobedience, Law, and Morality," *The Monist* 54 (1970): 536–55; "Some Notes on Moral and Legal Obligation," in *Human Rights* (Amintaphil I), ed. E. H. Pollock (Buffalo: Jay Stewart Publications, 1971), pp. 291–96; "The Justification of Egalitarian Justice," *American Philosophical Quarterly* 8 (1971): 331–41; "The Normative Structure of Action," *Review of Metaphysics* 25 (1971): 238–61; "Moral Rationality," Lindley Lecture, University of Kansas, 1972; "Morality and Autonomy in Education," in *Educational Judgments*, ed. J. F. Doyle (London: Routledge and Kegan Paul, 1973), pp. 33–45; "The 'Is-Ought' Problem Resolved," *Proceedings and Addresses of the American Philosophical Association* 47 (1974): 34–61; "Reasons and Conscience: The Claims of the Selective Conscientious Objector," in *Philosophy, Morality, and International Affairs*, ed. V. Held et al. (New York: Oxford University Press, 1974), pp. 89–117; "Civil Liberties as Effective Powers," in *Moral Values in Contemporary Public Life*, ed. R. B. Ashmore and L. C. Rice (Milwaukee: Marquette University Press, 1975), pp. 3–10; "Action and Rights: A Reply," *Ethics* 86 (1976): 288–93; "The Golden Rule Rationalized," *Midwest Studies in Philosophy*, vol. 3 (1978), in press.

2 (p. xii) N. Fotion, "Gewirth and Categorial Consistency," *Philosophical Quarterly* 18 (1968): 262–64; W. Gregory Lycan, "Hare, Singer, and Gewirth on Universalizability," *Philosophical Quarterly* 19 (1969): 135–44; George C. Christie, "Some Notes on the Nature of Institutional Obligations," in *Human Rights* (Amintaphil I), ed. E. H. Pollock, pp. 275–80; Donald R. Burrill, "Professor Gewirth's Principle of Moral Rightness," in Pollock, pp. 281–85; Thomas E. Davitt, "Response to 'Obligation: Political, Legal, Moral' by Alan Gewirth," in Pollock, pp. 286–90; D. E. Geels, "How to be a Consistent Racist," *The Personalist* 52 (1971): 662–79; James Corcoran, "Gewirth's Deontologism," *Ethics* 83 (1973): 313–21; Douglas den Uyl, "Gewirth's PCC and Ethical Egoism," *The Personalist* 56 (1975): 432–47; Robert Simon, "The

Trouble with Categorial Consistency, *Philosophical Studies* 27 (1975): 271–77; Colin Davies, "Egoism and Consistency," *Australasian Journal of Philosophy* 53 (1975): 19–27; Laszlo Versenyi, "On Deriving Categorical Imperatives from the Concept of Action," *Ethics* 86 (1976): 265–73; James O. Grunebaum, "Gewirth and a Reluctant Protagonist," *Ethics* 86 (1976): 274–77; Henry B. Veatch, "Paying Heed to Gewirth's Principle of Categorial Consistency," *Ethics* 86 (1976): 278–87.

1. The Problem of Justification

1 (p. 4) This point is not affected by the contentions of recent philosophers of science that some sorts of empirical facts cannot be ascertained independent of scientific theories or frameworks. See Thomas S. Kuhn, *The Structure of Scientific Revolutions*, 2d ed. (Chicago: University of Chicago Press, 1970); Norwood R. Hanson, *Patterns of Discovery* (Cambridge: Cambridge University Press, 1965); Paul Feyerabend, *Against Method* (London: NLB, 1975). Cf. the important critique of Kuhn's concept of a 'paradigm' in Dudley Shapere, "The Structure of Scientific Revolutions," *Philosophical Review* 73 (1964): 383 ff. I have discussed some of these issues in "Positive 'Ethics' and Normative 'Science'," *Philosophical Review* 69 (1960): 311 ff.

2 (p. 6) David Hume, *Treatise of Human Nature*, 3.1.1,2 (ed. Selby Bigge, pp. 458, 472). See ibid., 2.3.3 (p. 415). See also Hume, *Enquiry concerning the Principles of Morals* sec. 9, pt. 1 (ed. Selby-Bigge, pp. 271 ff.).

3 (p. 6) *Enquiry concerning the Principles of Morals*, secs. 7, 9 (pp. 254–55, 270).

4 (p. 8) See William H. Gass, "The Case of the Obliging Stranger," *Philosophical Review* 66 (1957): 193 ff.; J. R. Lucas, "Ethical Intuitionism II," *Philosophy* 46 (1971): 9–10; Renford Bambrough, "A Proof of the Objectivity of Morals," *American Journal of Jurisprudence* 14 (1969): 37 ff.; R. F. Holland, "Moral Scepticism," *Aristotelian Society Supplementary Volume* 41 (1967): 185 ff.; G. J. Warnock, *The Object of Morality* (London: Methuen, 1971), pp. 122–25.

5 (p. 9) See Douglas M. Kelley, *22 Cells in Nuremberg: A Psychiatrist Examines the Nazi Criminals* (New York: Greenberg Publisher, 1947). See also Maria Jahoda, *Current Concepts of Positive Mental Health* (New York: Basic Books, 1958), especially pp. 77–80. Cf. Hannah Arendt, *Eichmann in Jerusalem: A Report on the Banality of Evil* (New York: Viking Press, 1963).

6. (p. 9) Kurt Baier, *The Moral Point of View* (Ithaca, N.Y.: Cornell University Press, 1958), pp. 200–201. For similar statements, see Stephen E. Toulmin, *An Examination of the Place of Reason in Ethics* (Cambridge: University Press, 1950), p. 145, and S. I. Benn and R. S. Peters, *Social Principles and the Democratic State* (London: George Allen and Unwin, 1959), p. 56.

7 (p. 9) Philippa Foot, "Morality and Art," *Proceedings of the British Academy* 56 (1970): 132. See also Mrs. Foot's other important papers, "Moral Arguments," *Mind* 67 (1958): 502–13, and "Moral Beliefs," *Proceedings of the Aristotelian Society* 58 (1958–59): 83–104.

8 (p. 11) For two different examples of this defense of a plurality of principles, see A. C. Ewing, *The Definition of Goodness* (New York: Macmillan, 1947), pp. 203 ff., and Brian Barry, *Political Argument* (London: Routledge and Kegan Paul, 1965), pp. 4–8, 286–87.

9 (p. 14) Isaiah Berlin, *Four Essays on Liberty* (London: Oxford University

Press, 1969), p. li; see also pp. 167 ff. Recent expressions of similar views can be found in D. D. Raphael, "The Standard of Morals," *Proceedings of the Aristotelian Society* 75 (1974–75): 1–12, and J. O. Urmson, "A Defense of Intuitionism," ibid., pp. 111–20.

10 (p. 15) *Philosophical Investigations*, trans G. E. M. Anscombe (Oxford: Basil Blackwell, 1953), 1.265. For a perceptive discussion of problems of justification, see Henry B. Veatch, "The Rational Justification of Moral Principles: Can There Be Such a Thing?" *Review of Metaphysics* 29 (1975): 217–38.

11 (p. 18) See Nelson Goodman, *Fact, Fiction, and Forecast* (Indianapolis and New York: Bobbs-Merrill Co., 1965), pp. 63–64; John Rawls, *A Theory of Justice* (Cambridge: Harvard University Press, 1971), pp. 20–21, 48–51, 120, 579. See also Roderick Chisholm, *Perceiving* (Ithaca, N.Y.: Cornell University Press, 1957), pp. 32, 96–97.

12 (p. 19) See Baier, *Moral Point of View*, chap. 12; Kai Nielsen, "Why Should I Be Moral?" *Methodos* 15 (1963): 275 ff.; D. A. Lloyd-Thomas, "Why Should I Be Moral?" *Philosophy* 45 (1970): 128 ff. For a different approach to this question, see my "Must One Play the Moral Language Game?" *American Philosophical Quarterly* 7 (1970): 107 ff.

13 (p. 20) Rawls, *Theory of Justice*, chaps. 1–4. See especially pp. 14, 143, 293, 401 ff., 413 ff.

14 (p. 20) See Roderick Firth, "Ethical Absolutism and the Ideal Observer," *Philosophy and Phenomenological Research* 12 (1952): 317 ff.; Richard B. Brandt, *Ethical Theory* (Englewood Cliffs, N.J.: Prentice-Hall, 1959), chap. 10; John Rawls, "Outline of a Decision Procedure for Ethics," *Philosophical Review* 60 (1951): 177 ff.; Paul W. Taylor, *Normative Discourse* (Englewood Cliffs, N.J.: Prentice-Hall, 1961), chap. 6; Baier, *Moral Point of View*, chaps. 7–8.

15 (p. 23) *Treatise of Human Nature*, 1.3.6 (ed. Selby-Bigge, p. 179). Cf. ibid. 1.3.8, 1.4.1 (pp. 103, 183).

16 (p. 30) Max Weber, *The Theory of Social and Economic Organization*, trans. A. M. Henderson and Talcott Parsons (New York: Free Press, 1964), pp. 115 ff. Weber notes that the traditional and affectual types of action are "very close to the borderline of what can justifiably be called meaningfully oriented action," the former because it is sometimes "almost automatic," the latter because it may be an "uncontrolled reaction" (p. 116). These qualifications are similar to the restrictions noted above, especially in the distinction between occurrent and dispositional choices and purposes. See also Talcott Parsons and Edward A. Shils, eds., *Toward a General Theory of Action* (New York: Harper and Row, 1962). Four recent philosophical approaches to action are discussed in Richard J. Bernstein, *Praxis and Action* (Philadelphia: University of Pennsylvania Press, 1971).

17 (p. 33) See Aristotle *Nicomachean Ethics* 3.1.1110a 10 ff. On the problem of translating Aristotle's *hekousion* and *akousion* as 'voluntary' and 'involuntary', see W. F. R. Hardie, *Aristotle's Ethical Theory* (Oxford: Clarendon Press, 1968), pp. 152–53.

18 (p. 33) Lionel Robbins, *An Essay on the Nature and Significance of Economic Science* (London: Macmillan, 1952), pp. 15, 30.

19 (p. 34) See Robert Nozick, "Coercion," in *Philosophy, Science, and Method: Essays in Honor of Ernest Nagel*, ed. S. Morgenbesser, P. Suppes, and M. White (New York: St. Martin's Press, 1969), pp. 447 f.; cf. pp. 450 ff.

20 (p. 35) For this view, see Hans Kelsen, *General Theory of Law and State* (Cambridge: Harvard University Press, 1949), p. 65, and the essays by P. J. Fitzgerald and H. L. A. Hart in *Oxford Essays in Jurisprudence*, ed. A. G. Guest (Oxford: Clarendon Press, 1961), pp. 4, 5, 45. Cf. Barbara Wootton, *Crime and the Criminal Law* (London: Stevens and Sons, 1963), pp. 47 ff.

21 (p. 39) See I I. A. Prichard, *Moral Obligation* (Oxford: Clarendon Press, 1949), p. 10: "when, or rather so far as, we act from a sense of obligation, we have no purpose or end. By a 'purpose' or 'end' we really mean something the existence of which leads us to act." See also D. Z. Phillips and H. O. Mounce, *Moral Practices* (London: Routledge and Kegan Paul, 1970), pp. 34 ff.

22 (p. 39) See Charles Taylor, *The Explanation of Behavior* (London: Routledge and Kegan Paul, 1964), pp. 51, 60; Roderick Chisholm, "Freedom and Action," in *Freedom and Determinism*, ed. K. Lehrer (New York: Random House, 1966), pp. 29–30; R. B. Brandt and Jaegwon Kim, "Wants as Explanations of Actions," *Journal of Philosophy* 60 (1963): 425 ff.

23 (p. 39) On this distinction, see T. F. Daveney, "Wanting," *Philosophical Quarterly* 11 (1961): 135 ff., and J. C. B. Gosling, *Pleasure and Desire* (Oxford: Clarendon Press, 1969), chap. 6.

24 (p. 41) These two quotations are, respectively, from Ives Hendricks, *Facts and Theories of Psychoanalysis* (New York: Alfred A. Knopf, 1958), p. 158, and Erich Fromm, *Escape from Freedom* (New York: Rinehart, 1941), p. 142.

25 (p. 43) I borrow this convenient expression from Peter Geach, *Mental Acts* (London: Routledge and Kegan Paul, 1957), pp. 80 ff. See also Anthony Kenny, *Action, Emotion and Will* (London: Routledge and Kegan Paul, 1963), chap. 10.

26 (p. 45) *Topics* 1.1.

2. THE NORMATIVE STRUCTURE OF ACTION

1 (p. 50) Carl R. Rogers, *On Becoming a Person* (Boston: Houghton Mifflin Co., 1961), p. 170.

2 (p. 51) Cf. W. D. Ross, *The Right and the Good* (Oxford: Clarendon Press, 1930), pp. 255 ff.; P. T. Geach, "Good and Evil," *Analysis* 17 (1956): 33 ff. See, however, the repeated predicative use of 'good' in Genesis 1: "and God saw that it was good."

3 (p. 53) See Erich Fromm, *Escape from Freedom* (New York: Rinehart, 1941), and E. R. Dodds, *The Greeks and the Irrational* (Berkeley and Los Angeles: University of California Press, 1951), chap. 8. For an individual life-history of dependency, see Andrew H. Malcolm, "For This Convict, 'Freedom' Is Another Word for 'Fear,'" *New York Times*, 20 November 1974, pp. 41, 51: "Mr. Ferguson . . . has spent almost 39 of his 40 years inside state walls. Once he was an orphan. Later he was a patient. Now he is a convict. But soon he will be free. And Mr. Ferguson is afraid. 'I don't know how to live outside,' he says, 'my home is inside.'"

4 (p. 57) See Otto Fenichel, *The Psychoanalytic Theory of Neurosis* (New York: W. W. Norton, 1945), pp. 73–74, 358 ff.

5 (p. 62) The first quotation is from Thomas Hobbes, *Leviathan*, chap. 11; the second is from Aristotle, *Nicomachean Ethics* 1.7. 1098a18.

6 (p. 63) Cf. A. H. Maslow, *Motivation and Personality* (New York: Harper and Brothers, 1954), pp. 80 ff.; Charlotte Towle, *Common Human Needs*, rev. ed. (New York: National Association of Social Workers, 1957).

7 (p. 65) Cf. the slightly different list in John W. Salmond, *Jurisprudence*, 5th ed. (London: Stevens and Haynes, 1916), p. 185, where the concept of a 'legal right' is analyzed. Salmond does not list what I have called the 'nature' of a right, but he lists both the 'content' and the 'object' of a right, the former consisting in the act or omission that is obligatory for the respondent, the latter in the thing to which the act or omission relates.

8 (p. 67) See Wesley N. Hohfeld, *Fundamental Legal Conceptions as Applied in Judicial Reasoning* (New Haven: Yale University Press, 1964), pp. 41 ff.; H. L. A. Hart, "Are There Any Natural Rights?" *Philosophical Review* 64 (1955): 179.

9 (p. 70) The sources of these quotations are, respectively: (*a*) Clark L. Hull, *Principles of Behavior* (New York: Appleton-Century-Crofts, 1943), pp. 25–26; (*b*) A. J. Ayer, *The Problem of Knowledge* (Harmondsworth: Penguin Books, 1956), p. 35; (*c*) R. Rorty, in *Review of Metaphysics* 24 (1970): 119; (*d*) S. Blackburn, *Reason and Prediction* (Cambridge: University Press, 1973), p. 1; (*e*) R. J. Fogelin, *Evidence and Meaning* (London: Routledge and Kegan Paul, 1967), p. 69; (*f*) ibid., p. 130 n; (*g*) D. Lewis, in *Philosophy* 44 (1969): 253; (*h*) R. Palter, in *Journal of Philosophy* 20 (1973): 253; (*i*) A. Plantinga, *The Nature of Necessity* (Oxford: Clarendon Press, 1974), p. 221; (*j*) B. F. Skinner, *The Behavior of Organisms* (New York: Appleton-Century-Crofts, 1938), p. 17; (*k*) J. L. Austin, *How to Do Things with Words* (Oxford: Clarendon Press, 1962), p. 140.

10 (p. 70) Cf. Roderick Firth's critique of Roderick Chisholm's 'ethical' interpretation of epistemic terms, according to which "'It would be *unreasonable* for S to accept *h*' means that non-*h* is more worthy of S's belief than *h*," and "if it is unreasonable for S to accept *h*, then S ought to *refrain* from accepting it" (Chisholm, *Perceiving: A Philosophical Study* [Ithaca, N.Y.: Cornell University Press, 1957], pp. 5, 13; emphases in original). Firth's critique is in "Chisholm and the Ethics of Belief," *Philosophical Review* 68 (1959): 493–506. See also Chisholm, *Theory of Knowledge* (Englewood Cliffs, N.J.: Prentice-Hall, 1966), pp. 11 ff. The critique would not be justified, however, if the criteria on which Chisholm based his uses of 'worthy' and 'ought' were epistemic rather than 'ethical.' This would require a major change in his epistemological theory.

11 (p. 75) Cf. D. D. Raphael in *Political Theory and the Rights of Man*, ed. Raphael (London: Macmillan, 1967), pp. 108–10.

12 (p. 75) See Hart, "Are There Any Natural Rights?" pp. 180–81.

13 (p. 83) See John Hospers, "Baier and Medlin on Ethical Egoism," *Philosophical Studies* 12 (1961): 10 ff. Cf. D. Kading and M. Kramer, "Mr. Hospers' Defense of Impersonal Egoism," *Philosophical Studies* 15 (1964): 44 ff. My discussion in this section is indebted to the important paper by Brian Medlin, "Ultimate Principles and Ethical Egoism," *Australasian Journal of Philosophy* 35 (1957): 44 ff. For reference to similar arguments, see Edward W. Hirst, *Self and Neighbour* (London: Macmillan, 1919), pp. 4–6.

14 (p. 84) See Jesse Kalin, "In Defense of Egoism," in *Morality and Rational Self-Interest*, ed. David P. Gauthier (Englewood Cliffs, N.J.: Prentice-Hall, 1970), pp. 64–87, and J. A. Brunton, "The Devil Is Not a Fool; or, Egoism Revisited," *American Philosophical Quarterly* 12 (1975): 321 ff. See also the valuable critique by George R. Carlson, "Ethical Egoism Reconsidered," *American Philosophical Quarterly* 10 (1973): 25 ff., to which I am also indebted.

15 (p. 89) See Henry B. Veatch, "Paying Heed to Gewirth's Principle of

Categorial Consistency," *Ethics* 86 (1976): 278 ff., especially pp. 281–82. I have previously dealt with the amoralist in "Must One Play the Moral Language-Game?" *American Philosophical Quarterly* 7 (1970): 107 ff.

16 (p. 95) Karl Marx, *On the Jewish Question*, in *Writings of the Young Marx on Philosophy and Society*, ed. and trans. L. D. Easton and K. H. Guddat (Garden City, N.Y.: Doubleday and Co., 1967), pp. 235 ff.

17 (p. 96) Cf. R. M. Hare, *Freedom and Reason* (Oxford: Clarendon Press, 1963), pp. 104 ff.

18 (p. 97) See, for example, Albert Camus, *The Rebel*, including such a passage as the following from the introduction: "Our purpose is to find out whether innocence, the moment it becomes involved in action, can avoid committing murder. We can act only in terms of our own time, among the people who surround us. We shall know nothing until we know whether we have the right to kill our fellowmen, or the right to let them be killed. In that every action today leads to murder, direct or indirect, we cannot act until we know whether or why we have the right to kill" (trans. Anthony Bower [New York: Vintage Books, 1956], p. 4).

19 (p. 98) For the thesis of the peculiar modernity of the concept of rights, see Hart, "Are There Any Natural Rights?" pp. 176–77, 182; Isaiah Berlin, *Four Essays on Liberty* (London: Oxford University Press, 1969), p. 129. For the denial of the concept of rights in Roman law, see Henry Sumner Maine, *Dissertations on Early Law and Custom* (London: John Murray, 1891), pp. 365–66, 390; Michel Villey, *Leçons d'histoire de la philosophie du droit* (Paris: Librairie Dalloz, 1957), chaps. 11, 14; W. W. Buckland, *A Text-Book of Roman Law from Augustus to Justinian* (Cambridge: University Press, 1963), p. 58; H. F. Jolowicz, *Roman Foundations of Modern Law* (Oxford: Clarendon Press, 1957), pp. 66–67.

20 (p. 99) See, for example, the elucidation of various passages in the Hebrew Bible in terms of rights in *Judaism and Human Rights*, ed. Milton R. Konvitz (New York: W. W. Norton and Co., 1972), pp. 13–18. See also Hayim S. Nahmani, *Human Rights in the Old Testament* (Tel Aviv: Joshua Chaichik Publishing House, 1964).

21. (p. 100) Villey, *Leçons d'histoire*, pp. 214, 216, 218–19, 259. Buckland, *Text-Book of Roman Law*, pp. 61, 77, 86–94 (rights of citizens and others), pp. 102–6 (rights of fathers), pp. 122–23 (rights of adopted children), pp. 181–90 (property rights), pp. 405–11 (rights deriving from contracts and other personal transactions), pp. 674–78 (actions for civil rights *in rem*). In Buckland's briefer *Manual of Roman Private Law* (Cambridge: University Press, 1928), the concept of a right is used throughout. See also the copious references to this concept in Jolowicz, *Roman Foundations*, passim.

22 (p. 100) C. H. McIlwain, *The Growth of Political Thought in the West* (New York: Macmillan Co., 1932), p. 182. For detailed citations on this point, see R. W. and A. J. Carlyle, *A History of Mediaeval Political Theory in the West* (Edinburgh: William Blackwood and Sons, 1903 et seq.), 3:52 ff.

23 (p. 101) See the discussions of property in Plato *Laws* 5. 737E ff.; 9.913A ff.; Aristotle *Politics* 1.4 ff., 1253b23 ff. On the claims to political authority see *Politics* 3.12–13, 1283a10 ff. On the claims of the democrats see Plato *Republic* 8.557B; Aristotle *Politics* 6.1, 1317b10.

24 (p. 101) Gregory Vlastos, "Isonomia," *American Journal of Philology* 74 (1953): 355. See also Vlastos, "Ισονομία Πολιτική," in *Isonomia*, ed. J. Mau and E. G. Schmidt (Berlin: Akademie-Verlag, 1964), pp. 1–35. These two im-

portant essays also give a rounded account of the controversies over the interpretation of *isonomia* as it occurs in ancient Greek writings. See also Martin Ostwald, *Nomos and the Beginnings of the Athenian Democracy* (Oxford: Clarendon Press, 1969), pp. 96 ff. At p. 113, n. 1, Ostwald writes: "It is noteworthy that ἰσονομία comes closer than any other Greek word to expressing the modern notion of 'rights' in the sense in which we speak of the 'rights of man,' 'rights of a citizen,' 'Bill of Rights,' etc."

25 (p. 101) *Suppliant Women* 429 ff. I owe this reference to A. W. H. Adkins, *Moral Values and Political Behaviour in Ancient Greece* (London: Chatto and Windus, 1972), p. 104.

26 (p. 101) B. Malinowski, *Crime and Custom in Savage Society* (London: Routledge and Kegan Paul, 1926), p. 19. The subsequent quotations in this paragraph are from pp. 23, 74. For other discussions of rights in primitive legal systems, see E. Adamson Hoebel, *The Law of Primitive Man* (Cambridge, Mass.: Harvard University Press, 1954), especially chap. 4; Max Gluckman, *The Judicial Process among the Barotse of Northern Rhodesia* (Manchester: Manchester University Press, 1955), especially pp. 166 ff.; Gluckman, *Politics, Law and Ritual in Tribal Society* (Oxford: Basil Blackwell, 1965), chap. 2; E. Sidney Hartland, *Primitive Law* (London: Methuen, 1924), chaps. 3, 4.

27 (p. 102) See, e.g., George Santayana, "Hypostatic Ethics," in *Readings in Ethical Theory*, ed. W. Sellars and J. Hospers (New York: Appleton-Century-Crofts, 1952), p. 268; Hare, *Freedom and Reason*, p. 111; M. G. Singer, *Generalization in Ethics* (New York: Alfred A. Knopf, 1961), p. 40.

28 (p. 103) Hart, "Are There Any Natural Rights?"

29 (p. 105) Cf. J. S. Mill, *A System of Logic*, book 3, chap. 5, sec. 3; H. L. A. Hart and A. M. Honoré, *Causation in the Law* (Oxford: Clarendon, Press, 1959), pp. 15–18.

30 (p. 106) Cf. Ch. Perelman, *The Idea of Justice and the Problem of Argument* (London: Routledge and Kegan Paul, 1963), pp. 11–29, 36–45.

31 (p. 107) See Perelman, *Idea of Justice*, pp. 45–59; S. I. Benn and R. S. Peters, *Social Principles and the Democratic State* (London: George Allen and Unwin, 1959), p. 116. See also the discussion of an analogous point in the reasoning of judges in Edward H. Levi, *An Introduction to Legal Reasoning* (Chicago: University of Chicago Press, 1949), pp. 2–3: "The finding of similarity or difference is the key step in the legal process. . . . The problem for the law is: When will it be just to treat different cases as though they were the same? A working legal system must therefore be willing to pick out key similarities and to reason from them to the justice of applying a common classification. The existence of some facts in common brings into play the general rule. If this is really reasoning, then by common standards, thought of in terms of closed systems, it is imperfect unless some overall rule has announced that this common and ascertainable similarity is to be decisive. But no such fixed prior rule exists." Cf. the discussion of 'criteria of equality' in the school segregation cases, in Albert P. Blaustein and Clarence C. Ferguson, Jr., *Desegregation and the Law* (New York: Vintage Books, 1962), chap. 8.

32 (p. 108) See M. G. Singer, *Generalization in Ethics* (New York: Alfred A. Knopf, 1961), pp. 20 ff.; H. L. A. Hart, *The Concept of Law* (Oxford: Clarendon Press, 1961), pp. 155, 156, 159.

33 (p. 108) See F. A. Hayek, *The Constitution of Liberty* (Chicago: University of Chicago Press, 1960), pp. 154, 209–10; Hare, *Freedom and*

Reason, p. 107. Cf. Kurt Baier, *The Moral Point of View* (Ithaca, N.Y.: Cornell University Press, 1958), p. 202.

34 (p. 108) John Rawls, *A Theory of Justice* (Cambridge, Mass.: Harvard University Press, 1971), chap. 3.

35 (p. 109) See, for example, Kenneth J. Arrow, *Social Choice and Individual Values*, 2d ed. (New York: John Wiley and Sons, 1963), pp. 4, 11, 22–23, 30–31, 38, 72, 111; Abram Bergson, *Essays in Normative Economics* (Cambridge, Mass.: Harvard University Press, 1966), pp. 9 ff., 29 ff., 51 ff., 199 ff.; Anthony Downs, *An Economic Theory of Democracy* (New York: Harper and Row, 1957); pp. 17–20; James M. Buchanan and Gordon Tullock, *The Calculus of Consent* (Ann Arbor: University of Michigan Press, 1962), pp. 7, 23–24, 27–28, 96, 265, 312; Duncan Black, *The Theory of Committees and Elections* (Cambridge University Press, 1958), chap. 9; Robert A. Dahl and Charles E. Lindblom, *Politics, Economics, and Welfare* (New York: Harper and Row, 1953), chap. 2, esp. pp. 41–49.

36 (p. 113) Cf. Ernest Nagel, *The Structure of Science* (New York: Harcourt, Brace and World, 1961), pp. 559 ff.; Quentin Gibson, *The Logic of Social Enquiry* (London: Routledge and Kegan Paul, 1960), pp. 123, 187.

37 (p. 113) See H. L. A. Hart, "The Ascription of Rights and Responsibilities," in *Logic and Language*, first series, ed. A. Flew (Oxford: Basil Blackwell, 1955), pp. 145 ff.

38 (p. 120) *Politics* 1.2, 1252a30; 1.5, 1254b15 ff.; 1.13, 1260a12.

39 (p. 121) See Aristotle *Nicomachean Ethics* 5.3, 1131a18 ff.

40 (p. 128) Frederick Engels, *Anti-Dühring: Herr Eugen Dühring's Revolution in Science* (New York: International Publishers, 1966), part 1, chap. 10 (pp. 108–9).

3. The Principle of Generic Consistency

1 (p. 142) I first presented the Principle of Proportionality in "The Non-Trivializability of Universalizability," *Australasian Journal of Philosophy* 47 (1969): 126. Norman C. Gillespie has, with due acknowledgments, taken over my statement and application of the principle and has used it to discuss the problem of abortion, in "Abortion and Human Rights", *Ethics* 87 (1977): 237 ff. I wish in turn to acknowledge my indebtedness to Gillespie's discussion of the problem.

2 (p. 144) Jeremy Bentham, *An Introduction to the Principles of Morals and Legislation* (New York: Hafner Publishing Co., 1948), chap. 17, sec. 4, n. 1 (p. 311).

3 (p. 159) Aristotle *Nicomachean Ethics* 1.1.1094a2. Ralph Barton Perry, *General Theory of Value* (Cambridge, Mass.: Harvard University Press, 1926), chap. 5.

4 (p. 172) W. V. Quine, "Two Dogmas of Empiricism," in *From a Logical Point of View* (New York: Harper and Row, 1963), pp. 20–46. I have discussed these objections and related issues in "The Distinction between Analytic and Synthetic Truths," *Journal of Philosophy* 50 (1953): 397–425. For Quine's replies to some of my comments, see his *Word and Object* (Cambridge, Mass.: M.I.T. Press, 1960), pp. 65 n, 206–7 nn.

5 (p. 172) See W. V. Quine, "Necessary Truth," in *The Ways of Paradox* (New York: Random House, 1966), p. 56; and Richard Rorty, "Criteria and Necessity," *Noûs* 7 (1973): 313 ff.

6 (p. 173) See J. L. Austin, *Philosophical Papers* (Oxford: Clarendon Press, 1961), pp. 33 ff.; Hilary Putnam, "The Analytic and the Synthetic," in *Minnesota Studies in the Philosophy of Science*, vol. 3, ed. H. Feigl and G. Maxwell (Minneapolis: University of Minnesota Press, 1962), pp. 364 ff.

7 (p. 175) I have previously argued for this in "The Distinction between Analytic and Synthetic Truths"; see especially pp. 419–24. With this should be compared the thesis that the basis of some necessary truths is found in the things spoken of rather than in the way we speak of them. On this distinction between modality *de re* and *de dicto*, see W. Kneale, "Modality De Dicto and De Re," in *Logic, Methodology, and Philosophy of Science*, ed. E. Nagel, P. Suppes, and A. Tarski (Stanford, Calif.: Stanford University Press, 1962), pp. 622 ff.; Alvin Plantinga, *The Nature of Necessity* (Oxford: Clarendon Press, 1974).

8 (p. 178) For this objection, see especially George Nakhnikian, "On the Naturalistic Fallacy," in *Morality and the Language of Conduct*, ed. H. N. Castañeda and G. Nakhnikian (Detroit: Wayne University Press, 1963), pp. 153–55. See also R. M. Hare, *The Language of Morals* (Oxford: Clarendon Press, 1952), pp. 41–42; Jonathan Harrison, *Our Knowledge of Right and Wrong* (London: George Allen and Unwin, 1971), chap. 4; Henry H. Jack, "Moral Principles Are Not Tautologies," *Proceedings of the Seventh Inter-American Congress of Philosophy* (Quebec: Les Presses de l'Université Laval, 1968), 2:92 ff.

9 (p. 180) See John Laird, *An Enquiry into Moral Notions* (London: George Allen and Unwin, 1935), p. 107; Charles A. Baylis, *Ethics* (New York: Henry Holt, 1958), p. 96; Kurt Baier, *The Moral Point of View* (Ithaca, N.Y.: Cornell University Press, 1958), p. 10.

10 (p. 183) *Nicomachean Ethics* 2.6.1106b36. Cf. Aristotle's emphasis on the difficulties of applying this general principle to particular cases (ibid., 2.9.1109a23 ff).

11 (p. 184) *Treatise of Human Nature*, 3.1.1 (ed. Selby-Bigge, p. 462, penultimate paragraph).

12 (p. 190) *Treatise of Human Nature*, 3.1.1 (ed. Selby-Bigge, p. 457).

13 (p. 195) See Francis Hutcheson, *Illustrations upon the Moral Sense*, section 1, reprinted in *British Moralists*, ed. L. A. Selby-Bigge (Oxford: Clarendon Press, 1897), 1:404 ff.; and in D. D. Raphael, ed., *British Moralists 1650–1800* (Oxford: Clarendon Press, 1969), 1:308 ff. Hutcheson's terminology was called to contemporary attention by William K. Frankena in his important article, "Obligation and Motivation in Recent Moral Philosophy," in *Essays in Moral Philosophy*, ed. A. I. Melden (Seattle: University of Washington Press, 1958), pp. 40 ff.; see p. 44. For a brief critique of the distinction, see Philippa Foot, "'Is Morality a System of Hypothetical Imperatives?' A Reply to Mr. Holmes," *Analysis* 35 (1974–75): 53 ff. I deal below with some phases of this critique.

14 (p. 195) Plato *Gorgias* 448 ff., 453 ff., 462 ff.; *Phaedrus* 260 ff., 266 ff. Aristotle *Rhetoric* 1.1.1355a4 ff.

4. DIRECT APPLICATIONS OF THE PRINCIPLE

1 (p. 201) Kant, *Foundations of the Metaphysics of Morals*, sec. 2 (Akad. ed., pp. 421 ff.; trans. Lewis White Beck [New York: Liberal Arts Press, 1959], pp. 39 ff.).

2 (p. 201) See John W. Salmond, *Jurisprudence*, 5th ed. (London: Stevens and Haynes, 1916), pp. 202 ff.; W. D. Lamont, *The Principles of Moral Judgment* (Oxford: Clarendon Press, 1946), pp. 70–71, 76.

3 (p. 202) On the distinction between formal and material theories of deontological ethics, see my article "Ethics," *Encyclopaedia Britannica*, 15th ed. (1974), 6:990–94.

4 (p. 203) See J. S. Mill, *Utilitarianism*, chap. 4; Henry Sidgwick, *The Methods of Ethics*, 7th ed. (London: Macmillan, 1907), pp. 420–21, 497–98.

5 (p. 207) For these distinctions see John Rees, *Equality* (London: Macmillan, 1971), pp. 91 ff.; Brian Barry, *Political Argument* (London: Routledge and Kegan Paul, 1965), pp. 119 ff.; John Wilson, *Equality* (London: Hutchinson, 1966), pp. 81 ff.; Richard Wollheim, "Equality," *Proceedings of the Aristotelian Society* 56 (1955–56): 281 ff.

6 (p. 208) See Aristotle *Nicomachean Ethics* 2.1, 2, 4. 1103a31 ff., 1104a27 ff., 1105a17 ff.

7 (p. 218) Kant, *Foundations of the Metaphysics of Morals*, sec. 2 (Akad. ed., pp. 423–24; trans. L. W. Beck, pp. 41–42), and Sidgwick, *Methods of Ethics*, p. 389 n. For Sidgwick's utilitarian answer, see ibid., pp. 436–37. His objection is, however, subject to my above argument (2.10) about the agent's necessary claim to the rights of freedom and well-being.

8 (p. 220) Cf. Myles Brand, "The Language of Not Doing," *American Philosophical Quarterly* 8 (1971): 45 ff.

9 (p. 222) See H. L. A. Hart and A. M. Honoré, *Causation in the Law* (Oxford: Clarendon Press, 1959), pp. 31 ff.

10 (p. 224) For an example of the generalizing tendency, see J. L. Mackie, "Causes and Conditions," *American Philosophical Quarterly* 2 (1965): 245; for the particularizing tendency, see Hart and Honoré, *Causation in the Law*, pp. 106–7.

11 (p. 227) See Robert Nozick, *Anarchy, State, and Utopia* (New York: Basic Books, 1974), pp. 30–33, 170, 173, 179 n, 238.

12 (p. 228) *On Liberty*, chap. 1 (London: J. M. Dent and Sons, 1936), p. 74. Cf. Sidgwick, *Methods of Ethics*, p. 437. See also James M. Ratcliffe, ed., *The Good Samaritan and the Law* (Garden City, N.Y.: Doubleday, 1966).

13 (p. 232) *On Liberty*, chap. 1, pp. 72–73. For recent discussions of Mill's concept of harm, see J. C. Rees, "A Re-Reading of Mill on Liberty," *Political Studies* 8 (1960): 113 ff.; Ted Honderich, *Punishment: The Supposed Justifications* (London: Hutchinson and Co., 1969), chap. 6; D. G. Brown, "Mill on Liberty and Morality," *Philosophical Review* 81 (1972): 142 ff.

14 (p. 232) For the first view, see Richard Taylor, *Freedom, Anarchy, and the Law* (Englewood Cliffs, N.J.: Prentice-Hall, 1973), pp. 63 ff.; for the second, Richard Wollheim, "John Stuart Mill and the Limits of State Action," *Social Research* 39 (1973): 1 ff.

15 (p. 235) The reference to 'tendencies' in rule-utilitarian theories goes back at least to Francis Hutcheson, *An Inquiry concerning Moral Good and Evil*, 7. 6 (in L. A. Selby-Bigge, ed., *British Moralists* [Oxford: Clarendon Press, 1897], 1:160). For recent discussions, see David Lyons, *Forms and Limits of Utilitarianism* (Oxford: Clarendon Press, 1965), pp. 3 ff., 28; Anthony Quinton, *Utilitarian Ethics* (London: Macmillan, 1973), pp. 47–48. For a critique of the view that individual actions, as against kinds of action, do not also have tendencies, see T. S. Champlin and A. D. M. Walker,

"Tendencies, Frequencies and Classical Utilitarianism," *Analysis* 35 (1974): 8–12. For W. D. Ross, see *The Right and the Good* (Oxford: Clarendon Press, 1930), pp. 28 ff.

16 (p. 242) Cf. the valuable discussion of this subject in John Rawls, *A Theory of Justice* (Cambridge, Mass.: Harvard University Press, 1971), pp. 178 f., 440 ff.

17 (p. 243) Although I depart from various other philosophers in the ways I relate the prudential virtues to morality, my discussion of these virtues reflects the doctrines found in Plato, Aristotle, and Spinoza as well as in such contemporary philosophers as Philippa Foot; see especially her "Moral Beliefs," *Proceedings of the Aristotelian Society* 59 (1958–59): 97 ff. See also P. T. Geach, *The Virtues* (Cambridge: Cambridge University Press, 1977).

18 (p. 245) For one phase of these difficulties, consider the recent discussions of equality of opportunity with regard to education and its presumed effects. See James S. Coleman et al., *Equality of Educational Opportunity* (Washington, D.C.: United States Government Printing Office, 1966); Frederick Mosteller and Daniel P. Moynihan, eds., *On Equality of Educational Opportunity* (New York: Random House, 1972); Ivan Illich, *De-Schooling Society* (New York: Harper and Row, 1971); Christopher Jencks et al., *Inequality: A Reassessment of the Effects of Family and Schooling in America* (New York: Harper and Row, 1972).

19 (p. 248) See, for example, A. H. Maslow, *Toward a Psychology of Being*, 2d ed. (New York: Van Nostrand Reinhold Co., 1968), especially chaps. 6, 10. Cf. John Dewey, *Human Nature and Conduct* (New York: Henry Holt, 1922), pp. 54 ff.; *Reconstruction in Philosophy* (New York: Henry Holt, 1920), pp. 170–72; *The Quest for Certainty* (New York: G. P. Putnam's Sons, 1929), chap. 9 and pp. 279 ff.

20 (p. 257) *Civil Liberties* (American Civil Liberties Union), no. 303 (July 1974), p. 9.

21 (p. 270) See Hans von Hentig, "Remarks on the Interaction of Perpetrator and Victim," and Marvin E. Wolfgang, "Victim-Precipitated Criminal Homicide," in *Victimology*, ed. E. Drapkin and E. Viano (Lexington, Mass.: D. C. Heath, 1974), pp. 45 ff., 79 ff. Cf. Eric Berne, *Transactional Analysis in Psychotherapy* (New York: Grove Press, 1916), and idem, *Games People Play: The Psychology of Human Relationships* (New York: Grove Press, 1967).

5. Indirect Applications of the Principle

1 (p. 279) *Summa theologica* 2.1. qu. 95, a. 2.

2 (p. 280) For a fine statement of this problem in a related context, see Gregory Vlastos, "Justice and Equality," in *Social Justice*, ed. R. B. Brandt (Englewood Cliffs, N.J.: Prentice-Hall, 1962), pp. 39–40.

3 (p. 289) Cf. Grant McConnell, *Private Power and American Democracy* (New York: Alfred A. Knopf, 1966), and the essays by McConnell and Sanford A. Lakoff in *Nomos XI: Voluntary Associations*, ed. J. R. Pennock and J. W. Chapman (New York: Atherton Press, 1969), pp. 147 ff., 170 ff.

4 (p. 290) Cf. Robert Nozick, *Anarchy, State, and Utopia* (New York: Basic Books, 1974), chap. 2.

5 (p. 293) See Aristotle *Nicomachean Ethics* 5.2.1030b30 ff.

6 (p. 299) John Locke, *Two Treatises of Government*, secs. 7–13. Cf. Hans Kelsen, *General Theory of Law and State* (Cambridge, Mass.: Harvard University Press, 1949), pp. 338–39.

7 (p. 301) It must be emphasized that the above discussion focuses on the requirements of a system of criminal justice that is in accordance with the *PGC*. In view of the serious flaws that mar the actual administration of criminal justice in the United States, important qualifications would be required in order to apply the discussion to the system as it actually operates. See, for example, J. S. Campbell, J. R. Sahid, and D. P. Stang, *Law and Order Reconsidered*, Report of the Task Force on Law and Law Enforcement to the National Commission on the Causes and Prevention of Violence (New York: Bantam Books, 1970), esp. part 3, pp. 263 ff.

8 (p. 304) Cf. H. L. A. Hart, *The Concept of Law* (Oxford: Clarendon Press, 1961), pp. 54 ff., 83 ff.

9 (p. 313) These positions are interestingly developed, respectively, in Nozick, *Anarchy, State, and Utopia*, pp. 150 ff., and John Rawls, *A Theory of Justice* (Cambridge, Mass.: Harvard University Press, 1971), pp. 60 ff., 104, 302.

10 (p. 315) See Herbert Spencer, *The Principles of Ethics* (New York: D. Appleton, 1897), 2: 376 ff.; *Social Statics Abridged and Revised* (New York: D. Appleton, 1897), pp. 144 ff.; *The Man versus the State* (Caldwell, Idaho: Caxton Printers, 1945), pp. 22 ff. See also John Hospers, *Libertarianism* (Los Angeles: Nash Publishing, 1971), pp. 299 ff., and Nozick, *Anarchy, State, and Utopia*, pp. 30, 31, 170, 173, 179n, 238.

11 (p. 316) See Maurice Cranston, *What Are Human Rights?* (London: Bodley Head, 1973), pp. 66 ff. See also his contribution to D. D. Raphael, ed., *Political Theory and the Rights of Man* (London: Macmillan, 1967), pp. 96 ff. For the 'weaker' sense of the universality of rights referred to below, see Raphael in *Political Theory and the Rights of Man*, pp. 65 ff., 112.

12 (p. 326) John Stuart Mill, *On Liberty* (London: J. M. Dent and Sons, (1936), p. 132. See also pp. 75–76, 79, 132. This aggregative utilitarian criterion is not the only one invoked by Mill as to justified legal interference with individual freedom, but it is a pervasive one for him.

13 (p. 327) J. S. Mill, *Utilitarianism*, chap. 5 (London: J. M. Dent and Sons, 1936), p. 46. Kant gives a similar but more restricted definition of 'juridical duty': "only a particular kind of duty, *juridical duty*, implies corresponding rights of other people to exercise compulsion" (*Doctrine of Virtue*, trans. Mary J. Gregor [New York: Harper and Row, 1964], pp. 40–41).

14 (p. 328) *The City of God*, book 19, chap. 21.

15 (p. 331) For the 'natural lottery' argument, see Rawls, *Theory of Justice*, pp. 72 ff. See also Hastings Rashdall, *The Theory of Good and Evil* (Oxford: Clarendon Press, 1907), 1:250 ff. This position has also been argued in a series of important papers by Herbert Spiegelberg, including "A Defense of Human Equality," *Philosophical Review* 53 (1944): 101 ff.; "'Accident of Birth': A Non-Utilitarian Motif in Mill's Philosophy," *Journal of the History of Ideas* 22 (1961): 475 ff.; "Ethics for Fellows in the Fate of Existence," in *Mid-Twentieth Century American Philosophy*, ed. P. A. Bertocci (New York: Humanities Press, 1974), pp. 193 ff.; "Good Fortune Obligates: Albert Schweitzer's Second Ethical Principle," *Ethics* 85 (1975): 227 ff. For a reply to the natural lottery argument, see Nozick, *Anarchy, State, and Utopia*, pp. 213 ff.

16 (p. 334) For part of the first argument see Kurt Baier, *The Moral Point of View* (Ithaca, N.Y.: Cornell University Press, 1958), chap. 9. The second argument is in Marcus G. Singer, *Generalization in Ethics* (New York: Alfred A. Knopf, 1961), pp. 311 ff. The third argument is suggested by Aristotle *Nicomachean Ethics* 5. 11, 1138a17–20. Relevant to the question of duties to oneself are Aristotle's discussions (ibid., chaps. 9, 11) of whether a person can voluntarily be treated unjustly and whether he can be unjust to himself. For the fourth argument, see Leonard Nelson, *System of Ethics*, trans. N. Guterman (New Haven: Yale University Press, 1956), pp. 134–35; also Kant, *Doctrine of Virtue*, p. 44 (Acad. ed., pp. 384–85), although Kant uses the argument not against duties to oneself but against there being a duty to pursue one's own happiness. The fifth argument is in John Stuart Mill, *On Liberty*, chap. 4 (London: J. M. Dent and Sons, 1936), p. 135.

17 (p. 340) Rawls, *Theory of Justice*, p. 43.

18 (p. 341) See, on the one hand, *Theory of Justice*, pp. 63, 242, 244, 302, where Rawls maintains "the absolute weight of liberty with respect to social and economic advantages" and holds that "liberty can be restricted only for the sake of liberty itself." See, on the other hand, ibid., pp. 152, 247, 542, where he says, for example, "The denial of equal liberty can be defended only if it is necessary to raise the level of civilization so that in due course these freedoms can be enjoyed." The extent of 'due course' is not indicated.

19 (p. 348) I have dealt with these issues in "Starvation and Human Rights," to be published in *Moral Philosophy for the Twenty-first Century*, ed. Kenneth M. Sayre (Notre Dame, Ind.: University of Notre Dame Press, forthcoming).

20 (p. 360) Jean Piaget, *The Moral Judgment of the Child* (Glencoe, Ill.: Free Press, 1948), p. 404.

21 (p. 360) For explications of these concepts, see Charles Morris, *Foundations of the Theory of Signs* (Chicago: University of Chicago Press, 1938).

22 (p. 362) Cf. my "Meta-ethics and Normative Ethics," *Mind* 69 (1960): 187–205, and "Meta-ethics and Moral Neutrality," *Ethics* 78 (1968): 214–25.

23 (p. 364) Cf. A. J. Ayer, *Language, Truth, and Logic* (London: V. Gollancz, 1948), pp. 110–12; Charles L. Stevenson, *Ethics and Language* (New Haven: Yale University Press, 1944), pp. 30–31, 134–38. The position of R. M. Hare is more complex; see *Freedom and Reason*, pp. 97 ff., 105 ff. The noncognitivist tenet goes back to David Hume; see *Treatise of Human Nature*, 3.1.1 (ed. Selby-Bigge, pp. 463–69); *Enquiry concerning the Principles of Morals*, Appendix 1 (ed. Selby-Bigge, pp. 286–94).

24 (p. 364) John Locke, *Essay concerning Human Understanding*, 3.11. 15–18; 4.4.5–9.

INDEX

Abilities: as practical goods, 58–59; first-order and second-order, 59, 60, 233; second-order, as constituting well-being, 60–61, 207, 211–12, 233–34, 240–41

Abortion, 142–44

Abstractness, 127; and concept of action, 29

Achievemental mode of purposive action, 58, 62, 63, 68

Action: as subject matter of morality, 21–22, 24–26, 32–33, 37; reasons for, 23, 28, 30, 31, 35, 36, 37; strict sense of, 27; generic features of, 27–41; intentional, 29; four types of social, 30; involves value judgments, 44–45, 48–54; and right-claims, 63–103; and judgments about actions, 139; varying descriptions of, 169–70; justifying reasons central to, 194–95; distinguished from inaction and nonaction, 219–20, 267–68; inclusiveness of, 346–47. *See also* Interaction; Transaction

Actor, 129, 264, 265

Adkins, A. W. H., 373

Advertiser, 154–55, 157

Aesthete, 22, 23, 346–47

Agent, 26–27, 30, 31, 124, 129, 130–33, 171, 219-21; in social roles and institutions, 27–28, 273–74, 301–2; prospective, 27, 35, 62, 68, 111–12, 141; standpoint of, 44, 54, 71, 73, 82, 94, 114–15, 123, 125–26; rational, 44, 46, 88–89, 136–37, 138, 153–54, 159, 171–76, 227, 322, 335, 364–65; contrasted with

egoist, 82, 88–89; standpoint external to, 96–97, 114, 125–26, 160–61; children as potential, 120, 141; abilities of, 120; degrees of being, 120–25, 136, 140–45; superior, 120, 124–25; distinguished from recipient, 130–33, 220, 243, 255, 268–70, 285–86, 301; prospective and potential, distinguished, 141; empirical, 291; political, 310

Aggregative-distributive distinction, 200, 215–16, 218, 228, 236, 302, 318, 325, 326–27, 342. *See also* Utilitarianism

Alienation, 13, 34

Altruist, 57, 59, 71

Amoralist, 29, 89–95

Analytic truth of *PGC*, 171–87

Anarchy, 272, 306, 307

Animals, 120, 122, 140, 144–45, 243

Apodictic reasoning, 44, 102, 161

Appetitive-reciprocal consistency. *See* Consistency; Golden Rule

Arbitrariness: attributed to moral judgments, 7; reason as only sure way of avoiding, 22, 23, 111, 150, 175, 193, 339; definitions as having, 24, 175; of contingent right-claims, 78, 356; of criteria of relevant similarity, 107; avoided by necessary connections, 111, 170, 232–33, 356; avoided by criteria of relevant similarity, 150, 204, 302; acceptance of rationality does not have, 195; of criteria of harm, 231–32; of 'natural lottery,' 331; avoided by argument for *PGC*, 356

Inequalities: in concept of action, 119–20, 124–25; justified by *PGC*, 148, 165, 277–78, 279–80, 287–88, 302; economic, 208–9, 214, 246, 290, 311, 312–15, 350

Institution, 27, 102, 137, 200, 208, 230, 234–35, 241, 247, 253, 259, 266–67, 289; defined, 274; functional and organizational, 275–77, 300; morality as, 280–81, 361; requirements of, 344–45; autonomy of, 360–61; established and other, 361

Instrumental justification of social rules, 281–82, 290–92; static and dynamic, 292, 312; internal and external, 296, 299, 314, 327

Insult, 242

Intellectuals, 3, 59, 160, 346

Intention, 38, 39–40, 42, 50, 51. *See also* Purposiveness; Wanting

Interaction, 130, 273. *See also* Action; Transaction

Intuitionism, 8, 9, 14, 187, 234, 339

'Is-ought' problem, 16, 18, 25, 57, 159; resolved by argument for *PGC*, 102, 149, 155–59, 160–61, 355, 357. *See also* Circularity; Logical gaps

Isonomia, 101, 372–73

Jack, Henry H., 375

Jahoda, Maria, 368

Jefferson, Thomas, 77, 280

Jolowicz, H. F., 362

Judge, 274, 301–2

Justice: formal, 106, 161–62; distributive, 121, 201, 202, 203, 204–5; *PGC* as principle of, 161–62, 201, 202, 203, 204–5, 243, 254, 318, 322, 354; and beneficence, 228; as distribution according to merit, 287–88; retributive, distributive, and redistributive, 293–94, 315; general formula of, 293; requires uniformity, 300; relation of, to method of consent, 322; criminal, 378

Justification: as establishment of rightness, 7–8, 12; and noncogniti-

vism, 7, 13–14; rational, excludes arbitrariness, 7, 47; coherence view of, 11–12; and human control, 12, 278–79; internal and external relations of, 13–14; internal to moral judgments, 13–14; "appeals to something independent," 15; formal difficulties of, 15–16; inductive, 17–21; reflexive methods of, 20–21; conclusive, 22; reason as basis of, 23, 25, 47; action as basis of, 25, 26; and dialectically necessary method, 46–47, 114; of rights, 65, 66, 69, 72, 73–74, 104; not necessarily connected with justice, 71; and practical 'oughts,' 79, 90, 92; of criterion of relevant similarities, 107–11, 277–78; sufficient, 113, 115; rational, of *PGC*, 148–50, 153, 359; of use of value concepts, 159; central to action, 194; distinguished from motivation, 195; of social rules, 273, 278, 281–82; general and specific objects of, 278–79; procedural and instrumental, 281–82; optional-procedural, 283–90, 304; necessary-procedural, 283–84, 304–11; static-instrumental, 291–304, 312; dynamic-instrumental, 292, 312–27; sequence of, 359–61; 'external,' of an entire field, why required, 360–61

Kading, D., 371

Kalin, Jesse, 371

Kant, Immanuel, 2, 30, 201, 218, 243, 322, 346, 375, 376, 378, 379

Kelley, Douglas M., 368

Kelsen, Hans, 370, 378

Kenny, Anthony, 370

Kierkegaard, Sören, 2

Kim, Jaegwon, 370

Kneale, William, 375

Knowledge: of relevant circumstances, 31, 120, 122, 132, 244, 250, 258, 259–62, 284; scientific, needed for avoiding harms, 212

Kramer, M., 371

Kuhn, Thomas S., 368